The JOWETT JUPITER

the car that leaped to fame

New edition
by
EDMUND NANKIVELL

Books by the same author:
The Jowett Jupiter, the Car that Leaped to Fame (1981 edition)
The Complete Jowett History – with Paul Clark and others
Jowett Javelin and Jupiter: the Complete Story – with Geoff McAuley
The Jowett Jupiter, a Car for Road, Rally and Race
Jowett Jupiter Special Body, from Abbott & Beutler to Rochdale & Worblaufen

This edition produced and distributed on behalf of Edmund Nankivell by Veloce Publishing Ltd.
Original edition published in 1981 by B T Batsford.

All images herein are chosen for their historical importance.
The author makes no apology for the variable quality of the photographs included in this work.

British Library Cataloguing-in-Publication Data
A catalogue record for this book is available from the British Library.
ISBN: 978-1-845849-12-2
UPC: 6-36847-04912-6

Printed in India by Replika Press Pvt. Ltd.

NEW EDITION by EDMUND NANKIVELL

The JOWETT JUPITER

the car that leaped to fame

This book is dedicated to Malcolm Bergin and Ted Miller.

Malcolm produced the very first Jupiter Register with full details and history, and although mainly, but not entirely, about cars based in New Zealand, with his historical research he pioneered the way ahead.

Ted, tirelessly and accurately, chased down long-lost Jupiters in the USA, finding more than the rest of us put together.

"You must Trust what you cannot Trace"
– seen on a glass rolling pin dated to about 1850 and described as a love token

Some have likened the Jowett Jupiter to a fine wine:–
A lively expressive nose dominated by exotic notes, complemented by hints of passion.
A zesty burst filled with passion – racy and providing a crisp, lingering finish.

The author's maxim:– eschew obfuscation.

Contents

Abbreviations

AC = Auto Club
CJ = Collection Joves
BARC = British Automobile Racing Club
bhp = Brake Horsepower (power measured on a 'Brake' test apparatus = 0.7457kW in modern terms
   (so 62.5bhp = 46.6kW)
ERA = English Racing Automobiles – racing car manufacturer active from 1933 to 1954
FIA = Fédération Internationale de l'Automobile (International Automobile Federation)
FCCA = Four Cylinder Club of America – founded about 1945
HST = High Speed Trial. A minimum speed is set for each class, it gives the ordinary owner of a normal sports car a
   chance to show his skill in driving. Often the duration is 1 hour.
JCLtd = Jowett Cars Ltd
JELtd = Jowett Engineering Ltd
MC = Motor Club
MCC = Motor Cycling Club (not Marylebone Cricket Club!) – founded in 1901 for the sporting motorist
NMM = National Motor Museum
RSAC = Royal Scottish Automobile Club – the home of motorsport in Scotland
SCCA = Sports Car Club of America
TEAC = Thames Estuary Automobile Club

Acknowledgements

First and foremost, thanks must be recorded to George Mitchell who suggested the original book, supplied the Jowett Factory Records information having rescued it from Jowett Engineering Ltd on their close, opened his customer files on Jupiters, and contributed elsewhere, notably the section on engine numbers.

Secondly, essential assistance was rendered in ways small and large by several former Jowett employees amongst whom particular mention must be made of Donald Bastow, Charles Grandfield, Phill Green, Cliff Howarth, Reg Korner, Ken Shackleton, Charles Phillip Stephenson, and the works drivers Marcel Becquart, Ted Booth, Bert Hadley, George Phillips and Bill Robinson.

The competition history would hardly have been possible without recourse to Peter Dixon's collection of relevant magazines of the period and I would further like to thank Peter for his help in this and other aspects of the contents, together with his part in arranging the original publication and its funding. Terry O'Neil's book *Runways & Racers, Sports car races held on military airfields in America 1952-1954* (Veloce) was very helpful, and my thanks also go to FCCA historian Bill Wilkman, with his tireless research into FCCA's events covering the period in question.

I am grateful to *The Autocar*, *Autosport*, and in particular *Motor Sport* for permission to reproduce certain extracts; to Malcolm Wood for permission to search through the records and use the photographs of C H Wood (Bfd) Ltd; to the National Motor Museum for permission to inspect their material and for the use of photographs in their collection; and to Jonathan Wood then of *Classic Car* magazine regarding aspects of Jowett company history.

It would not have been possible to complete this book, covering as it does so many aspects, without the help of many people too numerous to mention by name – Jupiter owners past and present – in many countries of the world. My sincere thanks to all those who have loaned photographs, searched their attics and their memories, and supplied relevant information and I hope they feel they have played their part in the creation of this book. I must list, furthermore, John Blazé for camerawork, draughtsmanship and encouragement; Malcom Bergin for the inspiration and the New Zealand angle; Roger Gambell for information on the R4 Jupiters; Ted Miller for super-human feats of Jupiter tracing in the USA, Bruce Polain (Australia) and Jacques Touzet (Portugal). All photos come from the author's collection. It has not been possible in every case to trace the original photographer and if any copyright has been infringed the sincerest apologies are offered. Especial thanks are to C H Wood, Charles Dunn, Guy Griffiths, Klemantaski and *Motor Sport* magazine.

Finally, publication of the original version was only possible thanks to the efforts of the Jupiter Owners' Auto Club as a whole, of Club officials maintaining links with owners in many countries and so tracing and reporting Jupiter history through the Club's magazine *By Jupiter*. The same can be said of the Jowett Car Club Ltd and its magazine *The Jowetteer*, The New Zealand Jowett club's *Flat Four*, the Australian club's *The Javelin*, and the excellent topical publication *Jowett Sport* edited by Mike Smailes and Geoff McAuley covering Jowetts in action in the 1970s, 1980s and more.

Throughout this book a number in parenthesis indicates a Jupiter chassis number.

Prologue: Gordon Wilkins and the Jupiter R1

Gordon Wilkins after Le Mans 1952
(From *The Autocar* July 1952)

The Jowett Jupiter which Marcel Becquart and I shared at Le Mans in 1952 has excellent handling characteristics. Weight distribution is right and the steering is first class.

Modifications to the tooth form of the rack and pinion and the revision of pivots for the steering and suspension have contributed to quick, light and direct control. With fuel tanks full or nearly empty, the R1 can be twitched into a slide and out again under perfect control; if anything it understeers slightly but the control is always light and the response immediate.

At Le Mans we were repeatedly held up by bigger cars on the winding stretches and between Mulsanne and Arnage we several times had to re-pass cars which had overtaken us on the straight. There was nothing faster than the Jupiter through the corners.

The thick drifting mist brought a strange sense of isolation and unreality during the night hours, heightened by the fact that I found myself passing Ferraris, Talbots, and other fast cars which loomed up suddenly and were left behind. An open car is undoubtedly at an advantage in such conditions and one of the Jupiters passed a Mercedes – probably the car driven by Hermann Lang the ultimate winner – who was losing 40 seconds a lap at the worst period. At one time the White House bends could be taken at 100mph or more; two laps later the maximum speed would be nearer 50. Long practice in England's winters undoubtedly helps, and Briggs Cunningham said to me afterwards: I wished I had been born an Englishman last night. You fellows seem to go through the fog as though it wasn't there.

Gordon Wilkins in the 1952 Le Mans driving an R1-type Jupiter.
(LAT Photographic)

Gordon Wilkins (1912–2007) was, in his heyday, the doyen of British motoring journalists. He spent more than seven decades writing and broadcasting about cars. He was for a time technical editor at *The Autocar* magazine, having begun his professional life in 1933 when in his twenties, and was still attending motor shows and reporting on them to motoring magazines well into his nineties. He combined writing with participation in motor sport, including trials, rallies and races – his first Le Mans was the 1939 event and he drove a Jupiter in the 1951 Monte Carlo International Rally, and co-drove a Jupiter in the 1951 and 1952 Le Mans. Fluent in French and German, he worked extensively throughout Europe.

1: The Jowett Jupiter

Bradford in Yorkshire had, throughout the nineteenth century, been considered the 'worsted capital of the world' and even in the 1940s and 1950s wool textiles were still a major industry there, although synthetic fibres were by then challenging its supremacy. Thanks to abundant coal and iron in the region, Bradford also developed as an engineering town, and one engineering establishment that flourished was the car firm established in 1906 by the Jowett brothers Willie and Ben. During the inter-war years Jowett Cars Ltd expanded into a new site near the village of Idle just to the north of, and soon to be engulfed by, Bradford, and it was at this factory at Idle that the Jupiters were developed, built, tested, and in the case of the Factory cars, housed.

Bradford was far from the natural centre of the British motor industry, and this ensured for Jowett cars an interesting and sometimes quirky individualism not to be found in cars of other makes. For a while Jowett could attract clever engineers and designers such as Gerry Palmer, Frank Salter and Donald Bastow to its higher echelons; as regards the lower and middle levels of design Jowett were forced to grow their own and so there could not be the free interplay of ideas as at Coventry then.

In 1939 car building was abandoned for the war's duration and the company quadrupled its size to about 2000 people under the energetic management of Calcott Reilly, a man ambitious for further peace-time expansion through the spearhead of the Palmer-designed Javelin saloon car. Charles Clore, as chairman, came and went, buying the Jowett brothers' majority shareholding and then in 1947 selling it to the privately-owned merchant bank Lazard Brothers who then installed Wilfred Sainsbury as non-executive director, and George Wansbrough in place of Clore. Two years later Jowett were rocked by three high-level changes: Palmer returned to MG to be replaced by Roy Lunn, a young designer destined for great things in Detroit but at this time with only three years' experience in the motor industry Calcott Reilly went to the Cyclemaster moped firm – perhaps crucially taking with him Jowetts then Works Manager. Finally, in a move that was to result in the arrival of Arthur Jopling on the board, Wansbrough, having given the green light to the Jupiter project, left abruptly after some of his share dealings unconnected with Jowett met with the disapproval of Lazards.

The actual concept of the Jupiter is attributed to the

journalist Laurence Pomeroy, who after WW2 began promoting the idea of a sports car capable of standing up to the challenge of German and Italian cars in the medium capacity field. There were soon very promising early competition results for the Jowett Javelin, such as its excellent 2-litre class win in the 24 Hours of Spa race of

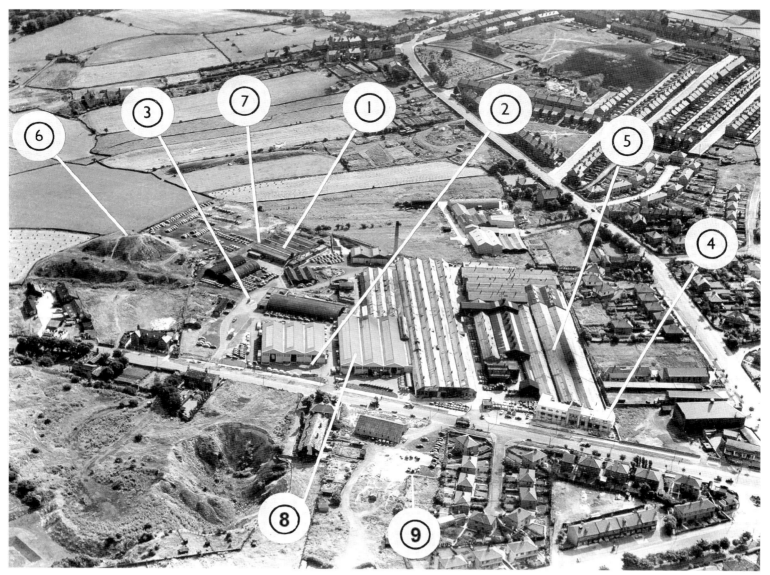

Aerial view of the Jowett Works post World-War 2: (1) Experimental Department. (2) Here Jupiter No 1 was photographed by C H Wood just after its completion. (3) Weighbridge – near where the Farina Jupiter HAK 317 was photographed. (4) Main offices. (5) Factory production. (6) Spion Kop quarry spoil-heap: motorcycle trials tracks can just be made out. (7) Here was taken the group photo of Jupiter No 1 with the Experimental Department staff. (8) Machine shop, where crank cases and crankshafts were machined. (9) Staff car park. (C H Wood)

1949 (2 places ahead of the Delage that won the 4-litre class) and a class win in the 1949 Monte Carlo Rally to ensure that Pomeroy's idea was taken up; and when the famous Austrian engineer, Robert Eberan von Eberhorst, arrived in England in May 1949 plans were already under way for the construction of a chassis to be produced by ERA using Javelin components. Eberhorst gave the Jowett programme new impetus and of course the project was subjected to a number of radical changes before the ERA-Javelin, as it was initially called (ERA car, Javelin engine), was ready for the October 1949 London Motor Show. At the show Jowett exhibited the ERA tubular chassis on which anti-roll bars were visible front and rear; Jowett liked the chassis but were not attracted to the complete car, a coupé that did not exist for long apart from the artwork shown opposite and its brief appearance in the lower ground floor of Jowett's London showroom during the show.

As it happens, the first Jowett Jupiter model had been introduced in 1935, a side-valve flat four Saloon of 10HP rating. It was not a success and was replaced the following March by the Peregrine model.

This book is only concerned with the Jowett Javelin Jupiter (as it was initially called) sports convertible and its derivatives produced between 1949 and 1954. In total 827 standard-bodied cars were built by Jowett

The 1949 ERA-Javelin coupé, the first car on the Jupiter chassis. Body was by Seary & McReady. (H M Bentley & Partners)

during those years, of which 733 were Mk1 and 94 Mk1a. We can add three rolling chassis that received standard coachwork outside the Jowett factory, making 828 standard Jupiters that once existed. Jowett shipped a net 74 fully equipped rolling chassis of which we know of 64 having been built. Most were early Jupiters, as Jowett initially had difficulty getting the bodies made: a slow process forming the panel-work from flat sheet using wheeling machines. Then rubber-bed presses were employed and Jupiter production got going on a good scale. A few of these special-bodied Jupiters received bodies closely resembling standard from the hands of various constructors, but at least 22 had bodywork fitted by coachbuilders with national or international reputations such as Abbott, Beutler, Ghia Aigle, Richard Mead, Stabilimenti Farina, Harold Radford and Worblaufen. Even Rochdale were involved to some extent. Other lesser-known constructors built what they wanted on these chassis. Some 18 or so attracted the attention of the new breed of specialist constructor that inhabited the Thames valley region in the early 1950s: Lionel Rawson, Coachcraft of Egham, Maurice Gomm, Charles Robinson and others who tended to be influenced by the work of the more advanced Italian designers such as the Ferrari by Touring of Milan-influenced Willment FHC Jupiter (725) intended for the 1953 Monte Carlo Rally but not finished in time.

Another group, of whom the two Lancashire-based

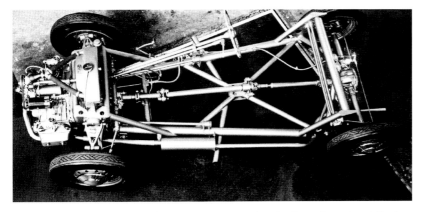
Out of the strong came forth sweetness: the Jupiter chassis at Earls Court 1949. Torsion-bar springs inherited from the Javelin give the suspension low unsprung weight. (NBS Publications)

The first Jupiter (25) in private hands. Body by Rawson, registered December 1950 for Sir Hugh Bell. 1963 photo by its then owner Robert Joint.

Two views of the Jupiter No 1 at the Jowett Works showing hood stowed and hood raised. (C H Wood)

bodywork was a rarity that tended to be engaged in with more enthusiasm than concinnity.

Whereas in 1950 coachbuilders had been looked to for Jupiter sales, by the end of 1951 when production got going, Jowett's lower price made it almost impossible for outside constructors, for the price differential in Britain was about £400.

Jowett's Experimental Department went on to build three special Jupiters, known as the R1 (see Chapter 3) on slightly modified Eberhorst Jupiter chassis for racing purposes (mainly Le Mans 1951 and 1952) and one survives in authentic condition. Three Jupiters type R4 (Chapter 8) were also built (two survive) but these are not on the Eberhorst frame; the design was by Roy Lunn and Phil Stephenson, and one was tested at just over 100mph. Interestingly an authentic Mk1a was built up with all correct components in 1956. It survives in good order.

The Jupiter chassis was designed by Professor Dr Dipl Ing Robert Eberan von Eberhorst when Chief Engineer at ERA Ltd, at Dunstable "where the birth of the Jupiter

concerns KW Bodies and J E Farr & Son, with Harold Radford of London, were in general long established firms, whose normal output might be Rolls-Royce bodies for cars, hearses, utilities and such like for whom sports car originated from". It is reported that six chassis were built by ERA: one was shown at the 1949 London Motor Show whilst the coupé, unwanted by Jowett, was on show at Jowett's London showroom. Of these six, Jowett received five whilst the other was used by Leslie Johnson as a road-test vehicle, fitted with very basic bodywork. Next, the Jupiter No 1 (E0/SA/1R) received the definitive Jupiter shape at Jowett from the pen of Chief Bodywork Designer Reg Korner, and was first seen in public at the British Motor and Engineering Show in New York in April 1950.

After the first eight Factory Jupiters, (bodies fabricated from flat sheet by an outside coachbuilder it is thought) Jupiter body panels, 14 per car, were obtained pressed but unfinished from the Western Manufacturing Estate Ltd (a company formed from the ashes of the failed Miles Aircraft Company) at Woodley Aerodrome near Reading, pressed on their aircraft-type rubber-bed sheet-aluminium presses. These panels then went to Jowett's Clayton plant where the 14 pressings were hand-welded into 11 panels (the bonnet was made from 3, the tail panel made from 2) and formed into body-sets on their respective body-frames (with their unique body number), then etched and primed before being transported the six miles to the main factory behind a Bradford driveaway-chassis vehicle. Jowett constructed the tubular chassis frames at their main factory after the five from ERA had been used.

The front wing-line, the 'swoop' that swoops across the door to the tail, has an interesting history, and some early appearances were from the highly skilled hands of Italian coachbuilders, as an example the 1942 Alfa Romeo Coupé by Bertone and other Italian cars of the time. It appeared on the Jaguar XK120 of October 1948 perhaps a little high, and the Lea Francis Westland Tourer of 1950.

The Jowett Factory Records were obtained by George Mitchell in 1963 and, in addition to the information listed at the end of this book, they show the name of the agent or dealer making the original sale and the original body

Alfa Romeo 6C of 1942 by Bertone. (Bonhams)

An Italian car of 1946-47. (CJ)

and upholstery colours, whilst for home sales the names and addresses of first owners are given.

Every effort has been made to ensure accuracy throughout this work but no responsibility can be accepted for any errors and their consequences. Some of the minor competitive events in particular presented many headaches due to the way they were reported: a "Jowett" in a saloon car event could be a Javelin or a Jupiter running closed. The same competitor could, like Albert Wake, have appeared at different times in a Javelin, or a standard Jupiter or a FHC Jupiter. These cars might be owned simultaneously or consecutively, and a Javelin owner might borrow a Jupiter for an event and of course the reverse!

2: The Jupiter Experiment

William 'Bill' Boddy in his road test of early Jupiter GKY 106 (19) for *Motor Sport* December 1950, after remarking that the Jupiter's performance figures were not very different from the pre-war 1½-litre Meadows-engined HRG, he found himself pleasantly surprised at the handling of the car in the teeming rain that prevailed on the day of the test, noting the high average speed he was able to maintain on a 400-mile round trip.

There was comment on "the steering and suspension with cornering that builds up confidence" and he liked the balance between over- and under-steer. "The tail breaks away first, tail skids easily corrected, seemed to occur rather frequently, probably because fallen leaves made the wet roads more than usually slippery and the rear Goodyears were rather worn. This tendency kept the driver alert". Three months later *Motor Sport* bought a Jupiter (98) and further articles praising the handling, long-distance high-average-speed capabilities, coupled with low driver fatigue and very good fuel economy followed. In 1953 the magazine purchased a Mk1a (972) so their sentiments can be taken as genuine.

A man insistent upon his lack of humbug in his road-test reports was John Bolster, who road tested for *Autosport*. About the day also teeming with rain, that he borrowed his test Jupiter (76), he wrote (18th January 1952) that he did not anticipate much excitement as for him "the luxuriously equipped and solidly constructed body had more of the American convertible than the British 2-seater...and with only 1½ litres of engine it did not seem likely that this would be a brilliant performer. A conscientious tester should discover what happens in extreme driving conditions...accordingly whenever it was safe to do so I flung the spray-enveloped Jupiter through the curves to the best of my ability. I was utterly dumbfounded by the result for the machine simply stuck to the road, and followed the road with complete accuracy".

"Here was a challenge, so I turned off the radio, sat up straight, and entered the next corner at an entirely impossible speed. A very gentle four-wheel drift was the result, and the course was held without any appreciable correction on the steering". He later reflected (*Autosport* 26 December 1952) "it has roadholding and steering of great merit. Even on wet roads it can be cornered at the

Eberhorst united with Jupiter No 1 at his then home in Heston, near Hounslow. (Archive Sloniger)

Below: GKY 106 as prepared for *Motor Sport*. It would soon be used in the 1951 Monte Carlo Rally. (Jowett Cars Ltd)

Above: Fine and mellow. HKU 56 was enthusiastically tested by John Bolster for *Autosport* of January 1952. (© The Klemantaski Collection)

highest speeds and I soon acquired the most abundant confidence in its behaviour. I have driven many faster cars but something intangible about this one made it appeal to me very much and I returned it with much regret".

The opposite view was reported by Tom McCahill in *Meccanix Illustrated* (British edition November 1951) where he wrote "...this little pancake-powered egg-beater...corners and steers worse than any Detroit family bus" and continued "The manufacturers in Merry Albion have us tagged for a bunch of dopes who wouldn't know a sports car if it ran over us". But *Road and Track* (March 1953) looked at two Jupiters and disagreed, as did Dick Hayward writing in the magazine *Motor Sports World*: "Seldom have I read a more unjust evaluation of the handling behaviour of an automobile...this little beauty not only cornered superbly but recovered straight as an arrow out of four-wheel slides, hands off!" Encouraged by Newton Small, Hayward sold his MG TD, bought a Jupiter, and continued "She is all I expected and more. She has better manners than anything I have driven and that includes a couple of Tom's top ten".

Eberhorst was one of the Jupiter's severest critics, remarking to his friend L J Roy Taylor (himself a Jupiter owner then) "Don't hold the car against me, it is not one of my best efforts". This, though, must be received in the light of the professor's unhappiness at ERA, as he told me, with the poor facilities to develop a new car, and the need – always a restriction for a designer – to use existing components.

Bert Hadley commented 25 years later: "I found the Javelin a fantastic car to drive in 1951-52, it was a credit to its designers way back in 1948. The roadholding was incredible and it could easily have contained a power unit with 50% more power. And the Jupiter – well its roadholding was again quite amazing and a credit to the chassis designed by Eberhorst. I can recall driving a Jupiter flat-out in the RAC Rally and it never put a foot wrong".

Bill Robinson took the class in the 1951 Monte Carlo Rally in his Jupiter GKY 256 (18) now lost to us. In his view "The Jupiter's handling was really outstanding in

tight street racing and particularly on adverse surfaces. A mug could drive one faster than other cars, the grip was uncanny in snow: the tyres seem to burn in, and on black ice while other cars were skidding around one could pass them effortlessly!"

The last word shall come from *Autosport* magazine's photographer George Phillips. Offered a Jupiter drive in the 1952 Silverstone Production Sports Car event by Charles Grandfield, he visited Idle, was shown over the car, and reported "I had always looked upon the Jupiter as a bit of a giggle – until I drove one". He had a high regard for his MG TD and could happily throw it about, but he felt he did not do the Jupiter full justice because "the built-in oversteer of the TD was hard to forget. The Jupiter was so much better than the TD, I could have done better with more experience...every swerve I went through I thought 'Christ I could do better than that'".

If in its day the Jupiter could arouse such enthusiasm it is worth enquiring why this should have been so. But apart from its Javelin inheritance it had no pedigree visible to the naked eye. Jowett's Experimental Department, enlarged in 1948 by Charles Grandfield, had done a lot of good work with the Javelin suspension system,

Bert Hadley in the 1951 RAC TT at Dundrod on his way to his class win. (CJ)

its response, front-to-rear interaction, and the like. Woodhead-Monroe the shock absorber people had been very helpful and the Javelin handled well, having a good coordinated system.

For the Jupiter, Jowetts seem to have divined a market gap for a comfortable, reasonably quick touring car and mounted thick (16g) aluminium panelling on a sturdy steel bodyframe; this was then fitted to the chassis designed up to a particular, calculated value of torsional stiffness and other factors, rather than down to a minimum weight. But if there was such a market gap, time quickly ran out, for initially the supply of panels made on aircraft presses depended upon pauses in demand from the aircraft industry. So it was not until the early part of 1952 that the delivery of Jupiters was reduced to months rather than years.

The Jupiter experiment may be regarded as having been promising but not wholly successful in its entirety. The car remains something of an enigma: touring car, sports car or competition car? Its engine although fairly highly tuned for its period, anything less than its 62.5bhp would have been unacceptable. The car does of course require competent handling in spite of the above, because in its day it was being compared with contemporary cars and things improved with time and development. It was clearly more congenial than inveterate oversteerers like the Porsche 356, the MG TD notwithstanding its massive chassis, or the HRG whose good handling was at the expense of its bodywork – efforts to provide the HRG chassis with a modern enveloping shape resulted in even shorter coachwork life.

The experiment began in 1949 at ERA with the unique chassis design of Eberhorst. By all accounts a charming and cultured man, an academic reared in the money-no-object racing workshops of Adolf Hitler's Germany, engineering for economic production in post-war Britain must have been a new experience for him. He took the suspension units and power train from the Jowett Javelin and added to them a chassis frame of which the front structure (crucial to the car's special properties) was only possible by the adoption of the Javelin's horizontal

Robert Eberan von Eberhorst (left) at the British Grand Prix, Silverstone 19th July 1952. (Guy Griffiths)

opposed engine, short in length and low in weight and centre of gravity.

Jupiter chassis tubes were welded in a longitudinal rotating jig. The chassis was crafted from a high chromium/molybdenum steel, lighter than normal steel for the same strength, helpful for today's Jupiter restorers as the steel is also highly rust-resistant.

Gerry Palmer, the Javelin's designer, had not been against a relatively large amount of body roll in his design, and to maintain the Javelin's good handling he had sensibly provided it with an extra front suspension adjustment – track-rod ball height – that when correctly set eliminated steering geometry changes as the suspension deflected under cornering. The Jupiter rolls rather less than the Javelin but the adjustment was retained. Also inherited from the Javelin was its all-round torsion rod springing, which minimises unsprung weight; and finally a well-located live rear axle for which Eberhorst again provided a rigid structure plus a Panhard rod. But his special contribution was the chassis front structure with its trailing diagonal struts providing a more rigid anchorage for the front

Silverstone 10th May 1952. George Phillips in Bert Hadley's 1951 Le Mans Jupiter HAK 366 (131). (Guy Griffiths)

and resistant to scaling and rusting. A version was evolved for bicycle frames such as the well-known Reynolds 531 tubing.

The Jupiter was found not to have the twin vices of chassis steering – where under hard cornering the chassis may twist to alter the steering geometry to oversteer – and suspension steering – where suspension deflection can produce a similar destabilising effect under cornering. Certain MG models for an example suffered from the first, and the second was commonly countered in sports cars by having a suspension with hardly any travel, such as the HRG that was sometimes called 'the springless wonder' and the Morgan Plus 4. The Jupiter's excellent road manners were not at the expense of riding comfort and it was therefore possible to conceive a car with some luxury.

suspension than can be possible with a vertical inline engine which would intrude here. A rarity in those days, the rack-and-pinion steering unit was a good example of its type and well-secured to the front structure.

The chassis turned out to be just a little less torsionally rigid than might have been hoped for, taking into account its sophistication, but the front structure did ensure that any twisting would not upset steering geometry. This lack of torsional rigidity led Reg Korner to design the body such that the coachwork was mounted on a steel bodyframe that still allowed scuttle shake and door sticking to take place, easily cured by cross-bracing and stiffening the mounts between chassis and bodyframe.

The construction of the chassis from straight lengths of largely two sizes of tubing was pivotal for, although it meant it could be produced at the Jowett Idle factory, it could never be as cheap as a £20-or-so pressed steel frame; so it would never be built in high volume and it could never be made by Briggs, the Javelin's body constructor. The 'chromolly' tubing widely used for aeroplane spars and racing car chassis was a lightweight grade of chromium and molybdenum steel very weldable

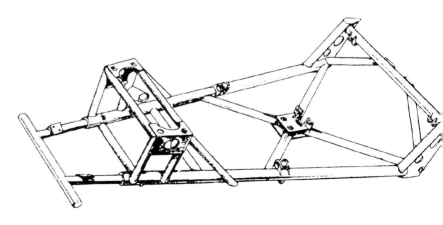

The basic Eberhorst Jupiter frame, showing the front structure on the left. (JCLtd)

There are compromises in the design of all cars and the Jupiter was no exception. The position of the engine close to but forward of the front axle line has two disadvantages: its mass does not contribute to the weight over the driven wheels, indeed slightly subtracts from it, and in its position its inertia contributes less to opposing or slowing down the onset of a spin should the tail break away. The Achilles heel was however the engine inherited from the Javelin – Gerry Palmer's one and only engine design one might add. It lacked two things helpful to any successful engine: crankcase rigidity and good cooling.

Nevertheless this power unit is integral to the design and experimenters have generally found to their chagrin that alternative engines (with the exception of flat-four units) destroy the car's handling qualities. Jowett had problems extracting more than 62.5bhp reliably, but Leao Padman in New Zealand was soon able to demonstrate 90bhp could be obtained reliably and the limit is probably not yet known even now; however more than the usual level of care and forethought will always be an important ingredient in a successful Jupiter engine. Jowett, though, in solving liner sinkage and crankshaft breakage rather late, could not contemplate much increased power for the R1 design and therefore developed its handling capability to the maximum, further stiffening the chassis by a subtle alteration to the central cruciform bracing, and by the perforated pressed-steel stiffening arch or stress panel that formed the bulkhead.

The stress panel used in the R1 may have been the first instance of consequence of the use on a racing car of a technique that was common aircraft practice at the time. Five years later Len Terry, no doubt independently, adopted it on his Formula 1 designs (Lotus 16 etc) up until the introduction of the monocoque.

Detail of the perforated stress panel as used on the Jupiter R1, an idea intended for the Jupiter Mk2 design – see Ch8. (Peter Dixon)

The skin and beneath
The general style of Korner's Jupiter can be traced to a series of Italian designs from around 1944 on Alfa Romeo chassis and a few others such as the 1947 Lancia Aprilia Langenthal cabriolet. Here were to be found the flowing front wing line taken across the door to intersect with the leading edge of the rear wing. In spite of the difficulty of accurately hanging such doors, these elegant designs were repeated for a time, strongly influencing the XK120 of 1948. London-born Reg Korner's brief was design a body with similarities to this Jaguar: the result was widely liked. That it *was* liked is amply borne out by the amount of space photographic editors allotted it – so helpful for historians – in magazines of the period, often in greater measure than can otherwise have been warranted: a good example is *Motor Trend*'s review of the New York show: out of 100 models on display 14 photographs were printed of which three were of the Jupiter; only one other car was pictured even twice. Stylistically therefore the Jupiter was well received.

Chassis
The chassis is made from straight lengths of chromium-molybdenum steel tubing, 3-inch diameter 16swg for the main side-members and 2-inch 18swg for the struts and torsional stiffness members, electric welded. The welder Peter Dear told me that the first efforts "came out goodness knows what shape" so they kept altering the jigs until the chassis sprang into the right shape on removal. For the Mk1a from Chassis 940 there were modifications at the front for the altered steering rack housing, and at the rear to accommodate the revised boot/petrol tank arrangement.

Front suspension
Independent, by unequal length arm, transverse link, with longitudinal silicon manganese steel torsion rod springs. Up to late 1952 the front suspension was the so-called 'metal-bush' type, giving a very firm ride. Then the so-called 'rubber-bush' front suspension was introduced, using Metalastik rubber bushes, quite an early car to have this feature. The telescopic front shock absorbers were now fixed at the top onto the front structure, whereas in the earlier type the shock absorbers were fixed at the top to the upper link; the two types of shock absorber are not interchangeable. Afficionados at the time said the handling of the later type was not quite so good. The last 170 or

so Jupiters built including all Mk1a had the later type, but some Jupiters that started life as metal-bushed have been changed to rubber-bushed. A few intrepid experimenters have replaced the front rubber bushes with bushes made from Nylatron, with noticeably improved results.

Steering

The Javelin front hubs are reversed, bringing the steering arms out at the rear of the hubs instead of the front. This enabled an ERA-designed rack-and-pinion steering unit to be solidly attached to the unyielding chassis front structure above the gearbox. A revised rack housing was evolved for the R1s in 1952 and this appeared on the 1953 Mk1a, requiring a minor chassis alteration. These adjustments are provided: Camber Angle by shims behind the upper link bracket; Tracking by adjustment of steering rod length; and by adjusting the height of the steering ball above the steering arm changes in steering geometry as the suspension deflects can be eliminated. Front ride height is controllable by torsion-rod tension adjustment. There is no adjustment for castor angle. The steering on the Jupiter is very positive and not heavy, even with radial tyres fitted.

Brakes

At initial Jupiter introduction in 1950, the Girling hydromechanical system was adopted as on the Javelin and other makes. The front leading-trailing brake shoes were hydraulically operated while the rear leading-trailing shoes were mechanically operated. The master cylinder was part of a floating link mechanism such that if the hydraulics failed the rear brakes were still actuated. Total friction area was 88¾ sq. inch. From January 1951 (Jupiter 56) the braking system became full hydraulic (i.e. both front and rear) and friction area was increased to 122.8 sq. inch with twin leading shoes at the front. As the braking was good for the heavier Javelin, it is even better on the Jupiter.

Rear axle

The Jupiter has a conventional live rear axle by Salisbury (2HA for hydromechanical, 3HA for full hydraulic) well located by a rubber-bushed transverse stay – the Panhard

Rod – and parallel trailing arms of equal length. Torsion rod springs are as for the front but transverse, running the full width of the chassis, damped by Woodhead Monroe telescopic shock absorbers, the final-drive ratio is 4.56:1 on standard Jupiters, 4.1:1 on the R1. Tyres are 5:50x16 on ventilated disc wheels giving 17mph per 1000rpm in top gear.

Gearbox

Four forward speeds and reverse. Synchromesh on 2nd, 3rd and top. A well-engineered steering column gear shift lever is provided on all Jupiters except the R4s. Floor change was initially offered but never provided, although two Jupiters have been modified for floor shift, one central and the other right-hand. Early Jupiters had gearboxes manufactured by Henry Meadows Ltd, later Jupiters had gearboxes manufactured by Jowett.

Engine

Four horizontally-opposed cylinders. The die-cast aluminium alloy crankcase is split vertically down its centre-line. The four semi-wet liners are a push-fit into the crankcase and have a bore of 72.5mm which, with the 90mm stroke, give a swept volume of 1,486cc. The overhead valves are push-rod operated by a central camshaft. The gas-flowed heads are cast iron, exhausting into a system somewhat more efficient than the Javelin's. Twin carburettors were initially Zenith 30VIG but following competition experience, from about chassis 657, were changed to 30VM in abandonment of the troublesome accelerator pump. Later experimenters have very successfully fitted single-choke Weber type 32IMPE and 32ICH as well as Dell'Ortos.

From about September 1952 Jowett fitted the Series III engine with many detail improvements. Other changes included relocating the SU pump from the scuttle to low down amidships following vapour-lock experience in hot climates; the single air cleaner behind the radiator was replaced at Chassis 590 by individual air cleaners above the carburettors, and the chassis-mounted oil cooler, prone to leaks, was replaced by a more conventionally mounted type for shipments to hot countries.

Jupiter engine bay is shown here with the earlier and more aerodynamic type of engine splash-guards. This Jupiter (264) was new in Gibralter and returned to the UK in 1955. (Alan Beedon)

Coachwork

The bodywork is supported by a complex sheet-steel bodyframe assembly, itself mounted at three points on each side of the chassis in bonded rubber 'silentbloc' units bolted to brackets on the chassis. The bodyframe is best understood by reference to the figure on the following page: it comprises a dash panel (firewall or bulkhead) to the front, a cowl panel subassembly which is the only externally visible part of the bodyframe supporting the bonnet, door hinges and the windscreen. The trafficator arms protrude through it when energised (not LHD USA models). The door sills run aft to the door lock pillars, floor support channels, tail frame, side valances, tail cross-brace assembly and so forth. This whole assembly, largely hidden except for the cowl panel, is the chief area for corrosion as the chassis frame material shows good resistance to such attack. The main

modification was to the Mk1a, and the 1953 Mk1 after about chassis 861, when a tubular cross-brace structure was integrally fitted, running from the rear face of the front structure to the dash panel, and thence to the door top hinges. A recommendation from the Factory to combat steering kick with front-end vibration was the replacement of the Silentbloc front and centre bodymount bushes with something more rigid such as hard-wood blocks – this with the cross-bracing provides a more rigid attachment of the bodyframe to the chassis. A flat strip cross-bracing to the firewall was an after-market modification for the same purpose. The body is made from eleven panels formed from 16swg aluminium. The four one-piece wings are flanged and brass-bolted to the main panels and separated by anti-squeak piping visible externally. To the front the bonnet is hinged at the bodyframe and it incorporates an inner steel stiffening framework and support mount. It has openings for the three grilles and two headlamps.

Bonnet hinges and their mounting boxes are fully adjustable. Door frames are of steel and feature winding windows with fixed quarter-lights whilst the doors are aluminium-skinned. The steel-framed removable windscreen has a Vee of two separate flat pieces of glass, usually laminated, which in the Mk1 is set in a 3-piece chromed brass surround.

The tail section (Mk1) is one large aluminium panel running from the cockpit down to the sills immediately behind the doors and to the tail extremity itself, supported at its front edge by being folded over the waist rail and riveted to it. On the Mk1 there is the small spare-wheel door which carries the number plate, the spare wheel being supported by a steel cradle beneath the fuel tank.

The hood, of double-duck originally (today we prefer German mohair hooding or vinyl) which *Motor Sport** quoted as their 'standard of excellence' for a number

---

*As late as September 1966 'Bill' Boddy terminated a lengthy correspondence in *Motor Sport* on the pros and cons of open cars such as Morgans and Sprites with "What is wanted is a really quick to erect hood giving coupé comfort when it's up. Which is best in this respect? Perhaps the late lamented Jowett Jupiter".

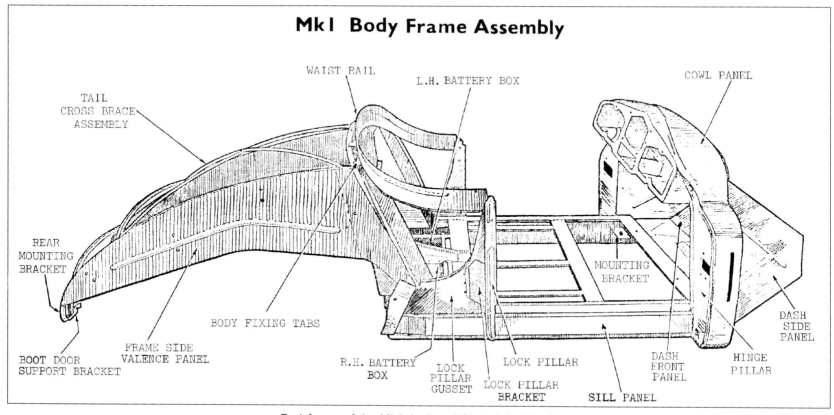

Bodyframe of the Mk1 Jupiter. (JCLtd, John Blazé)

of years, features a frame comprising two main hinged, double-jointed oak side-pieces which meet the tops of the windows, and three hoops running across the width. As original the hood would be fitted with a small glass window in a cast aluminium frame, however this often replaced by a larger clear plastic window. The hood is normally wind and rain proof, and can be folded onto the tail section (cabriolet mode) or more correctly folded out of sight behind the seat.

Within the car is a hide-covered bench seat, the leather seat covering covers a specially shaped Dunlopillo foam base and the seat is capable of accommodating two in comfort and certainly three occasionally. The seat-back tilts forward to access the aluminium boot void (Mk1 Jupiters), and a pair of suitcases ('Revelation cases') that fit were available and listed in the Spare Parts book, although

none have ever shown up. Fore-and-aft seat adjustment is provided but not tilt. The floor is plywood and carpeted.

On the Mk1a the fuel tank is relocated behind the seat, capacity reduced from ten gallons to eight. Its boot has somewhat larger capacity than that of the Mk1 and the spare wheel is accessed from the floor of the boot.

Colours
The Jupiter seat, the part you sit on, was upholstered in hide with the rest of the interior in matching vinyl. The colour was a warm tan colour (not grey Jaguar beige) although red came in, very sparingly at first, towards the end of 1951 when cars finished in copper (also called copper-bronze) were normally trimmed in red. Jupiters could be had in any colour including primer although the most popular colours were red, copper, turquoise-blue

The Jupiter production line at the Jowett factory, 28th March 1952. The leading two Jupiters have their bodies basically in place, the other two await body fitment. Jupiters were built on a simple line by moving their chassis from boxes to boxes (strong, specially made from wood) until wheels fitted. John Berryman in the front Jupiter. At the back a Javelin can just be made out. (C H Wood)

First the engine and drive train were fitted, with the car just pushed from station to station. Then the body frame and body and its trim and the seat were fitted. Finally the hood framing was hand-crafted to the bodywork with wooden pieces attached to the hinging, and the coach-trimmer then created and fitted the hood covering. (As it is a handbuilt car, replacement hoods must always be fitted to the car under restoration).

(a sort of green) and various greens including Bottle, Connaught, and British Racing. The 1953 brochure listed these colours: metallichrome turquoise with red upholstery and beige hood, metallichrome Connaught Green with beige upholstery and beige hood, Ivory with red upholstery and black hood, and Scarlet with beige upholstery and hood. The wing piping always matched the hood, indeed was made from the duck material folded over twisted string in the normal method of the time.

Each body-panel set, hand fitted to the bodyframe at the Jowett's Clayton plant six miles from its main factory, was sprayed as a unit. The chassis with just the front and rear suspension and axles and wheels fitted was then pushed into the final assembly shop.

The seemly prototype Mk1a (560) the only Mk1a with the bonnet strake – showing raked hood line and the higher tail profile due to its externally-accessed boot. (C H Wood)

When finished, fluids were added and the car driven off the end of the line for a short road test which included reversing up a slope to check for jumping out of reverse.

Dimensions
Wheelbase 93 inches (236cm)
Track front 32 inches (132cm)
Track rear 50½ inches (128cm)
Ground clearance 8 inches (20cm)
Overall length 168 inches (427cm)
Width 62 inches (157cm)

Height 56 inches (142cm)
Turning circle 31 feet (9.4m)
Kerb weight usually given as 17cwt (1895lb, 853kg) – but 2100lb (945kg) would be closer for a production Jupiter. Engine: Four cylinders horizontally opposed: bore 72.5mm, stroke 90mm, swept volume 1485cc. Compression ratio 7.6:1 (or 8:1 depending upon fuel available). Maximum power 60.5bhp at 4500rpm

This long-stroke engine was designed when the old RAC HP formula was still in force in the UK, making the engine 13HP for tax purposes.

Summary of Road Test performances from contemporary magazines

Magazine	Car	Weight	Best gear acceleration mph, seconds			Standing-start acceleration mph, seconds				Standing quarter mile	Top speed	Fuel consumption
		lbs	10-30	20-40	30-50	0-30	0-50	0-60	0-70	secs	mph	m.p.g
Motor Nov 1950	GKY106 (Mk1)	2462 as tested		5.8	7.8	5.1	11.7	18.0	29.6	20.5	86.1	25.1
Autocar Dec 1950	GKY107 (Mk1)	2107 curb	5.5	5.1	7.6	5.7	13.1	20.4	30.3		90	27-30
Motor Sport Dec 1950	GKY106 (Mk1)					5.0	11.9	17.0	29.0		88	25-28
Mechanix Illustrated Sept 1951	Early Mk1					5.4	11.9	15.3	21.3		89	
Country Life Dec 1951	Mk1		6.8	5.8				18.5			87.8	26.2
Autosport Jan 1952	HKU 56 (Mk1)	2075 curb					10.5	14.2	21.0	21.0	88	23
Autocar Jan 1953	HKW197 (Mk1a)	2535 as tested	4.9	7.4	7.6	4.9	11.7	16.8	24.5	20.7	85	21-26
Road and Track Mar 1953	Mk1	2382 as tested				4.1	10.4	15.1	22.9	20.44	86.2	31
Autocourse Spring 1953	Mk1a	2072						18.5			88.3	25.8
Measham 1954	HKW197 (Mk1a)			8.0	8.0	4.8	11.0	15.5	21.0		92.5	21-23 Driven hard
*Geoff McAuley 1976	NXH709 (Mk1a)	2027 as tested		4.2	4.4	4.5	8.2	11.0	14.4	18.4	95.5	28-32

* This fast Jupiter of enthusiast and HSCC competitor Geoff McAuley benefitted from his knowledge of engine tuning and a degree of lightening of his car.

Comparison with other cars of the period

Comparisons cannot be made with precision as prices and specifications fluctuated yearly or more frequently. So this inexhaustive list should not be seen as a retrospective buyers' guide. These comparative data from various sources may, however, help the reader to place the Jupiter in the scheme of things in its era.
NB 1-cwt = 112-lb = 50.8-Kgm

Year	Car	Engine capacity litres	Max power bhp	Dry weight cwt	Top speed mph	Length feet	Turning circle feet	UK pre-tax price
1950	Lea Francis 14HP Sports	1.75	77		87-90			£1275
1951	Jupiter	1.5	60	19	88	13½	31	£895
	AC Sports Tourer	2.0	76	25	85	15½	39	£1098
	Austin A40 Sports	1.2	50	19	80	13½	37	£565
	HRG Type 1500	1.5	60	14½	84	12	32	£895
	MG TD	1.25	54	18½	83	12	31¼	£470
	Morgan Plus 4	2.1	68	15½	85	12	33	£590
	Porsche 356	1.3	44	14½	90	13	29	
	Singer Roadster	1.5	58	16¼	73	13	33	
1952	Jupiter Mk1	1.5	62.5	19	90	13½	31	£825
	Jupiter Mk1a	1.5	62.5	19	90	13½	31	£895
	Allard Palm Beach	1.5	47	16½	85	13	28	£800
	Allard Palm Beach	2.25	68	17	90+	13	28	£865
	Austin A40 Sports	1.2	50	19	80	13½	37	£586
	HRG Type 1500	1.5	62	14½	84	12	32	£895
	MG TD	1.25	54	18½	83	12	31¼	£530
	Morgan Plus 4	2.1	68	15½	85	12	33	£620
	Simca Sport	1.22	50	18½	85	14	31	
1953	Jupiter Mk1a	1.5	62.5	19	90	13½	31	£725
	Jupiter R4	1.5	64	14	100	11½	31	£545
	AC Ace	2.0	85		100+			£915
	HRG Type 1500	1.5	62	14½	84	12	32	£895
	Porsche 356	1.5	55	14½	95	13	29	£1260
	Porsche Super	1.5	70	14½	100+	13	29	
	Singer Roadster	1.5	58	16¼	73	13	33	£519
	Triumph TR2	2.0	90	17¾	100	11¾	32	£625
1978	Triumph Spitfire USA version	1.5	57	15½	94	12½	24	

Good Jupiter Works and private race and rally results summary 1950 to 1953

Event	Registration	Crew	Result
Le Mans 24-25 June 1950	GKW 111	Wise / Wisdom	Class winner
Production Sports Car race up to 2-litre Silverstone 26th August 1950	GKW 111	Horace Grimley	Class 5th
RAC TT Dundrod 16 September 1950	GKW 111	Tom Wisdom	Retired when leading
Monte Carlo International Rally 23-31 January 1951	GKY 256 GKY 106	Robinson / Ellison Wilkins / Baxter	Class winner Class 2nd
Tulip International Rally 23-28 April 1951	GKY 256	Robinson / Leck	Class 7th
Lisbon International Rally 2-7 May 1951	BF–17–18	Nogueira	Outright winner
BRDC 1-hour Production Sports Car Race, Silverstone 5th May 1951	GKW 111	Bert Hadley	Retired when leading
Morecambe National Rally 25-26 May 1951	GKW 111 (hood raised)	Tommy Wise	Best Performance by any production closed car
RAC National Rally 4-9 June 1951	HAK 117 GKY 256	Imhoff / Wick Becquart / Lunn	Class 4th Class 5th
Swiss Production Sports Car race Bremgarten, 26th May 1951	BE 13382	Theo Gurzeler	Class winner
Rheineck/Waltzenhauzer Hill-climb 17th June 1951	BE 13382	Theo Gurzeler	Class winner
Le Mans 23-24 June 1951 standard Jupiter	HAK 365	Becquart / Wilkins	Class winner
Rallye de l'Iseran 18-19 August 1951	251–0–81	Armangaud	Overall winner
RAC TT Dundrod 15th September 1951	HAK 366 GKW 111	Bert Hadley Tommy Wise	Class winner Class 2nd
Queen Catharine Monteur Cup for 1½-litre cars, Watkins Glen 15th September 1951	HAK 364 (R1)	George Weaver	Winner – awarded the cup
Monte Carlo International Rally) FHC 22-29 January 1952) Jupiters	582–R–74 MTJ 300	Becquart / Ziegler Ellison / Mason	Class 2nd retired
RAC International Rally 31st March – 5th April 1952	LHR 2 NNK 560	Booth / Bowes Mr & Mrs Still	Class 8th Class 36th
BRDC Production Sports Car race Silverstone 10 May 1952	HAK 366	George Phillips	Class 3rd
British Empire Trophy, Isle of Man 29th May 1952	GKY 256 ZL 6262	Robinson Joe Kelly	Class 3rd Class 6th
Prix de Monte Carlo 2-litre sports car race 1st June 1952 R1 Jupiter	HAK 364	Marcel Becquart	Class 4th
Le Mans 14-15 June 1952. R1 Jupiter	HKW 49	Becquart / Wilkins	Class winner
FCCA Lake Tahoe Rally Sept. 1952	Mk1 Jupiter	Hunter Hackney	Overall Winner
Monte Carlo International Rally) FHC 20-27 January 1953) Jupiters	LOL 1 582–R–74	Grounds / Hay Becquart / Ziegler	Class 4th Class 15th
MCC/Daily Express National Rally 11-14 November 1953	NLX 909	A D C Gordon	Class 3rd

Jowett records by Mk1 Jupiters unless otherwise stated. Mostly in the era

Event	Registration	Crew	Result
Le Mans 1950	GKW 111	Tom Wisdom / Tommy Wise	1819.725 miles in 24 hours
Le Mans 1951	HAK 364 (R1)	Tom Wisdom	Fastest lap 6m 2.0s at 83.373mph
Le Mans 1952	HAK 365	Bert Hadley	Fastest lap 6m 13.7s at 80.60mph
	HAK 364 (R1)	Maurice Gatsonides	Fastest lap 5m 51.4s at 85.86mph
	HKY 48 (R1)	Hadley / Wise	1000 miles in 12hr 33m 1.8s
Monaco 1951	GKY 256	Robinson / Ellison	2m 31s at 47.2mph
circuit 1952	HAK 364 (R1)	Marcel Becquart	2m 12.1s at 54.0mph
Rest & Be 1951	JGA 123	K B Miller	81.9 sec
Thankful 1951	GKY 256	Marcel Becquart	82.1 sec
Hillclimb 1952	GKY 107	Bert Hadley	81.6 sec
Dundrod 1950	GKW 111	Tom Wisdom	6m 28.0 sec
1951	GKW 111	Tommy Wise	6m 17.0 sec
1951	HAK 366	Bert Hadley	6m 21.0 sec
Winfield 1951	GKW 111	Tommy Wise	1m 46 sec
Silverstone 1952	HAK 366	George Phillips	Full circuit: 2m 26 sec
1957	JKW 537 (R4)	Alf Thomas	Club circuit 1m 24 sec
1976	FVG 332	Peter Dixon	Club circuit 1m 26 sec
Prescott 1952	HAK 366	Bert Hadley	53.77 sec
Bo'ness 1952	GKW 111	Bill Brearley	46.9 sec
Goodwood 1952	HKY 344	John Lewis	2m 16.8 sec av of 5 laps, st/start
Standing Km 1952	Mk1 Jupiter	Hunter Hackney (USA)	37.3sec
Standing 1950	GKY 106	*The Motor* magazine	20.5sec
¼-mile 1953	Mk1 Jupiter	Hunter Hackney (USA)	20.1sec
1965	E1 SA 182R	Vic Morrison (NZ)	19.43sec
1967	E1 SA 72R	Ed Wolf (Australia)	19.5sec
1976	NXH 709	Geoff McAuley (GB)	18.4sec

Eberhorst had this to say about chassis tubes: "*The tube is the only element that gives, at the same time, the best torsional and bending rigidity, and you have to have both. I always thought that torsional rigidity was an essential part of road stability, and you can't beat the special properties of tubes for that*". And on ERA he was to say "*Leslie Johnson was a charming chap but the company had no tools, no test beds and no money! I was loaned out, first of all to Jowett, for whom I designed the Jupiter chassis frame by drawing it out in chalk on the shop floor – where mice played! After working at Auto Union and even Cisitalia, that was a crazy way to design a car*".

The year 1950 was no ill-time for the Jupiter to race at Le Mans; its win when just three complete Jupiters existed would surprise Jowett as much as the rest of the watching world. Nevertheless the Jupiter in its road-going form was to be a day-to-day car for most buyers, or maybe used occasionally in local races, rallies, trials or similar. Its power was not up there with the latest most competitive cars but there are several accounts by first or early owners that its handling was far better than contemporary machines.

The author Ernest Dudley, of his "Armchair Detective" novels, owned a Jupiter (14) from new. His daughter remembered how well it handled, much better than his previous car, a TR2. She told me he was a bad driver but the Jupiter always went around corners on all four wheels and she felt safe in it, and Dudley never crashed his Jupiter. Ian Forbes, second owner of coupé Jupiter (28) he raced to a class win at Goodwood, asserted many years later it was the best handling car he had ever owned, before or since. The Jupiter excelled in events where there was a premium on handling, such as the six laps of the Monaco Grand Prix street circuit which completed

Monaco street circuit 1952 sports car race: Marcel Becquart (wearing 10) in the R1. (Copyright Archive Maurice Louche)

the 1951 Monte Carlo Rally, and the day of driving tests on loose surfaces in the 1951 International Lisbon Rally.

For this book the two big events in France, the *Rallye Automobile Monte Carlo* and *Les Vingt Quatre Heures du Mans*, underline the commitment of France to that new-fangled gadget the horseless carriage. One notes that certain car-related terms are of French origin: garage, chauffeur, cabriolet, carburettor, coupé, chicane, tonneau and limousine, while several USA-founded makes of car have French names: Chevrolet is an obvious one, Pontiacq is a town in France, and then there is Cadillac – Frenchman Antoine Laumet the *Sieur de Cadillac* is credited with founding Detroit city.

The International Monte Carlo Rally (organised it is true by Automobile Club de Monaco) began in 1911 as a means of testing the latest improvements and innovations to cars and to improving their durability and suitability for winter touring. Since the *automobilistes* who set off from all over Europe were wealthy people an added attraction were the gaming tables at the destination. The Le Mans 24-hour race commenced in 1923 with the idea of developing road cars for fast road touring reliability with its night racing intended to stress the electrics, rather a weak point in those dim and distant days. Participants had to balance speed against the cars' ability to run for 24 hours as if on a long-distance tour, hence those complicated rules about re-starting on the button after a pit-stop, driver repairs and re-fuelling. It was the well-appointed Jupiter – sublime in every sense of the word with its glass winding windows, quick-to-raise and lower

Excellent class win at the 1950 Le Mans just achieved, notice memories of Churchill still fresh: Mike Wilson (dark glasses, Jowett's time keeper) standing on the left, then Reg Phillips, Tommy Wise toasting the victory, Charlie Clowes (beret), then Tom Wisdom also quenching his thirst and finally Roy Lunn far right. (© The Klemantaski Collection)

hood, and high quality interior trimming that appealed to discerning motorists. And the string of good competition successes also helped. Amongst early Jupiter owners with 'celebrity' status one could mention two-and-four-wheels world champion John Surtees (his very first road car), glitterati such as the actor Peter Ustinov and the film comedian Red Skelton. There was Gerald Lascelles the Queen's cousin, Jimmy Shand the Scottish accordion player and bandleader, Peter Craven world speedway champion 1955 and 1962, Budge Rogers the Bedford and England Rugby Football player, and Aubrey Forshaw who advised Ian Fleming on all motoring matters for 007. Light heavy-weight then heavy-weight champion boxer

Don Cockell had one from new, as did Frank Masefield Baker who went on to become Mayor of Brighton. W Tee, proprietor of *Motor Sport* had a Mk1 and then a Mk1a when it became available. Sir William Lithgow, chairman of his own shipbuilding company, an engineer and technologist by inclination, owned a Jupiter from new. Even, it is rumoured, Colin Chapman in his bachelor days was for a time a Jupiter owner.

The excellent survival rate of the 900 or so Jupiters originally built speaks for itself with a good 45% of production still with us, many in very-well-restored condition.

A typical meeting of Jowett owners in Britain. There were more Jupiters off-camera. Photo taken in 2013. (CJ)

3: The Leap to Fame – Le Mans and the R1 Jupiters

Leslie Johnson's modest fee of £12,000 reputed to have been paid for the design, development and construction of the half-dozen ERA-Jupiter chassis gave Jowett the basis of a far better sports car than they could have designed themselves. It appealed to some quite respectable international drivers, amongst whom were George Weaver, the American Le Mans veteran, Tom Wisdom the well-known motoring journalist who had won a Coupes des Alpes in the 1936 Alpine Trial in the then new Jaguar SS100, Marcel Becquart who had won the Monte Carlo Rally outright with Hotchkiss in 1950, and Bert Hadley who passed up Jaguar drives (including Le Mans 1951 where Bill Lyons wanted to pair him with the emergent Stirling Moss) for the 1½-litre outsider.

Money was always tight at Jowett thanks to the failure of the Javelin to break even (except in 1951) for a variety of reasons and it is enduringly to the credit of Charles Grandfield, Jowett's Engineering Manager, that he was able to get the competition programme going and sustain it at the level he did. Indeed, without his organisational skills, the best results could not have been possible. He personally translated the complex Le Mans and Monte Carlo regulations and ensured that everyone concerned had a copy of the sections relevant to them. In the RAC rallies, mechanics and caches of spares and tyres would be concealed in suitable woodlands along the routes in a form of rule-avoidance that was indulged in by all the teams with a real chance of collecting top honours. Generally it was tyres that were required as Javelins and Jupiters driven hard had quite an appetite for road rubber. If the Javelin lost money, and the good old Bradford made it, the financial contribution of the Jupiter could only be small – for what could something like 900 cars do amongst 64,000 except announce the existence of the marque – and this they certainly did. The Jupiter leaped to prominence with its record-breaking class win in the 1950 Le Mans and, seven months later, thanks to some very experienced winter-weather driving and six quick laps of the Monaco circuit, Jupiters took first and second in class in the Monte Carlo International Rally. Bearing in mind the Javelin's first-time-out wins in the 1949 Monte and its Spa 24-hour race, Jowetts may be forgiven for thinking that to enter was to win.

In British production sports car racing the main rivals were initially the Works and quasi-Works MG; although of

One week before the race: twin fuel tanks, faired headlight caps, special wheel hubs with Alfin drums, quick-release bonnet catches, ultra-light seats. L to R: Horace Grimley, Roy Lunn, Charles Grandfield. (C H Wood)

24-hour Grand Prix d'Endurance were classified in three ways. Firstly there was the general classification, on total distance covered in the 24 hours with the winner awarded the Long Distance Cup. Secondly there was the Index of Performance, a classification (effectively on a handicap basis) according to the degree by which competitors improve upon a minimum distance calculated from the engine capacity with the winner receiving the Index of Performance Cup. Thirdly was the Biennial Cup, awarded on an index basis but confined to entrants who qualified by having exceeded their minimum performance in the previous year's race. Competitors who achieved their minimum calculated performance were automatically invited to the following year's race.

The rules are many and complex and in part are designed to encourage manufacturers to improve all aspects of their products, hence the night racing that places the maximum demand on the electrical components. Refuelling can only take place in the pits, using fuel supplied by the organisers, and only after a certain distance has been covered. On entering the pits the engine must be switched off and can only be fired up by use of the starter-motor. The starting handle hole is sealed before the race and a push start leads to instant disqualification. If a car breaks down out on the circuit the driver himself could work on the car out on the circuit but

slightly less capacity their engines were 'staged' to about the same power as the Jupiter's. By contrast in the USA there was available to the sporting MG owner a wider range of tuning options that could bring 80bhp within reach, at least for the duration of a race or two, and an increase to 1440cc was possible by fitting Lincoln pistons. Compared to the Jupiter, the HRG had a little more power at a little less weight. And Porsche were emerging.

Before considering the three Le Mans races 1950-1952 in detail, the 1½-litre class-winners of the 1937 to 1949 races are reviewed below and compared with the 1950 Jupiter. There was no race in 1936 or 1940-1948.

Year	1½-litre car	Win distance	Win speed
1937	Aston Martin	1720.378 miles	71.683mph
1938	Adler	1718.111 miles	71.587mph
1939	HRG	1619.280 miles	67.307mph
1949	HRG	1700.181 miles	70.842mph
1950	Jupiter	1819.725 miles	75.821mph

There were normally 60 starters, and the finishers of the

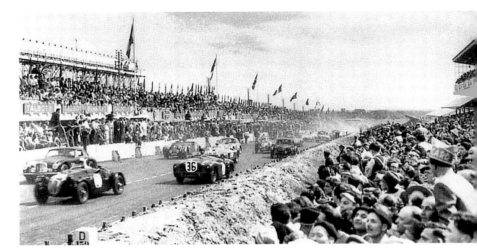

Just after the start of the 1950 Le Mans. (Washington Photo)

using only tools and spares carried. It could only be fixed in the pits if the driver first pushes it there unaided. These things did occasionally actually occur in these races!

In 1949 at the Spa 24-hour race a lightened (aluminium-bodied) but otherwise more-or-less correct Javelin driven by Tom Wisdom and Anthony Hume won their 2-litre Touring Car class, so Jowetts were tempted to try their luck at Le Mans, at a time when only three complete Jupiters existed. Their good pit-work owed more to wartime fire drill at the Factory than race experience, and earned the applause of those in a position to observe. The Jupiter for 1950 was the development model registered for the road as GKW 111, about 3-cwt lighter

than the production car was to be. It had special low-friction wheel bearings, an aero screen, and lightweight bucket seats. It was transported to the circuit on a lorry which had to be reversed up to a bank somewhere near the town of Le Mans as the only way of unloading the car.

The 1950 Le Mans was won outright by Louis Rosier in a 4483cc Talbot, after changing a rocker shaft himself and he driving for 23 hours out of the 24. A team of three XK120s made up Jaguar's first appearance at Le Mans, with Bert Hadley and Leslie Johnson maintaining third place for 21 hours in one of them until gearbox failure forced its retirement. The two XK120s running at the end finished 12th and 15th.

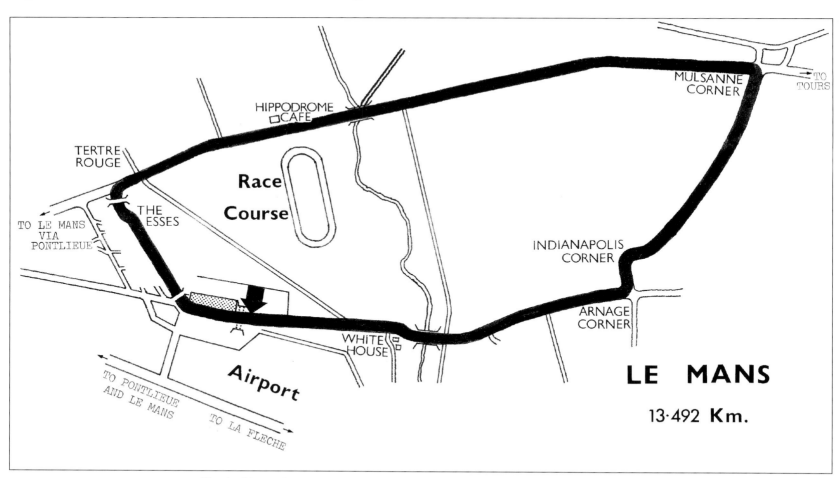

The Le Mans circuit in the 1950s, mostly on ordinary town roads. (John Blazé)

The two Jupiter drivers were Tom Wisdom and Tommy Wise, and so the car was nicknamed 'SAGACIOUS II' with the sobriquet sign-written on the car's bonnet for the race. Wisdom, in addition to being a very quick driver much in demand, was the motoring editor of the *Daily Herald*, the *Sunday People*, and *Sporting Life* (which accounts for that paper's excellent coverage of motor sport in those days), whilst Tommy Wise had much pre-war trials experience and five rallies under his belt.

The Jupiter could run for six hours without refuelling. Since Tommy Wise needed to pee more often, blistering barnacles! A pee-hole was created: a rubber tube running down his trouser to a tray. To a French paper the Jupiter was *une voiture avec pissoire*!

The Jupiter won its class at 16th overall out of 29 finishers with a class-record 220 laps – 1819.725 miles covered at 75.821mph, ahead of a 2443cc Riley, the George Phillips/Eric Winterbottom 1224cc MG TC (9 laps behind at class 2nd), a 2443cc Healey, a 1970cc Frazer Nash, and the 'clockwork mice' as the smaller-engined cars were called. The MG, which did not look like an MG with its much lightened special body – more

Tidings of comfort and joy for Chef d'Equipe Grandfield, far left. Next to him Tommy Wise, Mike Wilson (beret) Tom Wisdom, Roy Lunn and Horace Grimley. (© The Klemantaski Collection)

like the 1949 HRG – ran faultlessly but was no match for the Jupiter.

The Jupiter's fastest lap was said to have been at 80mph; it led the 1½-litre field for most of the race, so only briefly falling behind that MG when delayed at about 9pm with a broken fuel pipe causing a fuel leak. The 1491cc Simca-Gordinis of Gordini/Simon and Loyer/Behra were out after 14 and 50 laps respectively, and the Fiat retired after 75. The Jupiter made four pit-stops, only the fuel line problem costing as long as eight minutes. It was placed 11th in the Index of Performance but, significantly perhaps, I was told that by the time Tommy Wise had driven the car all the way back to the Factory it had a failing head gasket.

The 1950 Le Mans was followed seven months later by the equally spectacular 1-2 in class the Monte Carlo International Rally. So naturally the 1951 Le Mans beckoned.

Le Mans 1951 was run in the wettest after-dark conditions the event had seen, with seven hours of night driving to frighten the most courageous. It rained all day Friday and the Saturday morning, but although dry for the start, spectators sloshed around in the yellow mud. It was also the race where many British competitors were troubled by the lower than expected octane rating of the

Tom Wisdom and GKW 111 Le Mans 1950.
(© The Klemantaski Collection)

For competition, a lighter, narrower Jupiter with simpler coachwork was proposed and design began soon on the Jupiter type R1; so by early 1951 the sketch above had been produced by Phil Stephenson. The R1 was to be on the Eberhorst chassis, slightly narrowed, as the car would be a 2-seater not a 2/3 seater. So the essential chassis tubing was retained.

The 1:8 scale model made from Plasticine came next (top-right, photo taken by C H Wood on the 26th May 1951).

C H Wood photographed the finished race-ready car (right) in early June. It was so light that the passenger seat was not load-bearing as the regs did not say it should be. Styling is similar to the 1949 class-win HRG.

supplied fuel. As a consequence some improvisation took place in in certain camps. The event was to see the first outright win by a Jaguar.

The 1½-litre class contained four very rapid 1.4-litre 85bhp Simca-Gordinis entered by Amedée Gordini, plus the MG TD MkII in streamlined prototype MGA bodywork entered by George Phillips. Against these were pitted HAK 364 the new Jupiter type R1 to be driven by Wise and Wisdom wearing 41, plus a brace of lightweight 'standard' Jupiters which were HAK 366 (131) for Bert Hadley and Charles Goodacre (two former Austin Works drivers – Hadley was one of the fastest drivers of his day who had a soft spot for Jowett) and HAK 365 (132) for Marcel Becquart and Gordon Wilkins, their car lucky to

get a drive as it was the sixth reserve so with race number 66. All three cars were specially built for this Le Mans with somewhat tuned engines. The 'standard' Jupiters were made of thinner aluminium panels and a simplified bodyframe with many large lightening holes. Bench seat, bumpers and hood framing were of course removed with lightweight bucket seats installed.

The last two cars away were the Aston Martin of Reg Parnell and Tom Wisdom's Jupiter. After one lap it was Gonzales in his Talbot in the lead (to applause from spectators) followed by Stirling Moss in his Jaguar. Moss soon passed the Talbot and held the lead until his retirement sometime soon after midnight. In the Jupiter's class, the Simcas set up a murderous pace from the start, three of

Becquart in HAK 365 at scrutineering. On the left Jowett man T Hancock (good tenor voice in Jowett's choir) and the Zenith Carburettor man Charlie Clowes. (JCLtd)

them lapping at over 90mph (as fast or faster than the Aston Martins, Frazer Nashs and even some Ferraris) and were not expected to last the distance, while the MG TD settled down to about 82½mph average, hitting 107mph down the straights. The R1 Jupiter accelerated to match.

Retirements came quickly. The Hadley Jupiter was the second car out of the race after 19 laps at 78.5mph average, with a broken valve collar; he was most annoyed, he told me, because as a skilled mechanic in his own right, with the spare and a few tools he could have fixed it by the roadside. There was soon the first Simca retirement. After three hours the R1 and the MG were still on the same lap but then the MG made two pit stops in quick succession, thereafter continuing at a much reduced 67mph. After five hours the R1, which had exceeded 105mph down the Mulsanne Straight, having averaged 80.68mph for its 45 laps, suddenly developed a thirst for water and retired with a blown head-gasket, and the MG with a melted piston was soon to follow

The second Simca was already out and the third was soon to follow, leaving the Veyron/Monneret Simca well placed at nightfall eight laps ahead of the surviving Jupiter of Becquart/Wilkins and the 1100cc Porsche of Veuillet/

Mouche. At daybreak Becquart, by now nine laps behind the ever so fast Simca and three laps behind the Porsche did not have long to wait, for 1½ hours after headlights were switched off he passed the Simca slowly making its way to its pit – so all the highly-tuned Simca engines had failed – and that lucky so-and-so Marcel Becquart toured to finish, seven laps behind the Porsche which was in a different class – also in the closing hours the touring Jupiter, sole remaining car in its class, was passed by the very rapid and reliable 861cc DB Flat Twin of Bonnet/Bayol which finished one place higher than the Jupiter.

The class-winning Jupiter's position in the General Category was 23rd, a mere one lap behind the 4.3-litre Bentley Corniche of W S F Hay and Tommy Clarke.

The Le Mans race of 1951: some fastest laps:

Simca	37	5min 35.8sec	89.88mph
Simca	38	5min 20.8sec	94.08mph
Simca	39	5min 20.3sec	94.23mph
Simca	40	5min 27.4sec	92.19mph
MG TD	43	6min 00.1sec	83.81mph
Jupiter R1	41	6min 02.0sec	83.373mph
Hadley	42	6min 13.7sec	80.60mph
Becquart	66	6min 19.0sec	79.633mph

Jowetts could be reasonably satisfied with the way the R1 had closely matched the more highly tuned MG and accordingly it was shipped to the USA for the Queen Catharine Montour Cup, the race for 1½-litre sports cars, when Grandfield was assured that the New York and Chicago importer Max Hoffman could arrange a good enough driver for it.

This was at the **1951 Watkins Glen** over the weekend **14-15 September** and Hoffman got George Weaver to drive the R1. Jowett's top mechanic Horace Grimley ("worth six men" in Grandfield's estimation) was in attendance. The Glen was considered a difficult and hazardous course, mostly ordinary roads, which clearly suited the Jupiter. Weaver had dominated the first race in his Maserati V8R1 known as "Poison Lil" so the cameras

Straight no chaser – a famous victory for George Weaver in the ex-Le Mans R1 Jupiter now white. (*Motor Trend*)

55 seconds ahead of the second-placed Lester-MG. An HRG was third. Hugh Byfield was a sad 29th at 8 laps down on Weaver. Weaver's 68.96mph speed was 5mph faster than the previous year's winning speed. On his lap of honour he carried the race's Assistant Technical Inspector straddled across the back of the R1. It was not until Christmas Eve that Grimley reappeared in the Experimental Department, just in time to help with the demolition of a barrel of beer thoughtfully provided by Wisdom and Wise.

Watkins Glen was huge triumph for Jowett – to finish ahead of a Lester-MG was all but incredible, due to the R1's excellent handling on the difficult course and Weaver's superb driving. Jowett then put out a simple brochure on the R1 to see if there might be the possibility of overseas sales: power of 70bhp at 5000rpm was quoted from a compression ratio of 9.25:1 and with a special higher-lift camshaft – but no sales were made.

For the Le Mans of 1952 a further two R1's were built, all three needing all-enveloping front-end bodywork to comply with new regulations. Tom Bradley built the chassis (although a production-line welder, he did all the R1 chassis welding) together with Donald Wade, an ex-AJS Works motorcycle rider who worked on the R1s in his spare time; he later joined the Jaguar competitions department. Bill Poulter and Bill Egglestone constructed the body and the early car was updated as they proceeded. As usual, close attention to detail was required by Charles Grandfield, entailing perhaps 30 hours of polishing the engine's moving internals to stress-relieve and reduce oil drag. Phill Green drove ex Monte GKY 107 to Wolverhampton to collect four 10-gallon airflow tail fuel tanks and four water radiators beautifully made in aluminium to aircraft standards by Marston Excelsior who donated them to Jowett.

The practice R1, HAK 364, was accepted for Le Mans as the fourth reserve for Maurice Gatsonides, the very fast Dutch driver who had co-driven Nijevelt's Javelin in the Tulip Rally two months earlier (where they were robbed of a possible victory by a stuck radiator blind causing boiling) and Nijevelt.

and commentators were onto him as he drove the R1 in the Queen Catharine Montour 1½-litre race. Hugh Byfield had entered his standard Jupiter in the same event. There was a Le Mans-type line-up start and the 33 entrants were parked diagonally with the R1 about a dozen cars down from the front.

Two MGs were the first away followed by a 1400cc Siata, but by about four miles into the first lap George Weaver's flawless driving of the R1 Jupiter had caught all the cars ahead of him. He was pressed hard by the Lester-MG for most of the race and picked off the tail-enders in front of a crowd said to number 175,000. He never lost the lead, finishing the 11-lap race 1 minute

First, however, Becquart was to drive it on **1st June** in the **1951 Prix de Monte Carlo** race for sports cars of up to 2 litres (the F1 GP was on the following day!). The sports car event was run over 65 laps of the Monaco Grand Prix street circuit, a distance of about 127 miles. Stirling Moss took pole position with his Frazer Nash at 2min 4.7sec with Becquart on the fourth row with 2min 12.1sec; he finished a very creditable fourth in the 1½-litre class at ninth overall – 61 laps, 2hr 14min 12.1sec of very demanding driving. His average speed was 53.1mph. He finished ahead of two Ferraris (one driven by Castelotti), a BMW, a DB, a Veritas and others – see photo on page 28 (top). Of the R1, Becquart later told me "On such a twisty circuit I had no problem for road holding, just wishing the car could have been faster!". The winner was a 1.9-litre Gordini at 57.12mph.

The **1952 Le Mans 24-hour Grand Prix d'Endurance** on **14-15 June** contained a drama undimmed by the passage of time. The Jaguars, having been too hastily fitted with untried bodywork to meet the threat posed by Mercedes's post-war return to motor racing, quickly excluded themselves through overheating caused by the separate header tank required by the bodywork, a problem only recognised just before the race. One car was not modified and soon retired. Another was modified but the engine became damaged so it retired, as did Stirling Moss's Jaguar with mechanical failure.

The 2.3-litre Gordini led a Talbot for nine hours (French cars, French drivers!) but retired shortly before dawn, leaving the 4½-litre Talbot of Pierre Levegh to uphold French honour four laps ahead of the highest-placed Mercedes. The German car was unable to close the 21-minute gap as Levegh circulated relentlessly, determined to drive the entire 24 hours himself, even though at his last refuelling stop at 21 hours he was utterly exhausted and barely able to stand. With little more than an hour left, to the dismay of the partisan crowd, he missed a down-shift, the engine over-revved and broke a conrod, allowing the Mercedes (German cars, German drivers!) through to their 1–2 racing comeback a mere seven years after the war's end. The crowd did not take

Jupiter R1 in 1952 form, taxed and on the road. Even the dynamo pulley is lightweight. (C H Wood)

the German victory well, and no recording of their national anthem could be found to be played.

In opposition to the Jowetts in the 1½-litre class were a 1491cc Gordini, a 1484cc Porsche and a 1342cc OSCA, all faster than the Jupiters. Veuillet and Mouche were back with a factory-entered 1086cc Porsche and also in the same class was a very fast short-lived Simca (4 laps).

Thanks to last-minute withdrawals all the reserves were called up, therefore including Maurice Gatsonides, who hurriedly matt-painted his R1 (HAK 364 the practice R1) a bright orange (the Dutch Royal family is the House of Orange) distinguishing it from green (HKY 48) for Hadley and blue (HKY 49) for Becquart and Wilkins. As it happens the large round aircraft lights in the sides of the R1s were blue, green and orange, helping the R1s to be identified at night as they came into the pits.

There was no Sagacious II this year for Wisdom co-drove with Leslie Johnson the American Nash-engined Healey to third overall.

Jowetts had solved the gasket problem so raised the compression ratio to 9.25:1 but the crankshaft weakness was not yet understood and, although the R1s were capable it was said of 115mph on tow down the Mulsanne, the drivers had to be content with lower average speeds than they knew their competitors would use. The OSCA, designed by the Maserati brothers with bodywork by Vignale (said to have been built in only 10 days) and developing 93bhp for an all-up weight of only 1450lb, regarded the Loyer/Rinen Gordini and the Lechaise/Marin Porsche as their opposition. Extra air intakes were cut into the noses of the Yorkshire cars to allow plenty of cool air to reach the carburettor intakes. Fortuitously, as it turned out, the Becquart/Wilkins car missed the last practice session for the fitting of a new engine following a blow-up.

At 4pm as usual Charles Faroux flagged off the 57

Artistry in Motion. Le Mans 1952 soon after the start: Mau Gatsonides (No 64) leads Bert Hadley (No 46). No 47 is the Porsche 356SL of Lechaise/Marin while 48 is Damonte's very fast 1100cc OSCA. (Washington Photo)

starters and Gatsonides initially set the Jowett pace. An exhilarating lap was completed by him for the history books in 5min 51.4sec (85.86mph) but thereafter he settled into circulating with Hadley on his tail for 3½ hours averaging over 81mph. The Gordini, for the glory of France, led the class at nearly 94mph for its 134 minutes, to retire after 25 laps, leaving the OSCA just ahead of the 1½-litre Porsche on lap 22. Gatso and Hadley were on lap 21, but Becquart with 20 laps completed was already in the pits with the engine of his R1 not running properly.

At nightfall the OSCA was 11 seconds ahead of the Porsche on lap 57 whilst Hadley (lap 53) was keeping up with the 1100cc Porsche. Gatsonides was 2 laps behind Hadley while Becquart (the engine fault temporarily cured after several pit stops) was on his 44th lap but about to come in for a half-hour pit stop for a complete clear-out of carburettors, fuel lines and fuel tanks. Water and sand in the official petrol supplied were confirmed and officially admitted as the cause of the trouble.

After 7hrs 18mins 51.1sec, 68 laps at 77.9mph the crankshaft of the orange Jupiter broke, so Gatso, who had driven the whole time, was out. Hadley was on his 70th lap, three laps behind the 1½-litre Porsche, which in its turn was over a lap behind the OSCA. Becquart had completed 59 laps. Gatso was later to comment in his book *The Never Ending Race*: "This Le Mans reminds me of a very pleasant car with excellent roadholding and cornering, which enabled me several times to pass bigger and much faster cars on the bends".

At half time, 4am, the race between the OSCA and the Porsche intensified until the OSCA made a pit stop after 120 laps allowing the Porsche into the class lead. Hadley, 15 laps ahead of Becquart, was taking it easy as, he told me, he knew if he drove harder something in the Jupiter would break.

When the usual early morning fog developed, drifting across the roads in heavy swathes especially from Mulsanne to Arnage and thence to the pits, Hadley found he could best get around by following Becquart who was an unparalleled driver in foggy conditions sometimes so thick that the Mercs had to drive with their gull-wing doors open and flapping!

Left: Refuelling stop for Becquart's Jupiter type R1. A plombeur seals the filler cap. Right: Becquart back in the pits with the race over. (Both photos © The Klemantaski Collection)

Disaster again struck the Jowett team, for after nearly 16 hours of driving the Hadley/Wise R1 broke its crankshaft near Arnage. It had completed 149 laps at 78.6mph, and was six laps ahead of the 1100cc Porsche and a certain speeding 851cc Dyna-Panhard, and 14 laps ahead of the remaining Jupiter. Hadley's best lap was 6min 5.7sec.

The 1½-litre Porsche still led the class at 158 laps, but the OSCA was pressing hard and closing, and nearly an hour later was to set its fastest lap – 89.7mph – to snatch the class lead. Soon, though, the German car made two unscheduled pit stop on consecutive laps, thereafter proceeding at a speed reduced by about 10mph to 77mph. The Porsche, like the Jowett, was forced to play a waiting game; but the wait was short as after 168 laps the OSCA broke its clutch and in vain its driver took an hour to push the car the couple of miles back to the pits. Becquart, although no threat with a deficit of 21 laps, was slowly gaining on the Porsche when, with

4½ hours of the race left, Eugene Martin pit-stopped the Porsche and failed to switch off its engine. This led to his disqualification. He went to find the Clerk of the Course and said that he had switched off but the engine was 'running on'. He was wasting his time as he was not believed. An observer reported that in fact the starter-motor had failed so it could not re-start on the button.

Meanwhile, in the Jowett pit, a careful check of the records of the two engines that had broken their cranks revealed that the 48-hour life on test-bed simulation of racing conditions was reduced to precisely 24 hours of the real thing! Prudence not speed now required!

So while the pit staff endured the Tortures of Tantalus, Becquart in the sole surviving 1½-litre car showed he was champion at keeping her rolling as he once again toured to finish, the class win of 1751.586 miles achieved at an average speed of 72.94mph, unsurprisingly a lowly 15th in the Index of Performance and 9th and last in the Biennial Cup. About 19 laps had been lost through no fault of the car or drivers, the water and sand in the petrol helping to ensure no crank fracture!

Nevertheless Jowett had their third class win in three consecutive events and the successful car was transported to their showroom in Albemarle Street, London where it remained on show for two weeks – a laurel wreath on the front of the bonnet – and still covered in its Le Mans grime with dead flies on all forward-facing surfaces. It was then driven back to Bradford by Phill Green, very carefully! He remembered stopping at the Ram Jam Inn 8 miles north of Stamford, for lunch. On strip-down the crankshaft was crack-detected and found to have a crack beginning. The oval-webbed shaft was long overdue.

Jowetts never raced the R1s again, although they survived 1953 stored in the Experimental Department. Near the end of 1953 after the factory sell-off, International Harvester began moving their planners into the Experimental area, and when there was a shortage of space the three R1s, hand-built at a reputed cost of £5000 each, had to go. They were stripped down to their bare frames with main components put on the factory scrap-heap with their chassis cut into halves.

The management played safe to avoid the possibility of anything happening to a subsequent owner.

However, employees often took parts from the scrapheap and two apprentices took a fancy to the remains of the R1s: Tony Lockey paid about £5 for a bare frame for a V8 special he had in mind (never built, chassis almost certainly disposed of) whereas £30 bought Eric Price enough parts to reassemble a complete car, with the exception of the engine as these were scarce. The car was given a Vauxhall engine and registered for the road in 1962. Some years later the chassis was converted to take a Javelin engine and the discovery was made that by design or fluke it was the 1952 class winner of Becquart and Wilkins. Of the special Alfin hubs, one had traces of orange paint, one blue, and two of green. The car has since been accurately and entirely restored to its original state thanks to the untiring efforts of Peter Dixon, Dennis Sparrow and a specialist chassis-man, and even its original HKW 49 road-registration has been returned to it.

There was some rule-bending at Le Mans: only the actual driver of a car was permitted to work on his car, however advice and refreshments could be and were given. Small tools and components could be smuggled to the drivers cunningly hidden in bread rolls or pieces of fruit – so long as the pit watchman was distracted and not looking!

Le Mans was truly a 'Grand Prix d'Endurance' as the number of starters and finishers for our three races show:–

1950 – 60 starters and 29 finishers
1951 – 60 starters and 30 finishers
1952 – 57 starters and 17 finishers

To summarise, in the 1950 'Leap to Fame' race, at the finish all in front of the Jupiter were bigger-engined cars: an XK120 was one place 5 laps ahead yet a 2½-litre RMB Riley one place 7 laps behind. Things were not the same in 1951 with a 1086cc Porsche 20th with 210 laps, an 861cc DB Panhard 21st with 206 laps and the 1½-litre class-winning Jupiter 23rd with 203 laps; but a Bentley

was 22nd just one lap ahead of the Jupiter. It was similar in 1952 with the Jupiter's class-winning 210 laps (13th) bettered by 11th-placed 1086cc Porsche with 220 laps and an 851cc Dyna Panhard at 12th with 217 laps.

For the Jowett-free 1953 event the class-winning 1½-litre Porsche (overall 15th) covered 247 laps with the next-placed car, another Porsche, on the same lap at the finish. So Jowett would have had quite a lot to do to take a class win in 1953, which of course they were not in a position to attempt.

Rescued and running 1952 class-winning R1 Jupiter in 1962 with a new but not permanent registration. (Roger Barrett)

Peter Dixon in the fully-restored class-winning R1 Jupiter in the 2001 Le Mans Legends race. (Hugo Dixon)

4: The Major Rallies 1949 to 1953

Jowetts had a longer association with the Monte Carlo International Rally than with any other international event, extending from the first post-war Monte of 1949, through the Jupiter years and on into the mid-1950s, an association that was to be rewarded by two class wins, an overall fifth, and several other high placings. It began by Raymond Mays of ERA suggesting to Jowett that they should have a go at the Monte. Charles Grandfield had had some useful experience in the preparation side of rallying with the pre-war Austin teams, and so it came to pass that Jowett's first rally was with a Javelin and it was their first success when in the 1949 Monte Tommy Wise and Cuth Harrison finished class first at overall tenth to take the Riviera Cup. Gerry Palmer had gone too, for the ride, and paid his way by helping the Auto Club de Monaco with their arithmetic, for initially they had placed the Javelin 3rd in class.

In the 1950 event Jowett entered a team of three Works Javelins. One was crewed by Tommy Wise and Mike Wilson who at the finish were classified class fifteenth. Another was crewed by Captain John Minchin of Hendon's Police Driving School, photographer Louis Klemantaski,

and the motoring writer Eason Gibson. The third was entered by Bill Robinson and T Leck. On the last leg the screen wipers of Minchin's Javelin failed and John drove as fast as he could over the Col des Leques in falling snow with his head out of the window, while Klemantaski drove the last flat-out blind from Nice to Monte Carlo; they arrived apparently 15 seconds outside the time limit. The following year it was learned that there had been another error and the Javelin was officially re-classified as a finisher.

Becquart won the 1950 Monte outright in his 3½-litre Hotchkiss, giving that marque its record-breaking sixth successive Monte Carlo Rally outright win. This victory made him a big name in the motor sporting world especially the French motor sporting world.

For the **1951 Monte Carlo International Rally**, Grandfield replied with a team of three well-prepared Jupiters. This was the 21st International Monte Carlo Rally which took place from the **23rd** to **31st** of **January** and was filmed by Shell. Out of an unprecedented 362 entries 337 started, 65 of them – including four Jupiters – from Glasgow.

Tommy Wise (left) every inch the motor trader with the Javelin's designer Gerry Palmer at the Factory with the car prepared for the first post-war Monte in 1949. (C H Wood)

The rally was strictly confined to standard series-built passenger cars that had to correspond exactly to a model built by a recognised firm, described in that manufacturer's catalogue, and offered for sale through normal commercial channels. At least 30 had to have been built and be ready for delivery to the public by 1st November 1950 and the Jupiter qualified thanks to the rolling chassis ordered by accredited coachbuilders. Drophead and 'all-weather' bodywork was accepted provided the cars were closed before crossing the finishing line at Monaco and kept closed until after the Acceleration/Braking (A/B) and Speed/Regularity tests had been completed. Few deviations from the catalogued specification were permitted and there were penalties for faults and damage on arrival: for example a mudguard wrenched off or a car no longer having the specified dimensions due to a crash entailed a 5-point penalty; a headlamp not working 50 points and an all-weather body not closed on arrival 20 points. A new mountain section in France had been added for all competitors, as was the speed/regularity test on the Monaco Grand Prix circuit, devised in part to decide the finishing order if more than

one car should reach Monte Carlo without penalty.

There were six starts: Glasgow, Oslo, Stockholm, Lisbon, Palermo and Monte Carlo itself; each route was about 2000 miles in length and the cars had to average between 31½ and 41 mph to avoid penalisation, with 10 points per minute late or early at controls.

There were two final tests at Monaco. The Acceleration/Braking test was over 250 metres: from a standing start you had to accelerate to cross a 200-metre line, brake hard to stop, then reverse over it, and then accelerate 50 metres for a flying finish. The Speed/Regularity run comprised six laps of the 1.98-mile Monaco Grand Prix circuit, which had to be lapped as fast as possible with as little variation as possible between the last four laps. An additional penalty was applied for any lack of regularity between the first two laps. A complex formula was applied to calculate the regularity figure. It was his knowledge of this circuit that enabled local man Louis Chiron to improve the position of his Delahaye from 44th to 6th for example. However, one error like a fluffed gear change in the 250-metre A/B test could nullify over 3000 kilometres of faultless driving, for the time taken was counted as half a mark per second – at 30 marks to the minute easily the most burdensome test.

A 'flu epidemic was raging in Britain when on Tuesday 23rd January the Glasgow starters were flagged away from Blythswood Square, where the RSAC had its offices. Of the four Jupiters, three were the Works entries GKY 106 (19) for Tommy Wise and Jowett's Chief Experimental Engineer Horace Grimley, GKY 107 (21) for Gordon Wilkins (of *The Autocar*) and the BBC's Raymond Baxter who gave broadcasts from each control stop, and GKY 265 (18) of Robert Ellison and Bill Robinson, both Lancashire Jowett agents who had come to notice the previous year after some useful rally efforts in their Javelins. The ill-fated private entry JGA 123 (41) of K B Miller and F D Lang soon blew a head gasket and retired before the Carlisle control, whereas the other three crossed the Channel on the SS *Dinard* and followed the circuitous route northward through Belgium, Holland, then through Paris (where the rally crews were all well

At the Dover quayside on the way out: L to R at the front: Ellison, Wise, Grimley, Wilkins, Robinson, Baxter. (Robinson)

gradients, then over the 3800-foot Col des Leques to Grasse, then finally on to Nice and Monte Carlo. No less than 15 Gordini-tuned Simcas were the Jupiters' main threat in the 1½-litre category with top-flight French racing drivers at their wheels.

Robinson and Ellison shared the driving of GKY 256. There was a bag of cinders at both seating positions, needed about twice Robinson told me; this was typical of their careful winter rally technique. Robinson tended to drive the mountain and snow sections, and the crossing of the St Julien Pass on the Le Puy-Valence section had seen them blaze the trail for the other competitors, as the previous control had warned them to avoid the more direct route over the pass where the fresh snow-drifts were known to be up to 13 feet deep. However they took a wrong turning at one point and they headed over the pass by following the track made by a farm cart.

So they rushed some of the worst parts just to keep going and the Jupiter came safely through. The fresh, firm snow gave way to six inches to a foot of icy slush on the Digne-Grasse section and they found it difficult just to keep

entertained), arriving after relatively untaxing motoring at Clermont-Ferrand in the mountainous Massif Central on the Thursday.

That night the Jupiters travelled the last 430 miles through the new section over the Auvergne mountains up 1:8 gradients, to the 3400-foot Col du Pertuis, then descending to Valence in the Rhone Valley, followed by a climb through the Southern Alps to Gap, encountering a snow storm along the severely hilly and winding road to Digne again with 1:8

The three Works Jupiters prepared for the 1951 Monte Carlo Rally. Snow chains were slow to fit in those days, so two chained wheels were carried; one inside, one outside. Rope and shovel implies heavy snow anticipated. (JCLtd)

The Robinson/Ellison Jupiter (18) on the 75-mile Digne/Grasse section in the Provence-Alpes-Côte-d'Azur. The car on the left (possibly a photographer's) has pulled out of the way of the competitors. (LAT Photographic)

Below: Ellison drove in the Acceleration/Braking test on the wet quayside. Had to be with luggage – some of it! (LAT Photographic)

moving – at one point they passed a competitor cutting his way out of an entanglement of fallen telegraph wires. They could hear the wires snapping as they forced the Jupiter through, and fortunately there was no damage to it.

By contrast the route down the treacherous lower slopes from Grasse to Nice and Monaco was in heavy tropical rain.

The cars refuelled in Nice with only the tortuous run through the lower Corniche remaining between them and Monte Carlo; the Baxter/Wilkins Jupiter clocked in with a bare minute in hand thanks to the need to send radio reports to the BBC. According to *The Motor* his "nightly

broadcasts from various controls were an outstanding feature of this year's event". This was the second of Baxter's 14 consecutive Montes. He had flown Spitfires in the war and was especially noted for his ability to drive fast at night.

Tough though the road section undoubtedly was, of the 337 starters, 307 reached Monte Carlo, of whom 194, including six Javelins, had penalty points, whereas 113 cars including two Javelins and our three Works Jupiters had escaped penalties.

It was sleepy time down south as tired crews, including the penalty-free, began to check in at the famous "Arrivée" arch in the Boulevard Charles III to immediately take the Acceleration/Braking test on the quayside.

Early arrivals found the surface swimming with rainwater and it was felt that the later arrivals, principally from the Lisbon start, had the advantage for the water gradually disappeared during the day.

From the Lisbon start were R Thévenin with G Campion, their Jupiter shipped from Jowett 4th December 1950 – this was the very first private sale of a standard Jupiter (17). It completed the rally at 146th overall, class 43rd. The car survives nicely restored still in France. And from the Monte Carlo start were another two Jupiters: one was the Jupiter (42) of the Dutch pair Scheffer and Willing: they retired at the Brussels control after 2250 kilometres with a broken fan. This car also still survives, well restored, in Australia. The other Jupiter (52) to start at Monte Carlo was entered by the Spanish pair Fabricas Bas and Iglesias who had taken delivery of their Madrid-registered Jupiter just a fortnight before the off.

During the Acceleration/Braking test, Wise's Jupiter broke a petrol pipe on the suction side of the pump on one of the inevitable jerks in this test, and his Jupiter spluttered across the line to record 28.2sec so was therefore not amongst the best 50 to take part in the Regularity/Speed trial – which meant that the Jupiter team was out of the Charles Faroux Challenge Cup for a pre-nominated team of three. The Wise/Grimley Jupiter was still classified, but at 58th in the General Category.

Saturday was given over to an examination of the cars

and on Sunday the roads were closed for the Regularity/Speed test over the Monaco Grand Prix road circuit. Robinson had no racing experience, had not expected to match the Simcas, and was therefore surprised to clock his first flying lap at 2sec quicker than the best Simca lap up to that point. Ellison, seated beside him with the stopwatches, counselled caution but Robinson was right on the money for, catching sight of the 4½-litre Delahaye that had started half a minute before the Jupiter, he stunned the French spectators – and the Simca drivers – by closing the gap and cheekily passing it on the last corner of the final lap just past the Hôtel de Paris.

The highly-placed Javelin of Les Odell was also in with a shout having lost no road marks and recording 25.2sec in the A/B test.

1951 Monte: Regularity/Speed Test lap times on the Monte Carlo Grand Prix circuit were as follows:–

	Lap 3	Lap 4	Lap 5	Lap 6
Jupiter GKY 256 Robinson/Ellison	2min 32sec	2min 33sec	2min 31sec	2min 31sec
Best Simca M Scaron	2min 36sec	2min 35sec	2min 35sec	2min 34sec
Jupiter GKY 107 Wilkins/Baxter	2min 35sec	2min 36sec	2min 38sec	2min 35sec
Les Odell's Javelin John Marshall	2min 51sec	2min 50sec	2min 50sec	2min 50sec

Well went the day for Bill Robinson, the fastest British competitor in any car 'round the houses'. He drove the Jupiter to overall fourth best behind Louis Chiron, Gaston Gautruche and Pierre Levegh to clinch the class win at sixth in the General Category. The drivers ahead of him were in a 4485cc Delahaye, a 2867cc Citroën, and a 4482cc Talbot respectively. This revealed again the very advanced handling of the Jupiter in its day.

Wilkins fluffed his third timed lap to come 12th in this test, making him class 2nd at 10th overall, and Les Odell's Javelin placed class 4th at overall 26th behind a Simca Grand Sport. As a result Jowett still took the Manufacturer's Team Prize. Luck was surely

Above and left: Ain't Misbehavin' – Robinson in the Regularity/Speed test on the Monaco Grand Prix circuit. (ERPÉ Nice)

with GKY 256 for as Robinson engaged first gear and accelerated away to start the first of his six laps, he heard a clonk from the gearbox – but as all seemed well this was ignored. After the test, the rally being effectively over, he parked the Jupiter with all the other cars in the gas-works yard. But there was a drama to unfold! Maurice Trintignant was the Simca team leader and he was furious at the speed of Robinson's Jupiter! He lodged a complaint with the organisers, he was sure the Jupiter had a racing engine fitted. The Jupiter was ordered to a garage in Monaco for inspection but the gearbox had locked up and it could not

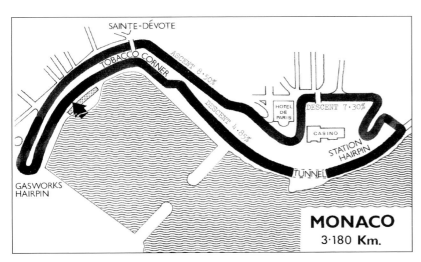

A solemn moment for the 1½-litre class winners as they receive their awards. (LAT Photographic)

be driven...and the car had to be towed there. A day and a half was spent dismantling, inspecting and measuring the engine components. As hydraulic tappets were expected but solid tappets fitted there was some difficulty, resolved by assurances from Horace Grimley, and eventually it was agreed that the engine was a standard production unit – which it was – producing a shade over 60bhp at 4500rpm. Horace then removed the gearbox and chipped out a broken half tooth to free the transmission – such is sometimes the margin between victory and defeat.

The car was entirely driveable again and was driven all the way back to Britain to return to Bradford via the London showroom with no further attention.

The Robinson/Ellison Jupiter shared 6th place in the General Category with Ken Wharton the 1950 British Trials champion; Ken scored 23.8sec in the A/B test but his meagre, for a 3½-litre car (Ford V8 Pilot), 15.86 points in the Regularity/Speed test brought him equality with the Jupiter at 27.76 points overall.

Robinson and Ellison won the following: the 1½-litre class and with it the Riviera Cup (for the best 1½-litre car). They class-won the Coupes Cibié plus the Calculateur Roadex Award and, equal with Ken Wharton, the Stuart Trophy, and finally the Tyresoles Challenge Cup awarded for the best performance by a member of the Monte Carlo Rally British Competitors Club.

If the driving part of the rally ended in the gas-works

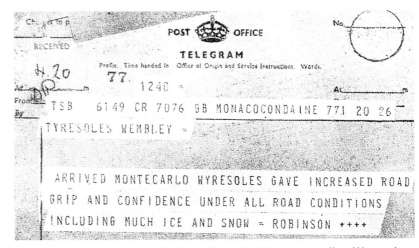

Robinson took time on arrival to telegraph his tyre supplier. Wyresoles were a favourite for winter rallyists. they were re-treads with coils of steel wire embedded and vulcanised into the tread for a good grip on ice. (Robinson)

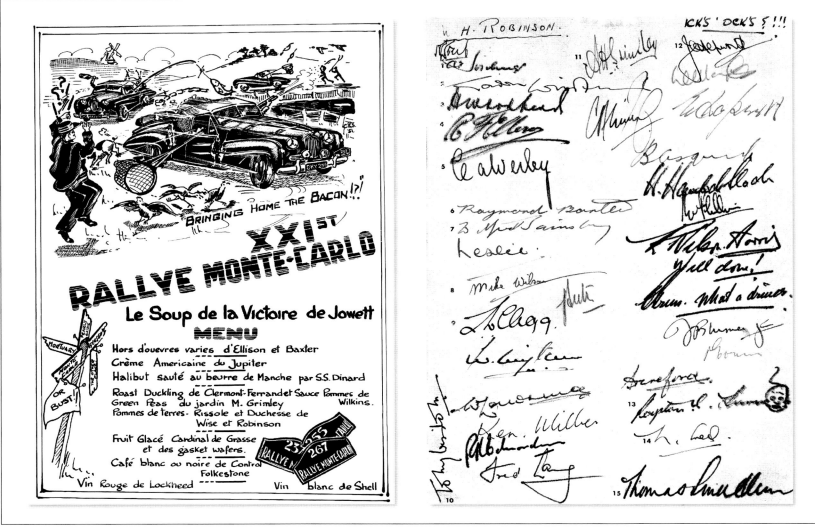

There was a celebratory dinner in Leeds on 21 February 1951. The mood of elation is well captured by this menu with its 'vin rouge de Lockheed' and 'vin blanc de Shell'. Lord Calverley of Bradford was amongst the guests. Other identified guests include Raymond Baxter, Gordon Wilkins, Tommy Wisdom, Bill Robinson, Bob Ellison, Royston C Lunn (the drawing is a reference to his alleged knowledge of the key to eternal youth, as Jowett people told me), Horace Grimley, Harry Woodhead, Mike Wilson, three Javelin rallyists R Nelson-Harris, Dr Thomas Smallhorn, and Fred Laing. Also present were J Hepworth of the Bradford firm of Hepolite piston-makers, Wilfred Sainsbury of Lazard Bros, Arthur Jopling Jowett MD, Norman Snell Jowett Company Secretary, and Jowett spares chargé d'affaires Albert Clegg. The signature "Leslie" – Leslie Johnson perhaps? (Artwork by Phil Stephenson)

yard on the Sunday, the social side was only beginning. The inspection of the prize-winning cars on the Monday was followed by cocktails given by the municipality at the Jardins Exotique, with a ball for the competitors in the

evening. On the Tuesday there took place the 'Concours de Confort' competition, and for British crews a dinner at the Metropole Hotel (the Jupiter team hotel) and on the Wednesday there was the parade of cars and the very ceremonial distribution of the 50 or more prizes, culminating in the dinner given by the International Sporting Club (CSI).

There is no doubt that this was another great victory for Jowett's Jupiter, at a time when only 18 standard Jupiters existed of which five were in the New World, and one, the Le Mans car, not eligible. Another went abroad to we know not where, so, out of the eleven remaining standard Jupiters, seven took part in this event which culminated, as we have seen, in a pair achieving first and second in their class, helped somewhat by their Wyresoles tyres with their 'steel claw thread that GRIPS'.

In the **1951 Tulip International Rally 23-28 April** there was one Jupiter amongst the 281 starters and 196 finishers for whom there were nine starts in eight countries. Jupiter GKY 256 (18), still a Works car at this time, was entered for Bill Robinson with his friend Towers Leck navigating; they were competing in the 1.1 to 1.5-litre Category II against 90 others including 13 Javelins and four MGs. In addition to the four categories based on engine size, a distinction was made between touring cars 'A' and sports cars 'B'. These were based on power/weight ratio: Category II had to have a ratio above 18.5Kg/bhp to be considered an 'A' touring car. On this basis a Jupiter was a 'B' and therefore its average speed on the special stages had to be 8% higher than the 'A' cars. Similarly in the final eliminating tests 'B' cars had their required times adjusted by 5%, and open cars had to run with their hoods closed. Between the special stages all cars had to average between 50 and 65km/hr to avoid penalties.

The 2000-mile route included four special stages, which were the 115-km Circuit du Puy-de-Dôme around Clermont Ferrand in the French Massif Centrale; the 140-km Route of the Fifteen Mountains in Alsace above the West bank of the Rhine; the similar 10-km test along the nearby Parcours du Bonhomme; and the 14-km Route of the Thousand Curves through Luxembourg and East Belgium. None of these special stages or the speeds to be maintained were disclosed until the start of the relevant stage, when a hieroglyphic route card would be handed to

1951 Tulip International: Bill Robinson's Jupiter at the final control. (CJ)

the car's navigator. Robinson in his Jupiter, Ian Appleyard (XK120 Jaguar NUB 120) and Goff Imhoff (Allard) formed the BARC team to compete for the Club award – and as all these three cleaned the road and stage sections they were awarded the trophy. All the other team entrants collected penalties. Sixty-two Category II cars finished of which 32 were unpenalised.

Friday 27th April was given over to the eliminating tests at Noordwijk in south west Netherlands (an area known for its tulip bulb fields) and Robinson in his third Tulip in a Jowett was confident of a win. He collected the Jupiter from the Parc Fermé in the morning and, although it started easily, unnoticed by him the tachometer drive cable had detached itself from the dynamo drive and had lodged in a position to jam the carburettor chokes closed. The engine was clearly running rich but the bonnet was now sealed and any repair except a supervised wheel change would result in exclusion. Robinson contrived to change the throttle cable without opening the bonnet as there was a spare taped in place but of course it was without the desired effect, so the tests had to be carried out at full choke with the engine producing plenty of smoke but unable to rev. So he scored 30,151 points to come seventh in his category. An MG was sixth at 29,917 while the best of the 14 Javelins scored 30,422 to place 9th and the ubiquitous John Gott (HRG) made 33,284 to place 24th. Robinson's time was less than 5% slower than his category's winner. Ian Appleyard won the rally outright.

The **1951 Lisbon International Rally 2–7 May** was run over nearly 2000 miles from ten starting points in nine countries such as Amsterdam, Frankfurt, London, Madrid and of course Lisbon. It attracted 69 starters, the two best-known being Ken Wharton in his 3½-litre Ford Pilot who had won in 1947 and 1949 and was runner-up in 1950, and Godfrey (Goff) Imhoff in his Allard. Ken was the best all-round British race, rally, hillclimb and trials exponent at that time, while by contrast Imhoff confined himself solely and frequently successfully to rallying. They both started from Frankfurt, and if these two failed to perform, then the event was expected to be won by a Portuguese. Imhoff was of the firm of radio and gramophone makers, the gramophone in the 'His Master's Voice' logo is an Imhoff.

There was only one serious accident; somewhere in Spain the Hotchkiss of Jose Ramos Gorge left the road and crashed heavily. The road section required 50km/hr to be maintained between controls and then there were three tests: at Figueira da Foz, then 100miles on at Gradil, and finally after another 35 miles at Estoril.

For these three tests the cars were divided into five groups by engine capacity; in this way an order in a General Category could be calculated which took into account engine size. These divisions were such that the lone Jupiter of the Portuguese driver Joaquim Filipe Nogueira (chassis 74, completely standard with no Factory support) which started from Lisbon had as competitors mainly Simcas, Volvos and Lancia Aprilias, whereas the three 1100cc Porsches ran in another group.

Went the day well for Nogueira. By the Estremoz control 15 competitors including Imhoff were eliminated at the effective end of what had been considered a notably difficult road section. From Estremoz the cars made their

Left: snapshot of Joaquim Filipe Nogueira. He went on to become one of the most successful Portuguese racing drivers, with a much-respected national and international career. (CJ)

way the 150 miles to Figueira da Foz, for the first of the penultimate day's three tests: here it was a timed 3-km sprint through streets closed to traffic. Nogueira had to repeat his run as during his first attempt he suddenly encountered a horse-drawn cart that somehow had slipped onto the course. In this test and the next one the winner of each group was allotted zero penalty points with the others marked in the proportion that they were slower than their group's best time. This first test was fast but somewhat dangerous due to the poor road surface that clearly suited the Jupiter for Nogueira class-won at 1min 33.7sec (about 72mph) compared with 1min 40.4sec of the Aprilia, 1min 41.6sec of the best Simca, and 1min 38.4sec of the best Porsche.

Film director Manoel de Oliveira at this point was in overall lead.

The second test, at Gradil another 100 miles south, was another timed street course over 3.3km, but here the Jupiter did not feature in the first five of its group, none of whom were penalised due to the closeness of their times – all within 0.6sec in three minutes. Indeed this was the experience of the top five competitors in four out of the five groups.

The cars then drove the 20 miles south to Lisbon, where they began to arrive a little after midday, and then on to Estoril, the elegant, glamorous resort 15 miles to the West of the capital, where an improvised circuit had been constructed for the Acceleration, Regularity and Braking test.

For this test, drivers had to accelerate along a 100-metre

straight with the last 25 metres timed, then lap the circuit four times as fast as possible with as little variation as possible, and then brake to a stop in the shortest distance after crossing a line. Nogueira again led his group with the same Aprilia second and a Simca third. Nogueira's points were lower than any other car in the rally except for the 3½-litre Ford Pilot of Clemente Meneres. This placed Nogueira second in the general category, which read:—

1. Meneres, Ford Pilot
2. Nogueira, Jupiter
3. da Fonseca, Simca
4. Ernesto Mattorell, Porsche
Ken Wharton in his Ford Pilot was 7th.

At Estoril on the final day of the rally there were a series of decisive tests and trials performed in front of cheering crowds, large once the early morning downpour had passed.

It was here that Nogueira showed that he was a great driver: resourceful, methodical and with the will to win. Six competitors were eliminated in the two days of tests leaving 48 finishers of whom 28 were Portuguese.

Final overall position	Driver	Car	Penalties
1	Joaquim Nogueira	Jupiter	16,296
2	Manuel Menéres	Ford Pilot	16,398
3	Conde Passanha	Allard	16,759
4	Emilio Christillin	Lancia Aurelia	16,918
5	Ernesto Mattorell	Porsche	17,132
6	Ken Wharton	Ford Pilot	17,407
7	Carlos da Fonseca	Simca	17,409

The final order in the general classification found Nogueira the winner, splendidly taking the only outright win in an International Rally for a Jupiter. He was also awarded the Automovél Club de Portugal Cup for the best-placed Portuguese driver.

The 1951 Morecambe National Rally 21–26 May

was its first as a full-scale event, with substantial support from the front-ranking rally specialists, possibly practising for next month's RAC Rally. There were six starts and 231 entrants. On the first day 250 miles had to be driven, culminating with tests at Morecambe, whilst on the second day an 80-mile road section through part of the Lake District included the 1-mile timed ascent of Tow Top in Cumbria (average gradient 1:10), followed by more driving tests on the return to Morecambe.

The talented rally specialist Goff Imhoff, who we have already met with his Cadillac-engined Allard, was beginning a brief flirtation with Jowett perhaps after seeing Nogueira in action. In this rally he drove his Jupiter (77) to do particularly well in the driving tests to finish 2nd in his class. Ted Booth with his special-bodied Jupiter (10) took part but in the final test his gear-change lever jammed in reverse and the movement in this unexpected direction so alarmed some marshals standing nearby that they leaped over the sea wall into the sands beyond! Tommy Wise, in the rebuilt ex-Le Mans GKW 111 now a road Jupiter owned by him, sensibly chose to run with the hood closed and was rewarded with 11th place in the general category. However, as all ten cars above him were open cars running open, he not only won the 1300 to 3000cc class for closed production cars but also took the award for the Best Performance in a Closed Production Car.

The first (**1951**) **RAC International Rally** (The 'Festival of Britain Rally') took place over the **4th to 9th June**. There were four starts all in the UK: 1700 road miles and tests at Silverstone, the Rest and Be Thankful hillclimb, a timed section embracing the up to 1:3.5 gradients of the Hardknott and Wrynose passes in the Lake District, driving tests at Blackpool, a speed trial at Eppynt in Wales, and the final test at Bournemouth. There was no General Category or first prize, and the four classes were just for open and closed cars of greater than or less than 1½-litres.

A team of three Jupiters had been mustered: GKY 256 (18) for Marcel Becquart (his only rally in a standard Jupiter) with Roy Lunn navigating; Goff Imhoff in his

The Jupiter team near Loch Ness after the Rest and Be Thankful Hillclimb. L to R: Roy Lunn, Goff Imhoff, Cyril Wick, Ted Booth, Derek Bowers. (Becquart)

Jupiter HAK 117 with Cyril Wick, and Ted Booth in his special-bodied Jupiter LHR 2 (10) with Derek Bowers handling the maps. Becquart was once described as the 'Scarlet Pimpernel of rallying' for 'no matter how hard one drove he was always at the next control ahead of one'. In 1948 his friend and usual co-driver on continental rallies, Henri Ziegler, had taken on the Geneva Jowett agency and at the Geneva Salon that year Becquart tested the Javelin demonstrator 'in a most electrifying manner' along the lakeside to determine how the car could be handled. But Hotchkiss were first and second in the 1949 Monte so he started his rally career in his 1939 Hotchkiss 686 Grand Sport to give that marque its sixth win in 1950. Lunn had joined Jowett from Aston Martin having worked with Claude Hill, the man responsible for the DB1, to take over the post of Chief Designer from the departing Gerald Palmer.

In the RAC Rally the class opposition to the Jupiters comprised five HRGs, eight MGs and four of the new Jensen-designed-and-built open Austin A40s.

For the 229 cars involved, the Silverstone test was more like a half-hour High Speed Trial, and it was on the short Club circuit too; a set number of laps dependent upon class had to be covered in 30 minutes, with one mark to be deducted for every second over the half-hour. The track rapidly became slippery with rubber dust, hot tarmac and spilled petrol. Alec Gordon's HRG slid happily at Stowe, whilst Booth's Jupiter once had a double-slide there.

Becquart had his Jupiter going so fast that Imhoff (77) had all his work cut out to catch him, hooting his horn at the slower stuff with his tyres screaming. The test was later annulled thanks to a muddle about the exact position of the finish line, and this had the effect of dropping Becquart two places in the final order. He was unable to match the HRGs on the 'Wee Rest' returning third-place 82.1sec behind JVS Brown and Nancy Mitchell. Imhoff recorded 9th place with 85.3sec but went on to pick up places by cleaning the Hardknott to Wrynose timed stretch to come third behind two MGs at the Blackpool driving test. The similarly powered but lighter if primitive HRGs were quicker on the hills whereas the Jupiter's superior handling was overwhelming on the zigzag 1.9-mile Eppynt speed trial. This trial was on army property: ideal Jupiter territory with an abundance of corners and switchbacks to make it interesting.

The class results here were:–
1. Becquart Jupiter 2min 14.2sec
2. Imhoff Jupiter 2min 15.4sec
3. Best HRG 2min 17.4sec
4. Booth Jupiter 2min 18.4sec

Two more HRGs were 5th and 6th.

Javelins had filled the first five places in the 1½-litre closed-car class on the 'Wee Rest' and now at Eppynt they took the top six.

The cars now headed south for the final driving tests on the Bournemouth promenade. In light drizzle Imhoff opened the proceedings to return 84.05sec but Becquart

Becquart (18) chasing hard at Silverstone. (LAT Photographic)

1951 RAC Rally: Ted Booth (10) at the final test at Bournemouth, temporary windscreen fitted. (Booth)

took the class with a perfect display of balanced sliding in and out of the chicanes with the minimum of braking to record the unbeaten 78.92sec.

Maurice Gatsonides, co-driver in van der Mark's Dutch Javelin, drove the LHD car in the 1½-litre closed-car class to equal 3rd, the driver having got his gears mixed up and missing a foul line. Dr Spare's 2nd-placed Javelin recorded 84.05sec behind a 1¼-litre MG saloon with 83.41sec.

Overall results placed Imhoff fourth in class behind two HRGs and an MG. Becquart came fifth and Ted Booth in his everyday car a creditable 12th. The Gatsonides Dutch Javelin finished second in its class behind the MG saloon, with two other Javelins fourth and fifth. The Gatso/van der Mark Javelin with a pair of other Dutch Javelins won the class team prize.

The Swedish **Rally to the Midnight Sun,** the second such event, was run from the **14th** to the **16th June 1951.** The Jupiter of K V Andersson was in it. He finished class sixth out of 36 finishers in his category. This rally was to evolve into the Swedish International Rally.

The **1951 Alpine International Rally** of the **13th** to the **21st July** was regarded in those days as the toughest of the European trials and had at times much

of the character of a road race. Unlike the other more gentlemanly rallies, quite difficult time schedules were set. It had just one start, at Marseilles and finished at Cannes. It would include 20 or more of Europe's highest mountain passes. Generally, only a small number of cars would complete the 2000 miles unpenalised (on times and condition of coachwork). All who completed it unpenalised received a *Coupe des Alpes*, with the final eliminator at Cannes deciding ties within classes.

In addition there were four separate tests with their own awards, but not contributing to the overall rally position. These four were: the Mont Ventoux 13½-mile regularity run, the Monza 1-km standing-start speed test at the Autodrome, the Falzarego 10-mile hillclimb on the third stage, and the Stelvio 9000-ft (8¾-mile) ascent with its 56 hairpin bends.

The *Criterium de la Montagne* traditionally attracted a strong British contingent and this year 31 of the 65 cars had British crews. In Jupiter GKW 111 (4) were Tommy Wise and Mike 'The Laugh' Wilson, long-time chairman of the BARC Yorkshire centre who even at his slimmest weighed 18½ stone so was a tight fit in the Jupiter, for Wise was no midget either.

Jupiter GKY 256 was entered by Bill Robinson, who probably owned the car (18) by now, with W James navigating. The high-mileage Javelin of Dr Smallhorn was another entrant – the car he used for his doctor's rounds. The third Jupiter was entered by Jean Armangaud, a Jowett sub-agent of Bordeaux. He went on to distinguish himself by his driving.

Also in the 1.1- to 1.5-litre class were six MGs, two HRGs, three Simcas and a Lancia. The start, from the Marseilles quayside in tropical heat, was at 8:30 in the morning. The first stage was a 450-mile run to the Mont Ventoux regularity test, then into Italy via the Turin Autostrade to Monza and the speed test at the Autodrome and then on to Milan. Robinson was unpenalised but both Wise, with electrical problems, and Armangaud were late at controls, as was Dr Smallhorn as his Javelin was having petrol feed problems. The Jupiters were not very successful on the Regularity Test where the HRG of

1951 Alpine, before the start at Marseilles. Two Jupiters and a Javelin side by side can be made out. (Cunane)

Below: The Wise/Wilson Jupiter with three tyres on the tail rack. Only wheels and tyres present at the start could be used during the rally. (Copyright Archive Maurice Louche)

those two famous motoring policemen J A Gott and G W Gillespie in their third Alpine with the same car headed the class with Wise fourth and Armangaud ninth.

At the Monza Standing Kilometre test Armangaud and Jupiter were in good form, winning the class at 40.4sec with an MG second at 41.0sec. Gott was third with 41.8, Jupiter men Wise was fifth with 42.0, while Robinson was class eighth with 42.2sec.

The second-day's stage included the difficult Dolomite road from Bolzano to Cortina and only four of the 1½-litre cars reached Cortina unpenalised, amongst them being Robinson in GKY 256. Armangaud had a good run also, without penalties for the day.

The third day's motoring covered 200 miles through the Dolomite mountains, starting and finishing at Cortina,

to be covered at higher speeds than average for the rest of the rally: for the smaller cars this meant maintaining very high down-hill speeds, expecting a great deal from the brakes, too much in fact for the Alfin drums on the hitherto unpenalised GKY 256 and they cracked right round from stud to stud to stud. Robinson, the 1½-litre favourite at that point, was obliged to retire. Wise, however, electrical problems temporarily in abeyance took GKW 111 up the Falzarego Pass in the class-winning time of 17min 2.8sec (37.2mph) behind a Simca. Armangaud again had a day without penalty, by now using the batteries from Robinson's Jupiter as his Jupiter was having dynamo trouble.

The fourth day took the cars northward from the Italian Tyrol into Austria over four mountain passes. Wise's electrical bothers were again slowing his Jupiter. At the end of the day, at Innsbruck, seven of the sixteen 1½-litre cars had retired and only one, the Gott/Gillespie HRG, was unpenalised. Drs Smallhorn and Lillicrap in their Javelin were having petrol feed problems on every piece of Alp according to a report in *The Autocar*.

From Innsbruck, the 450-mile fifth stage brought the survivors back to Italy through the Brenner pass, easy in spite of the poor weather, to the Mont Giovo Pass, a very different and fitting prelude to the nine-mile zigzag climb (ten hairpins in a 2-km stretch) to the summit of the Stelvio and the alarming, hurried, 14-mile descent to the Bonio time check. Then briefly into Switzerland through the clouded St Bernard Pass – visibility virtually zero – and across the French border to Chamonix.

Wise's Jupiter was again running well and he class-won the difficult Stelvio Ascent (20min 53.0sec) less than two minutes slower than Tom Wisdom in the ex-Le Mans 3-litre Aston Martin. Armangaud recorded a third place 21min 6.0sec behind an MG, while Smallhorn's Javelin, its high-altitude misfiring cured, recorded 23min 31.4sec one place ahead of Gott whose HRG recorded a poor sixth with 23min 33.4sec.

Alas, later that day, on the way to Aosta, two women cyclists shot out of a side turning in front of Wise's Jupiter. Wise managed to evade them but rammed a lorry disabling the Jupiter. One cyclist broke her shoulder, and John Gott, close behind, felt duty bound to take the injured girl to hospital, for which he was not penalised by the rally authorities. The luckless Wise spent the night in police custody.

Of the Jupiters, therefore, only Armangaud remained for the final 450-mile run south through the French Alps to Cannes. This run took in six peaks, two almost as high as the Stelvio, and a difficult route through the Iseran Pass (the highest motor route in Europe), then the Glandon some of which was on unmade roads complicated by avalanches, and the Galibier and Isoard mountain passes.

Hood lowered, Armangaud made a characteristically rapid ascent of the Galibier, but on the Isoard with almost all the hard work done, a serious boiling problem developed which sounded like a gasket blow, and he reached Cannes more than the permitted 30 minutes late.

Gott and his HRG were unpenalised after an immaculate drive, winning his Coupe des Alpes, and the Javelin of Dr Smallhorn was fifth out of the five survivors in his class and amongst the total of only 28 finishers of whom just ten were unpenalised, one of whom being Ian Appleyard who won his third Alpine Cup as well as the

1951 Alpine: Armangaud on the final day.
(Copyright Archive Maurice Louche)

Best Performance award in his Jaguar NUB 120.

The Jupiters could be content with three special awards: Tommy Wise winning the class in both the Stelvio and the Falzarego ascents, and Jean Armangaud winning the class in the Standing Km test at Monza, so the Jupiters were the fastest 1½-litre cars in the rally.

In the **1951 Rallye de l'Iseran 18–19 August** Jean Armangaud and Jupiter reappeared once more in this all-French rally in the Alps put on by the Auto Club de Savoie. In the two supplementary tests Armangaud had come overall third in the Standing Km (with 42.5sec) to two bigger-engined Citroën 11CVs with the best Peugeot (a 203) recording 44.6sec. In the 10-mile Côte de l'Iseran ascent the Jupiter clocked fourth place behind the Citroëns and the Peugeot 203. Nevertheless for the rally as a whole it was an outright win for Armangaud. Second was the Peugeot 203 – a car with similar engine power to the Jupiter's – while class third at overall ninth was Prestail's MG.

The **1951 MCC-*Daily Express* National Rally 7–10 November** was a national rally held over 1200 miles. Little can be said except that on a Yorkshire moor Ted Booth drove LRH 2 into a sheep, killing it and the nearside headlamp (there were of course penalties for damage). The only other Jupiter was the handsome but somewhat overweight FHC (99) KWX 770 of Edward Foulds, Jowett's Keighley agent, with K Jones. Although undistinguished, this first appearance in a rally of a saloon Jupiter was a foretaste of what was to come.

The **1952 Monte Carlo International Rally 22 to 29 January** saw sufficient snow, ice, fog and rain as almost to ensure that victory would be secured on the road section. The French Alps became littered with the wrecks of cars in what drivers agreed had been the toughest motoring adventure in years. It was snowing all across southern France right along the Mediterranean coast even into Monte Carlo itself. Consequently only 15 crews arrived unpenalised from 328 starters and 163 finishers.

Last year's rule allowing only cars with engines by the vehicles manufacturer had been rescinded, and there was a new rule allowing only closed cars. However as a gesture

The 1952 Monte: saloon Jupiters of Marcel Becquart (left) and Jean Latune prepared in Lisbon for the start. (Marcel Becquart)

to coachbuilders, individually built closed variations on series production open car chassis were permitted, with the proviso that the bodies must be completely finished for normal touring use and not constructed as rally-winning specials. Series production was defined as more than 50 examples shipped before October 1951. So Sydney Allard returned in a saloon version of one of his Allards powered by a 3.6-litre Ford engine. Crew were Guy Warburton and Tom Lush, with Sydney and Guy sharing the driving and Tom navigating and time-keeping. They won the rally outright (uniquely the driver driving a car of his own make) with Stirling Moss second in a Sunbeam Talbot.

It says something of the influence of the event and this rule, which only lasted for 1952 and 1953, that the construction of at least six saloon Jupiters can be attributed to it. Four of these saloon Jupiters made their rally debut in the 1952 Monte, one recording Jowetts highest place in the general category.

The most important of these saloon Jupiters was the Stabilimenti Farina of Marcel Becquart (59). Robert

Ellison entered with his Farr-bodied Jupiter (81) registered MTJ 300, and there was the Swiss-built Ghia Aigle saloon Jupiter (56) owned by Henri Ziegler the Geneva Jowett agent but to be driven by R Thévenin who was a garage proprietor of Bordeaux. All these Jupiters survive. The fourth saloon Jupiter (93) was entered by Jean Latune the long-time president of the Automobile Club de la Drôme of Valence, with co-driver J Vacher. His Jupiter was built by a coachbuilder near his home-town of Valence.

The Farina Jupiter of Becquart is the third such Jupiter to have been built and was his own personal car at the time. It was fully backed by the Jowett factory who for the rally rebuilt the engine to the latest specification, fitted a larger radiator, competition brake linings and brake fluid, and raised the riding height by three inches with other detail improvements.

The three French entrants, Becquart, Thévenin and Latune, were to start at Lisbon and were entered for the Charles Faroux Challenge Cup, the competition for nominated teams of three cars. Hopes for this cup were dashed from the outset as Thévenin did not set out for the start, blaming poor preparation by Plisson the Parisian Jowett agent. Becquart's mistress Mme Sigrand was also at the Lisbon start, she had entered with her Peugeot.

Robert Ellison in his Jupiter bodied by J E Farr of Blackburn had a competition engine loaned by Jowett, an extra fuel tank and a specially enlarged luggage locker which accommodated the two snow-chained spare wheels. The sole lightweight feature was the pair of Le Mans bucket seats also loaned by Jowett thanks to Horace Grimley. Walter Mason navigated; they started from Glasgow and also from that start was the Birmingham Jowett agent Frank Grounds in a Javelin fitted with wheels, headlamps and other parts no doubt including the engine transferred from his uncompleted saloon Jupiter (29).

Ellison had an uneventful run until soon after Bourges, by where all the rally routes had converged and where increasingly heavy snow was encountered. He stopped to fit the snow-chained wheels at Nevers 30 miles out of Bourges. Weather conditions deteriorated so suddenly and completely that almost all competitors were faced with equal difficulties on the final road sections – and from Clermont Ferrand through St Flour, Le Puy and on to Valance conditions were as bad as they had ever been on any Monte. Ellison, unfamiliar with driving on snow chains over-slid the Jupiter on a downhill right-hander near St Flour, 130 miles from Nevers, and as there was no bank or wall went 30 feet over the edge, turning over twice! He had completed 1640 miles and was not alone for the road between Bourges and Valence, at the best of times a twisty and rather dangerous one, resembled in places the dead car park of a long distance race being lined with stationary cars. In places the drivers met a barrage of whirling snowflakes, in others there was mist with visibility reduced to 20 to 30 feet through which it was not possible to maintain the average.

Ellison's Jupiter came to rest on a ledge about eight feet wide and soon had the front of a Citroën on its roof. The following day a local farmer arrived with a team of six oxen, attached them to the Jupiter with a chain, flicked the ear of the leader with a long stick and the car was back on the road in one minute flat.

After roughly straightening the roof and steering, and

Latune (93) at the summit of the Col des Lècques.
(Copyright Archive Maurice Louche)

1952 Monte on the Regularity Run: Marcel Becquart (59) getting away from La Turbie. The organisers required the white paint to be added for this test. (LAT Photographic)

with temporary screens fitted, Ellison continued to Monte Carlo arriving a day late.

The Latune Jupiter continued but with delays. At Valence only 17 cars were without penalty including Becquart's Farina, three Simcas and a Porsche. From Valence via Gap, Digne and Grasse it was only easier by comparison and few could have enjoyed the slippery slopes of the run down to the Riviera. On the Col des Lècques it was hardly possible to stand let alone drive fast.

The first car to reach the finishing control was Becquart's Farina. Mud-stained, it passed through the arrival arch dropping large lumps of melting snow onto the Condamine. It was unpenalised, one of now only 15, and so it qualified for the Regularity Run.

The Regularity Run, held for the first time over a twisty 75-km circuit in the hills around the Col de Braus at a required 28½ mph, was considered difficult in the wintry conditions almost the whole length being covered in snow. The results of this test were firstly to decide the final order of the unpenalised cars, and then influence the positions

of the subsequent 34 finishers. By way of example the experienced ice-racer Norlander (Javelin) vastly improved his position (80 points down on the road section) by being second in this test, collecting only 129 points. He was therefore placed 16th overall at class ninth although his total of 209 points was less than that of all but the best six of the unpenalised cars.

The Latune/Gay Jupiter had lost 380 points to come class 23rd at overall 58th and so was not amongst the 49 qualifiers for the Regularity Test. In Monaco, the heavy rain falling at the start of the test became blizzards up in the mountains. At a sharp right-hand bend near the Castillon tunnel more than half of the competitors spun, and it was on this section that Becquart lost a disproportionate amount of points to come equal seventh in the test with 162 points (but fifth out of the unpenalised cars) whereas Dr Angelvin in a Simca Sport (based on the 1951 production model but with many modifications 'suggested' by the ubiquitous Amédée Gordini) with 139 came fourth in the test and therefore third overall to win the 1½-litre class. However Becquart's overall fifth, at class second, was Jowett's highest placing ever in the Monte general category, but alas his only prize was the Coupe Cibié, awarded to first and second in each class, plus the Rally Plaquette awarded to the first six in the general category. Prize money was 50,000 Francs.

The **1952 RAC International Rally 31st March-6th April**, was the second such event. It was run early enough for there to be snow about. The two starts were Hastings and Scarborough and the routes were 1800 miles in length. The cars were divided into just three classes this year: Class 1 for all open cars, and classes 2 and 3 for closed cars of, respectively, less than and greater than 2½-litres. This was criticised as there was no class for the most popular engine size 1½-litre, and so likely to deter overseas competitors. Also of course it would favour bigger engine cars in the speed tests. The RAC countered this last criticism by announcing that speed test times would be adjusted through a formula based on engine size and, for the Mount Eppynt and Rest and Be Thankful ascents, Class 1 would be subdivided into three groups

– less than 1½-litre, 1½ to 2½-litre, and above 2½-litre. Class 2 was to have the same subdivisions. An average time would be computed for each class with those failing to reach the average being penalised. The contentious Olivers Mount test was treated as a Regularity Trial of two runs where marks put a premium on speed and regularity.

The cars were supposed to carry their entire luggage throughout even on the special tests and stages. Teams with support used clandestine luggage transporters away from the prying eyes of rally officials, and that would have included the Works-supported Jupiters and Javelins.

The entry list was 249 strong with eight Jupiters, 21 MGs, and some HRGs with Nancy Mitchell in one of them; nine Morgans with Peter Morgan in one, at least two Porsches and 26 XK120s. There were 13 Javelins including that of Dr Smallhorn. Maurice Tew was in a Humber and Mau Gatsonides in a Ford Consul.

The Jupiter entries were: E B Booth/D Bowers in LRH 2 (10); Bert Hadley/Bill Butler in GKY 107 (21); Tommy Wise/Mike Wilson in GKW 111 (4); L C Procter/J Randles were in PEH 796 (282); Bill Skelly in JGA 123 (41); Freddy Still/Mrs Still in NNK 560 (521). G M Sharp was entered and may have been in MAC 2 (522) which is known to have run. But Skelly, and also Nancy Binns with an unidentified Jupiter, both failed to start. Tommy Wise had by now bought the ex-Le Mans Jupiter GKW 111. Jupiter NNK 560 is at time of writing the author's tidy running Jupiter.

Realistically only the Works-supported entries of Hadley, Wise and Booth could expect to make a serious impression against the experienced and well-prepared opposition. Hadley, in the ill-fated Works Jupiter, had pre-war rally experience and was an accomplished trials exponent (in the Austin 'Grasshoppers' team) while co-driver Bill Butler had been a 1½-litre Singer trials driver. But Jowetts 'Sunday car' was their very best prepared rally Javelin HAK 743 for Marcel Becquart. Roy Lunn had to step in at the last moment as Becquart's co-driver and there were no navigational problems as Grandfield with his military efficiency had ensured that all preparations including maps on rollers (he told me) were complete.

The Jupiter (4) of Tommy Wise in the 1952 RAC Rally. It was testing the up-coming version of the front suspension, with rubber bushes instead of metal. (Guy Griffiths)

Hadley's Works Jupiter (the Experimental Department's road 'hack' (21) which was completely unprepared for the rally Becquart reported) already gave brake troubles on the way to the start but Roy Lunn, in convoy in the Javelin, sorted them out. Heavy snow fell in the south before the rally began which made it hard for some Hastings entrants to reach the starting control; but to the disgust of most competitors this led to the premature cancellation of the 10-lap Silverstone speed test on the first day, for the snow had thawed before the test would have begun.

The cars moved on to Castle Coombe via Bridport for a night-time driving test by the light of the car's own headlights, with best time of the evening coming equally from Ted Booth (10) and Ken Bancroft (Morgan). This test was almost speed-trial distance; however the first time Hadley used reverse gear it disappeared! His penalty meant he was virtually out of the rally before it had hardly started – and it so happened he did not need reverse again until the final scrutineering at Scarborough!

The following dawn saw a risky 2.2-mile speed test on the military roads of Mount Eppynt in Wales. Narrow and

The Works-entered Javelin for the 1952 RAC Rally, GKW 111 is parked behind. L to R: Lunn, Wise, Becquart and a paint wholesaler from Scarborough. (CJ)

Edinburgh (where Booth was now fifth in class whereas Hadley was 78th out of 81) the Rest and Be Thankful hill was climbed, and again Nancy Mitchell's HRG forced a Jupiter, this time Hadley's, into second place in their group. Best time of the day was Ian Appleyard's 71.6sec in Jaguar NUB 120; but it should be noted that Hadley's time of 81.6sec was faster than all in classes 2 and 3. The cars then looped east, through Kenmore at the end of Loch Ray and, in the dark, over the pass at Amulree where locals moved boulders onto the road a little faster than the RSAC could remove them.

The following day saw the ingenious Lake District Trials. The three stretches through Ulpha, Hardknott and Kirkstone had to be taken as fast as possible. They were of unequal length but had to be traversed in equal times – the aim was for consistency. Big-engined cars took the first seven places in this test (Ian Appleyard placing first) whilst equal eighth were two more Jaguars, an HRG and Bert Hadley's Jupiter. Then the 199 survivors motored

somewhat wavy in surface over similar territory as the 1951 rally, a passenger had to be carried and no practice was possible. In the up to 1½-litre open class the Jupiters of Wise and Hadley came second and third behind the HRG of Nancy Mitchell. Hadley had really tried his utmost here but unluckily both he and Bill Butler thought they had seen the 'Finish' board 800 yards before the true end of the test and so slowed too early.

Following the breakfast halt at the Victorian spa town of Llandrindod Wells, the cars moved on to Blackpool by way of the steep climb ascended non-stop up Bwylch-y-Groes (also known as the Hellfire Pass), and it was here that Merch's Porsche retired. From Blackpool, where Hadley's gearbox was hurriedly rebuilt, the route took the cars through the Lake District, familiarising the competitors with a test that lay two days ahead – and then on to the Scottish border. After the night in

1952 RAC rally. Freddie and Lorna Still somewhere in Scotland, with what looks like a Jaguar Mk VII following. (Brymer)

RAC Rally, Booth at the Scarborough signing-in. His car here has its final windscreen with three wiper arms. (Charles Dunn)

into Scarborough to find that at the end of the road section it was still anyone's rally: Class 1 was headed by K Bancroft (Morgan) with 60.0, but Ted Booth (10) was eighth with 64.2, while at 66.6 the lowest car in this category to qualify was J H Ray's Morgan.

Of the remaining Class 1 finishers F E Still and his Jupiter (521) came in a creditable 36th with 87.4 points well ahead of Nancy Mitchell with 102.6. Bert Hadley with 209.0 was classified a lowly equal 61st from 74 finishers in the class. The only Javelin in the 14 leading cars of Class 2 to qualify for Olivers Mount was that of Marcel Becquart at class fifth, with 74.6 points only 3.4 points behind his class leader.

The Olivers Mount Regularity Test was in two sections to be covered in the same time. The first, the slowest section, which contained a hairpin followed by a steep climb, had to be completed as fast as possible. This test saw the smaller-engined cars routed before they began as the inexperienced organisers had seen to it that marks for this test could swamp those for the previous five days of the rally. Tommy Wise's Jupiter had engine failure about 20 miles from the

finish, which had the enormous advantage of being close to his home in Harrogate. Ted Booth collected 161.2 points to finish 15th, one place below the HRG of J V S Brown (154.8). All the cars above them were 2-litres or more with the Cadillac Allard of Goff Imhoff winning the open-car class but a brilliant drive by Becquart took the Javelin up to class winner, actually 12.8 points above Class 3; therefore his was the Best Closed Car of both categories.

Results summary:
Castle Coombe Driving Test
Class 1 (open cars)

=1st	E B Booth	Jupiter	21.6sec
	K Bancroft	Morgan	
=2nd	J V S Brown	HRG	22.8sec
	R Rollings	Healey	

All closed cars were slower than these times

Mount Eppynt 2.2-mile Speed Test
Class 1 under 1½-litre group (open cars)

1st	N Mitchell	HRG	2min 45.2sec
2nd	T C Wise	Jupiter	2min 49.0sec
3rd	Bert Hadley	Jupiter	2min 50.4sec
4th	J V S Brown	HRG	2min 51.2sec

Class 2 under 1½-litre group (closed cars)

1st	M Becquart	Javelin	2min 53.6sec

Rest and Be Thankful Hillclimb
Class 1 under 1½-litre group (open cars)

1st	N Mitchell	HRG	80.4sec
2nd	Bert Hadley	Jupiter	81.6sec
3rd	A Gordon	HRG	83.6sec
4th	J Richmond	HRG	83.8sec

Class 2 under 1½-litre group (closed cars)

1st	M Becquart	Javelin	84.8sec

Olivers Mount Regularity Test
Marcel Becquart – Best Closed Car of the Rally.

The **1952 Lisbon International Rally 21–25 May** (the 6th such rally) saw Nancy Mitchell desert her HRG for a Javelin plus Joyce Leavens with the maps. There were two Jupiters, that of Joaquim Cordoso with Abreor Lopes (168), and Joaquim Nunes dos Santos (75). Out of at least 132 entrants there were just 24 finishers. The rally was won outright by Joaquim Filipe Nogueira who had deserted his Jupiter for a Porsche. The best Jowett results were: Coupe des Dames for Nancy Mitchell and Joyce Leavens in their Javelin, class 7th for Joaquim Cordoso and class 9th for dos Santos in their Jupiters.

The **1952 Alpine International Rally 11–16 May** (the 15th such rally) had been lengthened to 2060 miles, and for the first time it had a general classification calculated by an intricate formula that was seen to favour the smaller-engined cars. It was run over 34 Alpine passes. The 1½-litre cars had to maintain a general average of 35.4mph, with 40.5mph over the second day's 189-mile loop over the Dolomites.

The 20-strong 1½-litre contingent contained no less than eight Porsches and a British entry of three HRGs, two MGs, a Javelin and two Jupiters. Tommy wise was back with GKW 111 (4) while John Gott in his fifth Alpine had now swapped his HRG for the Works-prepared Jupiter HAK 366 (131) ex Le Mans of 1951, this being now the last surviving standard Jupiter from the Jowett Works racing era. GKW 111 had the latest oil cooler and, mindful of last year's accident with the cyclists, had a pair of horns mounted on the front bumper to supplement the characteristic whine of the engine. It would be the last international event for both these Jupiters.

The first and longest day's motoring took in five peaks in the 614 gruelling miles from Marseilles to Cortina, with a break for the Standing Start Acceleration Test at Monza, as usual the cars competing here for Monza's special award. This year, Wise notched 40.1sec while Gott recorded 40.2sec, both 2 seconds faster than their 1951 times, but too small an improvement on Armangaud's class winning time of that year. The best HRG (42.1sec), MG (46.2sec) and Bennett's Javelin (45.0sec) were outclassed by the quickest Porsche at 35.1sec and Butti's class-winning OSCA with 33.1sec.

Nevertheless the first day was penalty-free for the Jupiters – only the OSCA and three of the Porsches were also so distinguished – for there had already been seven retirements including both MGs. The Jupiters of Wise and Gott were a satisfactory 6th and 7th in the General Classification.

The second day was the 189-mile flat-out drive around the Dolomites, the roads there closed for the duration. The first 30 miles constituted a special timed test which Butti in his OSCA class-won at 45min 3sec. But the best Porsche time of 45min 24sec was not matched either by Wise (50min 14sec) or Gott (52min 21sec) nor the best HRG time which was 51min 6sec.

Again the two Jupiters were unpenalised at the end of a day that saw the retirements of the OSCA and two of the three previously unpenalised Porsches. This left Nathan's Porsche as the only other 1½-litre car with a clean sheet. Not bad so far!

But if the lessons of history are not fully appreciated they may have to be repeated: on the third day the rear Alfin brake drums of HAK 366 were found to be breaking away from their hubs, forcing Gott to retire. And a washer in the gearbox of GKW 111 failed leaving a bitterly disappointed Wise the choice of only two gears, the only known weakness of the Meadows gearbox. So at the end of the third day only 32 cars remained in this the toughest of the European rallies. Nathan and the Spanish driver went on to take 1st and 2nd for Porsche although both had penalties so did not qualify for Coupe des Alpes. Twenty-three crews finished out of the 83 starters. While the Porsches were faster than the Jupiters on the ascents they suffered from as yet unsolved braking and maybe handling deficiencies which meant that they could not match the Jupiters on the descents until the Alfin drums, adequate for the lesser rigours of sports car racing, failed under Alpine hammering.

Mau Gatsonides won the unlimited class in an XK120 to finish second overall.

The Rally of a 1000 Curves 29th June 1952 was

Snapshot taken at an impromptu stop in the 1952 International Alpine Rally: John Gott's Jupiter ex-1951-Le Mans ahead of an HRG. Gott was the fastest in his class on the Stelvio ascent. (Gott)

put on by the Santa Anita, California chapter of the Four-Cylinder Club of America (FCCA). Cars of various makes including MGs, Jaguars, Hillmans, Austins, Sunbeam Talbots and the Jupiter of Hunter Hackney competed for the coveted plaque presented by the Club. A breakfast stop fortified the competitors for the gruelling test ahead. The route took the cars through the San Dimas canyon, the Pomona and Hastings ranch to end in Lacey Park at San Marino. The overall winner was the Hunter Hackney Jupiter with Tom Ingram navigating, ahead of four MGs, a Sunbeam Talbot, some Jaguars and sundry other British cars.

Much encouraged, Hunter Hackney entered the FCCA **Lake Tahoe Rally** of **September 1952**. This took the cars through the High Sierras of northern California. The 16-hour road section, difficult and demanding, incorporated everything from super-highways to dirt tracks and winding mountain passes that was just the kind of territory that suited the Jupiter, as did the last section which resembled a road race. The start was at 6am, they crossed the Mojave Desert and then the Inyo National Park climbing from 6000ft to 8042ft; lunch was 328 miles from the start. Soon they were on roads where surfaces

were either under repair or should have been. The summit of 9624ft was achieved through sinewy hairpins the equal of any Alpine Trial. Hackney won the road section outright. In the gymkhana tests Hackney tied 2nd but was easily the overall winner by 18.5 points ahead of a TD, a TC, another TD and an XK120. The son of a gun had big fun on the bayou! For this was another of the great victories for a Jupiter, and Hackney, having collected five trophies, became the 1952 FCCA Rally Champion.

The 1952 Tour de France Automobile International Rally of **9th–16th September** organised by the Automobile Club de Nice with help from *l'Equipe*, the paper responsible for the cycling Tour de France. It had three stages and was over 3438 exhausting miles. There were no manoeuvring tests so it emphasised speed. There were two hillclimbs (Col de Peyresourde and La Turbie) and four sprint tests – one on the Le Mans Mulsanne straight. Of the 110 cars that started only 57 finished. First in the 1½-litre class was Armangaud in an OSCA, fourth was Nogueira in a Porsche, and a class position between fifth and seventh from 39 starters in the class was Jean Latune in his coupé Jupiter (93) with André Thomas navigating. At 26th overall from 57 finishers this was a very commendable result.

The 1952 MCC-*Daily Express* National Rally 12th to **15th November.** The rally was over 1266 miles with eight starts with most Jupiters in Class B1 for sports cars of their Jupiter's engine size. Also in the class were HRGs and MGs. The entry list included eight Jupiters, and seven were confirmed runners amongst a total of 421. The Jupiters were:–

N Freedman/P Waring in MXA 506 (509)
L C Procter/S G Dyke in PEH 796 (282)
G M Sharp/G P Jolly in MAC 2 (522)
F E Still/J Carter in NNK 560 (521)
R I H Sievwright/C F Denvey in KDA 937 (748)
F Defty in RPF 16 (539)
F M Baker in MCD 28 (597)
R V Russell/S Eddy in HPY 696 (probably 487)
It is thought that HPY 696 did not run.

Freedman and Sievwright were in class B2 so presumably ran closed. There was a concours at Brighton after the rally and Baker, Defty, Russell and Still were entered, so presumably finished the rally. In other respects no Jupiters distinguished themselves, and much the same can be said, alas, for the 16 Javelins entered.

The 1952 Alpine had been the final rally for a Works-entered standard Jupiter, for following Becquart's triumph in the 1952 RAC, Jowett was to concentrate exclusively on the Javelin with the single exception of one more Monte for Becquart's Farina Jupiter.

The Touring Car Championship was begun in 1953 and it accelerated the trend toward rallies mainly for production saloon cars modified only slightly from standard in ways generally available to the public and recommended by the manufacturer. It was not Jowett policy to contend the championship, rather the aim was to keep Jowett favourably in the eye of the public and perhaps also the financiers in Lazards and Briggs who were soon to decide the fate of the struggling Yorkshire concern. So Becquart, now their only regular rally driver, was henceforward entered just for the Monte, the RAC and the Tulip.

1952 MCC-*Daily Express* Rally, Ian Sievwright and lady friend in his Jupiter with unusual 2-colour bodywork. (Charles Dunn)

The 1953 Monte Carlo International Rally of **20–27 January** run over much the same route as the previous year was revealed for what it was: a relatively simple rally partly dependent upon bad weather to sort out the drivers and cars. This year, apart from the fog along the way as it was unseasonably warm, the weather let the organisers down, for the snow that fell just before the start had either thawed or been cleared by the authorities by the time the rally cars arrived. Out of the 404 starters, 253 were unpenalised on the road section and had to be put through the acceleration/braking test that tended to favour the bigger-engined cars. The 100 best from this test were sent on the 46.2-mile Regularity Run on the Col de Braus circuit at 40.0kph, having to avoid penalty by passing a sequence of six controls at exact pre-determined times.

Becquart's Farina Jupiter had been prepared by Jowetts with considerable thoroughness for what they may have felt would be the last chance for a Jupiter to do well in international rallying: a Wills-ring engine was installed (to avoid even the possibility of a head gasket blow) but not tuned for more power as the regulations forbade this – but otherwise virtually to Le Mans specification, with new torsion bars, shock absorbers, cables, fuel lines blown through, wheels and iron brake drums crack-checked – could anything have been overlooked in the search for perfection?

Becquart was again part of a team of three Jowetts, the other two being Frank Grounds with his saloon Jupiter (29) registered LOL 1 after his wife Lola, and Javelin man Bob 'Fearless' Foster, the TT motorcyclist (and 350cc World Champion in 1950 for Velocette). Latune again entered his coupé Jupiter and reached Monte Carlo unpenalised as did the Becquart team. In the Acceleration/Braking Test all the Jowetts qualified for the 74-km Regularity Run. The Jowetts were at this point placed as follows:–

17th	Becquart/Zeigler	23.6sec Jupiter (59)
=50th	Foster/Holdsworth	24.9sec Javelin
=74th	F Grounds/Jack Hay	25.5sec Jupiter (29)
=79th	Latune/Gay	25.6sec Jupiter (93)

Fastest time, 21.8sec, was posted by Sydney Allard in his saloon Allard thanks to its extraordinary acceleration; second was von Frankenberg in his 1½-litre Porsche at 22.3sec, an astonishing time as all but four of the 30 other Porsches took more than 25.9sec therefore failing the test – similarly were the Simcas reduced in number.

The lavishly-prepared Works Javelin HAK 743 for Ginette Sigrand and Ginette Largeot competing for the Ladies Cup did not reach Monte Carlo, still placed =171st at class 50th.

For the Regularity Run, Marcel Becquart was poised for a good result but it was not to be for whilst on the Col de Braus itself about half way round, his Jupiter's cooling fan disintegrated and punctured the radiator. The Javelin of Foster/Holdsworth did badly on the run scoring a miserable 200 penalty points to finish 95th overall at 13th in class. The final rally order for the Jupiters was:–

1953 Monte: Becquart and Farina Jupiter in action on the Regularity Run. No snow this year. (Copyright Archive Maurice Louche)

Grounds/Hay	Class 4th	Overall 36th
Latune/Gay	Class 6th	Overall 56th
Becquart/Ziegler	Class 15th	Overall 98th

The class was won by a Peugeot. Overall winner was Gatsonides/Worledge in a Ford Zephyr but he later confessed to illegally having had its engine changed en route!

From 1954 the Monte Carlo Rally's ideal, to develop and test of the ability of cars to tour in winter, moved into a closer embrace with mass production, and the FIA regulation that more than 1000 examples had to have been built was implemented. There were therefore no more Monte Carlo rallies for Jupiters.

The 1953 RAC International Rally of 23–28 March had 195 starters. In effect it comprised a large number of diverse special tests spread about the country, connected by fairly innocuous road sections involving little more than everyday motoring tactics to cover the 1600 miles in the allotted times.

The Jupiter entrants were: Frank Masefield Baker/F T Marchant in MCD 28 (597); T G Cunane/A Ellis NTJ 930 (604?); Frank Defty/J J Ford RPF 16 (539);

Left front Ken Rawlings. Right front Frank Grounds and Jack Hay, whose daughter was Richard Burton's widow. Jack Hay was the motoring correspondent for the *Birmingham Post*. (Photo ERPÉ)

Mrs Lola Grounds/Mrs Doreen Reece LOL 1 (29); and A Ross/D Phillips YMC 900 (757). Plus the Jupiter MCD 545 (838) of A R Sandibanks is known to have run. There were two sports car classes: for under and over 1½-litres, and three touring car classes which included drophead cars running closed: for under 1.3, 1.3 to 1.6, and over 1.6-litre cars. Marcel Becquart was in the Works competition Javelin HAK 743.

Marking was based on the 'Standard Performance' i.e. the average of the best 10, with all below the average penalised. But the penalties were heavy and a deficit once incurred could not easily be made up. The first day's test, at Silverstone, was a ½-mile standing-start sprint from Woodcote, to stop before a foul line 60 yards past the finish line. The slightly-built Lola Grounds did badly in the braking part of this test in her hydro-mechanically braked saloon Jupiter.

In the Castle Coombe night manoeuvring test by the car's own lamps (forward into a bay, reverse into another bay, forward and away) Mrs Grounds, roof-light pointing skywards, was penalised for touching a pylon but the expert Cunane was good, in fact the best Jupiter in this and the Prescott tests. Becquart was third at Castle Coombe, but he had a partial engine seizure during the Ulpha/Hardknott regularity run – he had headed his class up to this point – and although he continued to post class fifth in the Goodwood acceleration/braking test, he could not make up the deficit. Bob Foster holed the sump of his Javelin on a Yorkshire road and did not finish. Baker was best in the tests and on the road, but although there were no Jupiters in the top 101 finishers things went better for Javelins in the 1.3 to 1.6-litre touring car class with a class first for E Elliott at 19th overall, and class third for Dr D Laing at 45th overall – but Becquart could only post 67th overall.

The **1953 International Tulip Rally** from **27th April** to **2nd May** was a double whammy for Jowett. The one Jupiter entry was that of A Kammeraat/A C Mostert, but amongst the many Javelins the Jowett rally Javelin HAK 743 was entered for Marcel Becquart and Henri Ziegler; this was now the only Works drive due to

1953 RAC Rally Goodwood test. Mrs Lola Grounds driving LOL 1. (LAT Photographic)

cutbacks at Bradford. Becquart had won the 1952 RAC in this car, and in July the same year Gordon Wilkins had won the first National Economy Run with 67.86mpg over 828 miles. For this, the 1953 Tulip, the car was in fine form. Becquart had a superb road section run, and was class leader at that point. The final test was a day of races. Becquart was declared the Class winner at 6th overall.

The racing enabled the rather nit-picking organisers to spot the cars that were bending the rules for extra performance, and they had a close look at the eight top-placed cars, and disqualified the two class leaders: Becquart's Javelin and Elliott's Sunbeam-Talbot. Earlier they had disqualified the Fords of Gatsonides, Mrs Nancy Mitchell and T C Harrison, and the Sunbeam-Talbot of Phillip Fotheringham-Parker, a Peugeot and another Ford, all on the issue of non-standard fittings, mostly it was said on trivial points. Becquart's Javelin was disqualified for having a Jupiter front/side exhaust pipe, but the organisers said they knew they were looking at a Jupiter engine. And Becquart later told me, the whole car was a cheat. The evidence is, in fact, that it was not HAK 743 at all, but JAK 863, a quite different rally-prepared Works Javelin wearing HAK 743 plates. This would never have happened had Charles Grandfield been in charge, but he had left in a huff after the appointment of Donald Bastow as Chief

Engineer, and Roy Lunn was now in charge of what was left of the competition programme.

But all was not lost – quite definitely not! For not only was the Javelin of Zuylen van Nijevelt and F M A Eschauzer now the class winner, it was also winner of the rally outright! So, flukily, Jowetts had their second International outright win, the other being the 1951 Lisbon as we have seen. But by now few Javelins and no Bradfords remained to be sold, the R4 Jupiter was under way and clearly intended for competition, and the Tulip Rally Javelin now with its true JAK 863 plates was sold to a Croydon sub-agent and tested by John Bolster of *Autosport*. He recorded 0 to 60 in 19.2sec whereas a normal Javelin would clock 0 to 60 in 22.4sec. The dealer entered it in the 1954 Monte, to scratch when it became clear that there were no more Javelins to be sold.

Becquart was furious about his disqualification for a car that was a cheat, as he was a rally organiser in his own right – he organised the Evian-Mont Blanc rally each year – and he contacted Jowett to say he could never drive for them again. So there were no more Works-supported rallies to come. And the Kammeraat/Mostert Jupiter? It finished the 1953 Tulip in 4th place in the up to 2-litre class. So Javelins posted 1-2-3 in their class, all Dutch, to take the One-Make Team Prize.

In the **1953 Alpine International Rally 10–16 July**, the two private Jupiters amongst the 101 starters did not uphold the high quality of the previous year's failures. The first stage, of 585 miles, took the competitors from Marseilles over Montgenèvre into Italy to Monza for the Standing Kilometre test held at night in bitter cold. The second stage route ran from Monza to Bergamo, then a time-check at Male over the Mendola Pass and then down into Bolzano to end at Cortina. Sadly, at Bolzano just 40 miles from Cortina the Jupiter HKU 756 (407) of Dr A E Bernstein/E Yates was seen being towed away, and shortly afterwards the Jupiter of T G Cunane/E de Vadder NTJ 930 (604?) retired with a blown head gasket.

Cunane repaired the gasket with rings cut from an oil

On the way home from the 1953 Alpine. Cunane with his bronze Jupiter somewhere in Luxembourg. (Cunane)

can and was able to drive home! The 1.6-litre class was dominated by Porsches.

The **1953 Lisbon International Rally 13-18 October** was the last international rally to have a participating Jupiter, FUD 194 of Maurice Tew (620). There were 57 entrants, 11 British. It was the toughest Lisbon so far partly due to the inclusion of three winding mountain sections of un-made roads and partly due to the weather which provided rain, fog, cloudbursts, mud, branches fallen and bridges swept away. At Lisbon there was an acceleration/braking test followed by five laps of a twisty round-the-houses circuit. The Jupiter finished overall 25th at between eighth and 12th in the 1.3 to 2.0-litre class which did not suit the Jupiter. Above Tew were five 1½-litre Porsches (most Porsche Supers) and two 1.9-litre Alfas. The Javelin of W B Edwards finished 26th in the General Category, one place below Tew's Jupiter.

The **1953 MCC-*Daily Express* National Rally 11-14 November** had no less than 401 starters and 321 finishers in what was primarily a navigation run, for the special tests although searching were not chassis-breakers. After 360 miles the routes from seven starts converged in Yorkshire at Harrogate for the rest of the rain-soaked 1225 miles through the Yorkshire, Cumbrian and Northumberland moors, the Scottish Lowlands, Wales and then down to Hastings for the finish.

The Jupiter entrants running open were:—
Mr & Mrs Yull .... in WP 8448 (229)
E L Taylor/Mrs J Simmonds in NPO 133 (651)
B G Wolfson/H Levinson ⎫
W S Underwood/J Taylor ⎭ in unidentified Jupiters

The Jupiter entrants running closed were:—
R Harrison/P Guest in LJW 979 (929)
Mr & Mrs Tew with FUD 194 (620)
A Gordon/P Steiner in NLX 909 (761)

The coupé Jupiter of Frank Grounds LOL 1 (29) was entered but could not start due to a sudden illness of Mrs Grounds.

There was a timed downhill braking test just after Harrogate, an uphill acceleration test at Brampton in Cumbria, a 20-mile regularity run near Penrith, and a stop/re-start test near the Bwlch-y-Groes which was attempted from the north in half a gale and horizontal rain. Cars then headed south to the manoeuvring tests on a hill just outside Hastings for competitors dead-tired after day and night driving. They then proceeded on into Hastings to the seafront in sight of the finish outside the Queens Hotel for a braking and garaging test. Underwood reached the first control but not the second, whilst E L Taylor lost 249.4 points at his third control and retired.

R Harrison and Jupiter (929) on returning to West Bromwich after class-winning the Concours d'Elégance in the 1953 MCC Rally. (Sidney Darby Ltd)

Bill Boddy for *Motor Sport* observed the hill test at Hastings in the rain, writing "*a revealing one in respect of weight distribution and awkward gear changes*" and continued:— "*J R Smith, hood up, made a lot of noise and spin, while Tew's Jupiter also gave evidence of being too light at the back...very excellent runs were put up by Gordon (Jupiter), Masefield-Baker (Javelin)...*".

The Wolfson/Levinson Jupiter is known to have reached the final tests at Hastings. All finishing Jupiters did well, scoring below the standard average for the class: Yull lost 46.8, Tew 38.25, while Harrison lost 22.65.

Gordon with 12.46 came eighth in the General Category and third in the 1101–1500cc Closed Production Car class – but annoyingly had he run in the equivalent open-car class, with his score he would have been placed second! A Javelin was 20th in the General Category. On the final day the rain cleared for the Concours d'Elégance held on the Marine Parade at Hastings: in the category for open cars in the before-tax price range of £550-£850, R Harrison's suitably scrubbed Jupiter recorded a very creditable class victory.

1953 MCC-*Daily Express* Rally, R Harrison (929) trying hard in the rain on the Hastings Hill Test. (Brymer)

5: Races and Speed Events 1950 to 1953

Silverstone 26th August 1950. Some famous drivers were gathered at the circuit for the six races of the day, including Ascari, Fangio, Leslie Johnson, Pierre Levegh, Moss and Nuvolari to name a few, and amongst the competing marques were Alfa-Romeo, Alta, Aston Martin, ERA, Ferrari, Frazer Nash, Jaguar, Lago-Talbot, Maserati and more. The V16 BRM made its very first race appearance – shearing a drive shaft on the start line – and on a humbler level Jowett in the person of Charles Grandfield their Engineering Manager had entered their revamped Le Mans class-winner GKW 111 (4) in the **1-hr Production Sports Car Race** for cars of up to 2-litres capacity. Horace Grimley, Chief Experimental Engineer, in his first and only major race, was to drive it in a 15-strong class of seven HRGs with John Gott in one of them, plus the MG TC of Harry Lester and the Works Stage IIC MG TDs for Dick Jacobs, Ted Lund and George Phillips.

Despite an un-nerving spin at Beckets, Grimley was not fussed, bringing the Jupiter to an indicative class 5th at 68.89mph behind the three MG TDs and the class winner the HRG of Gerry Ruddock (71.78mph), and fortunately just ahead of the HRG of Peter Clark for it rudely shook

off its spare wheel on the final lap. Five HRGs and two MGs did not finish, nor did C J Turner in his Javelin.

The three-hour 18th **RAC Tourist Trophy** race, of **16th September 1950**, was first run in 1905 and was the world's oldest established motor race. A new circuit had been devised being 7.416 miles of country lanes around Dundrod, near Belfast in Northern Ireland. The roads

1950 Silverstone 1-hour Production Sports Car race. Grimley at speed in the ex-Le Mans class-winner (4). (*Motor Sport*)

were narrow, very demanding, camber often the wrong way, the surface often rough, and to cap it all it always seemed to be raining. Lance Macklin said there never should have been a race there, but Stirling Moss wasn't fussed probably because he was so good in the wet! Eligibility was limited to unsupercharged production cars and virtually no modifications from standard or factory-available tuning options were allowed. It is not clear how Jowett circumvented the requirement for at least 20 examples to have been built for, although the Jupiter was a true production car – and in production – only three had been completed before the race, to which one could add the 11 rolling chassis that had been shipped. Another five standard Jupiters were 'in work' however.

In many ways the rules resembled those of Le Mans with only parts carried in the car could be used during the race with the standard jack carried to be used for any wheel changing.

The 1½-litre class comprised the Works MG TDII team of Lund, Jacobs and Phillips plus an HRG team with Peter Clark and an MG TC team. Amongst the individual entries was Tom Wisdom with GKW 111, described in the programme as a "Gowott Jupiter". Wisdom disheartened the MGs (their 9.3:1 compression ratios and other modifications only allowed by the RAC after much pressure) by getting down to 6min 28sec in (dry) practice compared with 6min 38sec for the quickest HRG (Peter Clark) and the best MG with 6min 48sec. Once again the Jupiter's superior handling was telling.

At the start Wisdom was the last away for the Jupiter was reluctant to fire up in the heavy rain that was now falling. The TDs had the class lead for the first lap, but on Lap 2 they were all overtaken by the fast moving Jupiter, and although the MGs were then wound up fully, the Jupiter continued to pull away from them. A 'Go faster' pit signal was continually posted for the MGs.

Alas having built up an impregnable lead, the Jupiter's engine broke its crankshaft, in the first instance of a trouble that was to cause headaches for Jowetts best brains for some time to come. This actual crank had survived a good 24 hours at Le Mans and much further

testing but its end had come no doubt assisted by the (probably illegal) compression ratio that had been raised to 8.75:1.

Stirling Moss in his XK120 won his first major production car race, a dazzling drive in the torrential rain that had descended for the entire afternoon.

Watkins Glen 23rd September 1950. The December 1950 issue of *Road and Track* alerts us to the 8-lap (52.8-mile) race for the Queen Catharine Monteur Cup – one of three races that day. The straked Jupiter which must be the very No 1 Jupiter, was raced by L Whiting Jr, and was seen to have some front-end damage taped up, perhaps a collision with a haybale in practice. In the race he retired on the fourth or fifth lap "with sounds indicating all was not well with the engine" in fact one report said the engine sounded sour from the beginning. This car was then to be passed around unrepaired through three owners until bought in 1968 and restored accurately except for its engine (a 238cu-inch Chevrolet), transmission and rear axle; it is now a USA 'show car'.

The **1951 BRDC 1-hr Production Sports Car Race** was on the **5th May** at **Silverstone**. Contesting the 1½-litre class were five Stage II MD TDs (Dick Jacobs, Ted Lund, George Phillips, Dalton, Biggar), three HRGs (Ruddock, J V S Brown, Keen), and the ex-Le Mans Jupiter GKW 111 this time driven by Bert Hadley.

May 1951 Bremgarten Sports Car Race. Gurzeler on his way to a good class win and the Preis von Bremgarten. (CJ)

Hadley took the class lead from the start and established himself with a 2nd-lap time of 2min 19sec, a time beaten only once, by Jacobs with 2min 18sec. Hadley maintained his class lead of between 2 and 5 seconds whilst Jacobs and Lund swapped 2nd and 3rd places until the tenth lap when Jacobs consolidated 2nd behind the flying Jupiter. The MG's speed crept up until the energetic Jacobs was on the Jupiter's tail and getting alongside at Club Corner. He had no hope of beating the Jupiter on speed but his driving forced Hadley to use 3rd gear more than he would have liked and alas, after 15 laps at 72.66mph Hadley had to retire with gasket failure shortly before Lund broke a valve and ruined his MG's engine. Fastest HRG lap was 2min 35sec. The winner was Dick Jacobs.

The **1951 Giant's Despair Hillclimb**, 12th May, in Wyoming Valley, Philadelphia, was competed in by 63 cars including 19 MGs, some supercharged so in a different class from the Jupiter of George C Rand. The Jupiter was only able to run once, ascending the hill in 1min 32.3sec to place 9th out of 18 in his class.

The **GP of Bern**, Switzerland on **17th May 1951** witnessed Theo Gurzeler (Jupiter 66) finish 5th behind 4 x Porsche 356 but ahead of a Cisitalia, another 356 and a BMW 315/1. Gurzeler had started in motor sport aged 25 in his first car, a Javelin, in the 1949 Develier-Rangiers hillclimb.

The **29th May 1951 Bremgarten Sports Car Race** for standard production cars was held on a 4.52-mile forest circuit near Bern. Gurzeler, (66) in a hard race against strong opposition from a streamlined HRG and five MG TDs, lapped the last two MGs as his Jupiter took the 1½-litre class at 68.89mph. Although later racing Glockler, Porsche, Abarth and more he always said that this was his best ever race.

The **1951 Rheineck/Walzen Hillclimb** on the 17th June saw the return of Gurzeler. Here in his Jupiter he won the 1½-litre sports car class with a time of 5min 53sec. A Javelin was 2nd in the 1½-litre saloon car class with 6min 37.0sec.

The **1951 BRDC British Empire Trophy** of the **14th**

June, an international event run on the Isle of Man for catalogue sports cars where at least ten examples should have been sold by the 1st of May. Sundry engine modifications, higher compression and any fuel were permitted and the full race distance was 35 of the 3.88-mile laps around a street course on the outskirts of Douglas. The 1½-litre class contained three 'staged' MGs but the rest could not strictly be described as catalogue sports cars: Bill Robinson who we have already met in the 1951 Monte Carlo Rally in a standard Jupiter was here driving his saloon Jupiter NTB 603 (37) with at least the engine and chassis as the factory intended whereas two Lester-MGs and Cooper-MGs were sports racers made in tiny quantities and were so basic in bodywork as to have twice the power/weight ratio of a standard Jupiter.

Robinson's best practice lap was 4min 19sec whereas Jacobs and Lund in their MGs had practised at 4min 5sec and Griffiths in the faster Lester-MG was only 8 seconds slower than Moss in his Frazer Nash at 3min 26sec. Goodyear persuaded Robinson to replace his Michelin S tyres he had used in practice with some very stiff tyres for the race. They upset the handling and knocked out

1951 British Empire Trophy on the Isle of Man. Robinson in his saloon Jupiter No 4 cornering hard. The white car is S Hill's Healey, No 5 is the MG of Dick Jacobs. (S R Keig)

the front shock absorbers to modify things to the point where spectators scattered at his approach. It was put out of its misery on the 11th lap near the top of Brae Hill when its engine seized, ending remarks by the race commentator John Bolster about the car's ugly (in his view) bodywork having been "constructed by a relative of Heath Robinson". It had averaged 54mph for 40 miles.

1951 Sports Car Club of America (SCCA) Burke Mountain Hillclimb on **24th June** was a 1¾-mile paved climb starting at 1900 feet and ascending to the summit at 3267 feet, where there is an excellent view of Vermont. Its sinuosity could have been designed for Jupiters for there were five hairpins and another five sharp curves. Class 4 (1 to 1½-litres) was won by Dexter Coffin in his stunning red Jupiter (61) with 4min 42.2sec ahead of a Porsche with 5min 4sec and an MG TD with 5min 12.9sec. A BMW in another class recorded 5min 2sec.

The 1951 SCCA meeting at Thompson Speedway. George Weaver (61) ahead of the MGs. (*Road and Track*)

The **1951 Rest and Be Thankful Hillclimb** of **July 7th** had K B Miller in Jupiter JGA 123 (41) class 8th with 81.89sec. Ted Lund's was the best 1250cc MG TDII at class 4th with 71.25sec behind three specials. Best HRG time was 84.27sec.

The **1951 SCCA National Meeting** on **21st** and **22nd July** comprised two days of races and speed trials at the 5/8th of a mile oval banked track at Thompson, Connecticut. In a 5-lap race for 1½-litre sports cars,

neat cornering produced a clear win for George Weaver driving Dexter Coffin's Jupiter (61) ahead of Hugh Byfield in another Jupiter and a collection MG TCs, MG TDs and similar cars.

BARC Goodwood 18th August 1951. Shortly before his Jupiter (110) was shipped to Singapore, F E N Wills entered it in a 5-lap scratch race at the Sussex circuit. He completed four laps with his best lap 2min 25.0sec. The race was won by the very rapid Mike Hawthorne in a blue Riley.

In the **1951 MCC (Motor Cycle Club) Silverstone** meeting of the **8th September**, the *Motor Sport* staff car, Jupiter HAK 268 (98), was noticed in the car park with their other staff car, a Morgan.

On the track in the first 1-hr High Speed Trial was Alf Thomas with JTM 100 (38) his open Rawson-bodied Jupiter in the up to 1½-litre class. He averaged 61.10mph, a higher speed than seven out of the eight HRGs taking part. Whilst not an actual race, these High Speed Trials certainly looked like them to the spectators: a not too arduous target speed was set and the drivers would lap as fast as they could to see by how much the target speed could be exceeded. Alf Thomas, one of the first motor-sporting Jowett agents, favoured events of this type.

In the **1951 YSCC (Yorkshire Sports Car Club) meeting** at **Croft** also on the **8th September**, in a race for saloon cars of up to 1½-litres, the Jupiter-engined Javelin of G P Mosby finished first at 58.09mph while second was a 1267cc wheel-hopping Morgan. Third was K N Lee

Two *Motor Sport* staff cars at the Silverstone car park. 8th September 1951. (*Motor Sport*)

in what was described as Jupiter, but we do not know if it was a genuine saloon Jupiter or a standard Jupiter running closed. K N Lee was for many years a prominent member of the Yorkshire Sports Car Club, so my money (but only just!) goes on the KW Saloon KWX 770 (99) of Edward Foulds the Keighley Jowett agent. He was known to have used it in the 1951 MCC Rally in November, and it was raced by its next owner Albert Wake in 1954.

The **1951 RAC Tourist Trophy** of the **15th September** was again on the Dundrod country lane circuit near Belfast. The date was very convenient for Jowett as the UK launch of the Jupiter was barely one month ahead at the October Earls Court Motor Show. A change this year was that only ten examples had to have been built, but an ambiguity in the regulations, maybe deliberate, allowed some non-production sports racers like Lester-MGs.

There were 37 participants in cars ranging from 747cc to 5420cc but the largest group was the 1101-1500cc category, made up of a trio of 1250cc MG TDs to Stage II for Ted Lund, George Phillips and Dick Jacobs, three more MGs and the Reece cousins' Cooper-MG against the Lester-MGs of Harry Lester and the wealthy racing man Jim Mayers with engines bored to 1467cc, plus no less than four Jupiters.

There were three Works Jupiters all ex-Le Mans although of course GKW 111 was in revamped road-car form for Tommy Wise, accompanied by the ex-1951 Le Mans HAK 365 for Tom Wisdom and HAK 366 for Bert Hadley, plus Bill Skelly in his privately-entered JGA 123 (41). The three Works Jupiters had the advantages of lighter weight and Le Mans fuel tankage and would be able to complete the race without re-fuelling.

The race was run on a complicated handicap basis – a set distance proportional to engine capacity had to be covered in the shortest time, implemented by credit laps and a staggered start. The Jupiters and the Lester-MGs had one less credit lap than the 1250cc MGs and the Cooper-MG which were started 2min 45sec after the 1467/1486cc cars, thus receiving a net lead of about 60% of a lap. At the finish, however, class positions were decided purely on an average speed basis – the race was

The 1951 RAC-TT Dundrod, the start. The Lester-MG is about to swoop round the Jupiters. (*Autocourse*)

run nominally over 43 laps, nearly 319 miles. Under the handicapping this was the target distance for cars of over 5 litres, a sliding scale meant that the 1½-litre cars had a target of 40 laps. The race ended when the first car completed its target.

Bill Skelly (41) and Dick Jacobs battle it out in the early stages of the 1951 RAC-TT Dundrod. (*Autosport*)

73

1951 RAC-TT Dundrod: Hadley on his way to his class win. A commentator wrote "The Jupiters with their characteristic whine mopped up the opposition". (© The Klemantaski Collection)

to its pit with a broken rocker.

The three Jupiters of Hadley (131), Wisdom (132) and Wise (4) continued to circulate with just 45 seconds between them. On lap 14 the Mayers Lester-MG retired with run engine bearings to join the MGs of Colleen (gasket) and Phillips (clutch) in the dead car park with nearly two-thirds of the race still ahead.

After two hours racing, Hadley in the leading Jupiter was amongst the faster MGs; Wise was 40 seconds behind Hadley but a bare 2 seconds behind Wisdom who was, however, about to make a 3-minute pit stop with a misfiring problem and to take on oil. Skelly had been lapped by the Works Jupiters, while Reece in his little Cooper-MG was 3½-minutes ahead of the leading Jupiter on handicap. Four laps later Hadley slipped past the Loens MG and within another two laps Wise was also past what would be the highest-placed MG.

At the three-hour point (28 laps) the Jupiters of Hadley and Wise were still circulating like contented clockwork, 40 seconds between them, with Hadley a reduced 26 seconds behind what one commentator wrote was the "ugly but regular" Cooper-MG. Tommy Wise in his rapid Jupiter GKW 111 had opened up a 1½-minute lead on the highest-placed MG.

Possibly as a check on how 'production' the cars really were, there was a timed Km stretch right after a half-mile straight itself just after a fastish right-hander (gradient 1:40 down).

For the start, the cars were lined up in echelon formation in front of their pits, drivers seated, engines stopped. At the fall of the flag the drivers pressed their starter buttons and were sent off in batches according to their time allowances.

The four Jupiters made a good start as did the Lester-MG of Mayers which swooped past the Jupiters as they were still leaving their pit area. Harry Lester's Lester-MG did not start well, but was on Wise's tail after one lap having already picked off Skelly. The three Works Jupiters led by Hadley accelerated and Wise, looking in his mirror saw Harry Lester recede and after ten laps a gap of 2½ minutes had opened up. By this time Mayers had lapped his team-mate and was a formidable 4 minutes ahead of Hadley in the leading Jupiter. One lap later Lester's car was seen slowly mis-firing its way back

Summary of the 1½-litre Class results for the 1951 RAC-TT at Dundrod

Driver and car	Class place	Overall place	Laps done	Average speed mph	Best lap	Speed mph	Speed through the timed km
Hadley, Jupiter (131)	1	18	35	68.71	6m 21s	70.07	91.20 mph
Wise, Jupiter (4)	2	19	35	68.59	6m 17s	70.82	92.90 mph
Reece, Cooper-MG	3	17	35	67.63	6m 24s	69.52	87.32 mph
Loens, MG	4	20	34	66.24	6m 33s	67.93	83.81 mph
Jacobs MG	5	21	34	65.26	6m 37s	67.25	81.98 mph
Lund, MG	6	22	33	64.62	6m 38s	67.08	80.44 mph
McCaldin, MG	7	23	33	63.36	6m 40s	66.74	82.54 mph
Skelly, Jupiter (41)	8	24	32	62.23	6m 54s	64.49	–
Wisdom, Jupiter (132)	–		30		6m 24s	69.52	90.63 mph
Mayers, Lester-MG	–	DNF	14		6m 04s	73.34	86.98 mph
Lester, Lester-MG	–	DNF	11		6m 36s	67.42	–

The race ended after about 3¾ hours when the XK120C of Stirling Moss became the first car to complete its target. Reece in his Cooper-MG crossed the finishing line 14 seconds ahead of Hadley and was placed ahead of him in the General Classification, although the Jupiters of both Hadley and Wise were placed above Reece in their class order as they had averaged higher speeds. The 1500cc cars had been required to cover 40 laps but due to the imbalance of the handicapping their race was over after 35. But since the two Jupiters had averaged a higher speed than Reece, it meant that had the race continued for their 40 laps the Jupiters would have passed Reece on lap 38 – hence the Jupiters' top two places in class.

Tom Wisdom's Jupiter was still running at the end but had lost nine minutes in four pit stops, the engine ailment requiring both water and oil from around the 2-hour mark. Thereafter a subdued HAK 365, smoking, lapped at the same speed as Skelly's Jupiter. Back in the Jowett pit Wisdom, who managed to finish but was not placed, had a blazing row with Grandfield, and in a 'right two-and-eight' very publicly called him all sorts of names, so he could never, nor would ever, drive for Jowett again. But this was a triumph for Jowett on the lines of 1949 Spa and Monte, 1950 Le Mans and the 1951 Monte and Lisbon rallies.

Robert Eberan-Eberhorst was in the Aston Martin pits to see his latest car the DB3 prototype – he was responsible for its chrome-molybdenum steel tubular chassis somewhat similar to that of the Jupiter, with transverse torsion-bar springing at both ends. The DB3 in the hands of Lance Macklin held second place until it ran a big end and retired, the cause being oil loss from an inadequate sump seal.

The **1951 Nottingham SCC Races** at **Gamston** on **6th October** demonstrated the trend in British sports car racing. At Club level, where regulations were plastic, the specialist sports-racing cars typified by Mike Hawthorne's Riley and Ken Downing's Connaught were supreme and it was rare for a private owner racing his own off-the-peg car to figure in the top places. However, at Gamston in Event 3, a 5-lapper for non-supercharged cars of up to 1½-litres, K N Downing (Connaught) came first with 75.46mph, P B Reece (Cooper-MG) came second with 73.51mph, so it was a very good third for Tommy Wise in Jupiter GKW 111 who averaged 72.55mph.

In the **1951 Sports Car Races** at the airfield circuit of **Winfield** on **13th October**, Tommy Wise entered Jupiter GKW 111 in two of the day's races. In the first race of the day, 5-laps for sports cars of up to 1½-litres, he drove the

Tommy Wise at Winfield October 1951 on his way to a good win.
Le Mans straps still there on the bonnet. (*Motor Sport*)

Jupiter hood down to third place behind Ken Downing in his Connaught and a Rover-engined special.

Later that day, hood up in a closed car 5-lap handicap race, Wise led all the way to an easy victory at 64.8mph from Ken Downing this time in a 2443cc Healey saloon, and another similar Healey saloon. Skelly in his Jupiter came 13th in this event and a Javelin 17th and last. So GKW 111 was a very fast Jupiter there!

Bill Boddy from *Motor Sport* was at Winfield that day, having achieved a running average of 46mph from London to Darlington in Jupiter HAK 268; he averaged 49mph on the way back after spending two nights at Darlington. He was pleased to report that his total distance of 676 Jupiter miles was covered at 28mpg.

The **Torrey Pines Races** of the **9th December 1951** put on by the California Sports Car Club near San Diego were on a 2.7-mile circuit situated on a gentle slope a few hundred feet from a cliff overlooking the Pacific Ocean. It had two straights, bordered by Eucalyptus trees, and plenty of sharp bends. One of these bends was the

undoing of newcomer-to-racing Newton Small (Jupiter), whose sweetly running and otherwise well-driven car spun on the last lap of the inaugural 10-lapper, losing his lead to an MG to finish second.

He was said to be 'way ahead' of the MG when he spun the car. His was the first Jupiter to be raced on the West Coast.

In the *Autosport* magazine review of the 1951 season (21st December) it remarked "Britain did not produce a 1½-litre machine capable of matching the Gordini Simcas, OSCAs, and Fiats in short-distance races, and considered that the R1 Jupiter appeared to be the best solution to the problem." The magazine warned that the 1.1-litre Porsche, so reliable at Le Mans, would be raced in 1½-litre form in 1952 and expressed the hope that the R1 be persevered with. Of course it was, but just for the single Le Mans event; however with the engine's power limit quickly reached, the opportunity to streamline the front, presented by a change in the regulations, was passed over.

For Britain, 1952 saw the arrival of the amateur Jupiter driver, to compete with a proliferation of production-based specials with initially only sparse interference from the continent, while in the USA in the production car events,

Photographers rushed to capture Newton's big slide, Torrey Pines December 1951. (LAT Photographic)

where Jupiters most usually joined issue, Porsche began to take the upper hand.

Vero Beach 8th March 1952. Races were on Florida's **Municipal Airport**. The 3.25-mile circuit had five right-hand bends one a hairpin, two left-handers and a fast kink past the grandstand. The inaugural 1 hour race had 22 starters grouped in several classes. Bill Smith in his "go-to-work" Jupiter "came in class third behind only Max Hoffman's Glockler Porsche and Koster's HRG". Behind the Jupiter were the five MGs some supercharged.

Jupiter owner Bill Lloyd was there, he wrote:–

"The Jupiter is a very nice little car, it corners like a demon, is very comfortable and stays up with the best of them".

Later that same day at the **Vero Beach Municipal Airport** there was another race. Run by the SCCA on a circuit slightly altered at 3.3-miles, there were 1-hr, 6-hr and 12-hr races with class divisions from 500cc to unlimited. In the 1-hr race the opposition to Richard Thierry's Jupiter included five MGs, a standard Porsche, a lightweight ex-Works Porsche for Max Hoffman and an Offenhauser-engined HRG (perhaps the same HRG that came second in the earlier event). Max Hoffman, the importer of VW, Porsche and Jowett, placed overall second on handicap, winning the 1½-litre class from the HRG and Thierry's Jupiter.

The **22nd March 1952 BARC Members Race Meeting** at **Goodwood** in Sussex was for sports cars only, and Bill Robinson entered GKY 256, (18) by now his very own Jupiter: its first two race outings were a 5-lap scratch race and a 5-lap handicap. There were seven sports racers in the scratch event – a pair of Lester-MGs for Mayers and Ruddock, a Cooper-MG for Davis, a Lamgia entered by Harry Lester, a Connaught for Ken Dowling and a pair of MG specials. The rest of the pack was made up of six MGs, two HRGs and the Jupiter of Bill Robinson.

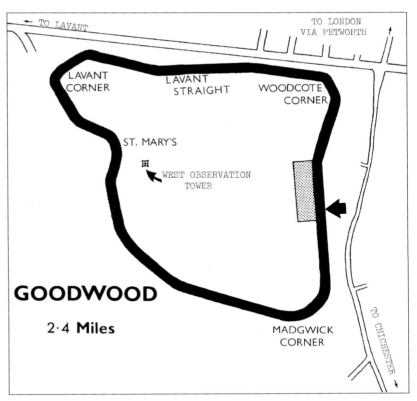

Goodwood circuit in 1952, formerly a Battle of Britain airfield. (John Blazé)

Goodwood 22 March 1952. The start: Bill Robinson and Jupiter on the right. The scratch car wearing 19 was the 2600cc blown Alfa of Nigel Mann. In front of him is the eventual winner, the Cooper-MG of F C Davis. (Guy Griffths)

Starting positions were picked by a ballot. A series of photos shows on Lap 1 Davis's Cooper-MG pulling away from the press, while on Lap 2 Robinson was holding his own with three of the 1426cc MGs and the Hurgs. Later pictures show a lonely Jupiter, and a partially-folded race plate suggests a brush with a straw bale, although the Jupiter seems to have finished ahead of T W Dargue's 1462cc silver MG Special, in fact out of 14 starters and 12 finishers he placed 8th. The handicap race had for the red Jupiter a more dramatic moment for, at nearly 100mph, Robinson saw the car's nose dip and the oil pressure gauge's needle flip to zero – the crankshaft had broken and split the block. Robinson's fastest lap was 2min 9.2sec, 66.9mph.

The **1952 fourth annual Palm Springs Road Race**, California, was on **23rd March**. The first race (10 laps, 23 miles) for production cars of up to 1½-litre was won by a Siata Sports, with an MG TD II second and the Jupiter of Bruce Mooney third from at least 15 finishers of which 6th, 7th, 8th and 10th were MGs. The other Jupiter was of the English driver Dennis Buckley but 'his mount sounded poorly' and he retired after three laps.

The fourth event was a Ladies' Handicap Race and Wanda Mooney (Jupiter) placed 6th behind five MGs. In May 1952 Bruce Mooney was again in action in a 100-mile race at Pebble Beach, to retire on lap 7.

In the **Turnberry Airfield Sprint 29th March 1952** W A Brearley was in action in the ex Le Mans Jupiter GKW 111, now borrowed by him from Tim Wise. Brearley drove GKW 111 to third place behind a special and an MG ahead of a Singer and two more MGs.

The **1952 BARC Ludgershall Hillclimb** on **5th April** saw Neil Freedman (Jupiter 509) in action. Hood raised, he won the 1½-litre closed-car class at 38.8sec.

The **1952 BARC Goodwood 4th April** races saw Joe Kelly in his Jupiter (120) in action in the Easter Handicap race. His best lap was 2min 17.0sec. The handicapping did not suit him as he placed 11th and last with the winner a DB2.

The year 1952 saw the BRDC taking over the Silverstone lease and they revised the circuit in various small ways. At

Silverstone 10th May 1952. Young Bill Skelly in the Production Sports Car race. A Frazer Nash is trying to pass. (Guy Griffiths)

Silverstone 10th May 1952. George Phillips had an enjoyable drive in the ex-Le Mans Jupiter (131). (Guy Griffiths)

the BRDC *Daily Express* **Production Car Races 10th May 1952**, in the Production Touring Car event, 1½-litre class, the three Javelins of Bert Hadley, Bennett, and John Marshall, had as sole company the 1¼-litre MG Saloon of MG man Dick Jacobs. Hadley's Javelin *"stepped off quite well suggesting lightweight"* he told me. *"It had lowered suspension and I could take most corners on full noise.*

One of the marshals said it looked terrifying in the corners but I liked it". It also had a rather special engine that had seen far too many hours on the Factory test bed. The Javelin was fast, indicating 105mph on the run down to Stowe and Hadley was well up in the field when with less than two laps remaining the inevitable happened and the top came off one of the pistons making a tremendous clatter. The pistons were experimental and long past their estimated life. What incompetence by Grandfield! Jacobs went on to win ahead of the remaining two Javelins.

By contrast, the Production Sports Car race, 1½-litre group, had 11 entrants: Leonard and Davis had doubled production and now there were **two** Cooper-MGs! There were Lester-MGs for Mayers and Ruddock while the genuine production-based contingent comprised MG TDs for Lund and Line, a 1.2-litre Austin A40 Sports, Sparrowe's 1.1-litre Morgan and three Jupiters. The Factory had loaned motor sportsman-photographer George Phillips the ex-Le Mans Jupiter HAK 366 (131),

Skelly was back once more with JGA 123 (41), and John Burness had entered Jupiter MUU 845 for C Le Strange Metcalf; again no HRGs for the TD/HRG battles were now waged elsewhere. The interest for spectators was whether the Coopers or the Lesters were the faster.

The start was Le Mans-type with cars lined up in order of practice times. George Phillips in HAK 366 left the other Jupiters and the rest of the production cars far behind: Mayers was the quicker of the Lester-MGs but in the effort of keeping up with the Coopers broke a conrod and deposited oil on the approach to Stowe. Then with the retirement of Leonard's Cooper-MG, Phillips was able to bring the lightweight Jupiter in at class 3rd at 70.25mph behind the remaining Cooper-MG (75.85) and Lester-MG (72.51mph). In the General Classification Stirling Moss (XK120C) was the overall winner and von Eberhorst-designed Aston Martin DB3s were 2nd, 3rd and 4th. The two privately entered Jupiters, lacking Works support finished poorly behind the MG TDs and the Morgan.

Silverstone Production Sports Car Race 1½-litre Class – 10 May 1952

Car	Driver	Class position	Overall position	Best practice lap	Average lap time	Race speed (mph)	Number of laps
Cooper-MG	Davis	1	16	2m 17s	2m 19s	75.85	16
Lester-MG	Ruddock	2	18	2m 28s	2m 25s	72.51	15
Jupiter HAK 366	Phillips	3	20	2m 29s	2m 30s	70.75	15
Morgan	Sparrowe	4	21	2m 37s	2m 37s	67.23	14
MG TD	Lund	5	22	2m 37s	2m 37s	67.05	14
MG TD	Line	6	23	2m 36s	2m 37s	66.99	14
Jupiter JGA 123	Skelly	7	24	2m 45s	2m 42s	64.82	14
Jupiter MUU 845	Metcalf	8	25	2m 47s	2m 47s	62.92	13
Austin	Christie	9	26	2m 50s	3m 00s	58.53	12

Silverstone Production Saloon Car Race 1½-litre Class – 10 May 1952

Car	Driver	Class position	Best practice lap	Average lap time	Race speed (mph)	Number of laps
1¼-litre MG	Jacobs	1	2m 45s	2m 46s	63.42	15
Javelin	Hadley	–	2m 45s	–	–	(13)
Javelin	Bennett	2	2m 46s	2m 47s	63.15	15
Javelin	Marshall	3	2m 48s	2m 49s	63.02	15

Prescott Hillclimb 18th May 1952. Eight hours of 880-yard hill-climbing in front of the largest crowd to assemble for a non-international event.

Climbs of this type are won by the cars that are quickest out of the corners and Hadley requested Jowett to provide him with a Jupiter fitted with lower gearing than standard. Jowett could easily have fitted a Javelin crown wheel and pinion assembly for example, but there seems to have been an issue between Hadley and Grandfield, perhaps because Hadley had the engineering experience that Grandfield lacked. Hadley, easily the fastest driver Jowett could expect to represent them, engaged the noted mechanic Harry Speirs of the Jowett Experimental Dept to ensure his Jupiter was properly prepared, unlike for example his 1952 RAC Rally Jupiter a few weeks back. Any road, the first event, for the smaller-capacity sports cars, attracted 19 entrants and the first good time was set by D F Ryder in a Cooper-MG at 53.17sec. Bert Hadley, with plenty of blue tyre smoke on Pardon Hairpin, urged the heavier ex-Le Mans Jupiter HAK 366 up in 53.77sec. Best time was set by Ruddock in a Lester-MG with 51.20s but still slower than the four-year-old HRG record. Hadley placed 4th in his class.

The 1952 Bridgehampton Annual Day Of Races put on by the SCCA on Long Island on the **24th May** featured two Jupiters, one of Hugh Byfield and the other was Bill Lloyd's ordinary road car for Richard Thierry. They were in the 10-lap Sagaponack Trophy race for 1½-litre stock sports cars. There were six MGs, two Porsches, a Siata and a Crosley. The two Porsches took an immediate lead to be chased hard by Thierry's Jupiter and the Siata, with the Siata slipping past the Jupiter on the fifth lap. Thierry finished 4th, ahead of the MGs in the next four places. Byfield had a poor race, falling back to retire on the ninth. The winning Porsche had originally been placed in the race for modified cars. Here is Bill Lloyd's full quote to a USA motoring magazine about his Jupiter *"It ran very well, beating all the MGs and coming behind the Porsches which cost $2000 dollars more than my go-to-work Jupiter which has proved to be one of the best compromises between a sports car and Detroit iron. The Jupiter is very*

nice little car, it corners like a demon, is very comfortable, and stays up with the best of them...".

The **1952 14th International British Empire Trophy Race** took place on **29th May** at Douglas, Isle of Man. It was a handicap race with 31 cars entered and 27 starting. The over 3-litre cars were on scratch, all Jaguars but for a solitary Allard. The 1½ to 3-litre cars were given one credit lap: they were six Frazer Nashs, Buncombe's Healey and no less a figure than Geoff Duke in a DB3. The by now familiar 1½-litre category was given four credit laps: there were Lester-MGs for Ruddock, Mayers and Griffith, Cooper-MGs with 1496cc engines for Davis and Leonard, three standard MG TDs for Llewellyn, Ted Lund and J T K Line, a TC for P Jackson, and very notably five Jupiters. Scratch distance was 52 laps 201.76 miles or for the 1½-litre cars 48 laps 186¼ miles.

The five Jupiters were of Bill Skelly (41), E W Cuff Miller and G A Dudley (651), J A Cowap (661), Bill Robinson (18) and Joe Kelly (120).

The Jupiter of Cowap did not start, while Dudley had crashed his Jupiter into a stone wall at Parkfield during the

Robinson and GKY 256 before the start of the 1952 British Empire Trophy. Behind is David Murray's XK120. Only one finishing XK120 averaged a higher speed than this Jupiter. (S R Keig)

previous day's practice, and so he also did not start, hence there were now three Jupiters to begin the race. Skelly (41) was starting at the back of the grid with the MG TC. Robinson's ex-Works Jupiter (18), now owned by him, had its engine specially built for the race by Leslie Armistead one of his own mechanics and barely run in by the start – therefore, mindful of last year's seizure he took the early part of the race carefully. The other Jupiter (120) with a good chance of finishing ahead of the MGs was that of the experienced Irish Grand Prix driver Joe Kelly.

Fastest race lap was posted by Geoff Duke in his DB3, naturally very popular with the local spectators who expected him to repeat his motorcycle wins. However the handicapping favoured the 1½-litre cars, specifically the Lester and Cooper MG-engined specials. So Griffith immediately took the class and race lead and these cars initially filled the first five places but after two laps the Jupiter of Joe Kelly replaced Mayers in fifth place as his Lester-MG was having steering difficulties.

After 40 minutes of racing Kelly still held class and race fifth and had averaged 57.42mph, a speed if maintained was sufficient to beat all the MGs. Five minutes later Davis retired his Cooper-MG with bearing failure, so Kelly's Jupiter moved up to 4th although lapped by the three leading MG-powered specials. Geoff Duke was fifth on handicap. Kelly at his average speed would have been passed by Duke after about 1½-hours racing but something was now slowing him for after holding class and race 4th for 20 minutes Kelly was passed by Duke and a temporarily recovered Mayers. Jupiter man

Robinson, now happy with his engine but unhappy about Kelly's dust in his eyes, put his goggles on, passed Kelly, and now at class 4th set out to at least win the "1½-litre Production Car" class.

After two hours racing, Leonard's Cooper-MG blew its head gasket, letting Robinson into class 3rd. Geoff Duke was then forced to retire and Mike Hawthorne (Frazer Nash) moved into his final position, third on handicap and fastest car to finish.

The race ended when Griffith, who had a splendid race leading all the way, completed his target 48th lap after just under three hours of driving. He was followed by Ruddock, second in class and overall.

This 1-2 by Cooper-MGs was followed in by Robinson, his Jupiter placing class 3rd at 7th overall. Behind him were the MG TDs of Line and Llewellyn with Joe Kelly's Jupiter class 6th at 10th overall on handicap but unlike Robinson, slower in average speed than three of the four

British Empire Trophy of 1952, Isle of Man. Bill Skelly, the 19-year-old son of a Motherwell, Scotland, garage owner, pressed by the Jupiter of Bill Robinson with its reversed foglight. (CJ)

finishing Jaguars. Robinson had finished behind the Frazer Nashs of Hawthorne and Salvadori and the XK120 Jaguar of Sir J S Douglas, but nearly a mile ahead of the second Jaguar and lapping the third (Bill Black) and the remaining MGs. Skelly had retired a few laps before the end with valve trouble thus saving him from last place. Three laps before the end Line's MG TC ran a big end bearing.

The advanced handling of the Jupiter was demonstrated by an incident early in the race. Robinson was passed by Stirling Moss in his Frazer Nash and a gap of about 50 yards opened up. Moss entered the chicane at the start of a very twisty part of the circuit and was slowed more than Robinson in his Jupiter. Robinson then closed on the Frazer Nash actually coming alongside at the apex of the corner opposite the Jolly Sailor pub. But Robinson resisted the temptation to pass Moss, who went on his merry way to get to within one second of Geoff Duke's best time, before retiring the Frazer Nash with variety of mechanical troubles.

Le Mans and Silverstone apart, there were no races for the Works Jupiters for reasons that are explored elsewhere, but amateur owner-drivers continued to contest lesser events often to good effect. At the **1952 Wirral MC Sprint** at **Rhydymwym** in Flintshire, Wales, on **30th March**, E P Scragg the noted Alta-Jaguar driver in a rare appearance in a car not with cycle wings, took his brother's Jupiter (565) to third in his class.

The **1952 Eight-Clubs Silverstone Races** on 7th June opened with a one-hour High Speed Trial for cars of up to 1½-litre, and amongst the qualifiers were the Jupiters of F E Still (521) and D Crowe. There is photographic evidence of the presence of Neil Freedman's Jupiter MXA 506 (509) and Jupiter LRU 504 which could be Crowe's car. It is worth mentioning that two weeks earlier the event's organisers had proposed a race at this meeting for Cooper-MGs, Lester-MGs and the R1 Jupiters to determine the fastest British 1½-litre sports car but the challenge was not taken up possibly because of the short

1952 British Empire Trophy analysis of results

Driver	Car	Engine size	1½-litre class position	Overall position	Race speed mph	Best lap
Griffith	Lester-MG	1½-litre	1	1	64.20	3m 31s
Ruddock	Lester-MG	1½-litre	2	2	64.07	3m 33s
Hawthorne	Frazer Nash	2-litre	–	3	67.88	
Salvadori	Frazer Nash	2-litre	–	4	67.31	
Mitchell	Frazer Nash	2-litre	–	5	66.79	
Douglas	Jaguar	3.4-litre	–	6	65.22	
Robinson	Jupiter	1½-litre	3	7	58.12	3m 55s
Line	MG TDII	1½-litre	4	8	56.61	4m 01s
Llewellyn	MG TDII	1½-litre	5	9	56.30	4m 02s
Kelly	Jupiter	1½-litre	6	10	56.30	3m 55s
Boshier	Jaguar	3.4-litre	–	11	57.84	
Black	Jaguar	3.4-litre	–	12	57.07	
Holt	Jaguar	3.4-litre	–	13	51.39	
Jackson	MG TC	1¼-litre	DNF	39 laps		4m 02s
Skelly	Jupiter	1½-litre	DNF	33 laps		4m 14s
Lund	MG TDII	1½-litre	DNF	10 laps		4m 07s

Eight-Clubs Silverstone races of 7th June 1952. We think it is
Crowe's Jupiter which is just ahead of Freddie Still's Jupiter.
(Guy Griffiths)

notice and, for Jowett, the proximity of Le Mans. The MG-
powered cars could lap the Club circuit at around 68+
mph at this time; but as to the R1, all one can say is that
as Alf Thomas could get the R4 Jupiter (of similar weight
and power but poorer handling than the R1s) round at
over 67mph, it could have been a close contest.

The veteran Irish Grand Prix driver Joe Kelly at Boreham 20 June 1952.
(Guy Griffiths)

On the **20th June 1952** the **West Essex Car Club** held
their second meeting of the year at the 3-mile Boreham
circuit and in the first race of the day Joe Kelly (120) drove
hard to third place behind Mayers (Lester-MG) and Davis
(Cooper-MG). Kelly's speed was 71.1mph.

For the **1952 BARC Members' Day** at **Goodwood**
on **26th July** there were two Jupiters present. John
Sykes raced HKY 133 (665) while John D Lewis raced
HKY 344 (718) – both Bradford-registered cars! Lewis
placed 4th in a 5-lap handicap race, with the actual
corrected speed of 63.16mph (best lap 2m 16.8sec).
In a 5-lap scratch race for cars of up to 1500cc, Sykes
was only faster than Betty Haig's MG; he had gasket
troubles and Jowett fitted a new engine for him free of
charge.

The **1952 National Six-hour Relay Race** held on
30th July, organised by the 750 MC on the Silverstone
Club circuit, was the second such event. The Queen's
cousin Gerald Lascelles told me he drove his Radford-
bodied Jupiter (8) nick-named the "Rabbit Hutch" for
70 laps under the pseudonym "G Davidson" in the
St Moritz Tobogganing Club's team; this team finished
overall fifth.

Overall fourth to finish was the Sporting Owner Drivers'
Club (familiarly known as the 'Sods' for reasons that baffle
me) in which Alf Thomas drove his special-bodied Jupiter
JTM 100 (38). A third Jupiter, that of F E Still (521) drove
in the Harrow CC team.

1952 6-hr Relay race. On the right the "Rabbit Hutch" chasing what is
thought to be a Buckler. (CJ)

At **Boreham** in **1952**, in the *Daily Mail* **West Essex CC International** on **2nd August**, there was a 100-mile race for Le Mans-type sports cars. Joe Kelly (120) had a spirited scrap with Sterry Ashby in his HRG Aerodynamic behind the usual 1½-litre sports-racers until after 10 laps, just 30 miles, the Jupiter retired with much emission of steam. C Swain's Jupiter (105) after a spin was 15th; Kelly was 21st and last.

In the **1952 Crimond Races**, put on by the Aberdeen and District MC on the **9th August**, R D Barrack (Jupiter) finished in a tidy third place in an 8-lap scratch race for 1.6-litre sports cars, behind a Cooper-MG and an MG.

1952 Shelsey Walsh Hillclimb took place on the **30th August**. The ascent was 1000 yards. Frank Grounds in his saloon-bodied Monte Carlo Jupiter (29) was timed at 61.55 and 61.89 seconds; five HRGs were faster, averaging 54.4 seconds. This was the only successful timed ascent by a Jupiter at Shelsey Walsh. In 1950 the Javelin of W H Osborn had been timed at 69.80 and 72.84 seconds.

RAF Croft Aerodrome 1952 Sprint Day was on **6th September**. The timed distance was 7/10ths of a mile on the old perimeter track. In the class for sports cars of up to 1½-litre W A Brearley (Jupiter, probably GKW 111) class-won with 37.91s, comfortably beating Richmond's HRG (38.87s) and the best MG (39.29s). The best Javelin was timed at 40.86s.

The 1952 Brighton International Speed Trials also on the **6th September** were held as usual along the seafront – the timed standing kilometre, with the speed measured over the last 88 yards. No times for the Jupiter are known, but these speeds are recorded for the 1½-litre class: A O Gosnell (HRG) 81.8mph, Neil Freedman (Jupiter 509) 79.3mph, best MG 78.8mph, and F M Baker's Javelin 75.0mph.

The following day, the **1952 BARC Brunton Hillclimb**. saw Neil Freedman again competing in his Jupiter.

The **1952 MCC Silverstone Race Meeting** on **13th September** was a good event for Jupiters. A chicane had been added to the approach to Woodcote. In the first 1-hour High Speed Trial first class awards were won by 11 cars including Neil Freedman (509), G M Sharp (Jupiter

Alf Thomas in his special-bodied Jupiter (38) at Silverstone on 13th September 1952. It is noticeable that the body is lower on the chassis than with the standard Jupiter. (LAT Photographic)

Neil Freedman (509) on his way to winning the *Motor Sport* Trophy, MCC Silverstone 13th September 1952. (LAT Photographic)

MAC 2) and Alf Thomas (Jupiter JTM 100). No award for R Brookes (Jupiter).

In Event 9, a 5-lap handicap race, C le Strange Metcalf, now in a 995cc Fiat Balilla, was on scratch with another similar car. Limit man L J Spiller, in a pre-war Hillman Minx saloon, hung grimly onto his lead up to the last lap when he was passed by Alf Thomas's fast-moving cream-coloured Jupiter, then by Neil Freedman's very competently handled green one. Both Jupiters had started off the same mark – Alf's winning speed was 57.29mph.

Event 10 was the *Motor Sport* Trophy, another 5-lap handicap, which Freedman won at 55.88mph, just ahead of Alf Thomas who was followed by Hely's Healey, Gibb's Riley, and Peter Morgan's Morgan.

Prescott International Hillclimb of the **14th September 1952** saw several Jupiters in action although good positions were not achieved. Most cars were racing cars and specials, and one event saw Ken Wharton in his supercharged Cooper-JAP lower the course record to 43.70 seconds. The table below shows some of the times recorded:–

The Swedish near-replica-R1 (6) photographed in 1953. (CJ)

Driver & car	Time 1 (secs)	Time 2 (secs)
Fastest HRG	54.33	54.55
Slowest HRG	56.43	58.44
A Jaguar	56.51	56.39
L Townson in Cowap's Jupiter (661)	57.64	58.00
Ian Sievwright in his Jupiter (748)	59.55	59.58
C F Eminson in his Jupiter (494)	64.55	64.69
A 1250cc MG	66.40	56.77
Javelin of A Black	68.07	65.31

It is very noteworthy that Hadley's time of 53.77s four months earlier was not approached by any of the Jupiters or any HRG or MG. Eminson's Jupiter (494), which had achieved class 3rd at the Attingham Speed Trial two weeks before, is known to have been entirely standard as delivered; it had the distinction of being photographed on the day to represent the Jupiter in Georgano's 1973 *Source Book on Racing and Sports Cars*.

Croft Speed Trial 14th September 1952 was put on by the Sheffield & Hallamshire Motor Club on a 1-mile circuit. There were two Jupiters taking part in this event, with a useful class 3rd notched by J Clarke in his unidentified Jupiter.

Also on the **14th September 1952** over in **Stockholm**, a day of international races was held on a 1.7-Km circuit laid out on Skarpnäck airfield. It attracted entries from England, Ireland, Holland, Belgium, Germany and the Scandinavian countries. In the 1½-litre Sports Car race, Nathan (Porsche) was the favourite but Wahlberg's Veritas displayed surprising speed and overtook the Nurburgring class winner and another Porsche. Fourth was R Berg in a 'Jupiter Le Mans' which can be taken to be the Sickla Karosserifabrik R1 near-replica (6). Places 5 to 7 were occupied by a Peugeot, a Siata and an HRG.

Snetterton 20th September 1952. The Aston Martin Owners' Club event included a half-hour High Speed Trial which had a compulsory pit-stop to change all spark plugs. First in Group 3 was the Jupiter MAC 2 of G M Sharp. A 2-litre Aston Martin came second. Sharp and Jupiter also received the award for Best Performer Of The Day. Teenager W T Smith in Jupiter ECF 494 (680) took a first class award in the High Speed Trial with only 3 points lost, and notched 5th in a 5-lapper. For 1953 he switched to a Jaguar, and in the 1955 RAC-TT Dundrod road race he died in a Connaught, one of three deaths in inevitably the last race at that very dangerous circuit.

In the **Bo'ness Hillclimb** of **20th September 1952** W A Brearley in the Jupiter reckoned to be GKW 111 came class sixth.

The **Snetterton Speed Trial** of **4th October 1952** saw W T Smith (680) again in action, this time with a hard-top fitted. In the 1101 to 1500cc closed-car class he posted third.

SCCA Turner Airforce Base 26th October 1952
in Albany, Georgia, USA. In the 12-lap 54-mile race for
the Keenan Sowega trophy for up to 1½-litre production
sports cars, in an early RHD Jupiter, Ashley Pace in his
very first race brilliantly class-won the trophy, ahead of
six MG TDs. Another Jupiter, that of D Manley, could only
complete 3 laps.

Torrey Pines Road Races 14th December 1952
was put on by the SCCA on the 2.6-mile circuit laid out
in 1951 at a disused US Army base near San Diego. The
day's first race, of 12 laps, was for novice drivers in two
classes – up to and above 1½ litres – and contained
two Jupiters: that of Jim Lambros and Hunter Hackney.
Hackney was a student at the University of Southern
California. The track allowed high speeds along the pit
straight but heavy braking was required for the following
corner, a corner of decreasing radius and reverse camber
that caught out many drivers including Lambros. At one
point during the race he broadsided his Jupiter on this
corner and smartly reversed onto the grass to avoid the
following MG TC which also spun. Two Singers narrowly
avoided the TC but a Siata was less lucky, putting itself
and the TC out of action. Lambros re-joined the race while
Hackney capped a successful season's rallying in his daily
transport, as we saw in the previous chapter, by securing
the first class-win for a Jupiter in West Coast racing. His
time was 32m 11.59s at 58.15mph and he was followed
home by a Crosley Sports and an MG TD. Hackney was
to say: *"Winning a race is a tribute to any car, but winning
a race in a car with 20,000 miles on the speedometer
and no work having been done on the engine is truly a
compliment to the fine building and engineering of the
Jowett cars...the high grade of workmanship and quality
engineering allowed very high lap times, while superior
brakes allowed me to increase my lap time in the closing
minutes of the race to make another victory for Jowett
cars; a tribute to a really fine sports car"*.

Jim Lambros was filmed and some footage of the
Jupiter racing appeared in the first *"The Fast and the
Furious"* film which was released in 1955 starring Dorothy
Malone and John Ireland. This film should not be confused
with a series of films of the same name which appeared
from 2001.

Over in Australia, Des Pinn, a young dentist of
Goulburn, NSW, bought a BRG Jupiter probably E1 SA
186R as this is the only appropriate BRG Jupiter sold new
in Sydney.

His BRG Jupiter was delivered in January 1952 and
registered AAJ 555 and he proceeded to tune it to a
legendary extent, as can be gauged from the need, for
other than round-town use, to change the spark plugs
after the engine had warmed up. Compression ratio was
raised, it was lightened by the removal of bumpers, spare
wheel, hood, windscreen, door linings and glass. Oversize
tyres were fitted. Normal top speed, estimated from the
tacho, was 104mph (6100rpm on standard tyres) and, at
the Mount Panorama circuit in Bathurst NSW it was once
timed at 111mph through the flying eighth on Bathurst's
aptly named Conrod Straight (slightly downhill with an
unpleasant hump about half-way) during an unofficial
practice session – for the car was not actually entered
for a race; such things were possible in those days. Des
remembers being disappointed with his lap times as the
climb up the mountain caught the car between gears.

At Castlereagh, an old aerodrome circuit marked by
oil-drums outside Sydney NSW, Des Pinn did brilliantly to
win a scratch race against XK120s and a sports Riley, and
it notched a Best Time of Day at a Mount Druitt meeting.
Des also participated in the Australian **Castrol Trophy
Reliability Trial** of **July 1952** in which he said the Jupiter
proved ideal *"During night running the cars encountered
a record snowfall on the NSW Central highlands. At one
stage the windscreen wipers froze to the screen and the
dash warning light that I had always joked about came
on"*. Although one of the leading cars at the time, Des
withdrew rather than risk damage as he intended to sell
the Jupiter at some time soon to help set up a dental
practice; in fact only a single car actually finished! In
retrospect Des considered the Jupiter outstanding in
handling but variable in reliability: he was twice let down
by gasket failure – caused by the raised compression ratio
maybe?

We are still in Australia for our last event of **1952**. This was at **Mount Druitt, NSW** on **28th December** and was probably for standard production cars although the level of tune would not have been strictly policed. G Kemp (Jupiter) came third behind the MG TD of D Chivas and the TC of R W Warnsley, both well-known names in Australian motor sport of the time.

The year 1953 saw the same sort of activity as had characterised 1952 and it is noticeable that Alf Thomas, and perhaps his garage which was less than 30 miles from the Silverstone circuit, was beginning to emerge as a nucleus of competitive Jupiter activity. In the UK the **1953** season opened as usual with the **BARC Members' Meeting** at **Goodwood** on the **21st March**. The circuit now had a chicane before the pits. Event 2 was a 5-lap scratch race which found G A Dudley (651) finishing 9th and Robbie MacKenzie-Low (544) 11th and last. John D Lewis (718) was also racing his Jupiter. Dudley's best lap was 2m 10.1s and Robbie's 2m 11.2s. Then in a handicap race, Dudley placed 4th behind a Riley Sprite, an MG Special and Betty Haig in her MG Magnette (all cars in

Madgwick Corner, Goodwood 21st March 1953. Three Jupiters: 10 (Mackenzie-Low), 11 (Dudley) and 23 (Lewis). No 2 is an RGS Atlanta, 14 an HRG, 1 a Cooper-Lea Francis, 6 an HRG lightweight special, 21 an MG TC Special, and on the grass is another MG Special. In front of Jupiter 10 is a Riley Sprite while to the right of Jupiter 11 are a Cooper-MG and a Tojeiro-MG. (Guy Griffiths)

this race were specials apart from the Jupiters). At one point John Lewis was up with MacKenzie-Low and on the outside on the Levant straight. Then trying to overtake round Woodcote Corner he lost it and damaged his Jupiter on some straw-bales. A Steward's Enquiry implicated MacKenzie-Low who was presumably dicing with Lewis. Dudley's best lap was 2m 8.3s.

At the **Trengwainton Hillclimb** on **6th April 1953** put on by the West Cornwall MC near Penzance on Easter Monday, Ken Crutch, a keen competitor in his Jupiter (602) and friend of Alf Thomas, placed 10th in the 2-litre class, with times of 34.11s and 33.84s. Also present but not competing was the FHC Jupiter LOL 1 (29) of Frank Grounds.

Bergstrom Airforce Base, Austin, Texas 12th April 1953 hosted a day of races. In Race 2 for all engine sizes, all that is known is that the Jupiter of J Saunders took part. But in Race 3 for cars of up to 1500cc the Jupiter of G Wright placed third behind a Porsche 356 Super and an MG TD but ahead of no less a driver than Caroll Shelby (Porsche) and, yes, seven MGs!

Charterhall Airfield Races over at **Winfield, Scotland** on **13th April 1953**. In a race for 1½-litre sports cars over five 2-mile laps, W A Brearley in the ex Le Mans Jupiter GKW 111, hood down, led two MGs to finish a very good first. In a 5-lap handicap race for saloon cars of all capacities, Brearley brought the Jupiter, hood raised, to second place, behind a Healey yet ahead of an Allard.

Also on **13th April 1953**, at the **BARC Brunton Hillclimb** near **Ludgershall**, Neil Freedman in his Jupiter (509) was again in action, results not known.

On **3rd May 1953** at **Phoenix Arizona**, the Four-Cylinder Club of America put on a day of races at the Luke Airforce base.

The club's name speaks for itself, putting on exciting events for the smaller European cars. Race 1 was for cars of up to 1500cc over

****

8 laps, 16 miles. The winner was 'Lammy' Lamoreux in his Singer SM 1500, followed by Cal Marks and then Hunter Hackney in their Jupiters, while following them were seven MGs, a couple of Porsche 356s, and two twin-cylinder Panhard Dynas which although less than 1-litre capacity could touch 81mph. Race 7 of 40 laps, 80 miles, was for the Governor's Cup, for all engine sizes. This time the class was hard-won by Hunter Hackney with Cal Marks second.

Bridgehampton (New York) Sports Car races on the **23rd May 1953**, promoted by the Sports Car Club of America (SCCA). It was the fifth of these annual events and the last to be held on public roads.

Race 1 for the Sagaponack Trophy was for stock production cars of up to 1½-litres, over 18 laps of the 4-mile circuit. The entry comprised six MG TDs, a Singer, five Porsches and the Jupiter of Pat Riedel. Pat finished sixth behind the five German cars but ahead of four MGs (two had been forced to retire) and the Singer.

At **Goodwood** on **2nd May 1953** there was a 5-lap handicap race for closed cars. Robbie MacKenzie-Low raced his Jupiter (544) with a pink hard-top fitted. His best lap was 2m 13.0s and, he told me, he thinks he finished fourth.

The **1953 Third National Six-hour Handicap Relay Race** was on the **29th August**, run as usual by the 750 MC. It was held this year on a special extended version of the Silverstone Club circuit, taking in the airfield's central runway to produce a lap length of 2½ miles. This was a true long-distance race for the amateur driver: the aim was to convey a sash around the circuit as many times as possible in the six hours. The cars and drivers could go out in any order and for any combination of laps.

The 'Jowett' team comprised D G Dixon (Javelin),

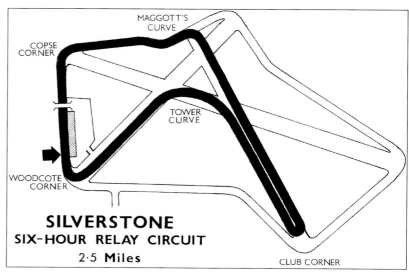

The Silverstone ex-airfield laid out for the Six-hour Relay Race showing the tight hairpin at the end of the central straight. (John Blazé)

Kenneth Crutch (Jupiter 602) and I A Forbes (Jupiter 28). Forbes scratched at the last minute, replaced by Tom Blackburn (Jupiter 846) who it turned out drove most of the race! It was a very wet day that day. The team finished 9th out of 33 starting and 31 finishing teams. A car christened 'Jehu' a special built by John Horridge on an unnumbered Jupiter frame powered by a Riley Sprite engine, ran in another team.

Over to California and the event on **16th August 1953** held on the **Moffett Naval Air Station** near Sunnyvale. In the NavCad Trophy for novices in all classes, the Jupiter of D Connelly placed 5th in his class behind a Simca 'Comp', an MG TD Special, and two Porsche 356s. Coming in after Connelly were no less than ten MGs and a Singer SM 1500.

Still in the USA, over to **New York** on **29th August 1953** and the **Floyd Bennett Naval Air Station** at **Sheepshead Bay**. The crowd was said to number 50,000 and the temperature was said to be 110°F (43°C). In the Sheepshead Bay Trophy race (20 laps 43 miles) for cars up to 1500cc retailing at less than $3000, there were 28 starters on the grid, mainly MGs but it was Wilbur (Lammy) Lamoreux in his distinctive yellow and blue

Bill Lloyd's RHD Jupiter with Richard Thierry seated in it, possibly at the 24 May 1952 Bridgehampton NY race. (Ossie Lyons)

Have mercy Mr Percy! The Lewis Jupiter after its affair at Goodwood back in March, where it brushed some strawbales, struck the wall they were supposed to protect, and then spun to face the direction of arrival. (Photo *Light Car* May 1953)

twin-carb Singer that jumped into the lead. At middle distance he was a good 30 lengths ahead of Bill Lloyd's white Mk1a Jupiter (963?) followed by a 'hoard of MGs'. Disaster struck Lammy on lap 17 as oil pressure failed and he was obliged to retire. This presented Bill Lloyd's Jupiter with the lead and he covered the remaining three laps to a good win, ahead of the 15 surviving MG TDs. Lammy's Singer although a DNF was generously awarded sixth on distance covered.

The **1953 Brighton Speed Trials** on the **7th September** was the usual Standing Kilometre run along the seafront. F M Baker again aired his Jupiter MCD 28 (597).

Goodwood 14th September 1953, the BARC Members' Meeting. In Event 3 a 5-lap handicap race for 1100-1500cc cars, J D Lewis (718) with his repaired Jupiter (from Goodwood six months back) came 6th out of 14 starters and 8 finishers. In Event 9, another 5-lap handicap race, he gained a 3rd place behind an MG and P S Bailey's special. Another MG was fourth.

The **Madera Road Races** of **October 1953** at California's Central Valley included two races for a

Jupiter whose engine had somehow been repositioned behind the front suspension. In the Novice race, driven by Bud Grosso, it took an immediate lead only to retire with ignition bothers. In its other race, this time with Bill Behel behind the wheel, it 'supplied the spectators with

The Jupiter of Cal Marks and staff of World Wide Import Inc., California Jowett agents. Far left, Hunter Hackney. Far right, Cal Marks. The owner with bow tie. (CJ)

some enchanting displays on the fast bends' but then the appalling handling forced the car to retire "for more development work on its steering geometry" said a report.

Long Beach, California, on the **3rd and 4th October 1953** witnessed two days of racing at the Reeves airfield 2.3-mile circuit, built on a man-made sand island. In Race 4 of six laps for up to 2-litre cars, J Carberry drove his Jupiter to third place behind a Porsche 356 and a Singer SM 1500 ahead of a brace of Dyna Panhards, three MGs and another Singer SM 1500. In Race 8 of eight laps for 1½-litre cars the Jupiters of Cal Marks and J Carberry finished third and fourth behind a Porsche 356 and a Singer 1500SM. Following them home was the Porsche that had won Race 2, and a mix of 13 MG TCs and TDs.

Over in Nevada now, at the **Stead Airforce Base** at **Reno** on **17th October 1953**, an event put on by the SCCA; in the novice race for cars of up to 1500cc although J Carberry placed 9th in his class he finished ahead of about 14 MGs. First and second places were taken by specials.

Back in California at the **March Airforce Base** at **Riverside** on **8th November 1953** organised by the SCCA, it was Carberry's day, for in Race 1 over 10 laps (35 miles) two Jupiters shone; Carberry class winner and Weissman class second. Class third was a Porsche, fourth a Siata 208S, fifth a Singer SM 1500. Race 3 was 30 laps 105 miles and Carberry's winning streak held with an extremely praiseworthy class win, with an MG TD second and Cal Marks in his Jupiter third. Next two places were filled by a Singer SM 1500 and a Porsche 356.

Over in **Fort Worth, Texas** on **6th December 1953**, in Race 3 over 15 laps 45 miles for cars of up to 2-litres, the Jupiter of J Saunders nicely won its class – an MG came second, a Singer SM 1500 third, followed by a Porsche 356 and several more MGs. The Jupiter of G Wright also ran. In Race 5 for all cars, 25 laps 75 miles, J Saunders again dominated his class finishing first ahead of a not always invincible Porsche 356 and an MG.

At the **Willow Springs, California, Hillclimb** of the **13th December 1953** a class win was recorded by an unidentified Jupiter.

Bill King, Activities Chairman of the Sports Car Club of America, with his Jupiter about 1953. (SCCA)

Rallying aside, there was only one Works-supported race for a Jupiter in 1953 and that by chance. MG-man Ted Lund had an entry for the **1953 RAC TT Nine-hour Race** at **Dundrod, Northern Ireland** on **5th September**, but for whatever reason his MG was not race-worthy. Spotting his friend Bill Robinson and daughter in their Jupiter GKY 256 driving through Wigan on their way to Belgium for a week's holiday he gave chase, stopped them, and proposed a Lund/Robinson entry for the Jupiter. It was instantly agreed, even though Robinson had by then decided to retire from motor sport. So the Jupiter continued on its way and in Belgium Robinson met the main Jowett agent who immediately telephoned Idle and the upshot was a competition engine was prepared for the car. On his way back from Dover, Robinson drove to Idle and collected the engine, stowing it beneath his passenger's feet – another instance of the Jupiter's notable carrying capacity!

For the race, fifty-four original entries became 45 by the time the programme was printed, and only 27 reached the start line, mostly British. Besides the Jupiter, its class comprised a Gordini, a Cooper-MG, a Lester-MG and two MGs, for the Porsches and USA-entered OSCA failed to materialise. Ninety-eight laps were required of the 1½-litre cars in a race that did hold a chance for the Jupiter.

It was only in practice that it was discovered that the engine supplied by Jowett had Javelin jets in its carbs, but with that corrected the car ran very well. Robinson lapped

In their successful competition Jupiters: Cal Marks (left) and Hunter Hackney (right) and trophies. (*Road and Track*)

at 2 seconds slower than Lund who knew the country-lane circuit intimately, and neither man noticed anything wrong with the new shock absorbers fitted for the race.

First race retirement was the Cooper-MG but after about two hours trouble struck the Jupiter. The front nearside shock absorber broke its upper fixing and Lund brought the car into the pits, but as it could not be corrected the damper was removed and Lund continued. Then, at around three hours the undamped wheel movements were sufficient to snap the nearside track rod and the wheel could move freely – only restrained by the castor action. When travelling at about 100mph past the pits the wheel moved with such vigour that it became virtually invisible! Lund had noticed it did not steer too

well on left-handers! The car was then black-flagged and retired. The 1488cc Gordini went on to win the class and the Series Production Award went to the George Phillips/ Roy Flower MG TDII. There were only 14 finishers in a race that was another triumph for the DB3 with Peter Collins and Pat Griffiths driving the winning one, whilst the Jupiter retired from representative racing and passed into history.

However GKY 256 was still driveable, Robinson maintaining that above 10mph the breakage could hardly be noticed and he drove the car back home without repair. It was then fixed and sold and its last licence was drawn in 1953 by a Mr Squires of Ulverston, Lancashire (five miles from Robinson's home town of Dalton). It is believed it was then sold abroad to disappear from our knowledge.

To complete the review of 1953 here is a quote from *Autosport* journalist and MG specialist Wilson McComb who, on 25th October 1953 was testing cars at the Goodwood circuit at the 6th Motor Show Test Day with the Guild of Motoring Writers:–

So to the last car of the day, the R4 Jupiter. Which had been besieged by eager journalists who were intrigued by its revolutionary appearance. The one at Goodwood was fitted with a hard top and did not have the plastic body, being in fact the Works 'hack'. There was nothing hackish about its performance, however, and in particular McC delighted in the overdrive. Just ahead of the normal gear lever protrudes another, more slender, lever; moving this forward engages overdrive 3rd, and backward engages overdrive top. The top gear overdrive was found to be so high that everything dies (ideal for petrol economy this!) but overdrive third produced an extra, super-close gear, great fun to use when cornering and of course demanding no use of the clutch. Approaching a tight bend one could change from top to overdrive third, then with a flick of the lever normal third when almost into the bend, and whip back into overdrive third when accelerating out of it. Playing tunes on it made the three laps pass all too quickly and it was with great sadness that McC handed back the last and most intriguing motor car.

His passenger added:–

*The R4 Jupiter possesses well-shaped bucket seats, but the toe-board was too far distant for useful bracing; at full chat around Goodwood bends in this incredibly lively vehicle, passenger's feet flailed vainly in search of a toe-hold. It is a driver's car – and we mean a **driver's car**.*

Finally in the 13th November 1953 *Autosport*. Donald Bastow explained:–

The overdrive ratio reasonably split the third–top gap. The OD switch was interlocked with the gear lever to give the quickest possible changes from overdrive top (switch again). I believe this was Roy Lunn's idea.

For more on the R4 see Chapter 8.

The original R4 Jupiter, photo taken 20th October 1953 somewhere on the Yorkshire moors. (C H Wood)

6: Other Rallies and Events 1951 to 1966

The **North Staffordshire Burnham Rally** to **Burnham-on-Sea** was very early in **March 1951**. Major L J Roy Taylor in his early Jupiter (51) took part. He told me he had ordered his Jupiter "off the drawing board" i.e. before he saw a completed car as he was a friend of Leslie Johnson and he also knew von Eberhorst.

Major L J Roy Taylor in the 1951 Burnham Rally in one of the final tests at Burnham. (LAT Photographic)

The second **Belgian GP** for **Production Sports Cars** at **Spa 20th May 1951** had a Jupiter running, driven by A Gendebien, brother of the more famous driver Olivier Gendebien a war-time resistance fighter who went on to win Le Mans four times for Ferrari. There were 100 cars and three races that day, result not known.

There were sports car races at **Zandvoort** in **The Netherlands** on the **10th June 1951**. Two Jupiters were entered: J Scheffer (42) of Amsterdam and H J Maas of Leeuwarden. Their race was won by an MG.

The **MCC Exeter Trial 29–29 December 1951** found Edward Foulds participating either in his saloon Jupiter (99) or more probably in his standard Jupiter (472) he already having taken delivery of it in November.

The **North Staffordshire Burnham Rally** to **Burnham-on-Sea 1–2 March 1952**. Major L J Roy Taylor again took part in his Jupiter (51). Taylor told the Author "*I laid open the back of my hand during the reversing tests at Weston-super-Mare with that awful gearchange*".

April 1952 in **Dallas, Texas**. The Foreign Auto & Sports Car Association had prepared a 100-mile rally course with tests. In the ¼-mile Standing Start trial Ian

Anderson (Jupiter) drove very well to win the 1250 to 1500cc class with 20.8s. Second was an MG TD with 21.4s.

The **London MC Little Rally 19th April 1952** was a pleasing day's motoring through the Surrey and Hampshire countryside for the 134 competitors, which included the open Abbott-bodied Jupiter (89) of Commander Milner.

The **Midlands Rally 19–20 April 1952** held over 200 miles, saw action from A B Hibbert and his Jupiter (586). They re-used the route laid out for the 1927 event. Hibbert went straight on to do the **Circuit of Ireland** a week later; and running closed he took equal third place in class with a Citroën and an Allard.

The **1952 Lancashire AC Morecambe Rally** held from **16th** to **18th May** had 300 entrants but the class division of 1.3 to 3.0 litres did not suit the Jupiters of L Pellowe

(485), Freddie & Lorna Still (521), R W Goodburn (618) and Ted Booth/Derek Bowers in LRH2 (12).

Booth did better than in the previous year's final driving test at Morecambe (see Chapter 4) and lost no marks – the marshals gave him a wide berth before letting him run!

The **Margate Rally** of **27–29 June 1952** organised by the Maidstone and Mid Kent Motor Club had 71 starters and was run over 300 miles including two secret checks though only a few lost marks at them. Following the completion of the road section, breakfast was taken at the Swan Hotel, Charing, followed by the Regularity Test which required competitors to follow a given route and to average 25mph passing two secret time checks: only six completed this without loss of marks. Then on the short final run into Margate many took the route through Canterbury (rather than the easier coastal route) with its schedules that proved harder to keep to. There were then four varied eliminating tests on the Margate seafront and the rally concluded with an official reception at the Winter

Kicking up some dust! Freddie and Lorna Still (560) in the 1952 Morecambe Rally. (Charles Dunn)

Freddie and Lorna Still during the Margate rally, their best result from nine events in 12 months. (Charles Dunn)

Gardens. In Class A amongst the 12 MGs, an HRG and a Morgan, were the Jupiters of Neil Freedman (509) and the eventual class winners Mr & Mrs Freddie Still in their Jupiter NNK 560 (521).

At Coatham Sands, Redcar, North Yorkshire, on **12 July 1952** there took place the **Flying Kilometre Speed Trials**. The Jupiter of R V Russell (almost certainly 487) won his class. Also on that day his Jupiter took part in the 1-mile races for the best time of 64.5s. Russell operated the nearby Thornaby Jowett agency.

The sixth **Evian-Mont Blanc Rally 24–27 July 1952** was organised by Marcel Becquart. It was for amateur drivers and was restricted to 100 French and 40 non-French competitors. The Jupiter of Englishman R W Austin is known to have taken part.

Also in **July 1952** was the **Four Cylinder Club of America's Scotchman's Drag Rally** in California. Over 111 miles from Laurel Canyon via Fillimore Drive, Santa Paula to Santa Barbara, 25 out of the 34 contestants finished within the time limit. Class III for 1250-1500cc cars was won by Don Broderick (Jupiter).

In the 8th **International Prescott Speed Hillclimb 14th September 1952**, Ian Sievright (748) placed 17th (from 19) in the Production Car handicap with times 59.55s and 59.58s. C F Eminson (Jupiter 494) and L Townson in J A Cowap's Jupiter (661) were also there.

The **London MC's 1952 London Rally 19–20 September** required 690 miles of driving from two starts, with four special tests included. The rally was of national status this year and was organised by Godfrey and Nina Imhoff. The 2-litre class, which was won by an HRG, contained the Jupiters of G A Dudley/E W Miller (651), T G Cunane/Mrs J O Cunane (NTJ 930), and Frank Masefield Baker with J Grantam-Brown (597); the reserve Neil Freedman (509) is thought to have run. The organiser Imhoff's Jupiter HAK 117 was seen near the start. Top Jowett result was by Mr & Mrs Leavens in their Javelin who won the best 'mixed crew' award.

The **Aston Martin Owners Club (AMOC) High Speed Trial** was at **Snetterton** on **20th September 1952**. You selected a speed and lost 1 point per minute if you were early or late. There was also a compulsory pit-stop of at least 2 minutes. Bill Smith in his Jupiter ECF 494 (680) only lost 3 points. In a 5-lap handicap race for sports and touring cars in full road trim, Smith in what was his first race finished 5th.

Also on **20th July** was the **SCCA Ivey Oil Rally in California**. It was an extremely hot day. The rally was a hidden-map treasure hunt – at the start a fragment of the map was provided enabling the first checkpoint to be located. At each checkpoint another map fragment was provided. The treasure was – a beer! Winner was Hunter Hackney (Jupiter). Curt Parker (Jupiter) was fifth, 18th was Bill Cochrane (Jupiter) but 37th out of 38 was Don Brodrick (Jupiter) having arrived at the wrong finish point and therefore had to open his escape kit.

The End-of Season **Castle Combe 20th September 1952** race meeting staged by the **Bristol Motor Club** included a 10-lap race for sports cars up to 1½-litres. It was over-subscribed and a special dispensation came from the RAC allowing it to run provided there was an echelon start. The race was notable for the first appearance on a British circuit of a Porsche. Of the 13 cars in the echelon Gillie Tyrer's BMW held the favoured position, while at the other end was C C Bannister's Porsche. The race became a procession with a German car at both ends, and by the 8th lap Tyrer had lapped J D Lewis's Jupiter (718).

The **Eastern Counties MC** staged a **Speed Trial** at **Snetterton** on **4th October 1952**. It was a Standing Start timed half-mile with cars in pairs. Bill Smith (680) hood up ran in the closed 1101-1500cc class of 12 runners: his best, 33.2s, placed him a good 3rd only behind two Riley specials but ahead of the rest including six MGs.

The **Bugatti Owners Club 1952 Welsh Rally** of **6–7 December** featured 324 winter miles plus a test in the Eppynt mountains and the Lystep hillclimb. Freddie and Lorna Still (521) are known to have participated while Ian Sievwright (748) finished overall 5th.

The **1952 Four Cylinder Club of America's** Economy Run, precise date unknown, was class-won by Don Broderick (Jupiter).

The **Cats Eyes Rally** of **31st January 1953** was a night navigation rally organised by the Thames Estuary Auto Club (TEAC) and sponsored by the makers of spectacles alleged to improve the wearer's night vision! Freddie and Lorna Still (521) took part.

On the **MacDill Airforce Base** in **Tampa, Florida,** on **21st February 1953** the Jupiters of Ashley Pace and W King were in action in a 12-lapper, but they did not make the first three places in their class.

The **Little Rally** of **18th April 1953** organised by Goff and Nina Imhoff for the London M C found the Jupiter of C W Yates, after 200 miles and some special tests, notching a praiseworthy class 2nd between two MGs.

The **Lancashire AC 1953 Morecambe Rally** of **15–17 May** included the Abbott-bodied FHC Jupiter (105) of C P Swain in both the rally itself and the Concours D'Elegance that followed. *The Autocar* correspondent (15th May 1953) covering the Concours wrote that this is "*a much more elegant car than the standard bodied Coupé*"!

The **1953 Felixstowe Coronation Rally** of **22–24 May** included, during its second day, high speed touring tests at Snetterton and driving tests at Felixstowe. Alec Gordon and P Steiner in NLX 909 (761) ran open while the Freedmans in MXA 506 (509) ran closed.

The **MCC** had a meeting at **Silverstone** on **20th June 1953**; in the first one-hour HST, first-class awards went to G M Sharp in Jupiter MAC 2 (522) and Maurice Tew (620) whilst Kenneth Crutch (602) who had bought his Jupiter new from the Alf Thomas Bedford agency qualified 2nd in his class. In the second HST Alf Thomas (38) received a first-class award as did a total of 34 cars. Event 8 a handicap race found Tew and E G Walsh (Javelin) taking part whilst Alf Thomas (38) had an outing in Event 9 another handicap race of 5 laps.

The **1953 Eastbourne Rally** was on **July 4th**. Amongst the nine MGs and others in the 1200–2000cc open-car class were the Jupiters of J C Checkley with the ex-Imhoff HAK 117 (77) and GAP 6 (242) of Robert Holmes, the very standard-looking open special-bodied Jupiter. In the equivalent closed-car class there was to be found the hard-topped standard Jupiter HKW 429 (544). This rally featured a concours at midnight after the dance!

The **1953 Brighton & Hove MC Brighton Rally** was staged on **11th July**. It required some quick laps of the Goodwood circuit in one of its tests. This was a good rally for Jupiters, as F M Baker (597) won the 1.3–2.0 litre open-car class, with Alec Gordon (761) coming second. Baker incurred fewer penalty points than the winners of four of the other six classes: a sometime Works Javelin and later BMC driver he, his Jupiter was Factory supported. He had, in the previous year's Brighton *Concours d'Elégance Ensemble*, entered his Jupiter with film and stage actress Dolores Gray, then of *Annie Get Your Gun*.

Also on the **11th July** was the **Southsea MC's Day of Driving Tests** on **Southsea Common**. It was a triumph for B Croucher (Jupiter) for out of 45 competitors in front

1953 Morecambe Rally. C P Swain's Abbott-bodied Jupiter
(National Motor Museum)

Above: 1953 Eastbourne Rally, Mr & Mrs Checkley with the ex-Imhoff Jupiter on the seafront for the final tests. Following behind is the Jupiter GAP 6 of Bob Holmes. (National Motor Museum)

Below: Bob Holmes and co-driver in the same test at Eastbourne, reversing into a 'garage'. Bob Holmes is the driver. This car is very good replica of standard bodywork. (National Motor Museum)

of a crowd of 3000 onlookers he won the Challenge Trophy for the best aggregate.

The **US Airforce Trophy Meeting** was at **Snetterton** (the former Norfolk USAF airfield) on the **25th July 1953**. Tom Blackburn (846) and D G Dixon (Javelin) took part in a half-hour reliability run. Rather optimistically Blackburn and Jupiter were entered in a 15-lap race for cars of up to 2-litres capacity which included the faster and lighter Cooper-Bristols and Frazer Nash Le Mans – in all 11 cars with 2-litre engines plus, yes, a Cooper-MG.

On the **26th July 1953** the **Southern Jowett Car Club (SJCC)** held their second **Plaistow Rally** for 17 Jowett entrants. First was E Walsh, Javelin, but second was Jack Bates in his Jupiter (315) and third was P Putt also in a Jupiter; Putt had won the SJCC driving tests event back on 21st June.

The **1953 Gosport Auto Club's Summer Rally** on **9th August** attracted 48 competitors. The three first-class awards went to a Riley Special, a Healey Silverstone, and Alec Gordon in his Jupiter (761).

The **London to Languedoc-Sète Touring Rally** was during **17–20 August 1953**. The 29 entrants followed a route that crossed France to take in Andorra, visits to wine cellars, and included a *Concours d'Elégance Ensemble*

Floyd Bennett Field, New York USA 29th August 1953. The original caption read: "*Wm Lloyd in his Jowett won the Sheepshead Bay Trophy Race after a determined effort*". (SCCA)

which recognised the "beauty of the car and its feminine accompaniment". Dr W E R Pitt's Jupiter (994) came third in the 'Car Only' Concours.

The London MC's **1953 London Rally, 11–12 September**, was again of national status. The entry list included 25 Jowetts, of which the Jupiter contingent is believed to have been: A Gordon/P Steiner (761), F M Baker (597), Maurice Tew (620), Mrs Lola Grounds/Mrs Doreen Reece (in the saloon-bodied Jupiter 29), R Goddard/Miss L E G Richardson (crewing Jupiter MXP 417), T A G Wright/P A Gundry-White (984) and Robbie Mackenzie-Low/Colin Davis (544). Colin Davis was the son of Sammy Davis the famous former racing driver and latterly motoring journalist (*The Autocar*). Colin "drove like stink...and holed the sump" forcing the car out of the rally. (Sammy Davis had coached Robbie on how to drive around Goodwood). The rally's Novice Award was won by T A G Wright in a nice example of a Mk1a Jupiter in competition.

The **Southern Jowett Car Club Rally** was held on the **13th September 1953** largely organised by Roy Clarkson. It involved seven tests spread over two Essex airfields (Gosfield and Earls Coln) with 50 road miles through narrow winding lanes between them. Class B, presumably restricted to Jupiters, was taken as follows: 1st B R Caerns (947), 2nd Alec Gordon (761), 3rd Jack Bates (315) and 4th H Flower (Jupiter).

The Midland Auto Club's **1953 *Birmingham Post* Rally 19–20 September** went from Birmingham's Civic Centre for 460 miles via lakeside driving tests at that rally favourite Llandrindod Wells, then on to Droitwich Spa. The 34 competitors in the over 1301cc class included the Jupiters of G M Tew (620) and Frank and Lola Grounds (29). The well-driven Grounds FHC Jupiter won its class.

The **Prescott Hillclimb on 20th September 1953** was put on as usual by the Bugatti Owners Club. The hill was ascended to no startling effect by John Horridge in 'Jehu' which failed to live up to its biblical counterpart; also that day Ian Sievwright (748) ascended Prescott to record a lowly Class 18th (101st overall) at 62.81s.

The **Lakeland Rally 26–27 September 1953**, but

actually held in Wales that year, had 130 competitors. Winner of Class B1 – and therefore of the Riley Trophy – was the Jupiter of W S Underwood.

The East Anglia MC's **1953 Clacton Rally** was also held on **26–27 September**. It was made interesting by the dense fog that, however, led to the cancellation of the Snetterton test. Class III was won by R B Goddard (Jupiter MXP 417). The 2-litre Touring Car Class was won by Lt Col F Basset in his Javelin.

The TEAC **Cats Eyes Rally** of **21st November 1953** (nicknamed the 'Kittens Eyes Rally' on account of its size) was as usual a night navigation map-reading run. N Roarke/E J Bardell (Jupiter) ran in the closed-car class, as did an A40 Sports.

At the **Torbay MC's 1953 Invitation Rally** on the **5th December** there were 51 entrants including the Jupiter of T G Cunane (Jupiter NTJ 930) who was noted as having done well in the 'Stop & Re-start' test but did not otherwise feature. A Javelin finished 6th.

The year 1954 was transitional for Jowett after its commercial reverses of 1952 and the first part of 1953. The decision had now been taken to sell the Jowett factory complete with plant and staff from management to floor-sweepers to the International Harvester Co (I H) for the manufacture of their light tractor, and consequently the factory commanded a high price. Tractors would come off the production line when the sub-contract work Jowett were doing for the Blackburn & General Aircraft Co had been moved to Howden Clough, Birstall, on the outskirts of Bradford. Jowett were to become purely a spares operation at Birstall. Jowett Cars Ltd became absorbed by Blackburn and its shareholders were paid pound for pound – so Jowett did not go bankrupt as is often reported and there were no redundancies. The name became Jowett Engineering in 1958, and it closed in 1963 when the promise of full spares and service for 10 years was completed.

Demand for Jupiters continued in 1954 and two small batches were assembled, although nothing further was possible after I H moved into the former Jowett factory in October that year, except to complete the last Jupiters.

Photo from a LHD Jupiter of the Jowett Works May 1954. The photographer's Bradford van at the back. (C H Wood)

The former Works Jupiters were scattered, GKY 256 possibly to Singapore and maybe was raced there. Interestingly, Alf Thomas bought the three R4 Jupiters. The final two years of Jowett Cars Ltd trading, 1953 and 1954, saw a return to profit with 31 Jupiters sold in 1954. The last one, sold on 4th November, was the 827th factory-bodied standard Jupiter – bought by a local Bradford garage, who, I was told, specifically wanted the very last one.

In 1954 there was no dearth of results as new names with Jupiters came onto the motor sporting scene. Halcyon days were not yet over!

Over in New Zealand at the Christchurch Motor Racing Club's **Lady Wigram Trophy Races** at **Wigram airbase 6th February 1954**, in a 25-mile handicap race for sports cars on the abrasive 2-mile course, "J L Holden's Jupiter was surprisingly fast but could not make up his handicap".

In Scotland now, at the **1954 Lothian Car Club's Driving Tests** on **21st February**, third overall was the Jupiter of C M M Gillespie – winner was an HRG.

The Scottish Sports Car Club's **1954 Moonbeam Rally** was on **19th February**. F D Laing (Jupiter) came fourth

in the 1.6-litre open-car class. It may be recalled that F D Laing co-drove with another Scotsman, Bill Skelly, in JGA 123 (41) in the 1951 Monte Carlo Rally, and furthermore we know Skelly had bought another Jupiter (976) in April 1953. Dear reader, please draw your own conclusion!

In the Nottingham Sports Car Club's **Pilkington Trophy Trial** on **21st February 1954**, one of three competitors to receive a First Class award was Mrs H J Curtis (Jupiter).

The first post-war **Intervarsity Speed Trial** was on **7th March 1954**. It was held on a narrow 0.8-mile course laid out on Little Gransden Aerodrome, Cambridgeshire, and comprised a succession of left-hand and right-hand 90° corners. Just the one run was allowed and the 1201–1500cc closed-car class results were as follows: 1st a Javelin (1m 28.4s); 2nd an MG (1m 29.8s); 3rd Flight-Lt C F Norris in Jupiter JWS 187 (probably 640) with 1m 30.9s.

The **1954 Bolton-le-Moors Car Club Day of Driving Tests** at **Blackpool** was on the **7th** of **March**. There were a dozen or so tests scattered around the town. In Class A amongst the Dellows, MGs etc were the Jupiters of L S Cordingley (908) and D L Lord (900) whilst in what was clearly a closed-car class were the Jupiters of Tom Blackburn (846), J W Waddington (910) and W S Underwood (possibly in the Abbott Coupé Jupiter No 105).

At the **Chiltern Car Club's Autocross** on **14th March 1954** the above 1300cc class was won by the Jupiter of D G Dixon (947).

Eastern Counties Motor Club 1954 Races at **Snetterton** was on **3rd April**. In the 1½-litre handicap race Albert Westwood (554) came third.

The **1954 Tunbridge Wells MC High Speed Trials** on **11th April** required two timed laps to be performed on the new 1.24-mile Brands Hatch circuit. I A Forbes in the 1.1–1.5-litre closed-car class came a nice second in the Coachcraft saloon Jupiter (28) at 53.39mph, just a whisker behind an Aston Martin at 53.40mph. Another Aston Martin was third.

Also on **11th April 1954** was the **Marconi Photographic Run** of 45 miles. The route card was a sheet of photographs. It was won by T Mosse in an unidentified Jupiter.

Eastern Counties Motor Club 1954 Autocross was on **28th April**. Class 2nd in the 1½-litre closed-car class was W T Smith (680) running hood raised with 1m 59.3s behind a VW with 1m 56.25s, whilst 3rd was a Javelin with 2m 0.0s.

The **1954 Bushmead Speed Trials** on **25th April** was a regular Bedford MC event in those days. The course was 2/3 mile with many corners. As would be expected Alf Thomas was there – almost certainly with his Jupiter JTM 100 (38). *Autosport* commented: *"The 1500cc open car class was won by Jim Pratt's immaculate Type 37 Bugatti, which beat modern MGs and Jupiters by a handsome margin"*.

Results Class 2a (1½-litre open)

1 Jim Pratt (Bugatti)	57.56sec
2 An HRG	59.90sec
3 Alf Thomas (Jupiter)	61.00sec

Results Class 2b (1½-litre closed)

1 Fl. Lt C F Norris (Jupiter JWS 187)	65.60sec
2 Ken Brierley (Javelin)	67.05sec
3 Mary Chapman (Jupiter)	82.35sec

In another class one of those new-fangled TR2s achieved 60.95 seconds.

In the **1954 BARC Members' Day** at **Goodwood** on the **1st May**, Race 1 was a 5-lap handicap event for closed cars in which the scratch car (that is, the fastest), an XK120 coupé, reached fifth place on lap 4 and drove very fast to second place when the chequered flag fell. However I A Forbes was well ahead to win in his "nimble special-bodied Jupiter" (28) while 3rd was a Ford and 4th was an Aston DB2-4. Forbes's best lap was 2m 15.2s (63.90mph). Also in the race were the Javelins of D H F Keen (5th with his best lap 2m 18s) and J de Norman (8th with best lap 2m 20.2s).

The **1954 Hants/Berks Autocross** on **16th May** was a timed trial on grass at Hill Farm, Farley Hill, Berkshire.

Both D G Dixon and R H Vivian took out the same Jupiter, believed to have been Dixon's 947.

The **Lancashire Auto Club's 1954 National Morecambe Rally** over **21–23 May** tempted Tom Blackburn (846) but his Jupiter broke its crankshaft during the second night.

In the **1954 Eight-Clubs Silverstone** meeting **29th May** there was a 40-minute High Speed Trial that saw several Jupiters in action. The trial required 21 laps to be covered at an average speed of greater than 50.65mph and included a pit-stop to swap the front wheels across, and to replace four spark plugs. The Jupiter participants were D G Dixon (947), Alf Thomas (Jupiter), K Hartridge (255), and C F Norris (JWS 187) whose 'brown Jupiter went round sounding his horn to qualify' as did Hartridge's. Event 10 was a 5-lap scratch race in which D G Dixon's Jupiter was entered to be driven by A Baker, a farmer who often raced his Land Rover at Silverstone (and he was eventually killed there racing it) whilst event 11, a 5-lap handicap, found the Jupiters of C F Norris (driving JWS 187) and D G Dixon (driven by R H Vivian) both on the limit mark.

The 26th **Bol d'Or** of 1954, run from **29–30 May** on the 6.3-Km Montléry circuit near Paris, was a miniature *Vingt Quatre Heures du Mans* for the private owner-driver. 'Jehu', the Horridge Jupiter-chassis special (BEN 775) was driven by John Horridge and Georges Trouis to a steady second place thanks to the reliability of its Riley engine and the retirement of several faster cars in the closing stages: the winning car went sick minutes before the end of the race but struggled across the finish line prior to expiring.

The **1954 ECMC Snetterton** was on **5th June**. Event 3 was a 5-lap race for production saloon cars. It provided an easy victory for D Woolley's Porsche which was so much faster on the straights that the driver could take it carefully and "deny the spectators the sight of the dreaded oversteer" on the corners. Second place was taken by Albert Wake's Jupiter coupé (99), was this a 'production' car?! He was ahead of another Porsche, an MG Magnette and a Javelin. In a ½-mile sprint for 1.2-litre to 1.5-litre closed cars, W T Smith (in a Jupiter

Albert Wake's coupé Jupiter when nearly new and owned by Edward Foulds. (Lansdown HK Bodies)

presumably 680 running closed) had a very good result to take first place.

The **Nottingham Sports Car Club** held a **sprint** at **Ossington Aerodrome** on **7th June 1954**. In the event for 1.1 to 1.5-litre saloon cars, Albert Wake was again in action in coupé Jupiter (99) and he placed second in his class.

At the **1954 Davidstow RAF Airfield Day of Races**, Cornwall, also held on the **7th June**, Alf Thomas took the R4 Jupiter JKW 537 to its first competitive outing. In pouring rain, in Heat 2 for 1500cc sports cars, from the back of the grid Thomas placed 5th from 10 starters. In Race 9 he placed 6th yet all in front of him were sports-racers: a pair of Connaughts, a pair of pocket-rocket Cooper-MGs and a Tojeiro, so the R4 was the fastest actual road car.

The **Aston Martin Owners Club St Horsfall Races** were on **24th July 1954**. Races 5 and 10a were a 5-lap handicap and a 5-lap scratch race for 1½-litre sports cars, where C F Norris pitted his Jupiter JWS 187 against an HRG, a Cooper-MG, a Lotus-MG and the like.

In the **1954 Nottingham Sports Car Club Silverstone Races** on **14th August**, there was action from C F Norris in his Jupiter and a new name, Max Trimble, in Jupiter JUN 592 (898). In their scratch race they were pitted against MGs, Lotuses, HRGs, a Porsche, and a Kieft.

BARC Members Day at Goodwood 21st August 1954 saw Max Trimble in action until his Jupiter broke its crankshaft during his race.

On **August 22nd 1954** the **Sporting Owner Drivers' Club** held an **Autocross** at Dunstable. Both C F Norris and his Jupiter JWS 187 were in good form, for in his event he equalled first place with an MG.

The **750 Motor Club's 1954 Six-hour Relay Handicap Race** was on **28th August**, a very wet day. Of the 40 teams that started, 39 finished. Ecurie Jupiter placed 11th, its Jupiters being those of Alf Thomas (R4, JKW 537), Peter Waring (NTF 510), D G Dixon (947), C F Norris (JWS 187) and Alf's son Barry Thomas in the open special Jupiter (38).

The **Southern Jowett Car Club** staged **Driving Tests** on **29th August 1954** at Tewin, Hertfordshire. U K Fleming in an unidentified Jupiter placed second, after a Javelin.

On the **26th** of **September 1954** the **Sporting Owner Drivers' Club** held another **Autocross** at Dunstable. This time C F Norris and his Jupiter JWS 187 were in even better form for he notched a class win.

1954 Charterhall Day of Races was on the **3rd September**. Jehu was again in action in a 10-lap race for cars of up to 1½-litre capacity. Our Jupiter-chassis special

Autocross 28th August 1954 at Dunstable. Flight-Lieutenant C F Norris drove his Jupiter to equal class first. (Richmond Pike)

with its Riley Sprite engine finished 2nd behind a Cooper-MG, ahead of a Riley Sprite.

The 50th Anniversary **London Motor Club's London Rally, 3rd** and **4th September 1954** saw Jupiter action from David Dixon (947) and Kenneth Brierley (564).

On **11th September 1954** the **Peterborough Motor Club** staged a day of races at Silverstone. Race 2 was a 5-lap handicap, with a Kieft-MG on scratch as the fastest, and a Lotus Mk VI, a Cooper-MG, some HRGs and the like plus the Jupiters of P Waring (NTF 510) and K Brierley (564). Waring was considered much the faster of the two Jupiters as he was given 20 seconds with the Lotus Mk VI while Brierley got a full minute's start.

On **4th October 1954** at **Aintree**, Albert Wake was again in action, finishing 3rd behind two 1488cc Porsches. Wake was said in the press to be in a Javelin for this race, but quite likely it was his coupé Jupiter (99) again. His

best lap was 2m 52.2s. In another race, Jehu was in action with its best lap 2m 48.0s.

On **10th October 1954** at **Bushmead**, Huntingdonshire, there was a day of sprints. In Class 2A, equal first were an HRG and a Tucker-MG with 57.1s, while in 3rd place was Alf Thomas (Jupiter) with 59.9s. Thomas was faster than a 2660cc Austin Healey (60.2s) and a TR2 (60.3s)

Staplefield Airfield near **Abridge** in **Essex** on **17th October 1954** had a 'Speed Hill Climb'. A G Davis was photographed in the ex-Works HAK 366 (131) on the gentle ¾-mile slope.

Over in **Macau 31st October 1954** there were races including a Grand Prix. The Jupiter of da Costa saw action, but sadly he crashed in practice and could not race. A photo in *Autosport* of December 3rd shows it was RHD, had an aeroscreen and bucket seats.

The **March Airforce Base** at **Riverside, California** on

Stapleford Hillclimb 17th October 1954. A G Davis driving the lightweight ex-Le Mans Jupiter which was the 1951 RAC-TT class winner. (Charles Dunn)

Below: MCC-Redex Rally November 1954 at Hastings. David Dixon in flat cap, Peter Harbin in woolly cap. (Charles Dunn)

7th November 1954 hosted a race meeting with a 1500cc 'Jupiter Special' taking part in three events. Race 1 of seven laps 24½ miles was for junior drivers in cars of up to 1500cc. M Stevens in the said 'Jupiter Special' held second place until the last lap when passed by an MG Special to place third in the modified 1½-litre class, and also third overall; ahead were an OSCA MTS and the MG Special. Fourth overall was a Porsche 356 running in the unmodified class so Stevens was faster than the Porsche. Race 5 of five laps was the Ladies' race, and now Jan Stevens drove the Jupiter to third place, ahead of five MGs and even a TR2 and an Aston Martin DB2. Race 6 was the big one, over 16 laps 52½ miles for up to 1500cc cars in three classes. W Thomas in the 'Jupiter Special' could only manage 10th in his modified 1500cc class. All above were the likes of four OSCAs, a VW Special, a Porsche America and a Beavis Offenhauser, but he did beat three MGs and a Porsche 356.

The MCC's **1954 National Redex Rally** was from the **10th** to **13th November**. Bill Boddy of *Motor Sport* spectated from a Jupiter (probably 972) at the

103

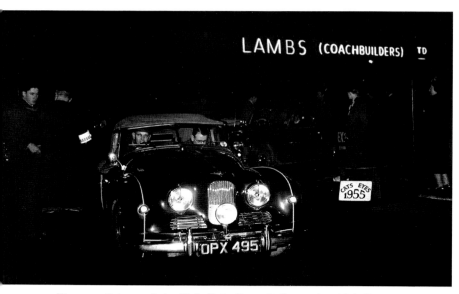

Thames Estuary Auto Club Cats Eyes Rally on the 19th February 1955,
Mr & Mrs D E Moore in Eric Jenner's Jupiter. This car (994) is still with
us in good running order. (Charles Dunn)

Bwlch-y-Groes ascent and the driving test at its summit – the climb of about 1¾ miles with severe gradients throughout (steepest is 1:4) is one of the highest mountain passes in Wales. Bill Boddy reported in his magazine that I Robertson's Jupiter had refused to start and was given time to cool off.

Now, down-country at Hastings where there were four tests, Bill Boddy noted that "Robertson's Jupiter was handled neatly but refused to repay such treatment, its offside back wheel spinning so furiously that from restart to finish the car only just moved". "Too much Redex" said a wag in the crowd.

Bill Boddy went on: 'D G Dixon, in odd headgear and a Jowett Jupiter, wasted many valuable seconds'. Actually it was Dixon's co-driver Peter Harbin in his woollen cap driving the Jupiter (947) as Dixon, an ex-Navy man, had drunk rum to alleviate his severe head-cold: Harbin was to remark: the rum was good for his cold but made him unable to drive or navigate! R J Hedges (unidentified Jupiter) with his co-driver a Miss Lockwood won a tidily-driven third class award.

Over in the USA in **January** or **February 1955** were the **Soapstone Trials**, Delaware Valley, Pennsylvania. There was ice, mud, and falling snow so a 'bouncer' was allowed in the cars. From 45 entrants, ten were disqualified for being too slow in practice (more than 6 minutes). Out of the remaining 35 starters, 10 failed to finish; but one who did, at 24th, was J Henry (Jupiter) with 7m 19.9s so it looks as if he got a little bit held up in the slippery stuff someplace! An MG was 25th with 9m 37.6s while the winner was a Morgan.

Thames Estuary Auto Club's **1955 Cats Eyes Rally** was on the **19th February**. Eric Jenner's Jupiter (994) is known to have taken part driven by Mr & Mrs D E Moore. See photo above.

The Cambridge University Auto Club's **1955 Intervarsity Speed Trial** at **Tempsford Airfield** near Biggleswade, Bedfordshire on the **6th March** was considered to be the traditional opener of the English speed season in those days; it was held that year over a ¾-mile twisty course in a biting wind. Event 4 was for closed cars, best of two runs. Winner was Alf Thomas in the ever so fast R4 Jupiter JKW 537 at 69.12s presumably with its hard-top fitted, second was Archie Scott-Brown

The R4 Jupiter with hard-top fitted. GB reminds us it had been abroad
on its proving run. (C H Wood)

August 1955 Snetterton in a 10-lap handicap event: the Beverley Motors saloon Jupiter wearing 168 is pressed by the MG. This Jupiter, driven by J F Hall, was completed by Maurice Gomm by October 1952 for Nigel Mann, sometime motor racing man, Alfa Romeo specialist and proprietor of Beverley Motors. (National Motor Museum)

in a Peugeot 203 (70.90s), third an MG Magnette with 75.58s, and fourth another Peugeot 203.

The R4's time in effect placed it third in the Sports Car Class ahead of a Cooper-MG (69.41s), an MG TF and an HRG, but running without the hardtop and screen would have made it unlikely that the R4 could have bettered second placed David Piper in his Lotus (66.15s). Astonishingly the R4 Jupiter was faster than all the cars in both the 1501–2500cc and over 2500cc classes. It is also known that Eddie Shrive with his Jupiter LMJ 517 (679) ran but we do not have a time for him.

In the **1955 Daffodil Rally** put on by the Warrington & District Motor Club on the **20th March**, the 1½-litre open-car class was won by D Lunt in an unidentified Jupiter.

In the **Horsham & District Motor Club's 1955** Spring Rally on the **27th March**, Jack Bates (Jupiter 315) won the award for the best performance in the class opposite that of the actual rally winner, plus the Team Award.

The **1955 MCC Easter Lands End Trial** was held over **8–9 April**. P Waring entered his Jupiter NTF 510 but the red Jupiter lost the use of both intermediate gears on the notorious Beggars Roost Hill, the half-mile boulder-strewn

climb near Lynton in Devon, and had to drive the 180-odd miles back to London using top gear only. Alf Thomas and his R4 Jupiter JKW 537 may have been in this event also.

The **Eight-Clubs 1955 Silverstone** on the **4th June** saw the Jupiters of P Waring (NTF 510) and K Brierley (564) in action. In Event 1, a 40-minute 24-lap High Speed Trial, both received First Class awards. In a 5-lap scratch race Brierley averaged 62.4mph to come a very fine second, while in a 5-lap handicap race he had to settle for third. After this event Waring sold his Jupiter, which had been his daily transport for over a year, in a move he later regretted, for he felt that although due to the under-column gear lever and rather slow gear change it was not well suited to the type of rally that was largely decided by 'comic' driving tests – as he was to put it to me – he considered that as a standard road car it had extraordinarily good handling characteristics that were very close to what one could regard as ideal.

At the **Sevenoaks and District Motor Club's Brands Hatch Sprint** on the **3rd** of **July 1955**, both R Blake and B Bisley had runs in the same unidentified Mk1a Jupiter.

The **750 Motor Club's 1955 Six-hour Relay Handicap Race** was on **9th July** this year. The very aptly-named 'Mixed Grilles' team contained a Talbot, a Darracq, an Aston Martin, a supercharged Morris Minor, and the Jupiter of Kenneth Brierley (564).

The **West Essex Car Club 1955 International Race Meeting** at Snetterton on **13th August** included a 10-lap handicap race for saloons. The Beverley Motors saloon Jupiter took part, driven by J F Hall; the race was comfortably won by a Porsche. This Jupiter had been announced on 10th October 1952 by a company owned by motor racing man Nigel Mann.

The MG Car Club's **Silver Jubilee Race Meeting and Pageant** at **Silverstone** on **27th August 1955** had a race for cars of any capacity and any make other than MG. The green Jupiter Mk1 (with the London registration NUL 895) of M G Harrison is known to have raced.

Brighton & Hove Motor Club held their **Golden Jubilee Speed Trials** on the **3rd September 1955** on Madeira Drive as usual – indeed Madeira Drive had been constructed in 1905 with the idea of holding speed trials on it. Horace Appleby took part in Jupiter MCD 28 (597) in a class that was won by a Porsche.

In the London Motor Club's **1955 National London Rally** of **16–17 September**, Horace Appleby took part, driving Jupiter MCD 28 (597) with John Baker navigating.

In Germany now, in **December 1955** in the British Army's 400-mile **Crossed Swords Rally**, including difficult forest roads, Lt John Doran (458) placed overall 2nd to an excellent finish a mere 2 points behind an Aston Martin.

Over in Victoria, Australia on a day in **May 1956** there was the **Templestowe Hillclimb**. Earl Pearce is known to have driven his Jupiter (136) in the 1½-litre class in this event with the time of 74.69s. He also took it up the **Rob Roy Hillclimb** in November 1956.

Mention should also be made of the single-seater, ladder-frame, supercharged (to 14psi) Javelin-engined Special, built by Arthur Wylie. In **December 1953** Stan Jones took it up the **Templestowe Hill** at a new record time of 61.51s to win him the championship. In 1968 the gifted engineer Bruce Polain lowered this time to 58.4s in the same car but with an even more developed engine. Besides

An early photo of the Wylie-Javelin taken at the Gnoo Blas circuit at Orange, NSW. Arthur Wylie on the left. (Gary Baker)

hillclimbs, the Wylie-Javelin, which first ran in 1951, was raced against the best in Australia and was timed in 1954 at 132mph, the fastest ever Jowett-powered car.

The **1956 MCC Silverstone** race meeting on the **30th** of **June** included a 1-hour blind. This opportunity for a long-distance dice was accepted by Barry Thomas (Alf's son) who gave the R4 Jupiter JKW 537 an airing. He also raced it in a 5-lap handicap that day.

In the **1956 Midland Rally** on the **8th July** organised by a Birmingham Motor Club, P Towers drove his Jupiter to a very useful overall third.

Also at **Silverstone** on **6th October 1956** the North Staffordshire Motor Club held their 'End of the Club Season' event. Alf Thomas was there with his R4 Jupiter and in one of his two handicap races he motored very fast into third place behind a TR2 and a Healey Silverstone. Perhaps this outing, believed to have been his first for 27 months, encouraged him to lay plans for the forthcoming season.

The **MCC National Rally** of **1956** was held over the **5th** to **10th November**. It was run over only 1250 miles this year and had 144 starters. Alan Dowsett, the third owner of MCD 28 (597) here drove the last Jupiter known to have participated in a National Rally. From 1959 the RAC Rally took over the MCC Rally's November spot.

The **Rob Roy Hillclimb** of **November 1956** in Victoria, Australia, saw some Jowett action. In the 1101–1500cc Touring Car Class, R O Robinson placed 2nd in his Javelin with a time of 43.66s, while in the equivalent Sports Car Class E Pearce was again in action with his Jupiter (136) to post 38.16s placing him class 6th. It is notable that Arthur Wylie in his Wylie-Javelin had posted 26.85s in February 1954 shortly after he had converted the car's rear end to De Dion suspension.

Still in Victoria, Australia, on **17th November 1956** there was again a **Templestowe Hillclimb**. Earl Pearce drove his Jupiter (136) in the 1101–1500cc Sports Car class with the time of 75.65s to 6th in his class while in the equivalent Touring Car Class, R O Robinson again placed 2nd in his Javelin with 78.86s.

Then came the Suez Crisis with petrol rationing in Britain from 29th November 1956 and consequently motor sport was suspended for the winter. Petrol rationing ended mid-May 1957.

So, in **May 1957** the **Cranleigh and District Motor Club** held a Versatility Trial and Jack Bates (315) drove to a well-driven class win.

Also in **May 1957** the **Bugatti OC Prescott Practice Weekend** found Miss E A Neale in action in Alf Thomas's R4 Jupiter JKW 537 with the best time of 59.74s up the hill.

The **1957 Eight-Clubs Silverstone** was on **1st June**, the summer's first really hot day. The first Half-hour High Speed Trial (Le Mans start, pit-stop for a plug change and front wheel swap-over, or to pour a half pint of oil somewhere near the oil filler hole!) saw first-class awards go to Miss E A Neale (Jupiter HAK 365 ex Le Mans), Alf

Alf Thomas in his R4 plays Chase the Ace at Silverstone on 22nd June 1957. (National Motor Museum)

Miss Neale racing the ex-Le Mans lightweight Jupiter (132) at Silverstone. (National Motor Museum)

Thomas (R4 Jupiter JKW 537) and K Brierley (Jupiter 564). A 5-lap scratch race was won by a fast-moving Ken Brierley (565) at 60.26mph with his fastest lap 61.98mph; he was followed by a 3-litre Lagonda and Nancy Mitchell driving an MG Magnette. This result did not do Brierley's handicapping any favours for in a subsequent 5-lap handicap race he had to settle for third place. Then in a 5-lap scratch race Alf Thomas in the R4 posted the fastest lap of 67.16mph to win at the race average of 65.22mph ahead of Mrs Scott-Moncrieff (Lotus-MG), a very potent 1500cc MG TD and a Morgan. In another 5-lap handicap race Miss Neale (again in the ex-Le Mans ex-Works Jupiter HAK 365) drove it to a tidily-driven third place.

BARC Members Day at **Aintree** was on **15th June 1957** on the 3-mile circuit within the horse-race venue and able to use the same grandstands. Race 7 was a 7-lap handicap event for 'closed' cars. R F Nanson (Jupiter, one assumes running closed) finished 2nd.

The 8th **MCC Silverstone meeting** on the **22nd June 1957** started with the traditional Half-hour High Speed Trial. The two lovers Alf Thomas (R4 Jupiter JKW 537) and Miss Neale (ex-Le Mans Jupiter HAK 365 chassis 132) took part. The third event was a 10-lap handicap race with Alf in the R4 on scratch giving 10 seconds to an MGA, a full minute to Miss Neale in HAK 356, and 1½ minutes to Ken Brierley now in his Javelin; at the chequered flag Alf was 4th with Miss Neale 5th. In the next event a TR3 on scratch gave the R4 Jupiter 15s, Miss Neale 45s and Brierley the benefit of a full minute, enabling him to come first at 60.12mph ahead of Peter Morgan in his Morgan Plus 4, Alf Thomas and then an MGA.

The final race was the *Motor Sport* Winners' Handicap for which Charles Bulmer produced his best handicapping of the day with practically the whole field attempting to cross the finish line together. By Lap 4 it was clear that Alf Thomas in the R4 was too fast for all except a C-Type Jaguar that stormed through the pack and caught the little R4 on the last bend to win by a length. Peter Morgan, yes he, was 3rd, and an MGA 4th. So the MGA was no match for the Jowett Jupiter R4!

The **1957 Midland Motoring Enthusiasts Club's Silverstone** meeting was on **29th June**. Event 4 was a 6-lap scratch race for sports cars of up to 1½-litres and it resolved itself into two races, one in the van for the lightweight sports racers that were now proliferating (mostly Cooper-Climaxes and Lotus-Climaxes) and another astern for the more normal road machinery. The 'second' race was led by the redoubtable R4 of Alf Thomas, once again too fast for his challenger, the second-placed J Trafford in his MGA.

Over in the Far East there was the **1957 Shell Malayan Motor Rally**, starting on the **3rd August**; 800 miles to be covered in three days. It is known that the Jupiter of M A Johnson of Penang participated.

The **750 Motor Club's 1957 Six-hour Relay Handicap Race** was on **17th August**. The race was run on Silverstone's 2½-mile special circuit: the normal club circuit plus the central runway with a very tight hairpin known as Club Corner. The race was started at 1pm by Colin Chapman, the 750 MC president in those days, and the 'Team Individualist' which included the Jupiter of Ken Brierley (564) led from start to finish, mainly due to the lead built up by the team's Elva Courier. A Buckler also did quite some of the driving – with Ken Brierley's Jupiter seeing action whilst the others were refuelled and their drivers rested.

The **Lincoln District MC** and **Lincoln CC 1957 Lincoln Rally** was on **7th September**. The Jupiter of Ken Taylor (922) with Timms as map-man finished in a very nice overall second place. This Jupiter was later owned by Budge Rogers the Bedford & England Rugby player.

The **Mallory Park 1957 Day of Races** and a High Speed Trial was on **14th September**. Alf Thomas was there with his R4 Jupiter JKW 537 as was Miss Neale with the ex-Le Mans HAK 365. Alf was in the HST and also Event 4 a 5-lap scratch race. In Event 6, a 5-lap handicap race with a Lotus on scratch, Alf Thomas was given 1m 05s while Miss Neale was given 1m 20s; Alf Thomas was the winner. In Event 9 this time a 10-lap handicap race, our pair of inseparable Jupiter racers took part.

The last meeting of **1957** at **Silverstone** was put on by the North Staffordshire Motor Club on **5th October**. The fourth race of the day was a 6-lap scratch race for 1½-litre sports cars in which Alf Thomas in his usual R4 led until the last lap when I H S Smith, in his home-made MG XPEG-engined Wisp, very modern-looking in its glass-fibre body, just got past to leave the R4 Jupiter second. Third was a 1498cc Lester Riley, and Miss Neale in the Jupiter HAK 365 also ran. In a 5-lap handicap race Alf Thomas, given 45 seconds on the scratch car, could only manage 3rd place behind an Elva and a Tojeiro.

The Lancashire and Cheshire Car Club's end-of-season race meeting at **Oulton Park** on **12th October 1957** was

Frank Collins in 1958 with Fairthorpe. (Martin Collins)

held in brilliant sunshine. In a half-hour High Speed Trial that included a compulsory wheel change, just 12 out of 34 drivers beat the clock. One who did was Alf Thomas in the R4 while one who did not was Miss Neale in HAK 365.

The **Eight-clubs 1958 Silverstone Meeting** was on **8th June.** Frank 'Bunny' Collins in his Jupiter (468) ran in a 5-lap scratch race, as did A T Fryer in his rear-Jupiter-engined special, the 'Scientific'. In a 5-lap handicap race with a Lotus XI on scratch, Frank Collins in his Jupiter started on the same 1m 40s mark as a Lea-Francis and a Buckler Mk V, just 10 seconds before the 'Scientific'. Collins went on to be a Works Fairthorpe driver.

The **1958 MCC Silverstone** was on **2nd June.** Alf Thomas was there with his R4 Jupiter JKW 537 and Ken Brierley with his Jupiter (564). But it was a sign of changing times for Anne Neale had switched to a 1489cc MGA and Alf's son Barry was now racing a 1098cc Lotus. In Event 2, a Half-hour High Speed Trial, all four were in action with Miss Neale winning a First Class award. Event 4 was a 5-lap scratch race with Thomas father and son participating, and in Event 5 a 5-lap handicap race, Miss Neale in her MGA and Ken Brierley in his Jupiter saw action. They were given 1m 10s and 1m 15s from the scratch car a 1098cc Lotus-Climax.

The **1958 AMOC St John Horsfall Races** were at Silverstone on **12th July.** In a 5-lap scratch race for cars of up to 1½-litres, Alf Thomas in his trusty R4 (JKW 537) notched a very creditable third behind an Elva-Climax and a supercharged Lotus VI. Miss Neale was entered in

the half-hour 'blind' (as High Speed Trials had become known) in the R4 but there must have been a switch of drivers for, as the commentator put it, "Miss Neale has a black moustache!"

At the **1958 North Staffordshire Motor Club's Silverstone** meeting of **27th July,** Miss Neale was racing Alf Thomas's usual R4 Jupiter. Read on to find out why!

The **750 Motor Club's 1958 Six-hour Relay Handicap Race** was on **16th August,** again on Silverstone's extended circuit, and for only the second time a full Jupiter team was fielded – once more the catalyst was Alf Thomas. This was the climax of Alf Thomas's career as a fanatical Jupiter enthusiast for now he was able to field a team of no less than three R4 Jupiters. The steel-bodied prototype JKW 537 was joined by the two fabric/resin-bodied examples, one being the 1953 Motor Show example SWT 356, the other which was bought at the last minute from Jowett in dismantled form possibly to avoid tax. This third R4 was hurriedly assembled by Alf's mechanics, and driven to the race wearing HAK 365 plates from the ex-Le Mans 'standard' Jupiter. These two R4s were lighter than the prototype but not quite as fast, as Alf had spent much time improving the older car. One of the newer R4s

The three R4 Jupiters in Alf's racing colours at the Alf Thomas garage at Kempston near Bedford before the Six-hour Relay Handicap Race of 1958. Alf Thomas extreme left. (A & R Thomas)

The 1953 Earls Court Motor Show: this R4 Jupiter was later registered SWT 356. (Associated Press)

apparently lost a hub in practice but this was rectified in time for the start.

Barry Thomas drove the prototype JKW 537, Miss Neale drove the ex-Motor Show SWT 356 while Alf himself drove the assembled R4 wearing HAK 365 plates. Ken Brierley with his Jupiter was included in the team but it is unlikely he got to drive.

Promptly at 1pm Holland Birkett dropped the flag and the 21 drivers sprinted across the track to begin their first stint. After one hour's racing a localised rain shower drenched the back of the circuit, narrowly leaving the pit area dry and at this point the Jupiter team was equal sixth with the Morgan Plus 4 team (led by Peter Morgan) and two places behind the Porsche team led by Dennis Jenkinson. Half an hour later the Jupiters had moved up to share the lead with the TR2s of the Chilton Car Club and the Healeys and Friends team. However after two hours racing the Jaguar team was leading and the Jupiter team was ninth but still in touch at less than ¾ of a lap behind the leader.

Miss Neale drove her R4 (SWT 356) fast and without incident, but disaster was to strike Alf Thomas in the built-from-parts R4: on the run down to the Club Corner hairpin, the bonnet of his R4, lacking restraining straps,

snapped off, reared up and swung back striking Alf on the head. He lost control and the car rolled with Alf flung out onto the grass with the bonnet wrapped around his neck "like a lavatory seat" I was told, and lucky indeed was he to suffer only cuts and bruises.

The team sent out a car to see what had happened and to collect the all-important sash, and the race continued for the R4s although the team was no longer able to contest the lead. But that was not all, for with a few laps to go, Barry Thomas went off at Woodcote and had to abandon his somewhat damaged R4, returning to his pit on foot bearing the sash: Miss Neale went out again to finish the race, which resulted in the team still up there at 14th place out of the 20 finishing teams. Peter Morgan's team was 2nd but the Porsches (a 1300, a Super, a 1500 Carrera and 1600 Supers) must have had troubles of their own, for they finished below the R4s at 16th. However now two of the R4s were quite badly damaged and a shaken and depressed Thomas never raced again. All was not lost for the damaged R4s were later sold and repaired but the built-from spares example was later written off. The other two are still with us in good order – see Chapter 8 for more.

Perhaps it began with the speedboat *Pacific Spot*. Lean and hungry, the original Deep-V 'Grey Nurse' hull, she looked as fast as she turned out to be. Doug Syme of Christchurch, New Zealand, fitted a standard replacement Jupiter engine in her and then first set the Australasian Speed record in 1953 for V-hulls with this Jowett-powered boat at 53.775mph – indeed the world speed record was once unofficially exceeded at 58.6mph, although the hydroplane *Hydrophobia* was faster. Such was the boat's success that he contacted Jowett at Birstall with a view to purchasing a Le Mans specification R1 engine. Thanks to the intervention of George Green, Syme was supplied with a kit of parts to bring his engine up to R1 specification plus an oval-web crankshaft. With one or other form of the engine (which was stamped R1/438), Doug and boat won 76 championships, bringing home an astonishing 40 trophies in the 91 cubic inch class (34 cups, 2 teapots, 2 salvers and 2 barometers). When around 1962 he retired the boat as unbeatable the engine was removed, and after a brief sojourn in another boat it was bought by New Zealander Wayne Rout, and he and Vic Morrison fitted it to Wayne's Jupiter (27). The Jupiter took part in a road race in which it proved to be very fast (helped by its high back-axle ratio) but was forced to retire when a gearbox mainshaft washer broke. Wayne did not race again, selling his Jupiter (without the R1 engine) to Paul Illingworth. Inspired, Vic Morrison very thoroughly prepared his Jupiter (182) for competition. It became known as the 'Jaguar Eater' for reasons explored below.

Both Paul Illingworth and Vic Morrison participated in the **1964 Day of Races** at **Ruapuna Park**, near Christchurch in the South Island. Both Jupiters had more or less standard engines and in the half-dozen or so races Paul drove his Jupiter very shrewdly to consistently finish ahead of Vic Morrison.

For the next race day at the same circuit Vic had fitted single-choke Weber carburettors to the engine, a great improvement on the standard Zeniths, and in this form Jupiter 182 was able to finish ahead of Jupiter 27. Paul then ceased racing, and when Errol Blatchford raced his Jupiter (414) at Ruapuna a couple of times he too was no match for the Jaguar Eater. Usually in these events there would be 10 to 15 cars in each race, and in most cases the cars would be specials solely used for racing, whereas Vic's Jupiter was his only car at the time. The Benmore Circuit, for example, was 220 miles from Christchurch and Vic would drive there and back in full road trim for comfort at speed: with 14-inch wheels fitted, revs were at a constant 5500 rpm for hours on end. Windscreen, quarter-lights, window glass, hood assembly, spare wheel and its door, headlights, bench seat (in favour of an Austin 7 bucket) were removed in the pits on arrival.

Vic obtained the R1 pistons from Doug Syme; the half-race camshaft was a standard unit reground for more opening time. Gear-changing took place when the rev-counter needle was at the main-beam warning light,

roughly 7,000rpm. **Ruapuna** was a 1-mile oval circuit with one of the straights extended and doubled back to form a hairpin and a reverse corner – like the profile of a balled fist with a pointing index finger.

Here are some results for Vic Morrison and his 'Jaguar Eater' Jupiter (182).

South Canterbury Car Club **Craigmore Hillclimb 23rd August 1964**. His first event, with engine completely standard:– time 78.2s. **23rd March 1965**. Engine with R1 pistons, half-race cam, Weber carbs:– time 71.3s

12th August 1965. 60 thou planed off cylinder heads:– time now his best at 70.0s

22nd August 1965. Standard camshaft refitted:– time 70.5s

Canterbury Car Club **Ruapuna Racetrack 20th September 1964**. Race 7 for sports cars. Vic Morrison the winner ahead of a Buckler and an MGA 1600.

South Canterbury Car Club **Saltwater Creek Grass Circuit 25th October 1964**. In three races Vic Morrison placed two 3rds and a 4th.

Canterbury Car Club **Ruapuna Racetrack November 1964**. In the race for sports cars, Vic placed 2nd behind a Morgan, but ahead of a Buckler Mk 90 (with its NZ-designed body) and an MG Midget.

Nelson Car Club's **Tahuna Beach Circuit 4th, 5th January 1965**. In Race 2, a scratch race for 1201– 2000cc cars, Vic Morrison placed 5th out of 14. Event 10 was a sports car handicap race where Vic finished 2nd

Ruapuna race track 21st March 1965, Vic Morrison's well-handling Jupiter eats Jaguar. (Vic Morrison)

behind a Morgan, ahead of a Mistral-Consul. Race 11 was an open handicap which Vic won ahead of second-placed Ford 10 Special. Race 6 on the second day was a handicap event for sports and specials up to 1750cc, and Vic this time came 3rd behind the Morgan and the Mistral-Consul.

South Canterbury Car Club **Mayfield Grass Circuit February 1965**. Vic was the winner of Race 4 and placed third in Race 9.

Canterbury Car Club **Ruapuna Racetrack 21st March 1965**. Race 7 was a 6-lap handicap event and it was here that Vic Morrison and his Jupiter earned his sobriquet. He had to give the Jaguar XK150 saloon a 4-second start, yet passed it on the last lap at the hairpin to come fourth behind an XK120, an MG Midget and a Morgan Plus 4. Then in Race 15, a sports car handicap event, Vic now finished in second place, a mere half-bonnet behind the winning Buckler but ahead of the next-placed MG Midget and the Morgan Plus 4.

Canterbury Car Club **Standing Quarter Mile Trial** on **4th April 1965**. With the Jupiter in full road trim Vic was timed at 19.43s.

Southland Car Club **Benmore Clay Circuit April 1965**. In races 10 and 15 Vic placed third.

Canterbury Car Club **Ruapuna Racetrack** meeting of **9th May 1965**: in a sports car handicap race Vic crossed the line in second place between two Morgans.

Canterbury CC **Summit Road Hillclimb** also in **May 1965**. Vic timed at 37.54s and 36.98s compared with 34.49s by a blown MG TF.

Canterbury Car Club **Ruapuna Racetrack 13th June 1965**. Results not known, but Vic and his Jupiter's best lap was 64.6s compared with J Slater in an XK150 which clocked a hair's breadth faster with 64.3s.

Canterbury Car Club **Ruapuna Racetrack 9th October 1965 Day of Sprints**. With Vic's Jupiter in full road trim and standard camshaft re-fitted, his times for the 1-mile lap were:

Standing lap 75.57s; flying lap 67.92s.

Goodwood 21st March 1953, the Jupiter of Robbie MacKenzie-Low (544). Robbie in white overalls talking to G A Dudley. (R MacKenzie-Low)

British people in the colonies sometimes brought Jupiters with them. Here in Malaya Frank Wills (110) takes part in a hillclimb, in 1953. He also took part in sprints there, while back in August 1951 before emigrating he had driven his Jupiter at Goodwood. (Frank Wills)

One-way maximum speed was measured late in 1965 with Vic's Jupiter's hood up, standard camshaft but engine otherwise as modified, standard Jupiter wheels fitted. The speed was read from the car's speedometer previously calibrated on a rolling road dynamometer. Speeds through the gears at 5700rpm were 31mph, 51mph, 81mph and 97.5mph.

Over to Australia NSW now, and five weeks after my 1966 time limit but included here for convenience. **Castlereagh Sprints Day 5th February 1967**. Ed Wolf (72) was there:

For the Standing Quarter Mile, his time: 21.25s
For the Flying Eighth Mile his time: 6.38s.

Also there was Bruce Polain in the further-developed Wylie-Javelin single seater (Page 106). Bruce was a superb engineer, and his class-winning times were:

Standing Quarter Mile, timed at 15.50s
Flying Eighth Mile, timed at 4.29s.

These times were actually down on his times set five months earlier on the same track, when his times were:

Here is an unknown Jupiter coming to grief during the 15th October 1956 Dunlop Gap Hillclimb in Singapore put on by the Singapore Motor Club. Photo taken at a dangerous hairpin on the Sembawang Road where several other competitors came to grief. With its unlouvred bonnet this would be an early Jupiter. (Bai Yun)

Standing Quarter Mile, timed at 14.55s
Flying Eighth Mile, timed at 4.11 (109.5mph)

This Flying Eighth was a new record for the Australian Racing Drivers Club.

Eight-Clubs Silverstone 4th June 1955. Ken Brierley is in HKW 386 (564). Following behind is P Waring in his Jupiter NTF 510.
(NMM Charles Dunn)

7: Jupiters Yesterday and Today

Although a couple of Jupiters are known to be museum exhibits, many Jupiters remain cars in use for one purpose or another, with enthusiastic owners not only in Britain where spares and expertise are relatively plentiful, but in many of the countries to which the cars were originally exported, the list taking in Australia, New Zealand, Scandinavia, the USA, Belgium and France. Many owners derive satisfaction from the restoration of their cars as the Jupiter's method of construction – being hand-built throughout with the low-rust chassis and aluminium bodywork – lends itself to such an activity. The car is stylish, balanced but not aggressive, and the overall result is the high survival rate of the Jupiter, which is in excess of 45 per cent.

The article reproduced below, "25,000 Miles in a Jowett Jupiter" first appeared in the *Motor Sport* issue of November 1952, encapsulating the bitter-sweet impression that the model was to make on many of its owners. Mr William Boddy, then editor of *Motor Sport*, occasionally garnished his magazine with references to this early Jupiter (98 bought 28 March 1951); in June 1951 the fan incident was related (50 mph at 27 mpg on wet roads was averaged until its disintegration); not being overtaken on the run back to London from Darlington on 14th October that year after the races at Winfield; and, having spectated at Castle Coombe, a burn-up was alluded to in WB's instantly recognisable style: "...and went swiftly Londonwards in the *Motor Sport* Jupiter up with which Sydney Allard, now in a Ford Zephyr, very nearly kept". I am greatly indebted to Mr Boddy and *Motor Sport* for permission to reproduce the article.

25,000 miles in a Jowett Jupiter by W J Tee, Managing Director of *Motor Sport* magazine.
Twelve months ago I made a business trip which took me as far north as Tongue and completed in all a little under 2,000 miles in nine days. I returned so enthusiastic about the Jupiter that I felt I had better let a few weeks pass before I wrote about my experiences, lest I be carried away and exaggerate in singing the praises of this wonderful little thoroughbred. When I finally wrote them they were crowded out, our editor unable to find space.

Twelve months passed quickly, and with the speedometer showing 24,000 miles, we started off on the same trip. Safely home again, I am even more enthusiastic than before. Firstly, though, let me relate some of my experiences with the youngest member of the Jowett family.

A heavy shower of rain had fallen and the sun was just beginning to shine through as I caught sight of my red Jupiter standing in the market-place at Stamford, quietly waiting for me. My first impression was 'you little beauty!' and as time has gone on that first impression has grown until for me it is the prettiest car on the road.

The drive back to London was taken quietly, and proved uneventful – then a period of quiet running took the speedometer along to 2,000 miles. Only then did I start to push the rev-counter beyond 3,500rpm. It must be remembered that this Jupiter was one of the first to come from the Jowett factory, and I decided to return it to Bradford for a general overhaul at about 3,500 miles; so, at 7 o'clock one very beautiful spring morning, the editor and I left for Bradford. The speedometer seldom dropped below 80mph and we soon realised that this little car was making really exciting headway so we pushed along a little faster but never exceeding 5,500 revs. Then, just before Stamford, the engine began to falter. And finally we came to rest by the roadside a few miles on the London side of Stamford. Obviously the engine was starved of petrol. I have no explanation as to why I did it, but I walked to the back of the car and released the filler cap at the back – a small 'pop' startled me and I quickly realised that the quick-release cap fitted so tightly that it had formed a vacuum. Drilling two small holes has made certain that we are never caught like that again. Only a few minutes were wasted and on we sped, and at 9:50 we were 5 to 10 miles the Bradford side of Doncaster when I thought the car had disintegrated! Several very loud bangs and a violent shaking of the floor-boards, and a large bump appeared on the beautiful red bonnet, and the editor shouted 'for God's sake stop!'

In a flash the ignition was switched off and the gears disengaged. As we were travelling at very nearly 90mph when it happened, this easy-running little car quietly drifted a very long way before dying by the roadside, but

The *Motor Sport* Jupiter (98), Mrs Tee, and the Forth Bridge 420 miles from home. (*Motor Sport*)

we were at least a little nearer Bradford. Quite honestly I expected to see the engine in pieces and was surprised at not seeing a trail of parts in the driving-mirror. However, when the bonnet was lifted, we saw that the fan had come adrift, hit the underside of the bonnet – hence the bump – and then out of the bottom. Our luck was in, for although it had severed several wires and pipes, nothing vital was touched and the radiator was undamaged. When the fan belt was taken off, the car was cranked (the starter being quite dead), and it started straight away. Driving quietly, with the water temperature well up, we proceeded to Bradford, reaching the Works at about 11:30am.

Very shortly the car was ready for the road, and we drove to Bradford in a very lively Javelin to collect it, arriving at the Works only 3 hours and 55 minutes after leaving Romford. The large bump on the bonnet had been smoothed out and after a short run round the local roads with the tester, a quick glance at the factory and lunch, we left about 3pm expecting to be back in London not later than 7 o'clock – perhaps 6:30. Before we reached Doncaster, an ominous knock started and, although the oil pressure was well up so was the oil temperature, we decided to stop at the next garage to check oil and water.

Tee and the *Motor Sport* Jupiter at an event. (CJ)

This we did and to my amazement one quart of oil was needed to satisfy the dipstick. Out on the road again, only a further 10 miles completed, a most 'sickening' knock developed in a matter of seconds to a rhythmic thud and we had no big ends. We had to press on but oh! What a miserable drive and it was 11pm when Romford was reached, and anyone was welcome to the Jupiter by just taking it away.

Several months went by and at last the little red car was delivered to the office with the remarks "You'll find her all right now, we know the answers to the flying fans, blown gaskets, and big-ends – you won't have any more trouble" By the time 4,500 miles had been completed a gasket blew again and the front tyres were bald, and as the back tyres showed practically no wear, it was obvious that the tracking was at fault. I was getting a little 'browned off' for, after all, I had paid a lot of hard-earned money for this car and even the most optimistic would have to admit that I had been in trouble!

August 1951 saw the speedometer clocking 6,000 miles and the modifications that had been made looking

as if they were going to be successful. The new tyres on the front were showing signs of a little unnecessary wear, but by now Jowetts had the answer to correct tracking and the necessary adjustments made. Twelve months have quickly slipped by and the speedometer reads 25,750 miles, the last 20,000 being very nearly trouble free – 20,000 hard miles, for all of them have been completed in the service of *Motor Sport* – trials in the West Country, hillclimbs in the North, large and small race meetings and speed trials at nearly every track in England and Scotland. Thousands of miles in torrential rain, snow and fog, and most of them in darkness. Never once has the little red Jupiter failed to get us to the meeting – never once has it failed to get us home again. The Lucas equipment has never failed to excite the engine, announce our presence, and light our way, although we favour the small Marchal spot and fog-lights. Dunlop tyres: 5:50 on the front and 5:75 on the back, have never failed us, and the Girling Mintex-lined brakes always just managed to stop us in time. Hundreds of interesting incidents rush to mind but space allows only one.

One Thursday morning, at 9:30, we left for a visit to the Ferodo works at Chapel-en-le-Frith, arriving at the Palace Hotel, Buxton, at 1:10pm. After a wash and brush up and a very good lunch, we went to fulfil our appointment and a very enjoyable afternoon we had. The very fulfilling of this appointment reminds me of one of the strongest points that makes the Jupiter such a favourite for the businessman.

One is able to put on a cap, a muffler and gloves and enjoy the exhilaration of an open sports car and, by Jove! Only those who have experienced it know the thrill. Then, having reached the town, one can put up the hood, wind up the windows, and go about one's business in the town in what is virtually a closed car. A very enjoyable evening and first-class service at the Palace sent us on our way in a very good frame of mind. Up past Holme Moss television transmitter aerial all shrouded in thick mist. Through Huddersfield and Leeds, joining the A1 at Wetherby, leaving it just after Scotch Corner, and then into Scotland by what I think is the most impressive route, the A68 over Carter Bar. We mustn't forget the old-world Wellington Hotel, Riding Mill, where the service and lunch were fit for a king.

Arriving at Edinburgh about 4:30 we found that Queen Elizabeth was already there and the town full and wherever we went we received the same answer 'No room at the inn'. So we pushed on to Linlithgow but, before reaching it, we saw a large white house high up to our right and were admiring its position when a small board announce it as Bonsyde Hotel. We took the last room and enjoyed our stay, leaving on Sunday morning after completing our business at Bo'ness.

Through the Trossachs, with the sun blazing its welcome, unbelievably beautiful and peaceful – lunch was taken at Tchailoch Hotel beside the loch – and then on to spend the rest of the day and night at Killicrankie. Mine host of the Killicrankie Hotel has created an atmosphere of delicate charm and we were sorry to leave at 8:30 on the Monday morning, climbing to 1500 feet through Glen Garry to Kingussie and on to Inverness. It pays handsomely here to drive back along the west shores of Loch Ness to Drumnadrochit and then along Glen Urquhart and finally north to Beauly. The Drumnadrochit Hotel, with its vast windows, provides one with a 'view while you chew'. Then through Dingwall to Bonar bridge, that delightful little village at the head of Dornoch Firth. Tongue was reached by 5:15. The Bungalow Hotel was our home for two days; it is built of wood with little wooden chalets overlooking the Kyle and warmed by peat fires. Just to think of the smell of the peat, the warm welcome, the good food beautifully cooked, and the delightful bays explored, gives me a glow of contentment.

The Jupiter – the first the local garage had seen – created interest, and the loving care with which it was serviced was much appreciated. Thoroughly greased (one quart of oil, one pint of water and about 4-5 lbs in the tyres, was the first attention it had received since leaving Romford 1,150 miles away), and we were ready for the wildest run to be imagined in Britain. Driving right round the Kyle, leaving Ben Loyal first on our left and then on our right, one strikes due west to Hope. Even on a glorious

day one needs hope, for the boulder-strewn roads are wild; desolate scenery makes on feel that without the Jupiter purring quietly and effortlessly along all would be lost. Round Loch Eriboll, divinely blue and as lovely as any Italian lake, then through Durness and following the road southwest to Cape Wrath to Scourie, across the Kylestrome Ferry, on past Loch Assynt through the wildest and roughest country in our lovely Isle and finally dropping down into Ullapool. A memorable day's run, the Jupiter simply bounding along. A most delightful evening was spent at the Grand Hotel, Ullapool, where the staff make one feel so absolutely at home. The sunset at Ullapool with the Summer Isles silhouetted against the evening sky is one of the sights one never forgets.

Away next morning by 8:30 and, following Loch Broom for a short time, the road winds inland for a short way before returning to Little Loch Broom, and from there to Gairloch one passes through miles of the loveliest mountain loch and sea scenery available for man to see: Grunard Bay with its sandy inlets forming natural wind-breaks give such marvellous opportunities to sunbathe as we did. The steep hill out of Grunard Bay was levelled by the lively Jupiter which had to be checked before taken to the Aultbea Hotel right by the seashore off the direct route but worth the visit. A run by the side of Loch Maree, then through wild country with a single-track railway appearing and disappearing, past Strathcarron Station and across Lochcarron by Strome Ferry, arriving at Kyle of Lochalsh about 5pm with the most delightful views of Skye which looked mysterious, its mountains appearing unreal and ethereal. Most delightful was our stay at the Lochalsh Hotel – everyone going out of their way to make us comfortable.

Leaving about 10am we travelled along the same road we came in by, Skye looking quite different in the morning sun but just as mystical. The country was still quite wild but the road surface steadily improved. We reached Fort William for lunch at the Alexandra Hotel, then on to Ballachulish and so into Glencoe, bathed in brilliant sunshine. The high snow-posts, however, were a reminder of what a terrible reception a visitor can get in winter.

Through Inveraray with views of Loch Fyne the grandeur of which defy description, finally down the Rest-and-be-Thankful to Arrochar, where we arrived at about 5:30pm. Before putting the gallant little Jupiter away, I checked the tyres and water (OK), oil (a quart needed); a check-up of petrol purchased since leaving London showed that we were averaging 28 miles per gallon for the 1600 miles completed, surely a truly wonderful performance, for about 1000 of it had been run over mountain roads which were the worst I have driven on in Britain.

After the Rest-and-be-Thankful Hillclimb which is held in such beautiful surroundings that the racing becomes a secondary consideration, we followed the road to Glasgow by Loch Lomond. How lucky are the Scots living around Glasgow to have such glorious scenery so near at hand! So through Glasgow to Abington to spend a most comfortable night at the Abington Hotel where any visitor can always be assured of a warm welcome: good food and drink served under the watchful eye of the Chief.

Sunday morning dawned mistily. Obviously we were in for a really hot day and, my goodness, how hot it proved to be. When travelling at 90mph in the midlands later in the day even the wind blew hot, but at no time did the Jupiter overheat. With no special preparation we left Abington at 8:35 and ran without a stop to within 10 miles of Newark. Here we stopped for lunch and filled up with eight gallons of petrol and a pint of oil. This took an hour and we left at 1:45pm. At 4:45pm we stepped out of the Jupiter at Romford, having completed the 375 miles in 7 hours and 10 minutes driving time.Some friends said to my passenger: *"you must be dead tired"* but her reply was *"not a bit, I should be happy to drive straight back"*. I myself would have been quite happy to have driven back. I was very nearly as fresh as when I started and, do not forget, the drive from Huntingdon had been through traffic which was quite heavy on this hot Sunday afternoon.

To sum up, any motor car that, after completing 1,600-odd miles over rough roads of north and north-west Scotland, runs 375 miles with one stop of an hour at an average speed of 50mph, with such smoothness and such airy lightness of control to leave the driver and passenger as fresh as when they started, has indeed qualified to be considered one of the finest cars in the world – and I submit that, on the evidence, the Jupiter is definitely in that class.

***The Jupiter in Concours d'Elégance*, by John Parker, former chairman Jupiter Owners' Auto Club, writing in 1980**
There are perhaps only some dozen or so Jupiters currently competitive in Concours events. This is a pity as the car gives you several immediate advantages over the other competitors:

1. The initial eye appeal that only a distinctive-looking sports car has.
2. Once in true Concours condition it is an *easy* car to maintain as such – my own experience after four years of inter-club and national contests is that with very little extra effort it seems to get even better each year.
3. It is a delight to drive and even under the most adverse weather conditions you can still get to the events you are entered in – the mark of a true serious competitor. No organiser likes the entrant who only arrives if the weather suits him – if you have formally entered then make every effort to get there. If you have doubts then don't enter until the day – most events accept late entries.
4. Finally I consider the Jupiter is an economical car to buy, restore and maintain. It is possibly the least expensive way of being really competitive up there amongst the XK Jaguars, Healey Silverstones, Astons, Bentleys: on occasions I have beaten top Bentleys and even a Silver Ghost RR.

For me the results speak for themselves; after buying and restoring my own Jupiter EHH 707 (505) I have won to date 27 awards and had a tremendous amount of pleasure in showing my car to the public as an example of my own standard of workmanship.

I would like to offer some advice to would-be Jupiter competitors. Don't cut corners when restoring your

John Parker's self-restored Jupiter (505). (J Parker)

car – the art of Concours is to show your car as if it had just left the Factory – people want to see what it looked like when new. Get rid of those items your car has 'grown' over the years such as non-standard hood window, irrelevant instruments and over/undersize wheels and tyres. Try to avoid thinking of your Jupiter as a modern competitive sports car – it is not. In the 1950s it was a star of road and track but even a modern family car has superior performance now.

The Jupiter is a true sports car from another era and that it how it must be preserved – if you do this it will give you and others untold pleasure and perpetuate the model in its true light.

The Jupiter in Historic Racing, by Peter Dixon, former Chief Registrar of the Historic Sports Car Club

By the mid 1960s it had become apparent that the Vintage Sports Car Club were never going to accept the rarer more worthy sports cars of the early post-war era and that, unless a home could be found for these cars, they would continue to be destroyed or unsuitably modified. Thus initially there came into being the Griffiths Formula for such cars, and the foundational meeting was held on **14th May 1966** at the **Castle Coombe circuit**. There were on that day a race and two High Speed Trials thus inaugurating a new and successful arena of competition for sporting cars of the past. This was all thanks to the motor sport photographer Guy Griffiths who had become concerned that many great racing cars had fallen into disuse. He created the Griffiths

Formula as a way of keeping them in competition and from this came the founding of the Historic Sports Car Club (HSCC). There was a Jupiter taking part that inaugural day, the 14th May 1966, it was FVG 332 (876) then owned and driven by Frank Mockridge.

However, nothing more was heard in what became the HSCC until 1972 when the next owner of that same Jupiter, Peter Dixon decided that the Jupiter's inclusion in the then 'historically eligible' list was worth celebrating.

By this time the HSCC was holding number of race meetings a year under the auspices of friendly relevant clubs such as the Aston Martin Owners Club, the Bentley Drivers Club and the Jaguar Drivers Club for historic 1940 to 1960 cars and post-historic 1960 to 1964 cars. In sports-racing, with such as Lotus X1, D-type and Lister-Jaguars mixing it with road sports cars such as Frazer Nashs, AC Aces and Porsche 356s, the Jupiter was one of the oldest and smallest cars out there and not surprisingly one of the slowest, so eventually the races were split and the sports racers went their own faster way.

Left: Peter Dixon and FVG 332 at Silverstone 26/8/1972; Right: Peter Dixon (876) closely followed by the Porsche Speedster of D Mallet at Silverstone in 1978. (CJ)

The best Jupiter racing was undoubtedly when joined by more of its fellows as FVG 332 would normally beat either newcomers or cars not running well or not being raced in earnest. Otherwise it came a sporting last! But, as in its heyday, people commented generally about the excellent race handling of the Jupiter, its safety record and its noticeable reliability including my road drives to and from all track meetings (some 36 ten-lap races). What people failed to notice was that it had no equitable competition for the 1600cc Porsches were mostly running post-1960 American racing components giving over 100bhp where the catalogue stated 55 to 75bhp as standard for the cars of the equivalent period. The HRGs did not appear.

In 1978 the ex-Le Mans 1952 class-winning R1 Jupiter reappeared to be raced by Peter Dixon, who immediately found that whilst this very historic car had considerable potential, the ravages of previous restorers, engine swappers and butchers had created areas needing further restoration and chassis and suspension tuning of this 13cwt car. It was then put through a thorough and accurate restoration programme to become one of the

rarer showpieces of the now ever more popular and successful historic sports car racing movement. There appeared six categories racing in different championships to include production sports cars of their respective eras for example TRs 2 & 3, MGs T & A, and Morgans etc. This spread to mainland Europe, Australia and the USA, but it is interesting to note that the Lester-MG and Cooper-MG is non-existent, thus in its strict era the Jupiter has proved to be the racing survivor, and its lap times compare favourably with its times during its manufacturing life. It is not possible to cover anything like the sum of everyone's Jupiter activities but perhaps a sense of what Jupiter people do is presented.In its first race on the Brands Hatch Club Circuit, on 8 June 1978, Peter and Jupiter set the best lap of 1m 14s to equal the then 1600cc HSCC Roadsports lap record held by an MGA.

It is not possible to cover here all the events enjoyed by Jupiter people in the years following Peter Dixons start, but I hope to convey to the reader some of the flavour of what Jupiters have been able to achieve in modern times. Following Peter Dixon's lead with his Jupiter, which he raced continuously from 1972 to 1978 without accident or breakdown, various other owners made appearances in these races and other events. Amongst others, Pete Crosby (898), Geoff McAuley (947), Mike Smailes (650), Keith Clements (841), Tony Fewster (913), Ian Dearie and Kathy Watson (860), and Frank Woolley (859), all of whom regularly competed in North of England sprints and hillclimbs as well, on occasion, being joined by Roger Barrett in the surviving R1. Geoff McAuley was consistently the fastest with Mike Smailes running him close! These Jupiters formed the 'Team Northern' group which entered northern events at Castle Howard, Topcliffe, Scammonden, Harewood, Baitings Dam, and occasionally at Oulton Park, Prescott, Silverstone, Croft and Snetterton. The team was active from 1973 to at least 1989. Rallies were also entered, and Mike Smailes finished 2nd in his class of 12 in the **1983 Coronation Rally**.

At the **Brands Hatch** Club Circuit on the **30 April 1989** Mike Smailes (650) and Frank Woolley (859) saw action in the first Synter AMOC race for 1950s classic sports cars.

They were mixing it with C-type and D-type Jaguars, Aston Martins, Lolas, Lister-Jaguars, Lotuses and ACs, while the class opposition including two very quick Fraser Nashs soon became a two-horse race.

Mike Smailes had bought his Jupiter (650) in 1969 and it was on the road by **1971**. Almost immediately he entered the **Curtis Bennett Rally**. He was in the top 25 out of 120 starters after 5 time controls and 4 passage controls all clean but one, when forced to retire with gearbox bothers. He then developed the car for rallying and racing, a good example being the **Targa Rusticana Rally** of the **13th** and **14th October 1990** over 150 miles in Wales in the LLandidrod Wells region when Mike Smailes (650) with Nigel Booth finished the overall winner from 120 starters. Another outright win was with the JCC Jupiter team of Mike Smailes, Keith Clements (841), Frank Woolley (859) in the **1989 Eight Clubs Silverstone** team handicap five lap race. The Jupiter team beat 14 other teams. In **October 1997 Solway Historic Rally** for Classic Cars, Mike Smailes (with Bryan Smith) finished first in class at sixth overall. Then in the **Pye Motors Classic Illuminations Rally 25/26 October 1997**, Mike and Jupiter won his class. Mike reckoned he did over 100 events in this Jupiter before

Mike Smailes (650) on his way to a class win at the Brands Hatch Club Circuit. (Fred Scatley)

Here is Frank Woolley (859) who was close behind Mike Smailes at Brands on 30th April 1989. (Chris Harvey)

selling it to Ib Rasmussen who continues to use the car successfully in Danish events.

The inaugural **Pirelli Classic Marathon** of **19/26 June 1988** used some of the rally routes from the 1950s. It was a long and difficult event about reliability, endurance, and stamina. The start was on London's Tower Bridge then across the channel to the old semi-derelict Reims Grand Prix Circuit then on to Monza then Cortina d'Ampezzo in the Dolomites, then crossing Switzerland and France to Spa in Belgium before returning to London via Vissengen (Flushing) for the ferry home.

The two Jupiters entered were NXN 499 (650) of Mike Smailes with Keith Clements navigating and KDA 676 (723) of Malcolm Oliver with Bill Lock, while the Javelin of Geoff McAuley with Frank Woolley made up the team of three Jowetts. There were initially 10 cars in their class: 2 x MGA – should have been 72bhp but Bryan Halliday's was reported, possibly by Bryan himself to Mike Smailes, to have been a hefty 115bhp! Possibly an MGB engine fitted!! And also 2 x Sunbeam Rapier (67.5bhp), 2 x MG Magnette (64bhp) and an Alpine, all a bit younger than the Jowetts. The cars were supposed to be in standard form so the competition Jowetts had to have their trim, bumpers etc added. The rally required driving a good 2200 often very demanding miles in eight days, with the maximum an incredible 510 miles on the Monday and then 535 miles on the Saturday! There were eight special tests with penalty points for drivers who failed to maintain the times laid down between controls, some really difficult to keep to.

For the first time in years Monza unlocked its old iron gates leading to a cobbled courtyard that was the parc fermé for the Tuesday night halt, prior to a timed test round the circuit and a full-bore 'hillclimb' for nine miles, up the 48 hairpins of the Stelvio Pass; however the Stelvio as a timed test could not be timed due to factors beyond the organiser's control but it was still an exciting climb.

The Sunday's start of eight day's serious driving began at London Bridge and took the cars to Lydden airfield for the first timed test. Mike Smailes was just 1 second adrift of Bryan Halliday's hairy MGA's class-winning time, with

Smailes with navigator Clements on the Stelvio. (Chris Harvey)

Malcolm Oliver's next in class followed by the Javelin. After Lydden it was to Dover, across the channel and the night stop at Calais. Monday saw the cars tested at the Pévy hillclimb 12 miles from Reims before heading the 330 miles to Aix-Les-Bains in the Rhône-Alps for the next night stop. Tuesday took the cars over the border to the Pirelli Test Track just short of the night stop at Monza. At the test track Mike came class second behind that fast MGA but Malcolm Oliver's Jupiter suffered various problems so could not take the test and was given a large penalty marking – nevertheless he continued. On the Thursday Mike showed that with superior driving and handling he could beat the MGA; then on the Friday from Cortina – after driving right across Switzerland – there were two speed tests and a slap-up meal at the Mulhouse museum (with its Schlumpf Collection of Bugatties etc). Saturday was a 12-hour 535-mile blind across France to Spa in Belgium for a speed test before driving to the ferry in Vlissingen for the crossing. By now Mike had pulled up a slender points lead over Halliday's MGA which he managed to keep at the final test at Crystal Palace to an excellent win of his class. Geoff's Javelin placed 5th in class with Malcolm Oliver's a lowly 9th thanks to his Jupiter not being able to take the Pirelli Test Track test.

In the second **Pirelli Classic Marathon of 18-24 June**

1989 there were again three Jowetts: Geoff McAuley was back with a Javelin, this time his competition Javelin with the usual trim additions plus an overdrive. Wally Dale entered his Rochdale-bodied Jupiter which was fast-restored for the event after a 30-year lay-up, and Keith Clements entered his performance standard Jupiter NKD 258 (841).

There was a quite different route from 1988: London Tower Bridge to Eperheide in the Netherlands, Speyer in Germany, Merano and Cortina d'Ampezzo in Italy, to what was then Yugoslavia to tackle the infamous Passo della Moistrocca Climb in what is now Slovenia (the highest pass in that country) then back to Cortina d'Ampezzo where the rally finished.

If the "Pre-1963 up to 1600cc" class had been retained, the Javelin of Geoff McAuley and Frank Woolley would have been placed winners of that class with Wally Dale and Robin Barry 7th and Keith Clements

The Rochdale Jupiter on a tricky stretch of the 1989 Pirelli Marathon. Robin Barry drove, Wally Dale navigated. Brake fade on the longer descents was an on-going problem. (Mary Harvey)

Phew! Pirelli Marathon Rally of 1989. Keith Clements and Drummond Black (841). (Chris Harvey)

with Drummond Black having been delayed by serious back axle problems (solved by some deft welding by Drummond) 9th – they had been class leaders for the first six days! However the official classification turned out to incorporate all the 1600cc cars placing the Javelin 2nd, the Rochdale Jupiter of Wally Dale and Robin Barry 13th and Keith's Jupiter 17th.

By way of compensation the Javelin won a much-coveted *Coupe des Alpes* (Alpine Cup), awarded to all competitors who finished the event unpenalised having met all the road section and special test target times. This was the first and only time in the long history of the Alpine rallies that a Javelin had won this award. And the Rochdale finished ahead of a Lancia Aprilia, a Riley and two Lotus Cortinas.

In the 1990 (third) **Pirelli Classic Marathon** Keith Clements again entered his Jupiter NKD 258 (841), with Drummond Black navigating, teaming up with Trevor Spero in his Jupiter FPR 474 (584I) with Michael Appell navigating; and in the 1991 **Pirelli**

Classic Marathon Keith Clements again drove his Jupiter NKD 258, now with Michael Appell navigating, joined by Geoff McAuley and his Javelin. Best-placed Jowett in these events was Geoff McAuley's Javelin in 1989 at 24th overall, class 4th, while the best class finish was the Mike Smailes Jupiter in 1988 with their class win at 37th overall.

Wally Dale continued to use his Rochdale Jupiter in competition in such events as the **Coronation Rally** of **12 August 1989** finishing class 4th, 8-Clubs races at Silverstone, Prescott hillclimbs, an Oulton Park MG T-type race and finally a **Harewood Hillclimb** on **19th July 1992** to place class 14th.

The Californians Scott Renner and Jim Miller started racing Jowetts the same day in **1989** in Baja Mexico, in the trans-peninsula road race **Ensenada to San Felipe**. Jim raced his Jupiter (192) and Scott his Javelin. Cometh the hour, cometh the man! Jim reckons this must have been the best effort ever of any Jupiter racing in North America – while certainly being his personal best. With Ted Miller as a passenger they averaged over 71mph for around 150 miles through some of the most dangerous mountain roads Jim says he has ever driven at speed in

Scott Renner (798) at speed at a California event in 2011. (Jim Miller)

any car. There were multiple fatal fiery crashes where other vehicles went right off the steep cliffs or, catching a tyre in the soft shoulder, cartwheeled into the desert.

Scott Renner started racing his Jupiter (758) in 1991. So then Scott and Jim raced together doing three events a year at venues such as Riverside International, Laguna Seca, Sears Point, Monterey, and Willow Springs.

The two also took part in road races and hill climbs at Palm Springs and San Diego. At the end of 1995 Jim stopped racing but Scott went on doing one event a year.

Still in the USA, Derek Chambers has been, and Dave Burrows still is, very successful at classic car concours events, as are Mike Stout and John Kenna in Canada.

New Zealanders began Jupiter racing as early as **1952** for a photograph exists of the Jupiter of Dr Ken Orr in a Sports Car Handicap race at **Ohakea Aerodrome** that year. Races still take place there, for at one of its 40th Jubilee events in **April 1990** in Race 5 for Open Sports Cars and Specials, the Jupiters of Neil Moore (167) with its ex-Pacific Spot R1 engine, and Ian Leighton (286) saw action. In **1964** in a Le Mans-start **Waimate 50** 'round the houses' road race Vic Morrison (in the Jaguar-eater 182) was leading his class on lap 30 when power fell due to a stretched exhaust valve blamed on the use of aviation fuel. The exploits of Vic and some other New Zealanders

Jim Miller (192) in action in 1993 at The Monterey Historic Automobile Races at Laguna Seca Raceway. (Jim Miller)

are covered in Chapter 6. Jupiters were raced by Sid Bradford (219), Les Gourdie (448) and later Len Howman in the same car; and in the 1990s Les raced the entirely-rebuilt Jupiter 27.

In the 2000s Barry Emms was racing his Richard Mead Jupiter (249). John Holloway raced and rallied his red Jupiter (454) from the mid-1990s to the mid-2000s in events like Dunedin's **Southern Festival of Speed** for classic and historic vehicles, the **Ruapuna Raceway** being a favourite as well as the **Summit Road Hillclimb** near Sumner, Christchurch. Neil Moore continued to compete in his Jupiter (167) through to 2014 and beyond, concentrating on the North Island events at Pukekohe, Timaru, the Whenuapai Airbase, Hampton Downs, the Dunedin street races, Manfield – where in 2014 after four years of trying he cracked a lap time of 1m50s by setting a race lap a tad faster at 1m49.8s.

Vic Morrison, after successfully racing his original Jupiter (182) in the early to mid-1960s sold his Jupiter for a Javelin. But then in 1982 he bought the remains of a CD Bradford, CD2, and set about building a sports body for it, very Jupiter-like, something Jowett could have done, which he named CDR3. In the late 1980s Vic began racing it in Historic events around the South Island re-living earlier times in his Jupiter. The CDR3 was quite competitive and he had fun racing it through the 1990s.

The Australians also entered Jupiters in motor sport as early as 1952 – see Chapters 5 and 6. The Duckett Special (69) was built by Tasmanian Lyndon Duckett into a lightweight stripped sports-racer; he raced it a few times but it was laid up in 1956 following a burst top hose whilst racing at Albert Park, Melbourne. Ed Wolf bought it in 2002 and brought it up to Australian historic racing specification, and has used it in historic competition, its first outing in Ed's hands being on 26th January 2004.

The **1994 Targa Tasmania** was from **27 April** to **1 May**. A commentator wrote in the *Targa Times*: "For many enthusiasts who can remember that far back, Joe Caudo's 1951 Jupiter is what a real sports car should look like. And despite its age the Jupiter handles like the giants of today..."

Joe Caudo's Jupiter (422) won its class and was awarded the Targa Trophy in this 'Ultimate TT' seeing off a 1959 and a 1960 Porsche 356.

In addition to Joe Caudo, Doug Rath (431) just does

Neil Moore (167) in a street race, where even strawberries were on offer! (Vic Morrison)

Targa Tasmania 1994. Joe Caudo (422) going for it, with Christine Caudo navigating. (Bill Forsyth)

Doug Rath (431) takes a hairpin at a Leyburn Sprint. (CJ)

single-car sprints such as Queensland's **Leyburn Historic Sprints** in which his highest place was second in class.

Other competition work was carried out by Ed Wolf in his two Jupiters (69, 72) as described above, and also by Neil Hood (205). Tasmanian Paul Byrne (440) did a **Targa Tasmania** event in 2009; in the tour class he won the 'Best Classic' award. And Ed Wolf did a number of regularity runs and for the last 10 years there were always five or six entries per year at Wakefield Park at the **Golden Era Auto Racing Club** events.

In **1972** the North-East section of the Jowett Car Club UK encouraged all Jowetts to enter a series of competitive events which would take place principally but not entirely in their region of the UK; some events were sufficiently well attended for a Jowett class to be instigated for 'Team Northern'. My grateful thanks are to Geoff McAuley and Mike Smailes for their excellent *Jowett Sport* publications covering all this although here is just summarised the Jupiter component. In **1973** there were 11 events including hillclimbs for historics at **Castle Howard**, **Scammonden**, **Harewood** and **Baitings Dam**. Geoff McAuley (947) was generally quickest in these – even faster than the R1 in its first appearances after its initial reconstruction, usually driven by Roger Barrett. Other competitors in Jupiters were Mike Smailes (650) who was class-winner at the **Baitings Dam** climb in 1973, Pete

Crosby (898), Dave Marshall (242), Pete Dixon (876), Ken Lees (1013) and Ian Dearie in 1975 driving (30). Other events included races at **Snetterton**, **Ingliston** and **Oulton Park**. Mike Smailes historic-raced at **Snetterton** to a class second and at **Ingliston** to a class win.

For **1975** the Jupiters were joined by Frank Woolley (858) and Tony Fewster (913). Frank, Pete Dixon and Geoff McAuley raced at **Silverstone**, whilst there were sprints at **Croft** and **Curbrough**. Also **Castle Howard**, **Baitings Dam**, **Scammonden** and **Harewood** were visited with Geoff (when in his Jupiter) usually the fastest, while there was a race at **Silverstone** and at **Brands Hatch** for Pete Dixon and he also ascended **Prescott**. At a **Castle Howard** timed ascent in March the order was Ian Dearie, Geoff McAuley (Javelin), Pete Crosby and Tony Fewster – but in October at the same venue the order was Geoff McAuley now in his Jupiter, Ken Lees, Kathy Watson in Ken's Jupiter, and Tony Fewster. In **May 1975** at **Silverstone**, Frank Woolley was fastest Jupiter at class 3rd in a 5-lap handicap race ahead of Geoff McAuley and Pete Dixon whilst in a scratch race Geoff was the fastest Jupiter just ahead of Frank and then Pete. At the end of the season Pete Crosby raced in the HSCC Historic at **Ingliston**.

The **1976** season saw the same sort of events entered with four Jupiters in action at the **Harewood** Hillclimb and again four in an 8-Clubs **High Speed Trial** at **Silverstone** where Geoff McAuley won a first class award, with second class awards to Frank Woolley and Pete Dixon. At **Castle Howard** in April Ken Lees was the fastest Jupiter with Kathy Watson only 1sec slower still ahead of Tony Fewster; while at the same venue in October Geoff won his class, setting a record at 36.78sec ahead of Ken Lees, Tony Fewster and Kathy Watson. Historic racing continued with, in **1983**, **Harewood**, **Scammonden**, **Castle Donington** and **Snetterton** attended; at the **Harewood** hillclimb in June the class order was McAuley first, Smailes second, and with Ian Dearie (860) and Mike Chevers (652) also running. At the HSCC **Snetterton** event in October Geoff (947) was first in class with Mike Smailes third – Geoff McAuley in his lightened, tuned

Mike Smailes airborne in a Coronation Rally. (C Taylor)

Jupiter (known from its colour as 'The Brown Bomber' in a tilt to the legendary champion heavyweight boxer Joe Louis) was normally pre-eminent closely followed by Mike Smailes.

In the first **Coronation Rally**, of **August 1983**, with Geoff navigating, Mike drove this difficult rally over rugged Welsh terrain to finish a very hard-fought second in a class of 12. In July 1985 no less than five Jupiters contested the **Harewood** Hillclimb: Geoff McAuley, Mike Smailes, Frank Woolley, Malcolm Oliver (723) and Tony Fewster. In **August 1985**, the **Coronation Rally** entrants included four standard Jupiters and the R4 registered SWT 356. The Jupiter of Malcolm Oliver and Mike McKenna (723) placed class sixth, Ian Pritchett drove the R4 to fifth place, a mere one second behind the fourth-placed car. Third was Mike Smailes while Geoff McAuley with his son Richard navigating took the class. Again, at the end of the season, Pete Crosby raced in the HSCC Historic event at the **Ingliston** circuit.

The **1989** season began on **30th April** with the **Synter Series** of races at **Brands Hatch**: in the pre-1955 class of up to 2-litres Mike Smailes finished first with Frank Woolley second; while in the equivalent race at **Donnington** on June 11th Mike Smailes placed second with Mike Oliver third. On 24th June in the **Cumbrian Classic Caper** Mike won his class at sixth overall out of

85 entrants. In August there was another **Coronation Rally** where the Rochale-bodied Jupiter of Wally Dale finished fourth in class. At the **Curborough Sprint** of **October** the Jowett order was Geoff McAuley first, this time in his Javelin, followed by the Jupiters of Malcolm Oliver and Wally Dale. The season ended on **8th October** with 8-Clubs races at **Silverstone**, with Keith Clements (841), Mike Oliver and Wally Dale in Jupiter action, Keith earning a first class award in a High Speed Trial.

Competition in France: as we have seen in an earlier chapter, Jupiter 17 took part in the 1951 Monte Carlo crewed by R Thévenin and G Campion. The car was found in 1972 by Antoine Dominguez of Montauban and he had it professionally restored. He historic-raced it at **Angoulême** in Charente, SW France, and also in **May 1993** at the **Circuit Paul Armanac**, Nogaro, in the Midi-Pyrénées.

In 2009 it was sold to Cédric Purgue of St Sulpice, Gironde, who amongst other events took part in the **Vignes et Virages Rally** in Bordelais, in the Bordeaux region, on **2–3 April 2011**, and in **2012** the 3-day **Rallye des Bastides** in the Perigord.

Mike Chevers moved to Limoges, France in 2004 with

Circuit Paul Armanac Nogaro May 1993. Antoine Dominguez (17) in action. (CJ)

his Jupiter (652) a well-restored running car, and he used in competition there including two local rallies 2007-2008 and in street races at the **Circuit des Ramparts d'Angoulême**.

The 10-day **Classic Marathon** to Marrakesh in Morocco over **5-14 September 1998** was very much not for the faint-hearted! Keith Clements drove his Jupiter (841) and his daughter Amy navigated. Modifications included an overdrive and non-standard stronger wheels. The competitors drove from time control to time control within set times and to avoid penalties should not arrive early or late. The route took the participants from the Versailles start across France via the Massif Central, during which run the Jupiter sheared a trunnion bolt locating one of the front torsion bars; this meant driving quite some distance with reduced steering and brakes until with difficulty and after several efforts it was fixed. Then it was the ascent to Andorra and across the Pyrenees into Spain, where they had a puncture, then past Gibraltar to Algeciras for the short ferry trip across the straits to Tangier in Morocco for their fourth night stop, having driven about 1250 difficult miles in less than three days.

Amy Clements did most Classic Marathon navigation but 20% of the driving too, in all countries. (Clements)

For the first day in Morocco there were four very tight Regularity tests back to back and a tough and twisty 270-mile drive across two mountain ranges, the Rif and the Middle Atlas, for the night halt at Ifrane, a Moroccan ski resort no less.

With careful navigating by Amy and hard driving by Keith they managed to clean many of the tests in spite of brake fade problems. They now headed south across the High Atlas mountains through the Gorges du Ziz with the vast expanse of the Sahara ahead of them, when a mysterious gearbox problem struck – no oil in it! This Keith found was caused by the reverse gear shaft emerging from the casing to let out the oil; it was jury-rigged back in place to allow completion of the rally. There were timed tests on stony tracks leading into the desert amongst the Sahara dunes, with flying sand making navigation difficult and leading to the cancellation of a special test there. The night stop was at Erfoud where many of the cars, not just the Jupiter, were worked on.

There was now some very lively desert driving to the touristic Berber town of Ouarzazate. The next day's early start took the competitors along a twisty precipitous road through the incredible 100km Tizi-n-Tichka Gorge to reach Marrakesh soon after midday on Saturday 12th September. Then Sunday turned out to be the hardest day in Morocco, with a 315-mile drive along the length of the Middle Atlas Mountains, ending in a tortuously tight section through a pine forest shortly before the finish back at the ski resort of Ifrane. The Jupiter now lost the use of overdrive and there were electrical faults to deal with, as well as health problems as it turned out the bottled water everyone had drunk was of dubious origin.

On the Monday morning there was a non-competitive run back to Tangier for a buffet supper and prize-giving. The Jupiter in the Historic Sports Car Class (pre 1965 and less than 1650cc) was the oldest car in its group, finishing behind four MGAs and three Porsche 356s to place class 7th which was 38th overall out of 77 starters, but they did place a very creditable 9th overall in the 13 special tests having been joint first in eight of them. Keith received the Ancient Marathoneer award. They then crossed back to

Continued after Picture Gallery, page 133

Picture Gallery

Left: The Queen's Golden Jubilee celebrations in 2002 included a parade in London of 1952 cars. (CJ)

Below: A few of of the Jupiters at JOAC's Hetherset meeting of 2011. Extreme right: John and Sue Powter with their Richard Mead Jupiter (34). (CJ)

The Jupiter (126) of Jaak Jacobs at a 2013 classic car event at Zolder, Belgium. (Jacobs)

Pat Locker's Farina Jupiter (109) at a Goodwood classic car event in 2011. (Lockyer)

Left: Jupiters attending a classic car gathering in northern France in 2012. (CJ)

Below left: Claude Bernard at an event at Zolder, Belgium. (CB)

Below right: Cédric Purge in France with early Jupiter (17). (CP)

The Nankivell Jupiter (521) touring Scotland in 2007. (CJ)

Next generation Jupiter owner in the making! (Greg Jackson)

Jim Miller with Stars & Stripes (816) all the way from California to Pitlochry, Scotland, in 2000. (Scott Renner)

The Jupithon at Croft. In September 2012 a relay of some 30 Jupiters celebrated the London Olympic games by travelling about 1300 miles around the UK bearing a flag transferred at each of 25 stages rather like the Olympic torches. The white car is Fishburn's Jupiter Mk2. The Jupithon was completed with no hold-ups at all! (Peter Welch)

Prototype Jupiter (5) of Pat Lockyer, superbly
restored and running again by 2000. (Lockyer)

The lightweight very fast Jupiter (917) of Richard Gane at
Spa in 2014. (Richard Gane)

July 29th 1992 Edmund & Ghislaine Nankivell in their Jupiter (521) on
their way from Lewes to Brighton. (Peter Dixon)

Dr A Wijesurendra and his Jupiter (882) being exercised in Sri Lanka.
(Asoka Wijesurendra)

Left: West Africa 1955: some roads John Doran drove on were nothing more than grassy muddy tracks. Right: John Doran's Jupiter (458) at Bobo Dioulasso with French army officers. (Doran)

Spain, a luxurious hotel night stop and the long drive back to England.

This was not the first foray of a Jupiter in Africa, for back in 1955 Lt John Doran, on returning home from a spell with the British Army in West Africa, dared to drive his Jupiter, which he had bought in 1952 in Accra, all the way back to Blighty across, he hoped in vain, the Sahara desert.

But because permissions were not forthcoming, he instead started north from Accra via Lawra in NW Ghana then crossed into what were then the French territories of the Upper Volta.

John stayed at French army bases in Leo, Ouagadougou near the Sahara, then turning westward to Bobo Dioulasso, then into Sikasso in present-day Mali, then Bamako on the river Niger before finding his way to Dakar on the Senegal Atlantic coast. It was then a boat-trip to Marseilles and a drive across France to a Channel port and back to Blighty. His African mileage had been about 2000 with only one serious breakage, to a steering component, repaired thanks to the well-equipped workshop of a French-Canadian missionary just before reaching Ouagadougou.

For the Jupiter's 50th Le Mans anniversary in 2000 no less than 40 Jupiters gathered at Le Mans to attend the 24-hour race. One of the 1951 Le Mans 'standard' Jupiters, the well-restored Bert Hadley car (131), was given pride of place in the display of the Automobile Club de l'Ouest (ACO), and no less a figure was with us than Gordon Wilkins, who with Becquart had won the class in 1951 in the sister Jupiter (132) of the car on show. Jupiters came from the UK of course but also Holland, Belgium, Denmark, and even USA Jupiters were with us – notably Jim Miller and Scott Renner in Jim's Jupiter with its very special bumper-to-bumper 'Stars and Stripes' paintwork. This was the first of three 'Jupitours' to France organised by Ghislaine Nankivell. The 2003 Loire Valley Jupitour toured to Amboise, Chenonceux, and Blois where there was *Son et Lumiére* and a dinner at which Leonardo da Vinci paid us a visit, then on to Le Mans where we visited the ACO museum and drove some of the circuit before returning home. For the Alsace/Black Forest 20-Jupiter Jupitour in 2006 they visited Verdun taking in the amazing Franco/German 90th anniversary 'light and flames' evocation of the WW1 Verdun battle, then on to Titisee in the Black Forest before Alsace where some enjoyed folk-dancing and exploration whilst others went to the National Car Museum at Mulhouse to see amongst other exhibits the Schlumpf Bugatti collection. Then it was to Sedan and back home.

In 2012 Keith Clements and Scott Renner audaciously drove Keith's Jupiter (841) to no fewer than 13 countries and 12 capitals for an amazing 3750 miles in 21 days in aid of cancer research – and you may have read about the 1998 Classic Marathon earlier in this Chapter.

The talented Jupiter man Keith Clements had bought his 1952 Jupiter (841) in 1969 when a university student. It immediately needed engine and other work which he did – his introduction to Jupiter ownership and maintenance! It was used as his only transport for many years, for going to work, for holidays, even towing a Campervan whilst his daughter Amy grew up into a Jupiter owner in her own right. Then it was prepared for racing and rallying.

Keith's Jupiter had performed very well on some difficult summer rallies such as the 1989 Pirelli Marathon and winter rallies such as the three **LeJogs** of **1994–96**. His Jupiter has been on the road all its life and never been rebuilt, just repaired or fettled for performance and reliability. Keith's wife Jenny died of cancer late in 2011, and it was also 60 years since the Jupiter was made, and with 15 Jowetts going to Denmark he decided to extend that trip to aid cancer research, promote the marque and have a holiday. Scott Renner of California, Jupiter owner/ restorer/racer himself, decided to join Keith.

The intrepid pair started in London and travelled via France to Brussels to the Atomium, with a stopover at a Jupiter owner's house. Next day they went via Amsterdam to The Hague to see the International Court. After lunch with a Dutch Jowett owner, they went on to stay at a Jupiter owner's house in Northern Germany for maintenance and a few modifications to the transmission. The next day was spent in convoy with a Jupiter from Belgium and a 1930 Jowett from Holland spending the night just north of Hamburg where more modifications were required to the propshaft midship supports.

Then on to Denmark to meet a Jowett Bradford van driven all the way from Finland and the other Jowetts including a 1928 two-seater from Devon plus some Javelins and Jupiters. Then at Copenhagen they found the cause of their problems, a broken overdrive support plate; so a new plate was made.

Next they crossed by ferry into Sweden and Stockholm to spend the day mainly in the Vassa museum, before catching the ferry to Finland. They then drove up country to see a new Jupiter owner and help him rebuild and fire up his engine. They saw an amazing collection of cars and a private collection of a few thousand car badges before going to Naantalii for a sea cruise to a private island for two days.

Then it was to Helsinki, staying the night with Jowett friends, before taking the ferry to Tallinn in Estonia to meet a local car magazine journalist who guided them to see the Russian prison for a photo-shoot, then to a car rebuilder in Viimsi and a meal at the yacht club. The next day it was south to Parnu to their motel and to meet two classic car enthusiasts and watch the first race on the new

Scott Renner and Keith Clements outside the Helsinki Olympic Stadium built for the 1952 Games. (Clements)

Audru track, where there was some exciting superbike and sidecar racing Estonian and Latvian style.

They then crossed into Latvia and down to Riga to visit another car restorer and the car museum there. From the museum, after six hours driving, they arrived with a minute to spare for their appointment at the Vilnius Rotary club. They then visited the fabulous private collection of vehicles of a Lithuanian rally ace followed by a tour of the very beautiful city given by local car journalist. Some bodywork damage was sustained by a reversing van, but without delaying the plucky Jupiter men by too much the front suspension was fixed with the help of a plastic coffee cup. They then entered Poland across an unmade road carefully aiming between Belarus and that bit of Russia encircling Kalingrad. After a night in Augustow it was the long drive to Warsaw then to their hotel in Lotz which turned out to be a fairy-tale and horror-movie residence!

Then to Berlin where they visited the Brandenburg Gate – braving arrest by taking the Jupiter into the smoke-free city centre. Next it was south past Leipzig before going west leaving the drizzle of the north behind, stopping over in a castle on the top of Wettenberg.

Now the Jupiter's water pump decided to develop a leak and the battery lost charge but they carried on and made it to Bonn, then Nurburgring, then Luxembourg, then into Belgium to Spa and a quick visit to Jupiter owner Jaak Jacobs and a well-earned meal in his hometown Peer. They left the restaurant to find a flat tyre, but help was at hand from three Jowett owners.

The final day saw an end to their gastronomic tour at a patisserie in Dunkirk before the ferry and Tower Bridge in the wake of the London Olympic celebrations, then home.

The **Le Mans Classic** of **4–6 July 2014** saw two quick Jupiters in action. This is quite a strenuous event on the standard Le Mans circuit. Of the six classes (the organisers described each 'class' as a 'plateau') which ranged from 1923 to 1979 with no engine-capacity breaks, the Jupiter's plateau was 1949 to 1956, which

Richard Thorne in the 2010 Le Mans Classic. (RMC-CARS)

meant they were mixing it with C- and D-Type Jaguars, Mercedes 300SL, Austin Healeys, Allards and the like, whilst in the up to 1500cc capacity range were Lotus XI, Porsche 356, Keift MG and some very fast but tiny DB Panhards (the 'clockwork mice'). The two Jupiters were the blue car of Richard Gane and John Arnold (917) with engine work by Dave Harris which had already raced successfully at Silverstone in 2013 and 2014, and the green car of Richard Thorne and Roger Whiteside (921) which had raced at the **Classic Le Mans** in **2010** where, due to superior handling, it had finished his one race ahead of some Porsche 356s.

The **2014 Classic Le Mans** timetable was:– Day 1 Qualification and Night Practice, then on Day 2 a daylight race of about ¾-hour duration, then on Day 3 a night race in the wee small hours followed by another race in the morning. Richard Gane (917) qualified at an average speed of 99 mph with his best lap 103 mph (hitting 120 mph down the Mulsanne he said), faster than half his class including five Jaguars, four Austin Healeys, a trio of Porsche 356s, and a TR2 (in many ways the nearest type of car to the Jupiter in the event), while the Whiteside/ Thorne Jupiter (921) qualified at 82 mph, a best lap 83mph.

In the night practice session Richard Gane averaged 72¼ mph, faster than 43% of his class including five

Jupiter (841) at Berlin's Brandenburg Gate. (Clements)

Richard Gane's Jupiter (left) with Richard Thorne's Jupiter in the pits at Le Mans, July 2014. Keith Clements waving. (Noel Stokoe)

an OSCA and a Lotus Sebring. The Whiteside/Thorne Jupiter finished seven places below Gane at 50.2 mph yet by any standard, a very good all-round performance by the two Jupiters at the famous Sarthe circuit. Races followed at venues like Spa Francorchamps, Goodwood, Silverstone and more.

Scott Renner races each May in California at Sonoma (used to be Sears Point, then Infinion). For the 2015 event he wrote: *"Managed to catch a couple of faster guys and then used the handling in the corners to open gap. They'd catch me just at the esses, and then I would walk away through the curves. Tons of fun!"*

* * * * *

Jaguars, three Aston Martins and a couple of Porsche 356s. Richard Thorne's Jupiter finished practice faster than 11 bigger-engined cars including three Jaguars.

The racing involved a pit-stop to change drivers after 30 minutes driving. In **Race 1** The Roger Whiteside/Richard Thorne Jupiter finished ahead of 40% of the field at 9th in the up to 1500cc group, averaging 65mph, ahead of 30 cars including three Porsche and four Jaguars and the 2-litre TR2 crewed by Mestrot/Da Rocha. The Richard Gane/John Arnold Jupiter did not finish this race thanks to an electrical supply problem to its fuel pump, but in **Race 2** (the night race) at 64.7 mph they finished ahead of more than half the field of 65, behind just 7 of up to 1500cc cars and 4 seconds ahead of the Noyer/Dierick TR2. Richard Thorne's Jupiter finished another 17 places down but still ahead of 17 including four Austin Healeys, two of Morgan +4 and two Jaguars. In **Race 3**, with the track very wet from a thunderstorm, the Gane/Arnold Jupiter finished further up the field at 21 out of 66, averaging 57 mph, seeing off amongst others a Kieft-MG, two DB-Panhards, four Porsche 356s, even

How many Jupiters were built by Jowett?
The factory assembled 733 Mk1 and 94 Mk1a complete Jupiters = 827 standard Jupiters.

A net total of 74 driveable rolling chassis were delivered to coachbuilders, so a total of 901 Jupiters of both forms left the Jowett Factory between 1950 and 1954.

We can add the Mk1a Jupiter registered VWF 99 which was privately assembled from genuine components on an un-numbered Jupiter chassis before July 1958. This makes 828 standard Jupiters made as new cars. Then there is the Mk6 Rochdale-bodied Jupiter built by an enthusiast also on an un-numbered frame, registered JST 53 by 1955. So with the two new cars constructed outside the factory, the total becomes 903 Jupiters.

Furthermore, Jowett constructed the three Jupiter R1s on Eberhorst Jupiter frames (Jowett's very own special-bodied Jupiters!) so it can be argued that we did have an overall maximum of 905 Jupiters of all types.

This is where things get complicated, because three of the Rolling Chassis shipments were given genuine standard coachwork outside the Works but in the era (chassis 27 in NZ and chassis 91 and 113 in GB), which makes the number of standard Jupiters that once existed total 891.

Now the three Jupiter R4s built by Jowett were on a different frame, of which two survive; they are not included in the totals given here – see Chapter 8.

Of the Rolling Chassis shipments (see Chapter 9) there have been 64 successfully identified as having been built but it is reasonable to assume almost all were actually bodied as it is known the Factory had taken back five unused rolling chassis and built them into complete standard Jupiters. Although the one rolling chassis that went to Australia (36) and the one to New Zealand (115) hung around for decades, they are currently being fitted with standard bodywork from other degraded or scrapped Jupiters.

But that is not the end of the story because a small

Les Gourdie in action in New Zealand with his Jupiter (27) in a classic car event. (Gourdie)

number of Jupiters that left the factory with standard bodywork have, in modern times following their degeneration, been fitted with special bodies.

And the reverse has happened with a small number of Jupiters that were originally fitted with special bodies have in modern times, following their degeneration, been fitted with standard Jupiter bodywork from other degraded Jupiters, or in couple of cases, partly new replica standard bodywork.

Last question – how many Jupiters are known to have survived?

Counting up Jupiters known to exist or Jupiters heard from since about 1995 or later, we have the following totals of survivors, including the few conversions from Special to Standard or the reverse:

» Standard Jupiters known to us as runners or generally in good order or known to be under restoration: total 275.
» Special-bodied Jupiters known to us as runners or generally in good order or known to be under restoration: total 40.
» Standard Jupiters stored, not as runners but believed restorable and generally complete or nearly so: total 88.
» Special-bodied Jupiters stored, not as runners but believed restorable and generally complete or nearly so: total 7.

So the grand total of standard Jupiters believed to exist either as runners or restorable totals 363 which is 44% of production, while the total of special-bodied Jupiters believed to exist either as runners or restorable stands at 47 which is 63% of their manufacture.

This gives us the total of all Jupiters known to us still in existence both types = 410 plus the single remaining R1 = 411 all told, which is over 45% of production.

Yet there could be a few more awaiting discovery as Jupiters survive well!

8: History of the R4 Jupiters

The year 1953 began with much wailing and gnashing of teeth at Jowett, for in January the last few Javelin and Bradford bodies were received from the Briggs Doncaster factory. A lathering of snow coated a large number of unbuilt Javelin bodies stored to the side of the Jowett plant – would Briggs ever restart the flow when more were needed? As British Ford tightened its grip on the British arm of Briggs, the American-owned car body-building firm, Jowett's Experimental Department were informed that a new sports car, if ready in time for the Motor Show that next October, might save the Company. It would have to be cheap, easy to make and not require the services of Briggs. Much midnight oil was burned and by March 1953 it had been styled by Phil Stephenson, the inspiration probably being the Ferrari 166 MM Barchetta of Carozzeria Touring of Milan; by no means a plagiarism, rather it was an original and well-developed variation. The intention was to attack the MG Midget market.

This Jupiter R4, which we have already met in Chapters 5 and 6, had its origins in the so-called Mk2 Jupiter, a highly developed project under way at the very start of 1952. It used an 'attenuated' version of the Eberhorst

Jupiter frame as it was felt at Jowett that there were still sales and handling advantages to it. Very full detailed manufacturing drawings were produced showing lessons had been learned from the R1 Jupiter, and it was fully drawn up with its plasticine model made by the 21st of March 1952, showing that studying Italian designs seen at various Motor Shows had paid dividends, an example being the aforesaid Ferrari Barchetta by Touring of Milan seen at the 1949 Paris Motor Show and elsewhere. It was only natural, and to be expected, that having the Stabilimenti Farina FHC Jupiter (on chassis 7) dividing its time between the Jowett showroom and Jowett's Experimental Department would mean that Italian designs were inescapable.

The intensively-designed Mk2 Jupiter had by March 1952 its assembly drawings and Plasticine model photographed in Jowett's Experimental Department by C H Wood.

Three R4 Jupiters were built and ready for the 1953 Earls Court Motor Show:– for the stand, for the showroom, and for demonstration runs. The photo opposite was taken on 10th July 1953 in the Experimental Department.

Touring of Milan 1949 Ferrari 166 MM. (R M Auctions)

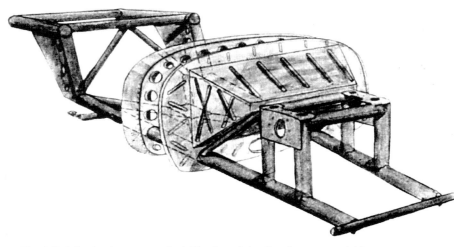

The Mk2 Jupiter's attenuated Eberhorst Jupiter frame would have looked like this, with its R1-type stress panel. (C H Wood)

Plasticine model of the proposed Mk2 Jupiter. (C H Wood)

R4 Jupiter No 1 completed by July 1953. (C H Wood)

The Mk2 Jupiter on its Eberhorst frame accurately built to Jowett's drawings by the skilled panel-man Allan Fishburn, and put on the road in 2012. (CJ)

Donald Bastow was now Chief Engineer and he had overall responsibility of the R4 project, but with the departure of Grandfield and Korner it was Roy Lunn who provided the biggest contribution. Now Donald Bastow, a brilliant engineer, after obtaining a first-class honours degree in mechanical engineering at University College, London, had been with Rolls-Royce where in 1933 he designed the first independent front suspension system fitted to an R-R. He told me he always preferred a small company so it is such a shame he did not join Jowett a year or two earlier. His prime task at Jowett was to design-out the many engineering problems which had been hanging around for some time as well as others that were beginning to show up. At the same time Frank Salter had re-joined Jowett as Technical Director with a similar brief to sort out production problems. Roy Lunn was proving to be a natural engineer, a very forceful sometimes impulsive character who was good at getting things done in a hurry. He provided a lot of ideas but still needed Bastow's guiding hand.

Work on the new design, for the future of Jowett, began in April 1952 and the highly skilled Experimental staff showed their worth, often making parts before they were drawn up! Designer-draughtsman PhilStephenson told me that, in full spate, he once completed no less than 47 separate drawings in a single 24-hour period. Wherever possible, elements from the CDs were incorporated as they were fully developed and tooled and it was still hoped that CD production would yet take place.

The R4 chassis was formed from box-section fabrications of exceptional depth, further reinforced by a welded-on scuttle and tail panel, the complete assembly having greater stiffness than the Jupiter Mk1 design yet being lighter. It was cart-sprung at the rear but retained the transverse torsion bars at the front as for the CD range of utility, van, pick-up and 2-door saloonall on their same chassis. Many years later Vic Morrison, the highly gifted Jowett enthusiast in New Zealand, built a very attractive Jupiter-like sports car on a CD chassis (his 'CDR3'), which Jowett might well have thought of! The R4 was

Underside of the first R4 Jupiter showing the overdrive and finned aluminium sump. This is the only period photo of the R4 chassis that I could find. Taken in the Experimental Department's workshop in August 1953, part of Jowett's 1950 Le Mans pit sign can be seen in the background on the right. (C H Wood)

intended to achieve 100mph, which it did, just! So initially 'Jupiter 100' was to be its name, later 'Jupiter R4' was chosen.

Phil Stephenson told me that it was one Friday in early spring of 1953 that the Experimental department's monthly staff's pay-cheques bounced, and although the matter was quickly settled Phil took the hint and during June he left. George Green the Sales manager, visiting the

USA that same month, had photographs of the R4 with him, and reported back that many could be sold there.

Since initially the new car was to be called the 'Jupiter 100' the first R4 is chassis 100/1 being registered JKW 537 in July 1953, and on the 10th of that month was photographed with 148 miles on its odometer and only aeroscreens fitted. It was being prepared for its continental proving run to be driven by Roy Lunn with Teddy Fannon as riding mechanic. Six weeks later it was again photographed having returned from France and Italy; its bonnet, now straightened after an incident in the latter country, was louvred, the gearbox now had an overdrive attached and 4766 miles were showing on the odometer.

Cockpit of the R4 after the fitting of the overdrive. The switch to the right of the steering wheel sounds the horn when tilted in any direction. (C H Wood)

This first R4, JKW 537, had its body entirely made from steel, but Lunn had other ambitions. When it became clear that Briggs were looking for ways to shed its commitment to Jowett, the Experimental Department looked into the use of "fabric reinforced plastic" for Javelin door and boot panels (an all-FRP Javelin was not,

however, contemplated). It was not fibreglass (fibreglass, or GRP – Glass Reinforced Polyester – was discovered in the late 1940s but not widely adopted until the mid-1950s). This FRP was very novel; it was a locally-made material supplied by Automold Plastics Ltd of Lancashire but experiments showed that this new material had highly inflammable vapours, the resins were not self-colourable and, taking days to cure, could and sometimes did self-ignite while curing. The finished product did not take paint readily and the paint would craze, only minimised by choosing white or near-white. It was brittle and inflammable, and could splinter and fragment on impact.

Undaunted, Jowett took the decision to use this material for the entire fronts of the two pre-production R4s, and all-night sessions laying up FRP for these cars bore fruit: panels from JKW 537 were used for moulds, but since they had not been originally designed for mould-work, it sometimes took many men to pull the mouldings off. Soon there were three R4 Jupiters, and a hardtop was made and fitted to JKW as was the new bonnet emblem for up to then an RAC badge had sufficed.

On the day in October that the 1953 Earls Court Motor Show opened, photographs of the prototype appeared in the *Manchester Guardian*, the *Daily Mail*, the *Daily Mirror* and the *Evening News*; Bastow and Lunn drove it south and Phill Green gave demonstration runs through London's streets. On the Jowett stand, attracting a lot of comment, stood one of the newer R4s: ivory with blue upholstery. Its electric cooling fan was noted, as was the change from rack-and-pinion to cam-and-lever steering. The R4 was awarded second place in a Sports Coachwork competition (below £800 division) to the TR2, with the MG TF third. It was the lowest-priced 100mph car at the show at £773 4s 2d after tax.

The third R4, Dove Grey with red interior, went to Jowett's Albemarle Street showroom, but apparently its dust sheets were never removed!

On 25 October 1953 JKW was tested by journalists at the Goodwood Test day, wearing its hardtop and full windscreen. On 13 November the Scottish Motor Show opened; although an R4 made the journey it was

Earls Court: Sir Edmund Hillary, who five months earlier had become the first man to ascend Everest, with his wife tries out the R4.
(Press Association)

Prototype Jupiter R4 engine bay. (C H Wood)

neither listed in the catalogue nor accompanied by any explanatory literature. So some folk at Jowett were seemingly not fully convinced the Jupiter R4, or Jowett for that matter, had a car-making future. The R4 chassis was based on the CD van chassis, as was the suspension. The pressed steel chassis supporting a 'cart-sprung' rear end was definitely a backward step from the Eberhorst chassis of the original Jupiter which set new standards of handling to make these cars still a joy to drive decades after conception.

By 1953's end Jowett were virtually no longer car makers although 28 Mk1a Jupiters were to be built and sold in 1954. Through the Briggs connection Ford head-hunted Roy Lunn and his illustrious career took a new turn when he joined Ford in January 1954 to design the 105E Anglia. He had his regrets for he was sure, he told me, that the R4 was a winner.

R4 Jupiter with ragtop. (C H Wood)

There was still some unfinished business: the soft top to be fitted to the Show car; this was carried out and a photographic session followed on Christmas Eve 1953.

A little development work continued after Roy Lunn's departure and this included a speed check on JKW by John Brace at MIRA. The 0-60 time of 12.6 seconds was obtained, and with the windscreen removed the 100mph mark was just achieved. JKW was then loaned to Frank Masefield-Baker of Ovingdean near Brighton for evaluation. Frank, who later served time as Brighton's mayor, had driven a Works Javelin in the 1953 Monte and he was instructed to use the car and report. He told me it was a bit rough with odd wiring everywhere (it was the prototype after all) but he thought it a 'cracking little motor car' and took it up to its maximum speed, an indicated 114mph, every time he went out in it.

Jowetts meanwhile temporarily forgot that Masefield-Baker had the car! Sometime in 1954 they wrote to him asking for it back as they had a buyer for it in the person of Alf Thomas of the Central Garage, Kempston, Bedford whose plans for the car centred on the club racing scene at Silverstone near him, as well as other events. Alf had crashed his first Jupiter, the Rawson-bodied JTM 100 (38) within a week or two of collecting it in 1951 and brushing with the Grim Reaper, a broken rib puncturing a lung. Nevertheless he continued to drive JTM 100 at Silverstone up to 1953 but with the acquisition of the R4 his son Barry would drive the light, fast but tail-happy earlier car although also driving the R4 on occasion. The JTM story is covered elsewhere.

Eric Turner was the chairman of the Blackburn & General Aircraft Co based in Brough, about 50 miles east of Birstall to where Jowett had moved after the sale of their factory to International Harvester. Blackburn & General had taken over Jowett Cars Ltd as Jowett were making components for that firm when they were not looking after the postwar Jowetts. Turner took a liking to the R4 and consequently the Show car (chassis R4/1) was registered for him on 2 July 1956 – SWT 356 – and he is known to have driven it on occasion the 50 miles from Brough where he lived to

Birstall. In 1958 the car appeared in Birstall for a minor Isopon repair to the front, and for a check-over as it was to be put up for sale.

After the Motor Show in 1953 the third R4, the Albemarle Street car, disappeared, to reappear in dismantled form in 1958 for sale. The buyer for both this one and SWT was Alf Thomas, including enough parts to put the dismantled R4 into functioning condition. Alf himself and one of his mechanics assembled the third R4 making an exhaust system for it and having it ready just in time for the **Six-Hour Relay Handicap Race** of **16 August 1958**. There was no time to register the rebuilt car so it was driven to the circuit wearing HAK 365 plates. As we have seen, Alf owned this ex-Le Mans 1951 class winner at the time and indeed Anne Neale had been racing it. So Alf could field a team of three R4s for the race!

Howden Clough 1958, Alf Thomas buying an R4. (A Neale)

The competition history of the R4s in the hands of the Thomases can be found in Chapter 6: it is known that Alf was initially critical of JKW's sometimes unpredictable handling. His son Barry told me 'the R4's handling was good but you had to get to know them – then you could chop them around corners very fast'. The R4 would slide easily and once in a race at Silverstone Alf was seen to

Barry Thomas racing the first R4 at Silverstone. (CJ)

take his hands off the steering wheel on a corner for which he was black-flagged.

Inspection of race results shows that JKW was quite a competitive 1½-litre car at the time, often quicker round the Silverstone Club circuit than the 1½-litre MGA, and where Alf had managed the occasional lap at 65mph in 1954 this had risen to 68mph, sustainable for a 5-lapper by 1956/57, faster than the TR2s when they first appeared. By 1958 the R4 is believed to have been able to put in the occasional lap at about 1min 24sec, around 69mph; by comparison in 1956 a Lotus-MG's winning speed might be 67.3mph (though a year later the Lotus-Climaxes were a full 10mph faster). And in 1956 a 1½-litre MG TF might lap the Silverstone Club circuit at 1min 29sec (62.65mph), an MGA might return a best of 1min 26.6sec and a Healey Silverstone might manage 1min 29sec around the circuit that bears its name. By 1958 the MGAs were clocking typically a 69.6mph fastest with a 67.7mph race average. So Alf Thomas and the R4 JKW 537 with 69mph were still up there with best of them!

One race at **Crystal Palace** is known for Alf Thomas and JKW; believed to have been the **BRSCC** meeting of **10 June 1957**. Whereas the Production Sports Car event was won by a Lotus-Ford, an eyewitness said that the R4 'saw off the TR3s'.

The original R4 engines differed in various respects from standard Jupiter engines. A fundamental problem with the Javelin/Jupiter is that the cylinder head studs are mounted at the top of the aluminium crankcase while the liners are seated at the bottom. Since steel expands less than aluminium, as the engine warms up the nip of the head gasket reduces ever so slightly, leading to the possibility of gasket blow. Donald Bastow had an ingenious solution. First he experimented with Wills Rings which were used on the later R1s so that they could operate reliably at 9.25:1 compression ratio, but concluded they were too fiddly for production. So he devised finned aluminium sleeves for the liners which would be shrunk on. This meant that the liner was seated via aluminium and the differential expansion would be eliminated. However it was established that the

Albemarle Street R4 Jupiter reassembled from spares and subsequently sold to Peter Michael had Wills Rings seals.

Other changes included lowering the water pump and flanging it to the top of the front timing cover. The R4 with a wheelbase shorter by 9 inches than the standard Jupiter weighed in at 1568lb (710kg) making it a very useful 330lb (159kg) lighter. Compression ratio was raised to 8.5:1 compared with 7.6 or 8:1 for the standard Jupiter, and the camshaft was retimed so that maximum power occurred at higher revs giving 64bhp at 5,000rpm. Gearing in direct top gear at 16¾mph per 1000rpm gave a theoretical maximum speed of 102–105mph in the optional overdrive top gear.

The R4's gearbox casing is quite different from the Javelin and Jupiter unit and is of the design developed for the Javelin-engined version of the CD Bradford. It is a casting that is unit with the clutch bell-housing, although components inside are the same as the normal Javelin/ Jupiter box. This allowed a floor gearchange between the bucket seats.

A still un-concluded development of 1957 by Paul Emery (well-known then for his ingenious and successful front-wheel-drive Emeryson 500cc single-seaters) was not for a Jowett but was for a 1½-litre Formula 1 engine based on the Javelin/Jupiter engine block but with double overhead cam cylinder heads. The head patterns and the aluminium heads themselves were made by Louis Giron. Louis was a racing driver and engineer who back in 1954 had cleverly designed for John Willment a one-off all-alloy twin-cam four cylinder four-carburettor engine for an experimental 500cc single seater, and he went on to become Chief Engineer at the National Motor Museum at Beaulieu. His twin-OHC version of the Jowett engine with its four Amal carburettors immediately produced 100bhp measured at the flywheel (fuel injection was to follow) but the crankcase halves cracked across the tops leading to the project's abandonment. Paul Emery later told me that with some subtle welding he was sure he could have overcome that. The heads first went to Alf Thomas, and after more ownership changes the as yet still unused heads survive in Australia.

On show at a UK Jowett meeting: would-be Formula 1 twin-cam heads before shipment to Australia. (CJ)

Nevertheless, as has been noted elsewhere in the report on the 1958 Six-hour Relay race, Alf had a second encounter with the Grim Reaper when the nine Dzus fasteners holding down the R4's front-end panel let go, leaving him in the cornfield badly bruised, so ultimately and with much reluctance he decided to give up racing, and in February 1960 he advertised all three R4s for sale as 'the only three made before the sad end of production of Jowett cars'. They were offered in damaged state exactly as they were after that race. Alf's Jowett days were now over and he was to die of cancer six years later.

Jowett owner and enthusiast Peter Michael, a student at that time preparing for what would be a brilliant career in electronics for which he was later knighted (he was one of the inventors of digital television), sold his mother's car without her knowledge to raise the £1500 or so Alf would accept for the trio. One car was immediately prepared for Mrs Michael and she took over the all-metal prototype JKW 537, with engine in a lower state of tune minus its overdrive, to be re-registered 4488 BY to seem to be a modern car – but not before its front end had once again served as a mould for the new bonnet set needed for the crashed

The original R4 with its new registration, photo taken about 1963 in North West London. (CJ)

R4 that was soon to be sold wearing JKW 537 plates. Peter Michael then fitted the overdrive into the Show car SWT 356 and registered it in his own name in March 1961.

For the superstitious, bad luck runs in threes, for within three years all three R4s were destined for what for normal cars could have been terminal accidents. The first instance was the Albemarle Street car wearing JKW 537 plates sold on a nebulous sale-or-return basis to a Glaswegian named Iain McCaskill.

On driving the car back home Iain lost it in a big way on the A739 switch-back road towards Bearsden (six miles North West of Glasgow) notorious for burn-ups, wrapping the car around a lamp post and bending the chassis literally into a U-shape. McCaskill's insurance company argued that the car was not yet his and so was not their responsibility, and likewise Peter Michael's

maintained the car was de facto sold – such are the ploys of insurance companies! The Scottish Jowett spares man George Mitchell got hold of the engine, which had an unstamped plinth and Wills Rings liner seals and it was to go into his Javelin. The ruined R4 was stripped of all things saleable: some parts went to Scottish Jowett spares man Charlie Moar and maybe the logbook went back to Peter Michael while a few bits went onto Iain McCaskill's sister's boyfriend's saloon Jupiter (35); the gearbox went to SWT 356's new owner as a spare and so forth. Iain was the nephew of the Miss Kate Cranston of the very posh Willow Tea Rooms in Glasgow's Sauchiehall Street. His sister's boyfriend was Balfour Rombach who (allegedly) after being rumbled for running a phoney hire-purchase company was gaoled for five years.

After a year or so Mrs Michael sold the true JKW wearing 4488 BY (its logbook endorsed with "made up from spare parts" and giving the chassis as R4/2) and around 1962 it was in the Watford area where its tachometer failed; the makers, AC, reported it was one of only three prototypes. The car seems to have been in the NW9 area of London by 1963 although soon to be sold to the Midlands; it was this new owner who crashed the car. It then appeared at Owens of Oakengate near Telford having been rolled and 'written off' to be resuscitated by a perceptive scrap-metal dealer named R G Kurswell of Picklescott, Shropshire, who was obliged to run the R4 untaxed and uninsured (there was no logbook) until the law caught up with him. In 1971 the car was owned by one R N Thomas of Bristol, who had bought it from some college youths of Cardiff or Swansea. Sometime before 1979 it was in the ownership of one George Bird of Shropshire who began its restoration, and finding the 100/1 chassis stamping concluded this was the true JKW 537, so its original registration was returned to it. At the time of writing it is in the hands of Jowett enthusiast Simon Wood by whom it is largely more and carefully restored.

Last to go was SWT 356 which Peter Michael sold to Alan George who registered it in his name in January

Restored and running R4 when owned by Norman Reeves: photo taken near Beaulieu in 1989. (CJ)

1964 but in February, going too fast (the car was being joy-ridden) he heavily crashed it into a railway bridge near Coventry. Ray Brown was in the passenger seat with Javelin-man Gordon Timms crammed into the back. Ray was the librarian of the old Southern Jowett Car Club (SJCC). Both Ray and Gordon required hospitalisation and the wreck went under a tarpaulin in the yard of Jowett dealer Ken Braddock in Leighton Buzzard: its front-end in fragments.

Around March 1967 it was reported to me as "hardly recognisable as a car" when it was bought by Arthur Rutland of Northants, who noted its odometer read 43,437 miles. Arthur very slowly and carefully restored the car although many years would elapse before it again saw the light of day as Mr Rutland did not enjoy good health – nevertheless he gave the car his devoted attention, gradually and meticulously restoring it to the point at which it could be trailered to the 1979 Alexandra Palace Classic Car Show virtually completed.

Its photo was worthy enough for the front cover of *Thoroughbred and Classic Cars* of September 1979, taken at Arthur Rutland's place. Arthur died that same year and the car passed to others who completed its restoration and today it is a very fine running car.

For example in June 2008 its new (UK) owner Keith Patchett drove it to the Louwman Museum in The Hague, in the Netherlands, said to be the world's oldest private collection of old vehicles open to the public (cars, motorcycles and coaches), put together by two generations of the Louwman family.But just as JKW 537 will always be associated with Alf Thomas who developed it and raced it over those years, so SWT 356 should be associated with Arthur Rutland who took it on when no one else would consider it, and who was finally cheated of driving the car to which he had selflessly applied himself for so long. So, of the three R4s that there once were, we have one very well restored and running, and another in the process of being very well restored.

Abridged data for the R4 Jupiter, from the brochure dated October 1953:

Length 139in. Maximum width 62.5in
Overall height unladen 54in.
Wheelbase 84in. Track front 52in, rear 49in.
Turning circle 31ft
Steering wheel turns from lock to lock 2½
Ground clearance 7½in under chassis
Kerb weight 14cwt (1568lb)
Maximum engine power 65bhp at 5,000rpm
Final drive is 4.44:1
Pressed steel wheels 4J x 15-inch (instead of the standard Jupiter's 16-inch).
Proposed extra equipment:–
Laycock de Normanville overdrive
Detachable plastic coupé top
Aero screens, Radio, Heater, tonneau cover.

Colours offered were Dove Grey with red interior and black hood, and Ivory with blue interior and black hood.

Price in 1954 was given as £773 4s 2d including tax. Its pre-tax price was £545 compared with £555 for the TR2.

At 16¾mph per 1000rpm its expected top speed without overdrive could be 92mph at 5500rpm.

In October 1953 JKW 537 was accurately speed-tested at the Motor Industry Research Association (MIRA) test ground at Nuneaton. With its windscreen removed it was able to just exceed 100mph in overdrive top.

In the spring of 1954 an R4 graced the cover of the French magazine *l'Automobile* with an appropriately stylish lady at the wheel.

Phill Green who was in charge of the road test R4 at the 1953 Earls Court show reliably informed me that "thousands" of orders were taken for the R4 at the show and that, of course, they could not be honoured.

9: Special-bodied Jupiters: the Coachbuilders

Initially, Jupiter body manufacture was a slow process with the few complete cars built from around January 1951 being reserved for export, necessary in order to get the steel ration for the Javelin increased. But fully equipped rolling chassis were available to British and overseas buyers, and the fully dimensioned drawings for coachbuilders were available from April 1950. There were 75 rolling chassis shipped out between 11 August 1950 and 2 March 1953 with 55 shipped out by June 1951. The overall survival rate of 63% (even higher than the 44% for the standard product) says something about the regard even the least attractive were held by their owners over the years.

In total about 50 went to British coachbuilders. They vary from the elegant Abbotts, Meads, Rawsons, Coachcrafts and the like through some very good tries to some odd individual designs.Nevertheless one should not turn up one's nose at bodywork that in its way is representative of the types that were being fitted to many other chassis at that time – at bottom these designs express the feel of the immediate post-war era, times long gone. For that was a time when, in the motor industry at large, chassis-building capacity outstripped body-building capacity, and for a while there were opportunities for many small concerns, just, at the few-off level, on chassis such as Healey, Alvis, Lea Francis as well as Bristol and Bentley.

The Jowett Jupiter rolling chassis were mechanically complete and some were even road-tested over a 100-mile road course near the factory. Jowetts initially hoped that outside coachbuilders could contribute much Jupiter construction but it emerged that the bespoke market was rather marginal for a 2/3 seater with its 1500cc engine capacity. The chassis were shipped with the instruments, bumpers, electrical equipment including the wiring harness, and grilles which it was hoped the coachbuilder would use, or fit a grille pattern that hinted at the Jowett design. Jowetts asked that they should approve the bodywork in which case they would cover it for the then industry-standard six-month warranty period.

Aesthetically, the newer continental ideas varied in influence from wholesale lift (Adams & Robinson) through more or less indirect (KW, Coachcraft) to second or third hand or none at all (JJ Armstrong). And there were two

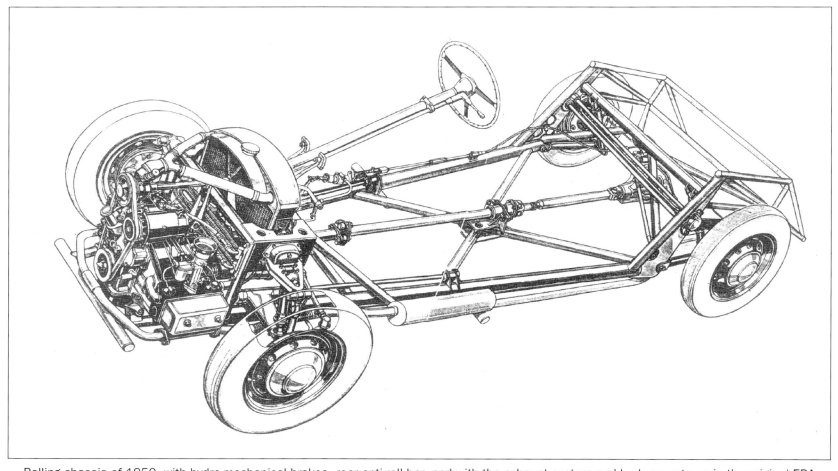

Rolling chassis of 1950, with hydro-mechanical brakes, rear anti-roll bar, and with the exhaust system and body mounts as in the original ERA form, but with tail structure for the fuel tank and spare wheel added. (LAT Photographic; drawing by Max Millar for *The Autocar*)

(Barnaby and Watling-Greenwood) which are a reminder that for the first 15 months Jupiters were for export only and the construction of near replicas could overcome this little local difficulty.

Three out of the four Swiss coachbuilders most active after WW2 built Jupiters, in fact they built bodies, mostly dropheads, on the majority of British cars with separate chassis, and of course on Fiat. As Switzerland was perhaps the healthiest European market at that time, there was enough custom to keep that handful of coachbuilders busy, although much of their bread-and-butter work was commercials. Only a few of them survived

into the 1960s. Of the fourteen chassis sent to mainland European coachbuilders all have been identified as having been built and nine survive, generally in very good order or under restoration, and that includes all four Jupiters built by Stabilimenti Farina of Turin.

Of the 75 rolling chassis delivered to the UK and the rest of the world, three are known to have received genuine standard Jupiter bodies outside the Factory and five are known not to have been bodied at all in the era. Of the remaining 67 chassis there are four unidentified examples that are known to have been built in the era, the rest we know more about. At the time of writing 47 coachbuilt Jupiters were known still to survive. A much more detailed account of these cars can be found in the book *Jowett Jupiter Special Body – from Abbott and Beutler to Rochdale and Worblaufen*, also by the present author.

Abbott

Abbott of Farnham, Surrey, are well-known for their Rolls and Bentley bodies, and the Abbott Healey of which about 77 were built in the early 1950s. Some lesser-known are the Lammas-Graham cars of 1936-38, the Atlanta, the Lagonda Rapier of 1934-35, Connaught L35R sports car of 1951 (12 laid down but possibly not all completed) and the open version of the Bristol 405 (43 built). Shooting brakes were produced like the Ford Farnham which were estate cars on modified Anglia and Zephyr cars. An XK120 four-seater tourer was made for a New Zealander.

In 1951 two open Jupiters (32, 89) were built by Abbott which resembled the Bugatti Type 57 when viewed from some angles. The latter (89) was driven in the 1952 Little Rally. In 1952 two fixed-head coupé versions (105, 247) followed, the first for C P Swain who used it in the 1953

Morecambe Rally; these two cars were offered at £2210 10s 0d (including tax) in old money. Both of the open and one of the two closed Abbott Jupiters (247) survive.

Adams & Robinson

The name Philip Fotheringham-Parker is still well-known in vintage car circles: he competed in a wide variety of pre-war events and cars (Fraser Nash and Alvis including a Works Silver Eagle at Brooklands) and post-war in ERA, Maserati, XK120 and Connaught. He is known to have visited Jowett vainly hoping for an R1 drive. With the Monte Carlo Rally rules changing in 1952 to allow only closed cars, he decided to have a compliant closed Jupiter built and he took delivery of chassis 725 in February 1952. Around that same time Roy Clarkson had the same idea: he was one of the best of the rally specialists of the day, who with his beautiful blue Type-212 Inter Ferrari with coachwork by Touring of Milan had rallied it (1951 Tulip, RASC Scottish, MCC) and raced it (a lowly 23rd in a Silverstone Production Car race). In his case he arranged with Peter Morgan to have a Morgan Plus 4 chassis also FHC-bodied to evaluate its suitability

Three saloon Jupiters. Left to right: Adams & Robinson (725), Flewitt (97) and Maurice Gomm (30). (CJ)

for rallying. So Fotheringham-Parker and Clarkson had their respective chassis delivered to the Pannells Farm, Chertsey, Surrey, workshop of Adams & Robinson for Charlie Robinson to fit coupé bodies influenced in construction (Superleggera – aluminium panelling on a light framework of small-bore steel tubing) and style by Clarkson's Ferrari. Both cars tended to replicate the sculptured curves of the afore-mentioned Ferrari, as Robinson already had an envied reputation for skill in multidirectional aluminium panel-work, typifying the highest standards of craftsmanship learned or developed in the wartime aircraft industry.

Both cars were intended for the 1953 Monte Carlo Rally so it was a race against time. Brilliant panel-man that he was, Charlie Robinson had no sense of time and his partner, the Mr Adams, would 'look after' nurses at a nearby nurses' home, allegedly, rather than gee-up Charlie. There was a funding issue also with the result that the Morgan was just, only just, ready in time to head for the Munich start, to retire while still in Germany. Maurice Gomm, who at that time shared the barn with Robinson, did what he could with both cars, but mainly the Morgan, perhaps explaining why that car has a very similar windscreen to the Beverley Motors saloon Jupiters Gomm was building at that time. Although the Jupiter's panelling was formed and in place on the tubing welded to the chassis, Fotherinham-Parker lost interest having missed the rally and realising that Jowett was in trouble and likely to cease car manufacture.

Robinson was now working on racing cars for John Willment, much easier to build than road cars; but he is also known at that time for Emerysons for Paul Emery, a Cooper-Triumph, Austin and MG specials, and a Pyecroft Jaguar. Willment began racing in the early 1950s with an Austin 7 Special, as many did then, and he had a series of specials built. He is perhaps best remembered for his part in JW Automotive which with his friend and partner, John Wyer, developed and ran Ford's GT40 sports racers. So Charlie Robinson moved full time to John Willment's place nearby, and the unfinished Jupiter came too. John Willment took a fancy to it and

persuaded Charlie to finish it, and between them finish it they did, and it was registered for the road on 1st August 1957 to Willment Bros Ltd of Isleworth, Middlesex. John continued as its owner-driver until February 1960. After a succession of owners, it was bought by the author in 1969 and after quite some necessary work it was put on the road in 1971 and has been on the road and a driven car ever since, for many years seeing use as his family's second car all the year round (it would have made a good Monte Carlo Rally participant) and having been to the Black Forest in Germany, Alsace and other destinations in France, while in the UK it has seen Cornwall, Wales and Scotland.

Armstrong
The *Carlisle Journal* of 13 June 1952 reported that the local firm of J J Armstrong had just completed a closed Jupiter (12) at their Thomas Street Garage. The company had been building vehicle bodies for 20 years but this was their first private car, the design being by Mr Armstrong himself. It was said to feature ample luggage space with a detachable shelf in the rear of the driving seat and a walnut instrument panel. It was upholstered in blue leather, to go well with the dark maroon of the body. For improved access, the bonnet lifts a full 90 degrees. This car was seen in London in 1970 still a daily-use car; but now after long storage periods it is currently under restoration.

Barnaby Bodybuilders of Hull
Cliff Golan of Barnaby Bodybuilders of Hull constructed a Jupiter (10) for Ted Booth to enter as part of the Jowett Team in the 1951 RAC International Rally. It had to resemble standard, which thanks to drawings supplied by Jowett it almost did, especially the front end but its body is noticeably lower on the chassis. It was registered on 12 April 1951 and it took part in the Morecambe National Rally in May and came 12th in the 1951 RAC Rally of June. Other 1951 events were the Yorkshire Sports Car Club races at Croft, the MCC-*Daily Express* Rally, and it also took part in the 1952 RAC International Rally, see

Ted Booth driving the Barnaby Jupiter (10) in the Olivers Mount Consistency Trial, Scarborough, in the 1952 RAC International Rally. (Charles Dunn)

Chapter 4. For some time now it has been a very nice restored and running car often at meetings.

Barrou, Jean
Only one Jupiter rolling chassis (93) was exported directly to France, and it is a safe assumption that this became the saloon Jupiter of Jean Latune of Valence in the Rhône-Alpes region. It is also a good assumption that it was built by his local coachbuilder Jean Barrou of Tournon-sur-Rhone. Marcel Becquart told me as much: that it was "built by a coachbuilder local to him". We know of his Jupiter as it was photographed in two Tour de France Automobile rallies (1951, 1952), two Monte Carlo rallies (1952, 1953), and the 1953 Lyon-Charbonières rally, see Chapter 4. It was then not heard from again. Its best result was class 5th in the 1952 Tour de France Automobile.

Barton Transport
The main business of Barton's Transport was constructing and operating coaches, but the firm did build, of all things, a camper body on Jupiter chassis 107 for the

firm's managing director, a Mr C Barton, to the design of his foreman Tommy Shirley. Mr & Mrs Barton are known to have toured to Switzerland in it in 1953, I was informed, where on the camper's radio they listened to the broadcast of the coronation of Queen Elizabeth. The Jupiter was sold in 1955 to disappear for good.

Bendall
Under the heading 'Carlisle Firm Improves Car' the *Cumberland News* of 15 March 1952 announced the completion of a neat and original open Jupiter (253) by James Bendall & Sons Ltd of Carlisle, a sheet-metal and car repair business of that town. Jim Bendall designed the body and thought of using the Riley front wings, while Douglas Workman and Jack Dodds of Armstrong & Fleming, the Jowett and Rover agency of Penrith (18 miles south of Carlisle) carried out the mechanical work. However the original customer for the car had a change of heart and withdrew, so Reg Sheppard drove it down to London to be auctioned. It was apparently sold to a movie starlet but the first known owner was cinemactor Peter Ustinov, who it is said took it to Hollywood with him for a couple of years. It later found its way to Jowett expert Dennis Sparrow who got it running well and he used it for some years before putting it into storage.

Beutler
The Swiss firm Gebruder Beutler of Thun in the canton of Bern built two drophead Jupiters, the award-winning (83) and the last Swiss-built Jupiter (291). A very eye-catching car, the first of their Jupiters was entered in the July 1951 International Automobile im Festkleid in Lucerne, a beauty contest for cars, where it was awarded second in its class after a 1400 Fiat built by Ghia of Turin. The first of their Jupiters is lost to us but the second was discovered in the 1970s still in Switzerland where it still resides today having been beautifully and sympathetically restored. It was even driven to Britain three times, in 1982, 1983 and 1984. Following the passing away of its restorer Ernst Oberholzer, this lovely car has not travelled outside its native land.

153

The restored Beutler Jupiter (291) of Ernst Oberholzer. (Oberholzer)

Gomm Jupiter on chassis 246 after its crash. (J Short)

Gomm Jupiter on chassis 30 looking good as always. (CJ)

Beverley Motors, Tidy Bros, Maurice Gomm
Nigel Mann of Beverley Motors, New Malden, Surrey, was a relative of the brewery firm that once bore his surname. He was a well-known and consistent competitor at Le Mans, Goodwood and other venues in a 2.5-litre Healey, his DB2 and a 2-6-litre Monza Alfa Romeo.

Besides offering individual coachwork on Alfa Romeo chassis, in 1952 Nigel Mann collected no less than six unsold Jupiter rolling chassis from Jowett dealers; they became the Gilliver Saloon, the Primrose Saloon, and bodies on chassis 30, 40, 113, and 246. The construction of three (two of their chassis numbers not identified) were mostly by a coachbuilder Tidy Bros of Wimbledon but completed by Maurice Gomm, who initially shared a barn with Charlie Robinson of Adams & Robinson before expanding into much larger premises where he traded as Gomm Metal Developments. Gomm had hand-built the very first – aluminium – Lolas and he completed the two Beverley Motors saloon Jupiters which late in 1952 were advertised in *Autosport* at £1,100 + tax, with a picture of one describing its colour as "primrose with blue wheels and upholstery". One of the Beverley Motors saloon Jupiters is known to have raced at Snetterton. A Beverley

Motors saloon was registered 53 CPA in December 1956 which of a certainty was chassis 40, but it is not thought to be the Snetterton car. This 1956-registered Jupiter was last licenced in October 1963, its then owner a serviceman is known to have been posted to Germany in 1964, and here the trail goes cold, for both Beverleys are now lost to us. The Gilliver saloon, first registered May 1955, is so-called as it is named after its only known owner. A photo shows it as a handsome closed car with a near-to-standard front end and a very neat fastback tail.

This car is reliably reported to have been scrapped in the mid-1960s.

In 1954 there remained the three unbuilt Beverley chassis. One (113) is known to have been built up into a standard Jupiter, the work completed in June 1954. The remaining two still unused chassis (30, 246) were bought in 1958 for £200 apiece and then resold to two intrepid airline pilots.

These pilots both got Maurice Gomm to build saloon bodies on them to their own quite differing designs. One (30) was put on the road in 1960 and survives to this day in excellent running order whilst the other which was only completed in 1964 was crashed after five years of daily use: it seems like its new owner was trying too hard!

Before a Jupiter enthusiast could get to it with some cash, a scrappie had unpicked the aluminium panelling and sold it off, leaving just the rolling chassis. Around 1970-72 this was very well re-bodied to standard form using panels from scrapped Jupiters. It, too, is in fine running order.

So, from the six chassis rounded up by Beverley Motors/Nigel Mann, three have vanished, while two are in standard coachwork and just the one special-bodied Jupiter (30) remains.

Boonacker
A Jupiter rolling chassis (85) was exhibited at the 1951 Amsterdam Motor Show and it went on to be bodied by the Dutch coachbuilder Boonacker in Haarlem, best known for building hearses. A nice closed car with cream coachwork and a dark green roof, it was in daily use at least up to 1958 before disappearing from our records.

Coachcraft of Egham, Pat Whittet
This Surrey-based coachworks also has a convoluted story to tell, having their origins, it is believed, as Coachcraft in 1934 and being involved with other related businesses from time to time; but cash-flow problems hit around the period of interest to us here bringing closure in 1954. They certainly built two saloon Jupiters (28, 48) and it is very likely that the open Jupiter (47) was built by them

too. The first (28) was panelled by Coachcraft but all mechanical work that needed doing was carried out by a small car-development business run by Pat Whittet, (based just 10 miles from Egham) almost certainly including the right-hand floor gear change which the car still has. Very early in its life the car suffered front-end damage and as the standard grilles were not available ex-stock from Jowett, Pat Whittet fitted a Ford Mk1 Zephyr front grille slightly modified. This can be seen in the image, below, of the Jupiter being raced at Goodwood on 1 May 1954 in a saloon car handicap event which the Jupiter won – its only race as it turned out.

Goodwood start line May 1954. Jupiter 28 and Javelin.
(National Motor Museum)

The driver was Ian Forbes, this Jupiter's third owner. In November 1955 Bob Graves of Old Coulsdon, Surrey, (then aged 25) bought the car and ran it for a while then stripped it down for a full makeover; in May 1964 he re-registered it CDG 63B. The engine was altered to have four Amal carburettors and he later fitted a supercharger, with liners using R1-type Wills Rings top seals. It was

Jupiter 28 about 1968. (Alan Wright)

reliable for it went on three trips to Spain. By 1966 it had a new owner and conventional carburettors and no supercharger.

For some years it looked good and went well and received further fettling including a new Zephyr grille. It was bought in 1990 by no less a figure than John Surtees, but by then the car was suffering from neglect. John just stored it but we did get its original registration returned to it. From 2012 it found new owners and professional restoration commenced in 2015.

Jupiter 48 began life with Pat Whittet who arranged for 'Farina-influenced' saloon coachwork to be fitted by Coachcraft of Egham. They made good progress until slowed by the afore-mentioned financial problems and the almost completed car went to another coachbuilder, King & Taylor of Godalming, Surrey for completion and trimming. Pat Whittet fitted a Wade Ventnor supercharger and special head gaskets, for the first owner R C Trussler was going to race the car but never did. It was still supercharged in 1958 when advertised for sale, but when the car was discovered by an enthusiast in 1972 the blower had been removed although still with the car. It was a runner in the 1970s and 1980s but then got laid up, to deteriorate considerably. Much of this deterioration has been rectified by the careful work of its current owner Simon Wood.

Jupiter 47 is a drophead with no confirmed

coachbuilder but from its construction, styling, and date and place of first owner and registration Coachcraft of Egham seems a likely identification. In 1960 it was owned for six months by Peter Michael (who also owned the three R4 Jupiters then), a close associate of Bob Graves he, the then owner of Coachcraft Jupiter Chassis 28. It was recoveredfrom a breakers yard in 1970 and dry-stored; as I write it is being restored.

Colinsons
See Rawson

Crouch
See Hodge

Epsom Motor Panels
This firm, said to be a "Three men and a dog" outfit, built a pleasant closed Jupiter body onto Chassis 49. Its Italianate construction and styling influenced by the Zagato Fiat 8V was completed in January 1952. It continued to be a running car and in use up to 1977 when it was taken off the road for some restoration work, still to be completed.

Farina
The very first special-bodied Jupiter (7) was by Stabilimenti Farina to the order of Jowett Cars Ltd, the first of four, all surviving. Colour maroon, it was completed by 5 October 1950 just ready in time for the Paris Salon where it attracted a lot of interest. Stabilimenti Farina was founded about 1919 by Giovanni Farina, older brother of Battista 'Pinin' Farina (who founded his own company Pininfarina in 1930), beginning by repairing then building horse-drawn then horse-less carriages. 'The Italian Look' is attributed to Pinin designs on Alfa Romeo, Lancia Astura and other chassis of about 1936–39. Post-war it was refined with the Cisitalia of 1946 and several other designs of which the best known are probably the Lancia Aurelia of 1948 and the Aurelia that followed. The two companies worked closely together and it is possible that by 1951 Stabilimenti was separate only in name. By 1953 the older company was absorbed into the younger one.

Good accessibility to luggage in the Farina Jupiter (7) Doors are pillarless. (C H Wood)

Jowett's Farina (7) was registered for the road on 30 March 1951 and in June that year Marcel Becquart visited the Factory and tested it around the Yorkshire Dales and decided he wanted one for himself. Farina (7) was bought from the Jowett London showroom about March 1952 and exported to what is now Malaysia but then a British colony, where it took part in various sporting events before being bought by a New Zealander who took it home with him in 1959 to be registered there in September. After much road use, development work and modification it was bought by Simon Wood in 2002 who imported it back to the UK with the intention of returning it to its original state.

Three other Farina Jupiters were constructed: Chassis 33 for the Hoffman Motor Car Co Inc of New York and Chicago – now under restoration in California from having a V8 bodged into it, Chassis 59 for Marcel Becquart to use in rallies such as the 1952 and 1953 Montes (see Chapter 4), and Chassis 109 for a French private owner:

this latter car came to Britain in 2001 and has been immaculately and sensitively restored. The Becquart Farina is also in excellent condition in New Zealand, to where it migrated around 1980.

Farr

JE Farr & Son Ltd of Blackburn Lancashire built four saloon Jupiters (81, 245, 252, 583). The first was for Robert Ellison to use in the 1952 Monte Carlo Rally. The *Blackburn Times* reported (4 January 1952) that "the two directors JE Farr and his son JS Farr have incorporated ideas which have come to them during the course of many years' experience in this type of work...they outlined their ideas to Mr Tom Edwards who transferred them to the drawing board". The first car's weight at 18cwt was a disappointment to Ellison, as was the price £1750. It took part in the 1952 Monte Carlo Rally (Ch4) but came to grief a day's drive from the finish; it has been beautifully restored and even sports its original rally plate.

Farr Jupiter 245, a road car into the 1960s, is now under restoration, while 252 after long storage is, as I write, also getting much needed restoration work. Their last car (583) was first used by one of the Farr family but is known not to have survived beyond the 1970s.

Flewitt

The coachbuilder Flewitt Ltd of Alma Street, Birmingham, were founded in 1905 building on some Rolls-Royce chassis from 1912; they were coach-building until 1957 and continued into the late 1960s doing bodywork repairs. In 1952 they bodied an XK120 chassis and in 1953 they completed the comely saloon Jupiter (97). This car sat in in a Jowett dealer's showroom until 1958. Then its first owner used it as his everyday car, teaching his wife to drive in it, before going abroad in 1965 when the car went into decline due to poor storage. This superbly crafted car is now under restoration.

Ghia Suisse

The Swiss coachbuilder Ghia Suisse of Aigle was a much smaller concern than its Italian namesake now owned by

Ford. The peripatetic Giovanni Michelotti (also known for designing the Triumph Herald and Spitfire amongst many other models and makes) was designing cars at Aigle when the very pleasant 3-seater cabriolet Jupiter was built on Chassis 31 to be shown in the 1951 Geneva Salon. It was in use in the 1950s but has since disappeared. Ghia Aigle went on to build an appealing FHC on Chassis 56 and after much road use it found its way to the a small collection at the Château de Sanxet 8 Km south of Bergerac in the south of France. A FHC Jowett bodied by Ghia Aigle appeared in a Swiss exhibition sometimes described as Javelin and sometimes a Jupiter; if a Jupiter it would have been on Chassis 95. It too is lost.

Gomm
See Beverley Motors

Grounds
Frank Grounds the Birmingham Jowett agent had a saloon Jupiter (29) built in his own coachworks, cunningly matching a Jupiter bonnet to Morris Oxford doors and thence to its quite lovely fastback coachwork. Frank and his wife Lola (for whom it was registered LOL 1) used it in a number of rallies including the 1953 Monte and RAC and class-winning the *Birmingham Post* rally (see Chapters 4 and 5).

Lola Grounds in a test in the 1953 RAC Rally. (*Autosport*)

It was then used as a daily driver by Lola for a number of years before they passed it on. This very good-looking car unmistakable a Jupiter is currently under restoration.

Hartwell
George Hartwell Ltd of Bournemouth, Hants, built an interesting open Jupiter on Chassis 250 for a Mr Vincent Louis Smith, a local hotelier. It incorporated a V-screen with horizontally split halves with the top panes openable. It had two sets of seats, a set for touring and set for rallying and it was noted for its good cornering at 90mph although it is not believed to have ever been rallied. A photo shows similarities between this Jupiter and the Hartwell Alpine (the car which led to the Sunbeam Alpine) that Hartwell was building on a Sunbeam 90 chassis at the time. This Jupiter's whereabouts are unknown.

Hodge – Crouch – Australian specials
The Australian motor-sporting driver John Crouch of John Crouch Motors, Sydney, was a major specialist dealer in the 1950s offering Bristol, Cooper and Dellow as well as Jupiter. In 1950 he very ambitiously imported we believe five Jupiter rolling chassis with the intention of having ash-framed but otherwise replica standard Jupiter bodies fitted to them. The actual work was to be done by S O Hodge who traded under the name Moorebank Motor Body Repairers based in a suburb of Sydney.

Chassis 13 and 16 are known to have had Hodge bodies fitted but Crouch was hit by Jowett Jupiters going into series production from about May 1951. Chassis 13 is known to have been crashed in 1958 or before – and its Hodge body was fitted temporarily to another ex-Crouch chassis (24) which amazingly had an Australian Vauxhall Tourer body fitted up to that point – but then, in the early 1960s the Hodge body was removed and a lovely JWF Italia fibre-glass kit-car body began to be fitted, a project never finished in its era but as I write is at last being completed.

Some creative Australian specials-builders got to work on other chassis connected with Crouch, the not unattractive Pudding-bowl Special (11) was raced a few times while Len

The Australian production of replica Jupiter bodies on chassis 13 and 16 in the Hodge workshop. (Crouch, Hodge)

Deaton had built a basic but not quite R1-like open special (22) which also went racing a few times. The chassis 13 and 16 both survive body-less and are to have rescued and repro standard Jupiter panels fitted to them.

Of the total of eight rolling chassis imported to Australia, just the one (69) still wears its original body, fitted by Tasmanian Lyndon Duckett into a lightweight stripped sports-racer. He did race his 'Duckett Special' and the car is still in fine form, developed to meet current Australian historic sports racing car specs and has seen some competition in the hands of its present owner Ed Wolf.

The Deaton Special (22) now only exists in photographs. (Ed Wolf)

Kanrell

The very first production Jupiter chassis (6) was imported into their country in August 1950 by the Swedish Jowett agent AB Motortillbehor of Stockholm, to be displayed at a motor show. It was soon bought by Rune Berg, then the owner of a fast MG TC with replica aluminium bodywork and later a standard Jupiter. This Jupiter chassis (6) was clothed in near-replica 1951 R1 bodywork by Karl-Gustav Kanrell. Factory drawings of the R1 arrived late, forcing Kanrell to work from photographs and it is evident that only front views were available to him; however an R1 engine was purchased from Jowett for £50 and used as a model for what were at times fruitless engine experiments.

The car's first outing was an international race at Skarpnacks Airfield in 1951, when Berg drove it to fifth place behind the Porsche Works team of four cars headed by Max Nathan – however at least the Jupiter was the only car not to have been lapped by the Germans. In the September 1952 event (Chapter 5) Berg placed fourth. The Jupiter is recorded as having been raced (on ice) by Rune Berg on Lake Flaten in 1953.

Kanrell himself never raced the Jupiter but recalled *"the roadholding was fantastic for its time, top speed as well. Many times I drove it at 170 and 180kph (106 and 112mph) on normal roads"*. Kanrell went on to become one of Sweden's leading racing mechanics and up to 1957 worked with Joakim Bonnier the Swedish sports car and F1 driver. Berg parted with the car in 1954 on getting married; its new owners are known to have used it in what they called 'hectic' ice races; perhaps it was around this time that the front-end bodywork was somewhat changed for the worse. After two more ownership changes and much storage, in 1998 it was bought by Danny Nash, brought to Britain, and its front end skilfully converted by Allan Fishburn back to original. It currently awaits the final completion of its restoration

KW Bodies Ltd

The firm of KW bodies of Blackpool goes back to about 1928 when it was Lansdowne HK of Fleetwood just 9 miles up the road from Blackpool. The "K" was a Mr

Kitchener who designed all three Jupiters (37, 99 and 103) which were all closed cars. The first was for Bill Robinson to go racing in, which he did in the 1951 BRDC British Empire Trophy on the Isle of Man (Ch5). Chassis 99 was built for Edward Foulds the Keighley Jowett agent and he rallied it (Ch6), most notably in the MCC Rally of November 1951 while its next owner Albert Wake raced it at several venues (Ch5). Of the third Jupiter very little is known, and it must be recorded that all three KW Jupiters are now lost to us.

Leacroft

In January 1955 Chilton Cars of Leighton Buzzard advertised a one-owner open 1950 Jupiter for sale at £455 with photograph, telling us that its special body had been built by Leacroft. This company is known to have been based near Staines, Middlesex, in the general region where Coachcraft, Maurice Gomm, and others who flourished in the 1950s and 1960s. If truly built on a 1950 chassis, as the price seems to confirm, then it would have been on chassis 50. It had a proper folding hood, bucket seats trimmed in brown leather, and an opening boot. It was an insurance write-off in 1963 after receiving a terminal side-swipe. This Jupiter is seriously missed.

Mead, Richard Mead

Richard Mead, initially based in Dorridge Warwickshire before moving 10 miles to Kenilworth, built six Jupiters (34, 87, 117, 248, 249 and 251). He is better known as the designer and builder of the P4 Rover 75-based 'Marauder' of which he also built six. He had re-bodied a pre-war Bentley, built a Lea Francis and many other cars such as shooting brakes and ambulances. He produced a sketch of his proposed Jupiter and circulated the Jowett dealers and consequently his sextet is a record for Jupiter specials by one coachbuilder.

All Mead Jupiters are open cars, well-thought-out, balanced, nimble-looking and are unmistakeably Jupiters. They are not all identical: one (34) has its boot externally accessible and a one-piece curved screen in place of the normal V-screen. The highest spec (251) has a true

Richard Mead's sketch of proposed Jupiter. (R Mead)

Richard Mead Jupiter on chassis 117. (CJ)

Richard Mead Jupiter on 248 in happier times. (CJ)

folding hood and winding windows and was offered at £1250 pre-tax, while the celluloid side-screen clip-on hood versions were £170 less.

All feature a bonnet that lifts significantly and usefully higher than that of the standard Jupiter.

Of the six Mead Jupiters built, 87 was scrapped many years ago, 248 lost its body also many years ago but survives in chassis form, and the other four are all with us in excellent running order – 249 went to New Zealand in 1953 with its first owner, and 251 found its way to Australia in 2012, so Mead Jupiters 34 and 117 are still in the UK.

New Moston Sheet Metal

The New Moston Sheet Metalwork Co, who-ever they were, may sound like the wrong people to be let loose on a Jupiter chassis (9) but not so! They produced an unexpected and charming open Jupiter with something of the Crosley Hotshot about it, and its charm is enhanced by it still being in unspoilt early condition. Its body is supported on the chassis by a sturdy steel tubular structure – one day for sure this Jupiter, a running car up to 1965, will come out of hiding and be restored.

Park

Wm Park (Coachbuilders) Ltd of Mortlake Road, Kew, London, built rather nice aluminium-on-ash hardtops for Mk1 Jupiters, one of which was used in competition on HKW 429 (544). At £130 they were well made but rather expensive and not many can have been sold, although Jupiter hardtops were also made available in California and Australia.

Radford, Seary and McReady

The coachbuilder Harold Radford & Co Ltd of South Kensington, London, may still be known for their 'woodie' utility bodies on Bentley and their upmarket Mini conversions including some hatch-back variants for the famous. The firm has relevance in the Jupiter story beyond their two dissimilar open Jupiters (8, 14) a relevance that reaches back into the pre-Jowett penumbra of the Jupiter's

The ERA-Javelin in the basement of the Jowett showroom during the 1949 Earls Court Motor Show. (Jowett Cars Ltd)

gestatory period in the summer/autumn of 1949, when it was an ERA project masterminded by Leslie Johnson. Perhaps the first functioning proto-Jowett under ERA's auspices was a running chassis for development driving, with a crude wooden-framed body like a park bench across the chassis, a box at the back with weights to get the centre of gravity right and a plywood-aluminium bonnet held onto the front cross-tube with Jubilee clips. Just fancy! It was test-driven in all weathers by David Hodkin wearing a flying suit often covering 400 miles in a day, occasionally being stopped by the police.

David Hodkin was Eberhorst's right-hand man under Leslie Johnson. Next, it was Seary & McReady, builder of the 'Rich Man's Utility' Bentleys who built up the ERA-Javelin, the first real body on the Eberhorst – what would later be called Jupiter – chassis, in time for the October 1949 Earls Court show. The only later intelligence we have on what **could** be this car is from a book on the London Metropolitan Police Traffic Department. Its author, Chief Inspector K Rivers, lists a 'Jowett ERA 1½-litre 13HP saloon' as being used for various duties from 1950 to 1955, before being transferred to the Met's driving school at Hendon for two years. We have no other tidings.

David Hodkin told me he also had a Seary and McReady Porsche-like saloon Jupiter for his personal use for about 18 months; again we have no further evidence on this car.

Both Radford's actual Jowett Jupiters were open cars from the initial Jowett batch (shipped in August 1950) of production rolling chassis. Gerald Lascelles, the Queen's cousin, ordered the first (8), notable for its short doors and high sills giving a stiff draught-free ride while its rear wheel-spats remind one of the ERA-Javelin depicted above. When Lascelles visited the car under construction the coachworks had the board 'Seary & McReady' but when he came to collect the car its sign read Harold Radford (Coachbuilders) Ltd. His car was registered in August 1951 and raced a few times at Goodwood and Silverstone. It is under sympathetic restoration as I write this.

Jupiter 14 had less straightforward origins. Elongated front and rear, as a two-seater it gives the appearance of great length (not in itself a problem) and although by the look of it surely it is a 1950/51 concept it was not, I was told, completed until 1953.

It was registered for the road in December 1955, when its first owner-driver was even more famous, being the prolific writer and broadcaster Ernest Dudley of the

Jupiter 14 in the mid-1960s when fitted with a one-piece curved windscreen. (Maidens)

'Armchair Detective' stories. Dudley wanted a car no one could recognise, and was very impressed by its handling: much better than the TR2 he had before, he was to say. It has been a running car most of its life and is often seen around.

Rawson, John Colinsons
Lionel Rawson restarted building cars immediately after Word War 2. A name was created using the first names of the sons of Rawson and his business partner hence the exact spelling John Colinsons – neither son had any further

Lionel Rawson working on one of his Jupiters. (Rawson)

Below: April 2013. The ex Alf Thomas Rawson Jupiter owned by Roberto Onofri at Lake Iseo in northern Italy. (Onofri)

connection with the firm. Rawson pioneered the fully opening front-hinged bonnet on a Jaguar SS100 he built in 1946 for Paul Pyecroft; this type of front later appeared on the DB2, E-type Jaguar and many other cars but not on the Jupiters he made (25, 35? 38 and 39). Mr Rawson should be remembered for building the 23 Healey Sportsmobile cars of 1948-50 and the Austin-Healey 'Streamliner' record-breaker (192.62mph) of 1954.

A deal was set up probably by Alf Thomas (38) for three open Jupiters to Rawson's design, to be constructed by him and his panel-man Arthur Jennings at their Works in Slough, Bucks. The three open cars (25, 38 and 39) were built side-by-side virtually identically, in style suggesting the DB1 of Aston Martin's Chief Engineer Claude Hill. Alf Thomas's Jupiter (38) was raced by him and his son with considerable success (see Chapters 5 and 6).

The first, 25, is being well restored, while both 38 and 39 have migrated, in very good order but separately, to Italy. The closed car 35 (now lost to us) is stylistically very similar to the others, but when I asked Lionel about it he was not sure if he had built it.

Since purchasing Jupiter 38 in 1989 Roberto Onofri had it re-sprayed its original cream and uses it in Mille Miglia retros, in Italy still being allowed to wear its original Alf Thomas registration JTM 100. It normally has a couple of outings in a year, and then rests in the Museo Mille Miglia in the Monastery of Saint Eufemia in the province of Brescia.

Rochdale

Rochdale Motor Panels & Engineering Ltd of that town have two Jupiters to their name. The first was 'Jehu' the Horridge Special, of which its Jowett connection was just its Eberhorst Jupiter frame, suspension and axles. Powered by a 1½-litre Riley Sprite engine it was used in six events 1953-55 but has since disappeared. Their other one is a real Jupiter, wearing a Rochdale Mk6 fibreglass kit-car body. It was assembled in 1954-55 on a spare un-numbered Jupiter chassis by a mechanical engineering student at Glasgow University with all mechanical components obtained from Jowett Engineering Ltd. Its

second owner, after making some improvements to it including a re-spray, took it on the 1989 Pirelli Marathon Retro (ch7) as well as in ten other motor sport events. It is still a handsome running Jupiter which may be seen around occasionally.

Seary & McReady
See Radford above.

Sommer
Erik Sommer was a Danish engineer who had begun importing cars into his country soon after the war and who handled Jaguar as well as Jowett. Experimentally he built various vehicles using a variety of imported components notably his S1 saloon, based on the Bradford van, and a front-wheel-drive van powered by an opposed-piston two-stroke engine designed by none other than Eberan von Eberhorst! Very successfully he imported some Bradford driveaway chassis and a fleet of taxis was created for Copenhagen. In 1951 he felt an urge to take on the Italians with special coachwork on sports chassis. He began modestly enough with a standard Jupiter (170) on which he fixed a suave hardtop; the car, it was said, was sold to a Swedish customer. That said, the car has not been heard from since.

The Sommer Jupiter on chassis 500. (Clausager)

Next, the only two LHD rolling chassis were ordered from Jowett with the first (500) arriving at the end of 1951.

So the beautiful Sommer Jupiter (500) was designed and built, it being the only LHD special-bodied Jupiter, with its standard Jupiter bonnet a smart car always in running order. The designers had a cunning way to get the bodywork right: the shape was perfected by constructing a lattice cage of steel rods on the chassis, cut and bent to shape until Sommer father and son were happy with the result. Thus their careful experiments were made at full size instead of the normal small models. The design was carried out by Erik and his son Ole with the aim of a car to rival the best from established sports-car design houses. There was a problem raised by Sommer's desire to bring the top speed up by 10% by superior aerodynamics so, like some other saloon Jupiters, the headroom for tall drivers is (only) just a little tight. Completed by January 1952, the car was registered with its first owner in the following October. The car still looks good and runs well.

As for the second LHD chassis ordered by Sommer (746), for this Erik Sommer is believed to have had ambitions for his own design of more aerodynamic front-end but regrettably his plans came to nought and the chassis was returned to Jowett to be built into a RHD standard car (937), ironically as a previously returned RHD chassis had been built into a LHD standard car.

Worblaufen

This Swiss coachbuilding firm of the town of that name founded in 1929 constructed a rather Teutonic but pleasing open Jupiter on Chassis 23 and exhibited it at the 1951 Geneva salon together with an equally attractive Javelin cabriolet. It has to be assumed that both cars found buyers in Switzerland. Cars they built post-war included Armstrong-Siddeley, Alfa Romeo, Bentley, Delage and others. Although several of Worblaufen's examples survive, with the firm continuing up to 1958, alas we have no further information on their two Jowetts.

This review is regrettably incomplete, not covering

Jupiter (65) re-bodied in 2012 for Bruno Cortini into an R1-Jupiter-type special. Bruno at the wheel. (Cortini)

some one-off examples, and one can only speculate on the ones known to have existed but now long gone. A saloon Jupiter, white with red top, a split screen and non-winding windows was reported in New Zealand many years ago. As already noted, Gordon Gilliver, way back when, owned a London-built saloon Jupiter with its standard-looking bonnet first registered in 1955 to a dental mechanic. As I write, remarkably there are 47 survivors known, with correct running gear and original coachwork, of which 40 are in running order or under restoration with 7 stored.

To add to these there are already some six interesting special-bodied Jupiters with bodywork fitted to chassis that once had standard bodies since decayed; to name a few there is the R1-type aluminium bodied Jupiter in Italy (65), the Nickri-bodied Jupiter (693) and the Fiorano-bodied Jupiter (449) both in the north of England and the amazing Jupiter Mk2 which Jowett designed and never built, put together by the world-class panel-man Allan Fishburn (944) see Chapter 8.

So – the special-bodied Jupiter lives on!

10: The Jupiter Register

These were the Jowett Factory Jupiters:

–	E0/SA/1R*	23 March 1950	New York USA show car. Privately raced at Watkins Glen
–	E0/SA/2R	October 1949	UK/Europe Exhibition chassis 1949–1953
GKW 111	E0/SA/4R	April 1950	1950 Le Mans and much more
GKU 764	E0/SA/5R*	March 1950	Factory road-development, then Wells Motor Sales Toronto
HAK 317	E0/SA/7R*	30 March 1951	Stabilimenti Farina body, in 1950 Paris Salon and Jowett London showroom
GKY 256	E0/SA/18R	Nov 1950	1951 Monte (class-winner) and more
GKY 106	E0/SA/19R	24 Nov 1950	Demonstrator, road-test car, then 1951 Monte
GKY 804	E0/SA/20R	26 Jan 1951	Motor Show Jowett stand and London showroom
GKY 107	E0/SA/21R	24 Nov 1950	Demonstrator then 1951 Monte, then Works 'hack'
HAK 364	E1/R1/1R	7 June 1951	1951/52 Le Mans, Prix de Monte Carlo, Watkins Glen
HAK 365	E1/SA/132R	7 June 1951	1951 Le Mans and more
HAK 366	E1/SA/131R*	7 June 1951	1951 Le Mans and more
HKU 56	E1/SA/76R*	16 Oct 1951	1951 London Motor Show demonstrator, road test car
HKU 92	E1/SA/255R*	20 July 1951	Jowett Cars Ltd Service dept 'hack' for two years
HKU 639	E1/SA/339R*	16 Oct 1951	Jowett show-room car and demonstrator
HKW 48	E2/R1/56R	20 May 1952	1952 Le Mans
HKW 49	E2/R1/62R*	20 May 1952	1952 Le Mans
HKW 197	E1/SB/560R	11 Feb 1952	Prototype Mk1a, road-test car
JAK 76	E2/SC/940R*	17 Nov 1952	1952 London Motor Show car
JAK 74	E2/SC/942R*	21 Oct 1952	Mk1a demonstrator and roadtest car
JKW 537	100/1*	July 1953	Prototype R4 Jupiter

* These Jupiters still exist

Approximate introduction of Bradford registration marks*

GKU December 1949
GKW April 1950
GKY September 1950
HAK February 1951
HKU June 1951
HKW December 1951
HKY April 1952
JAK September 1952
JKU January 1953
JKW May 1953
JKY August 1953
KAK December 1953
KKU March 1954
KKW May 1954
KKY September 1954
LAK December 1954

** From the book *Car Numbers* by Noel Woodall (Garnstone Press 1969)

Numbering systems

Jowett stamped four separate sets of numbers on Jupiters, two on the car and two on the engine. These were the chassis, body, engine and crankcase numbers.

Chassis number

Post-war Jowetts were allocated a chassis number arranged in a three-part code. The first part indicates the year of manufacture: E0 = 1950, E1 = 1951 up to E4. For the Jupiter the second part consists of S = Sports (P to indicate Passenger car for the Javelin and C is Commercial for the Bradford van) followed by A for Mk1 and C for Mk1a, followed by L if the car is Left-hand drive (only the prototype Mk1a E1 SB 560R was 'SB'). The third part is pure serial number starting from 1 (but some numbers were never allocated). The suffix R serves no known function, all Jupiters have it.

The chassis number on early Jupiters, before about chassis 41, was stamped on both sides of the 'front structure top plate' (radiator surround top face). All others were stamped on the left-hand bonnet catch bracket

close to the front cross-tube weld line. Complete cars were provided with a brass VIN plate mounted in the under-bonnet area. This is the same plate as used on Javelins and is a little ambiguous because, as applied to the Jupiter, the "Chassis Body No" is the number of the body panel set, while the "Model No" is the true chassis number, always a bigger number than the body number as not all Jupiter chassis received bodies at Jowett. The reason for this nomenclature is that this Javelin VIN plate was stamped this way since Javelins were received from Briggs as a "chassis-body" which is to say the Javelin chassis was unit with its body.

All factory-built Jupiters up to 939 (except 560) are Mk1 (that is, SA or SAL) with walnut instrument panel and internal luggage locker, while 940 to the end are Mk1a (that is, SC or SCL) with a metal instrument panel and externally accessible boot.

Body number

The body panels were hand-made, being only roughly shaped on rubber-bed presses at Western Manufacturing Estate Ltd, the name "Western" referring to its location on the Woodley aerodrome near Reading, Berkshire. These presses were normally used for aircraft aluminium panelling, so typical of the industry at that time. Jowett craftsmen had to iron out the ripples – a two-man job requiring rollers – then form the flanges, pierce them and carry out the final shaping on a car by which time the panels were in sets and not necessarily interchangeable. Consequently they were given their own serial number, stamped on all flanges. Because the bonnet was formed from three pressings and the tail panel from two, they carry the number stamped in three and two places respectively. The doors carry the number stamped on the steel strap behind the trim, and the trim panels themselves are sometimes found to have the number chalked on them. The firewall also carries the number. Bonnets supplied as spares carry a letter stamped on the three places plus the matching wings. So the Jupiter is a truly hand-built car which means the restoration can be and often has been very competently accomplished by amateurs.

The 'chassis-body No' stamped on the brass plate sometimes disagrees with the body-set number on early Jupiters, implying that at the start of production Jowetts tried to build Jupiters in a certain order, and stamped the brass plate too soon in the assembly process.

Engine number
This is stamped on the raised plinth forward of No 1 cylinder and *as original to a car* was identical to the full chassis number (the "Model No" on the brass VIN plate). Engines reconditioned by Jowett had their plinths ground clean and re-stamped using a variety of identifying codes. The not inconsiderable number of reconditioned engines built by Jowett Cars Ltd and Jowett Engineering Ltd is a comment on the reliability and development of the Javelin/Jupiter power unit: a score or more modifications to bearings and their lubrication were introduced during the engine's commercial life with improvements such as the all-metal liner bottom seal (from 1953) and the oval-web crankshaft (from 1955–1956) were introduced to the power unit which is capable of propelling Jupiters pretty reliably even today.

Crankcase number
The very earliest crankcases were sand-cast, but soon there was a change to gravity die-cast. Since the cases are common to the Javelin, numbering started from '1' in 1947, and Jupiter No 7 had crankcase 10546. The crankcase number is found stamped on both sides of the crankcase at the front, the same number on both halves as

the cases had to be machined as a matched pair. From about 1956 or later, sand-cast crankcases re-appeared for all-new engines and were numbered A1 to A100 or thereabouts; and B, D and H series are known. It is believed only about 500 such cases were made.

As we have seen in Chapter 7, at the time of writing, the survival rate of standard-bodied Jupiters from the 828 that had originally been built, there are at least 363 surviving, the majority in very good running order or under careful restoration. A further 47 special-bodied Jupiters exist either as running or project cars, and it is reasonable to suppose that there may yet be a few Jupiters out there awaiting discovery.

Jupiters in California and the Bulletin 149 engines.
Little is known of the import of new Jupiters into

The original American caption read: Ginny Baxter (left) and Jacqueline Du Bief, 1952 Olympic world's free-skating and figure-skating champions ... in a Jowett Jupiter sports car loaned to the stars by British Austin Ltd, Hollywood. (CJ)

Newton Small at the start of his Torrey Pines race in December 1951 in an early Angell Motors Californian Jupiter – no bonnet louvres. For more see Chapter 5. (Ted Miller Collection)

California, but it may not have been an altogether happy experience for some of them. The West Coast distributor, Angell Motors of Pasadena, imported more Jupiters by far than any other agent anywhere – the 34 imported during 1951 rose to about 24 per month for the first five months of 1952. Angell had around 39 western USA outlets covering not only California but 10 states in all. They imported several other makes of British cars and other European makes. They were responsible for persuading Jowett to make a left-hand-drive version of the Jupiter with flasher indicators in place of trafficators, and California-specification headlights were fitted locally.

A few Javelins were also imported to California. In mid-May 1952 the flow of Jupiters to Pasadena was interrupted although all must have been sold in the normal way for another 14 were dispatched from Bradford at the end of August. But around then Angell Motors went bankrupt and these Jupiters remained in bond until George Green, Jowett's technically competent Sales Director, visited in June 1953 to bring them back into the land of the living. It is not known to what extent the Jupiter's problems in

Californian road conditions of long high-speed cruising contributed to Angell's downfall, but it is known that a considerable number of special engines – the Bulletin 149 engines – were shipped to California with improvements that reduced the likelihood of head gasket failure.

Word Wide Import Inc. took over where Angell Motors left off, importing British cars like the Hillman Minx and Sunbeam Talbot, but although only bringing one more Jupiter to California they did sponsor Jupiter men Cal Marks and Hunter Hackney in motor sporting activities. The Jupiter they really wanted to import was the R4, George Green had shown them photos and a brochure, but it was not to happen. However they did provide support for Jupiter owners up to 1962 and thereafter what remained of their Jupiter spares went into private hands, ultimate being bought by cinemactor and Jupiter owner Walker Edmiston who in 1978 passed them on to Ted Miller.

The Jupiter Register reproduced here

The chassis number, shipment date and country (the first three items) are taken from the Jowett Factory Records. The GB Warranty Return Factory Records may provide additional information for GB cars. Chassis numbers suffixed "+" indicate that the car was shipped in Rolling Chassis form. If the car has not been heard from since leaving the Factory, that will be its only data, unless the Factory registered the car e.g. for Personal Export Jupiters where the registration mark will be included, but its destination was never in the Factory Records – these cars were bought free of the hefty purchase tax (c.58% in 1951) and could be driven in GB for up to 6 months (being the car's warranty period then!) before being returned to Jowett for servicing and export.

NB: Throughout this book, a plain number in brackets indicates a Jupiter chassis number.

All additional data indicate that the car has been heard from since leaving the Factory; following the country of shipment, this will be stated if known: present country, most recent sighting date, and brief history if applicable.

Country Abbreviations:–

A	Austria	I	Italy
AUS	Australia	IRL	Eire
B	Belgium	JAP	Japan
BR	Brazil	NL	Holland
CAN	Canada	NZ	New Zealand
CH	Switzerland	P	Portugal
D	West Germany	S	Sweden
DK	Denmark	SF	Finland
E	Spain	SGP	Singapore
F	France	USA	United States
GB	Great Britain	YV	Venezuela
HK	Hong Kong	ZA	Rep. Sth Africa

A curiosity of British car registrations is the number of "Identical triple digit" marks, like the 1950 Works Jupiter GKW 111. If I am not mistaken, in theory the random chance is 9 in 999 which is about 0.9%. But it happens that out of known first registrations by private British Jupiter owners nearly 4% were "identical triple digit" marks, suggesting there was an ambition at least by some owners to have their car registered with such a mark.

Ex-Works Jupiter (4) when owned by Dan Mercer c. 1954-55. (Dan Mercer)

E0SA 1R/29 Mar 1950/USA. First prototype. Shown at British Motor & Engineering Show New York April 1950. Raced at Watkins Glen the following Autumn. In 1968 found in depleted state; meticulous restoration by 2006 but Chevy 283 turbo engine/Muncie g/b Corvette IRS otherwise very original.

E0SA 2R+/Oct 1949/GB. Exhibition chassis shown 1949 at London, Glasgow, and 1950 Brussels, Geneva, and 1950–1953 London. Continuously updated and eventually built into complete car (1033) the last car built by JCLtd.

E0SA 3R+/Jan 1950/USA. Exhibition chassis at British Motor and Engineering Show New York April 1950. Transferred to Angell Motors Pasadena, to disappear after mid-1952.

E0SA 4R/Apr 1950/GB. Registered GKW 111: Class winner Le Mans 1950; then rebuilt to resemble the first production cars (17–21). Raced at Silverstone, RAC-TT at Dundrod, recce car for the 1951 Monte Carlo Rally, then more events in private hands. Scrapped c. 1964/5. Farewell, my Lovely!

E0SA 5R/29 Mar 1950/GB. Prototype car GKU 764 for Jowett to road-test, it toured Britain and France spring 1950 driven by H Grimley/C Grandfield. Seen July 1950 at Silverstone paddock before export to Canada. In 1958 rescued in a poor state. Restored, made LHD with floor gearchange, flashers. To GB in 1999; more restoration work, now a fine running car.

E0SA 6R+/11 Aug 1950/S. The first production chassis to be sold. Fitted with near-replica R1 body by Karl-Gustav Kanrell in Sweden. On 14/9/1952 placed 4th at race at Skarpnäck Airfield, Stockholm. To GB 1998 with new owner.

E0SA 7R+/14 Aug 1950/GB. Malaya/NZ. GB. FHC body by Stabilimenti Farina of Turin. In 1950 London and Paris motor shows. Briefly in Jowett's London showroom then north to the factory. Registered HAK 317 on 31 Mar 1951. To Singapore Aug 1952. To NZ in 1958 registered EQ 4747 then BY 3123. In 2002 back to GB for full restoration.

EOSA 8R+/16 Aug 1950/GB. Open bodywork by Harold Radford registered MGP 999 for Hon. Gerald Lascelles, the Queen's cousin, who raced and rallied it. On owner's honeymoon they toured the Dolomites in it. Known as the 'Rabbit Hutch' after its front grille, since modified. Restoration began in 1990. New owner from 2009 continued its restoration.

EOSA 9R+/18 Aug 1950/GB. Open Tourer body by Moston Sheet Metal Co reg'n AJM 470. Believed exists long stored.

EOSA 10R+/17 Aug 1950/GB. Open body by Barnaby Body-builders of Hull, near replica of standard, registered LRH 2 for Ted Booth for 1951 RAC Rally. Came 15th in the 1952 RAC Rally (Ch 4). In 1992 new owner restored it to a high standard.

EOSA 11R+/12 Sep 1950/AUS. Given the "Pudding Bowl" body in Australia and raced twice. Scrapped in the 1960s.

EOSA 12R+/21 Aug 1950/GB. Closed bodywork fitted by J J Armstrong of Carlisle. Reg: EHH 897. Car in daily use into the early 1970s. In 1994 bought by new owner for restoration.

EOSA 13R+/31 Aug 1950/AUS. Originally fitted with a frail but close replica of standard body by S O Hodge of Moorebank NSW. Chassis was body-less by 1969. Receiving in the hands of present owner a true replica of standard bodywork.

EOSA 14R+/28 Aug 1950/GB. Interesting Open Tourer body by Harold Radford built 1951 but only registered for the road (as WAR181) in Dec1955. First owner the author Ernest Dudley. After many owners it was bought in 1980 by present owner who completed its restoration into a fine running car.

EOSA 15R+/30 Aug 1950/AUS. Open car, the "Jock Walkem Special". Probably destroyed by the late 1950s.

EOSA 16R+/12 Sep 1950/AUS. Originally received a near but frail replica of standard body by S O Hodge of Moorebank NSW. By 1988 body removed and lost. Chassis bought 2009 for restoration to standard form.

EOSA 17R/4 Dec 1950/F. This was the first of batch of five production standard Jupiters but the only survivor. Chassis 17 to 21 all carried fore-and-aft strakes but otherwise standard production cars. This was the first Jupiter to be sold new – to M Thévenin of Bordeaux registered M-8660 and driven in the 1951 Monte Carlo Rally, see Ch 4. Found in south of France and professionally restored 1972-1993. Reg'n 1950-JB-82. Used in a few classic car races. Sold 2009 and 2015.

EOSA 18R/28 Sep 1950/GB. Jowett Works team car GKY 256. See Ch 4: in 1951 Monte Carlo Rally. Drivers R Ellison & W Robinson; Class win at 6th overall. In 1951 RAC Rally crewed by M Becquart & R Lunn to Class 4th. Then bought by Robinson and used in 1951 Tulip Rally (to Class 7th) and in 1952 raced at Goodwood (DNF, broke crank) and Isle of Man TT to Class 3rd, at overall 7th. Last heard from in Oct 1953.

EOSA 19R/24 Nov 1950/GB. Jowett Works team car GKY 106 in 1951 Monte Carlo Rally. Drivers T Wise & H Grimley; class position not known but 58th overall, see Ch 4. Used in some magazine road tests. Dismantled and very incomplete remains last seen in a breaker's yard in 1967.

EOSA 20R/26 Jan 1951/GB. Jowett show car GKY 804 for 1950, then the London showroom. Nothing more known.

EOSA 21R/24 Nov 1950/GB. Jowett Works team car GKY 107 See Ch 4: in 1951 Monte Carlo Rally. Drivers G Wilkins & R Baxter placed Class 2nd at 10th overall. Driven by B Hadley in 1952 RAC Rally, see Ch 4. Was Works 'hack' used to test R1 engines before Le Mans: once on the York-Scarborough dual carriageway Phill Green did 16 miles in 10 minutes (96mph). Around Nov 1951 Phill drove it from the Factory to Bridgewater and back in a day (6am to 11pm, this was 543 miles across country round trip) to return a faulty Krypton gas analyser. This car a tender at races such as the TT thanks to its ex-Monte Carlo Rally large tail rack, and also used to evaluate new designs of head gasket. Alleged rescued in depleted condition from a breakers yard in 1967 but since disappeared.

EOSA 22R+/12 Sep 1950/AUS. Built into the rather ugly Deaton Special which exists only in photos, so now lost to us.

EOSA 23R+/15 Sep 1950/CH. Believed was the lovely Worblaufen DHC depicted in *The Autocar* 16 Mar 1951 in the Geneva Show of March 1951. This very lovely car is lost to us.

E0SA 24R+/11 Oct 1950/AUS. Initially fitted with a 1947 Australian Vauxhall Tourer body, covering 70,000 miles in this form. In the early 1960s Bill Webb started to fit an attractive JWF 'Milano' fibreglass body to it. This project not finished in the era, but due to be completed by c. 2016 by new owner.

E0SA 25R+/10 Oct 1950/GB. Open body fitted by Lionel Rawson, registered GPY 859 for Sir Hugh Bell. After several owner-drivers, in 2010 new owner instigated major restoration completed 2016; bodywork by the Jaguar Heritage Trust.

E0SA 26R+/8 Nov 1950/JAP. Nothing more known.

E0SA 27R+/8 Nov 1950/JAP/SGP/NZ. Found c.1955 in Singapore by a New Zealand airman and brought to NZ still a chassis. Bought by an owner who fitted a standard Jupiter body to it, major parts imported new from GB; he made what he could not import. Car running in mid-1950s registered AP 4707. In 1962/63 fitted with an R1-spec. engine from the speedboat 'Pacific Spot'. Then fell on hard times, was involved in body-swapping with 4 other Jupiters. By 1994 a complete car again looking good, running well, was raced in 1998.

E0SA 28R+/8 Nov 1950/GB. Closed body fitted by Coachcraft of Egham registered PPF 746. Original customer was 6ft 6in so it has a high roof-line. Raced to a class win at Goodwood in May 1954. After re-work, re-registered CDG 63B – later back to original with Wills Rings top seals. Owned John Surtees 1990 to 2012 not run or restored by him. Auctioned 4 Sep 2014 for £38,525 to a Frenchman, he had it well restored.

E0SA 29R+/6 Nov 1950/GB. Closed body with standard bonnet built for rallying in the body-shop of first owner Frank Grounds, registered LOL 1. In the 1953 Monte Carlo Rally see Ch 4. Class-won the Sept 1953 Birmingham Post Rally, then was Mrs Lola Grounds's day-to-day car before re-registered SON 142 for sale in 1959. After some ownership changes, in 1999 new owner getting slow restoration carried out.

E0SA 30R+/8 Nov 1950/GB. Rolling chassis bought and stored by Nigel Mann. Closed body by Maurice Gomm only fitted in 1960 when registered 6504 MH. Always a runner but restoration needed on and off, and its owner from 2008 did much to improve it before selling it in 2011.

E0SA 31R+/9 Nov 1950/CH/GE 28077. Special drophead coachwork fitted by Ghia Suisse and shown at the March 1951 Geneva Motor Show. First owner P Strinati used it for three years. It has since disappeared.

E0SA 32R+/10 Nov 1950/GB. Drophead coachwork by Abbott of Farnham. registered PPL 373. A running car until autumn 1967. Owner from 1972, the car in storage or slow restoration.

E0SA 33R+/17 Nov 1950/USA. Closed body by Stabilimenti Farina. Believed for, and imported by, Max Hoffman who had a showroom in Chicago. Found in 1989 in Chicago with a V8 badly fitted, inserted through the cabin! Bought 1990 to California, since 2010 careful restoration under way as body and chassis had been grotesquely cut, now corrected.

E0SA 34R+/13 Nov 1950/GB. Very attractive open bodywork fitted by Richard Mead, one of six such Jupiters. Registered XRE 550 May 1952. Uniquely it has a single-piece bowed windscreen. Present owner bought it 1965 and it was running then – and is now – after its Big Sleep.

E0SA 35R+/17 Nov 1950/GB. This saloon-bodied car registered SNU 886 was daily transport from summer 1952 to late 1967 when its then owner crashed it. A surviving photo suggests from its style that its body may have been fitted by Lionel Rawson. There is no news of this car since 1967.

E0SA 36R+/23 Nov 1950/AUS. This chassis was never bodied in its era and as of modern times is now being fitted with standard Jupiter bodywork from written-off Jupiters.

E0SA 37R+/17 Nov 1950/GB. It received a saloon body by K W Bodies of Blackpool and registered NTB 603 for Bill Robinson, who raced it in June 1951 in the Isle of Man TT. See Ch 5. Sold soon after. Scrapped in 1964.

E0SA 38R+/17 Nov 1950/GB. Open body by Lionel Rawson registration JTM 100 fitted for Alf Thomas who went racing in it with success, see Ch 5. On the road

Feb 1951. Sold in April 1955 as Alf had bought an R4 for racing. JTM was used in competition by later owners before found in a breakers yard in 1966. Restored to a high standard then sold to Italy to owner who used it in some Mille Miglia Retro events 1997 to least 2002. It is kept in the Mille Miglia Museum in Brescia and is still taken out occasionally.

EOSA 39R+/20 Nov 1950/GB. Open body by Lionel Rawson on the road August 1951 registered EPR 900. By 1990 it again in a very high standard. Sold in 1997/8 to Greece, to a Greek millionaire collector. Sold in 2011 to a collector in Italy, believed in the Rome region. In February 2014 it was offered for sale at £59,000 but it is not known if sold.

EOSA 40R+/20 Nov 1950/GB. Closed body built by Tidy Bros of Wimbledon for Nigel Mann. Only first registered 53 CPA in December 1956, with its last licence drawn Oct 1963 and believed a running car into 1964. It has since disappeared.

EOSA 41R/19 Dec 1950/GB. Standard Jupiter reg'd JGA 123. It was in the 1951 Monte Carlo Rally Glasgow start to retire at Preston. Next owner Bill Skelly used it in competition e.g. 1951 RAC-TT at Dundrod, see Ch 5. After long storage it had a new owner in 2015 for restoration.

EOSA 42R/19 Dec 1950/NL/GB/AUS. Standard Jupiter reg'n GX-696 in the 1951 Monte Carlo Rally Dutch crew Scheffer and Willing. Back to Jowett 29 Aug 1952 for full updating, sold as a new car reg'n JKW 294. Bought October 1964, owner took it to Australia in 1968 reg'n KCW 706 then in 1999 changed to JKW-294. Normally in good running order with many sympathetic improvements such as high back axle.

EOSA 43R/29 Dec 1950/B. Nothing known of this car since it left the Factory.

EOSA 44R/4 Jan 1951/ Personal Export registered GKY 644 by Jowett for a Mrs Gardiner; no more known since its export.

EOSA 45R/5 Jan 1951/B. Nothing known since its shipment.

EOSA 46R+/31 Jan 1951/CY. Shipped as a rolling chassis

Bill Skelly (41) and a Lester-MG at the start of the 1951 RAC-TT at Dundrod. (LAT Photographic)

to "Pat Whittet & Co Surrey for Mr Graham, Ceylon". This is believed the completed car shipment date. Attractive open body fitted to this chassis in GB but its decayed remains found in Sri Lanka in 1970, its aluminium panelling having been made into buckets and its engine powering a local Javelin.

EOSA 47R+/27 Nov 1950/GB. Open tourer body believed fitted by Coachcraft of Egham. Registered RPB 882 Nov 1951 and in use to July 1960. Rescued from a beakers yard in 1970, stored since. As of 2015 it is to be restored.

EOSA 48R+/27 Nov 1950/GB. Closed body by Coachcraft of Egham but completed by King & Taylor, registered NPB 333 Dec 1951 with Wade-Ventor supercharger. A runner to 1966, with supercharger removed but kept with the car. Bought in 2001 and its difficult restoration is now in progress.

EOSA 49R+/29 Nov 1950/GB. Closed body by an unknown coachbuilder registered RPD 734. Still a runner in mid-1970s. Bought 2006 in reasonable and very-restorable condition.

E0SA 50R+/29 Dec 1950/GB. Open body by Leacroft – we think of Staines Middlesex. Registration unknown but the car reliably reported to be in daily use up to 1963 when it was an insurance write-off following a crash and so is now lost to us.

E0SA 51R/15 Jan 1951/GB. First of sizeable batch of complete Jupiters (most of 51 to 80). Registered NMA 507 new to Major L J Roy Taylor who had these mods: 4.1:1 rear axle, hand throttle, radio, bucket seats and – somehow – outside lid to boot. Used it in 3 competitive events. Sold early 1952 to Rex Catell, a time-keeper at Prescott. Scrapped in the mid-1960s.

E0SA 52R/5 Jan 1951/E. New in Spain reg'd M 86600. It has been identified as the 1951 Monte Carlo Rally Jupiter crewed by Fabricas Bas and Iglesias. That is all that is known of it.

E1SA 53R/22 Jan 1951/USA. Imported by the Hoffman Motor Car Co of New York. That is all we have on this car.

E0SA 54R/16 Jan 1951/USA. Imported by the Hoffman Motor Car Co of New York. That is all we have on this car.

E0SA 55R/16 Jan 1951/USA. Raced in SCCA events by its 2nd and 3rd owners E Curtis and D Freeman. Later bought by a Miss Gertrude Prior with 70,000 miles on odo. She continued to use it for a few years. Then car to Canada. In 2009 bought by a Californian in dismantled state. It is to be restored.

E0SA 56R+/5 Jan 1951/CH. Closed all-steel body by Ghia Suisse. Was Bordeaux-based Thévenin's entry for the 1952 Monte Carlo Rally, but scratched through poor preparation. By 1980 in the collection of Michel Dovaz 100km south of Paris still with its Geneva registration GE 52240, then to appear in the very imaginative Phantasme Automobile show of 1989-1990 in Sarlat. Finally it went to a small collection of cars at the Château de Sanxet near Bergerac where it remains.

E1SA 57R/24 Jan 1951/USA. Imported by the Hoffman Motor Car Co of New York. That is all we have on this car.

E1SAL 58R/22 Feb 1951/USA Ca. Imported by Angell Motors of Pasadena, the first LHD Jupiter. Believed assembled in Jowett's Experimental Dept workshop, converted from RHD. Owner from 2000 has started to restore this important car.

E1SA 59R+/16 Mar 1951/F. 482 R 74 Delivered to Turin to the Stabilimenti Farina workshops to be bodied for Marcel Becquart, see also (7, 33 and 109). Reg'n 482-R-74. In the 1952 Monte it finished class 2nd at 5th overall. In the 1953 Monte, after a mechanical delay, classified class 15th; see Ch 5. In 1967 it was bought by a Dutch collector who took it Holland reg'd DT-90-77, he then emigrated to NZ with some of his cars including this one, now reg'd LN 1950. In 1995 its odo read 17,212km (10,700 miles). Still same owner with this car in North Island looking good and running well.

E1SA 60R/24 Jan 1951/USA. Raced about six times by its 2nd owner Jerry van Voort in club races on Long Island, Bridgehampton etc. Present owner bought it in 1984.

E1SA 61R/29 Jan 1951/CAN. Bought in 1976 by owner based in Nova Scotia who carried out a full restoration to a good running standard. It moved to the USA when it changed hands thrice; owner in 2005 of Cincinnati had improvements to its braking. Car sold at auction in June 2015.

E1SA 62R/31 Jan 1951/USA NY. Known since 1962 in Alabama. In 2001 owner's son took it to Ca and following restoration uses it for shopping trips, etc, from 2009.

E1SA 63R/31 Jan 1951/USA. Imported by the Hoffman Motor Car Co of New York. Known from 1962 when in Columbus Ohio. A runner to 1975. Back to the UK in 1991, running by 1995 reg'n GFO 363. New owner in 2007, car a good runner.

E1SA 64R/31 Jan 1951/USA. Imported by the Hoffman Motor Car Co of New York. That is all we have on this car.

E1SA 65R/7 Feb 1951/USA. Imported by the Hoffman Motor Car Co of New York. Known from 1967 in the New York area, by 1969 rough and dismantled. Sold on eBay 2011 to Italy. By 2013 an aluminium near replica of the R1 was built on its chassis. A running car.

E1SA 66R/20 Feb 1951/CH. Raced at Bremgarten, Berne by T Gurzeler 17 May 51 to 4th place behind three Porsches but on 26 May 51 raced again at Bremgarten to victory in a 1500cc sports car race ahead of an HRG and at least four MGs; he also class-won a hillclimb in Switzerland on 17 Jun 51. Registration BE13381. See Ch 5. No more known of it.

E1SA 67R/7 Feb 1951/USA. Imported by the Hoffman Motor Car Co of New York. First owner was D van Voort of NY, brother of Jerry van Voort, see Ch 6. That is all on this Jupiter.

E1SA 68R/31 May 1951/S. Originally booked to CH but the car not collected even with its Swiss plates TI 642, so sold to the Stockholm agent. That is all we have on this car.

E1SA 69R+/5 Mar 1951/AUS. Built by Lyndon Duckett into lightweight stripped sports racer. He raced it to 1956. Made road legal in 1971. In 2002 new owner brought it up to Australian historic racing spec. with road registration 3009 SH; used in historic completion from 2004. For sale 2015.

E1SA 70R/7 Feb 1951/USA. Imported by the Hoffman Motor Car Co of New York. To California by 2000.

E1SA 71R/14 Feb 1951/CAN. Imported by Wells Motor Sales, Toronto, Canada. That is all we have on this car.

E1SA 72R/15 Feb 1951/AUS. Same owner since 1966. Laid up 1972, then after restoration back on the road in 1987. Used in historic competition in Australia.

E1SA 73R/15 Feb 1951/CH. Imported by Jos Stierli the Zurich agent. That is all we have on this car.

E1SA 74R/6 Mar 1951/P. Portuguese registration BF-17-18. Bought by Joaquim Filipe Fonseca Nogueira of South Lisbon. He won outright the 1951 Lisbon International Rally in this car, see Ch 4. Found in 1978, with a VW engine fitted. Jupiter engine from (281) was installed, and after several ownership changes and restoration work, owned by C Cruz of Lisbon from 2006 having been brought up to very good condition.

E1SA 75R/6 Mar 1951/P. Portuguese registration BF-17-17. It was driven to class 9th in the 1952 Lisbon International Rally by Joaquin Nunes dos Santos. see Ch 4. Found by Jose Martins in North Oporto in 1980 lacking engine parts and radiator.

E1SA 76R/16 Oct 1951/GB. Registered by Jowett HKU 56 in July 1951. It was the October 1951 London Motor Show demonstrator. Road-tested by John Bolster for *Autosport* 8 Jan 1952: Bolster thought very highly of it. Written in *Sport & Country* 6 Aug 1952 "300 miles with 3 stops in 10 hours". In early autumn 1953 this Jupiter was in the extended testing at the MIRA track to prove the new Series III engine, with 40,000 miles per car of continuous running. The driver lost it on a corner of the triangular circuit: it inverted in a ploughed field. Driver and car survived: A Jowett employee bought the wreck and rebuilt it, sold October 1953. After many owners and a stay in Northern Ireland 1964 to 1996 it was bought 1998 by present owner who always keeps it in very good order.

E1SA 77R/6 Mar 1951/GB. Registered by Jowett as HAK 117, as a direct sale to Alfred 'Goff' Imhoff, a London radio dealer and rally-man usually in Allards. In the 1951 Morecambe Rally it placed 2nd in class, see Chapter 4. A Jowett team car in the 1951 RAC Rally placing class 5th, one place behind Marcel Becquart in Jupiter GKY 256. J C Checkley was its next owner and he drove it in the July 1953 Eastbourne Rally, see Chapter 6. It was seen in London in 1959 but known to have been scrapped in the late 1960s.

E1SA 78R/8 Mar 1951/USA. Importer Hoffman Motor Car Co of New York. Originally no bonnet louvres so an unusual louvre pattern made. Moved to Arizona, Texas then Ca by 1972 where in 1999 last titled, then to Ohio. To GB in 2000 for body-off restoration to running order in 2013 reg'n 881 YUJ.

The Checkleys (77) in driving test 1953 Eastbourne Rally. (Charles Dunn)

E1SA 79R/10 Mar 1951/S. Imported by the Gothenburg agent Alpen & Gundersen. Nothing more known of this car.

E1SA 80R/10 Mar 1951/USA. Importer Hoffman Motor Car Co of NY. After stored 40 years found in Colorado in 2010. Poor nick: chassis cut for a foreign engine. To be restored.

E1SA 81R+/10 Mar 1951/GB. Light closed body by J E Farr & Sons Ltd of Blackburn Lancs reg'd MTJ 300 on 1 Jan 1952 for Ellison in the 1952 Monte. It left the road at St Flour so did not finish – for more see Ch 4. This its only sporting event and sold August 1952. Found in 1965/66. New owner in 1984 and well-restored and back on the road again. In 2002 it was re-united with its original Monte Carlo Rally plate. Then the owner's daughter took on the car, it seen around from time to time.

E1SA 82R/28 Feb 1951/CH. Imported by Jowett agent Fransisco Morani of Lugano. That is all we have on this car.

E1SA 83R+/9 Mar 1951/CH. Imported by Jowett agent Jos Stierli of Zurich. Lovely open body by Gebrüder Beutler fitted: it appeared in an *Automobil im Festkleid* (Concours d'Elegance) 10th July 1951 to come 2nd in its class (under SF20,000). Registration ZH-28648 known from photos in *Automobil Revue* 11 Jul 1951. That is all we have on this car.

E1SA 84R/28 Feb 1951/CH. Imported by Jowett agent Jos Stierli of Zurich. That is all we have on this car.

E1SA 85R+/20 Mar 1951/NL. Chassis imported by H G L Sieberg the Amsterdam Jowett agent. Four-seater closed body fitted by Boonacker of Haarlem. Registered NK-03-02 in 1952, a running car up to 1958. It is now lost to us.

E1SA 86R/10 Mar 1951/I. Imported by I.E.R.S.A of Florence. That is all we have on this car.

E1SA 87R+/13 Mar 1951/GB. Open body fitted by Richard Mead of Kenilworth, Warwicks. Registered MBJ 519 with warranty dated 27 Nov 1951 to a Mr Barker of Ipswich, director of a cereal firm. Last heard from in 1959 when sold to someone in Coventry for £325. Nothing more known.

E1SA 88R/20 Mar 1951/NL. Imported by H G L Sieberg the Amsterdam Jowett agent. In June 1952 to NZ with its Dutch owner, sold there Sept. 1953. These NZ reg'ns: EH 15 then MA 6051 then ME 1951. Restored by 1988, engine 1600cc and a 5-speed g/b. New owner in 2009, an excellent car.

E1SA 89R+/7 Mar 1951/GB. Open body by E D Abbott of Farnham, Surrey, reg'd RPA 7 for Commander Milner in the April 1952 London MC's 'Little Rally'. In May 1954 he in a London MC Sprint at Goodwood. Sold Dec 1954 with reg'n WPC 121. Current owner bought it in December 2013.

E1SA 90R/13 Mar 1951/ Personal Export car, reg'n HAK 183 by Jowett. Found in the USA in 1984. After 3 owners, in July 2014 to a buyer in Poland, needing restoration.

E1SA 91R+/16 Mar 1951/GB. Chassis bought by a coach-operator in Gainsborough, Lincs for a special body, but instead to a Bradford-area garage for a standard body to be fitted. Never used, sold in 1989 in poor nick. By 2013 its stripped chassis sold for a body (maybe standard?) to be fitted to it.

E1SA 92R/19 Mar 1951/USA. Importer the Hoffman Motor Car Co of New York. That is all we have on this car.

E1SA 93R+/16 Mar 1951/F. Shipped to the Paris Jowett agent J A Plisson. This the chassis believed bought by Jean Latune, President of the Automobile Club of Drôme who had a closed body fitted by coachbuilder Jean Barrou of Tournon-sur-Rhone registration 769-P-26. The Jupiter (see Ch 4) was in these competitions: Tour de France Automobile Aug/Sept 1951 to Class 9th from 35; the 1952 Monte to Class 23rd; Tour de France Automobile Sept 1952 to Class 5th from 39; 1953 Monte to Class 5th, the March 1953 Lyon Charbonières Rally now crewed by P Gay and M Trollinet, one of whom may have been its new owner. That is all we have on this elusive car.

E1SA 94R/19 Mar 1951/USA. Importer Hoffman Motor Car Co of NY. Three owners 1960-1970 known. In a poor state by 1970 and believed dismantled and scrapped. The bonnet, however, went onto Jupiter No1 q.v.

E1SA 95R+/18 Jun 1951/CH. Imported by the Jowett agent Fransisco Morani of Lugano. Could be the 3rd and last Ghia Suisse saloon-bodied Jupiter. A photo shows it with a Jupiter-like body with split V-screen. That is all we have.

E1SA 96R/19 Mar 1951/USA. Importer Hoffman Motor Car Co of NY. Known to have been in the same family since 1954. Owner in Ohio was last heard from in 1976.

E1SA 97R+/13 Jul 1951/GB. By 1953 an attractive closed body fitted by Flewitt Ltd of Birmingham. In Hebden's Jowett agency showroom to 1958 when reg'd HCW 83 in Oct for sale. Running car for c.7 years then stored. Bought 2002 and some difficult restoration work has been carried out.

E1SA 98R/28 Mar 1951/GB. Reg'n HAK 268 by Jowett for direct sale to W T Tee, proprietor of *Motor Sport* magazine. Next owner from 1963 ran it to 1981. As of 2013 the car in work or stored. It claims to have a floor-mounted gear change.

E1SA 99R+/12 Jun 1951/GB. Closed body by KW Bodies of Blackpool for the Keighley, Yorkshire, agent E Foulds with reg'n KWX 770. In the Nov 1951 MCC Rally (Ch 4). later raced by new owner A Wake at Silverstone on 5th June 1954 taking class 2nd, one of the five events he raced it including at Ossington and Aintree. Nothing more known.

E1SA 100R/19 Mar 1951/USA. Importer Hoffman Motor Car Co of NY. Owner 1972 in Washington DC. Professionally restored 1996-2000 by Treasured Motorcar Services of Reistertown Md. Reg'n LZO 474. owner now in Md, took this Jupiter to a high degree of originality. Stored from c. 2010.

E1SA 101R+/10 Jun 1951/GB. This chassis shipped to the West Lothian, Scotland, Jowett agent. Warranty return in the name of Elizabeth Sneddon of Caldercruix, Lanarkshire dated 4 Feb 1952 confirms the car was built. We have nothing more.

E1SA 102R/11 Mar 1951/S. Imported by the Swedish agent Nordiska Automobil A/B. To Denmark March 1959. After several owners and dismantlement, new owner from 2014 of Hillerød, Denmark had the car under restoration.

E1SA 103R+/15 Jun 1951/GB. This chassis shipped to the Lancaster Jowett agent, and while nothing definite is

known, it is a reasonable assumption that it is the third KW closed Jupiter, built for a Mr Green of Leeds. Nothing more is known.

E1SA 104R/21 Mar 1951/S. Imported by the Swedish agent Motortillbehor A/B. Owned by Carl Magnus Ring since about 1983 who still had it in 2010, modified but long stored.

E1SA 105R+/15 Jun 1951/GB. Closed body by E D Abbott of Farnham, reg'n CCP 966 Jan/Feb 1952 in Halifax. Price £2210 new included heater, radio and screen washers. C P Swain drove it in the 1953 Morecambe Rally (Ch 6). On 17May1966 while driven too fast, it went over a cliff in Wales killing the two young men in it. In 1996 confirmed wholly scrapped.

E1SA 106R/2 Apr 1951/Morocco. Imported by Auto Corp SA. Casablanca. First owner a Roger Di Marco who drove it in the Rallye du Maroc to a good place, including the final speed event on the Ring of Casablanca. Nothing more known.

E1SA 107R+/18 Jun 1951/GB. As new given a real camper body, fitted by Barton Transport, a bus company. Registered NAL 323 c. July 1952, it toured mainland Europe in 1953 as far as Switzerland. Sold 1955 and nothing more is known of it.

E1SA 108R+/2 Apr 1951/USA. Importer Hoffman Motor Car Co of NY. First heard from in 1991 in North Carolina. In 2013 the car still stored in N Carolina.

E1SA 109R+/6 Jul 1951/I. This chassis went to Turin to Stabilimenti Farina for H Pereire. Found 1991 near Paris in France. Bought 2001 to GB for a total excellent restoration. By 2003 on the road reg'n 707 PL and looking very good.

E1SA 110R/3 Sep 1951/Personal Export reg'n HAK 41 by Jowett. Date is the export date. Car running in the UK six months earlier for a Goodwood appearance in August 1951 in a 5-lap scratch race – owner F E N Wills. He took it to Singapore, reg'd there BB 1861. Nov 1951 in Singapore Gap Hillclimb to 3rd behind a BMW and an MG TC. Did several more events 1952, 1953 before being sold. That is all we have.

E1SA 111R/20 Dec 1951/GB. Should have been shipped

as a rolling chassis as all other odd-numbered chassis 81 to 119 were rolling chassis. Complete standard car registered NYD 273 in February 1952. Known from June 1964 as everyday transport. Always in good running order with developments. New owner from 2002 still uses it regularly.

E1SA 112R/11 Apr 1951/USA. Imported by Sanders Motor Sales, Texas. That is all we have on this car.

E1SA 113R+/5 Oct 1951/GB. This rolling chassis unbuilt until a standard body fitted via the Portsmouth Jowett agency, reg'd JRV 163 in June 1954. First owner kept the car to 1984 when sold with 24,272 miles on the odo. Still around and seen about.

E1SA 114R/2 Apr 1951/USA. Importer Hoffman Motor Car Co of NY. Ordered with an XK120 for Mary McBride of the firm McBride Construction Inc. Shipped as deck cargo so needed a re-spray. Owner in California from 2008 had it restored to excellent condition by Scott Renner. To GB in 2016.

E1SA 115R+/7 Aug 1951/NZ. This chassis never built in the era. Various owners acquired body parts from scrapped NZ Jupiters and from 2001 very slow restoration began, with registration JJ 1951 reserved for it.

E1SA 116R/10 Apr 1951/CH. Found in 1982 by Heinz Bolliger, an auto-mechanic of Rutlingen near Berne who did a superb restoration on it, in July 2002 reg'n BE 131 254. In 2013 sold locally in very good nick, re-registered BE 12305.

E1SA 117R+/7 Aug 1951/GB. Fitted with an open body by Richard Mead of Kenilworth, Warwicks, and in Feb 1952 reg'n TVW 999. First seen in 1962 as a running car. Bought 1994 for restoration, to be sold in 1999 a good runner.

E1SA 118R/10 Apr 1951/USA Tx. Shipped to Sanders Motor Sales of Texas. That is all we have on this car.

E1SA 119R+/25 Jun 1951/GB. Shipped to a Lancashire agent, but no warranty return so we know not if it was completed.

E1SA 120R/11 Apr 1951/IRL/Eire. Reg'n ZL 6262 by first owner V Ross, soon did a hillclimb near Dublin. By early 1952 sold to Irish driver Joe Kelly who used it the

1952 British Empire Trophy, Isle of Man, then on 14th April 1952 in a handicap race at Goodwood, then a race at Boreham – see Ch 5. Then sold to Northern Ireland in mid-1960s reg'n AIJ 1824 about 1967 and restored. Then to Scotland for more restoration reg'n AS 2209. Bought 2012 south to England, a runner.

E1SA 121R/6 Apr 1951/CH. This Jupiter was shipped to a Mr J Lancy c/o Jos Stierli of Zurich. Nothing more known.

E1SAL 122R/24 Apr 1951/USA. Shipped to Angell Motors of Pasadena. While known in 1967, it is now believed scrapped.

E1SAL 123R/24 Apr 1951/USA. Shipped to Angell Motors of Pasadena. Since 1968 owned by a Boeing engineer of Washington State who well-restored it from 2002.

E1SAL 124R/22 Jun 1951/USA. Chassis of this Angell Motors car now a special with Abarth motor, stored from 2007.

E1SAL 125R/24 Apr 1951/USA. Shipped to Angell Motors of Pasadena. Last driven in Ca in 1956. Then to Philadelphia a runner but stored from 1973. Bought 1987 by D Burrows of that town, by 1991 very well-restored, winning top awards at shows. Reg'n HB-44 (at rear) but JJUP51 at front.

E1SAL 126R/22 Jun 1951/USA. Shipped to Angell Motors of Pasadena. Found still in Ca in 1984 'a wreck' as chassis cut for a V8. To Belgium in 1994. In 1995 next owner restored it to a high standard, with aero-screens. In 2006 reg'n OBQ 354.

E1SAL 127R/23 Jun 1951/USA. Shipped to Angell Motors of Pasadena. In Ca 1984, a basket case. For sale in GB 2015.

E1SA 128R/30 Apr 1951/USA. Shipped to Sanders Motor Sales of Texas. That is all we have on this car.

E1SA 129R/30 Apr 1951/USA. Shipped to Sanders Motor Sales of Texas. Laid up 1965. Bought 1995 by J Womble of Tx who did much restoration on it. but work stopped in 2010.

E1SA 130R/29 May 1951/USA. Importer Hoffman Motor Car Co of New York. That is all we have on this car.

E1SA 131R/7 Jun 1951/GB. Lightweight car reg'n

Dave & Judith Burrows showing their Jupiter (125). (Burrows)

HAK 366 built by Jowett for Le Mans 1951 driven by Hadley/Goodacre. See Ch 3. Jowett team car 1951 RAC TT driven by Hadley to class win, and a 1952 race at Silverstone where G Phillips drove it to Class 3rd: see Ch 5. After more competition to 1954 (Ch 6) found in 1969 in poor state. Several owners worked on it. From 2000 new owner fully restored it to Le Mans specification for a prominent appearance at the ACO Clubhouse at the Le Mans circuit during the 24-hour race that year (the Jupiter's 50th) one of 40 Jupiters attending. It still has its many special features; the lightened bodywork with unstamped panels confirming its Experimental Dept build.
E1SA 132R/7 Jun 1951/GB. lightweight car reg'n HAK 365 built by Jowett for Le Mans 1951 driven to class win by Becquart/Wilkins. See Ch 3. Later sold to Alf Thomas and raced by Anne Neale at Silverstone and Mallory Park in 1957 (Ch 6). Last licence drawn in 1965 to a Miss Prior of Lewes who sold it in 1966 allegedly to an American who took it to Spain, last seen in 1970 near Torremolinos.
E1SA 133R/23 May 1951/USA. Importer Hoffman Motor Car Co of NY. Known from 1974, put in good running order from 1976. In 2005 bought by a Mr Jowett based in north-east USA.
E1SA 134R/30 Apr 1951/USA Tx. Shipped to Sanders

Motor Sales of Texas. Three owners in Indiana known. J Clifton, 1957-1969 raced it in SCCA C-Modified class with Corvette 283ci V8 with 3 speed g/b. In 1969 sold to G Tabron.
E1SA 135R/1 May 1951/USA Tx. Shipped to Sanders Motor Sales of Texas. That is all we have on this car.
E1SA 136R/4 May 1951/AUS. An early owner Earl Pearce used it in the Rob Roy Hillclimb Nov 1956. Restored c. 2004 and then sold 2009 to new owner.
E1SA 137R/23 May 1951/USA. Importer Hoffman Motor Car Co of NY. Known in Connecticut in 1974 but that's it.
E1SA 138R/11 May 1951/F. Imported by Plisson the Paris agent. That is all we have on this car.
E1SA 139R/23 May 1951/USA. Importer Hoffman Motor Car Co of NY. Known in Connecticut 1990 then Illinois 2002.
E1SA 140R/23 May 1951/USA. Importer Hoffman Motor Car Co of NY. Known in Alabama from 1952, used as everyday car for a number of years. To California to his son Scott Renner in 2000. After much work, restored by 2015.
E1SA 141R/23 May 1951/USA. Importer Hoffman Motor Car Co of NY. That is all we have on this car.
E1SA 142R/23 May 1951/USA. Importer Hoffman Motor Car Co of NY. That is all we have on this car.
E1SA 143R/30 May 1951/USA. Importer Hoffman Motor Car Co of NY. That is all we have on this car.
E1SA 144R/29 May 1951/USA. Importer Hoffman Motor Car Co of NY. Owner from 1958 fitted a Corvair Flat 6 engine in 1988. Sold 2004 to Tennessee. Well-restored to original power etc by Kip Motors of Dallas Tx, completed by 2007.
E1SA 145R/29 May 1951/USA. Importer Hoffman Motor Car Co of NY. That is all we have on this car.
E1SA 146R/23 May 1951/USA. Importer Hoffman Motor Car Co of NY. That is all we have on this car.
E1SA 147R/29 May 1951/USA. Importer Hoffman Motor Car Co of New York. Three owners known from 1981 to 1989. Then bought by Jim Miller in a very poor state, to be restored.
E1SA 148R/29 May 1951/USA. Imported by the Hoffman Motor Car Co of NY. That is all we have on this car.

E1SA 149R/29 May 1951/USA. Importer Hoffman Motor Car Co of NY. That is all we have on this car.

E1SA 150R/29 May 1951/USA. Importer Hoffman Motor Car Co of NY. That is all we have on this car.

E1SA 151R/29 May 1951/NL. Imported by Amsterdam agent H G L Sieberg. Known in use 1958-1963, and from 1981. Reg'n UX-70-15. New owner in 2005/6, the car looking good. Seen in a concours event in 2012.

E1SA 152R/5 Jun 1951/USA. Importer Hoffman Motor Car Co of NY. That is all we have on this car.

E1SA 153R/13 Jun 1951/F. Imported to Paris. Believed the car used by Armangaud in the 1951 Alpine Rally, see Ch 4. Well-restored from a crashed state 1995-1999 with Alfa 1500cc flat engine + a Ford Taunus gearbox. Next owner from 2001 used it in some classic car events. Sold 2011 still in France.

E1SA 154R/6 Jun 1951/A. Shipped to an address in Vienna. That is all the history we have on this car.

E1SA 155R/19 Jun 1951/U. Shipped to Barrere & Cia, Montevideo. The only Jupiter imported to Uruguay. Barrere had no Jowett-trained mechanics: maintenance sloppy, repairs poor. An angry owner shot wounded Barrere's Head Mechanic. This Jupiter crashed many years ago; we assume long gone.

E1SA 156R/4 Jun 1951/USA. Importer Hoffman Motor Car Co of NY. In Maryland from 1978. In 1980s a Volvo engine installed. Last heard from in 2001 when for sale in Colorado.

E1SA 157R/4 Jun 1951/USA. Importer Hoffman Motor Car Co of NY. A runner when known in 1983. In 1990 the owner was of Holbrook, NY. Last heard from in 2000.

E1SA 158R/4 Jun 1951/USA. Importer Hoffman Motor Car Co of NY. That is all we have on this car.

E1SA 159R/5 Jun 1951/USA. Importer Hoffman Motor Car Co of NY. First known in 1966. To Canada in 1982. Then sold in 2009 to California, dismantled but body in good order.

E1SA 160R/26 Jun 1951/NL. Early registration ST-18-16 (1955) then ET-1816 now CT-92304. Found 1973 with an early Porsche engine fitted, and returned to standard. New owner from 1982: as of May 2015 still a very nice runner.

E1SA 161R/18 Jun 1951/NZ. Registration CT 6895. By 1990 it a bare stripped chassis its bodywork on other Jupiters. Chassis complete in 2015, to be rebuilt in some form.

E1SA 162R/19 Jul 1951/AUS. Known about since first ownership. Reduced to a poor state by the late 1960s. Owner from 1992 began restoration c. 1976 and completed 2006, a very smart car registered JUP 51.

E1SA 163R/26 Jul 1951/AUS. Bought Tony George in 1984 after 14 years lying in the open. It was very well rebuilt and finished in 1994 to a very good running order.

E1SA 164R/26 Jul 1951/Cyprus/First owner Elpherios Prastitis of Famagusta used it in local events 1951-1955. Also used by S Sphaliotis in a Famagusta Rally. It was in storage in 1974 when the Turks invaded. The car believed lost to us.

E1SA 165R/26 Jul 1951/AUS. Known from 1970, registered RWS 205 in 1985. Restored c.1999 by C Warnes and used in rallies and hill-climbs. New owner from 2005.

E1SA 166R/12 Jul 1951/AUS. G White bought it in 1977 as a runner, approximately. Now restored and running.

E1SA 167R/19 Oct 1951/NZ. First owner Arthur Brownlee raced it at Tahuna Beach and other events. Found in 1965 then new owner from 1980 restored it, reg'n AW 25. With developed engines and even the R1 engine from the speedboat Pacific Spot, raced in Historic events in NZ from 1983 to now.

E1SA 168R/31 Aug 1951/P. Registered ID-17-85, in the 1952 Lisbon International Rally to class 7th by 2nd owner Joaquim Luis da Cunha with Silva Cardoza. Third owner was P Godinho who took it to Scotland with him when at Glasgow University. Around 1956 he had an accident near Carlisle and it was rebuilt by JELtd when with Edinburgh reg'n OSG 12. In 1964 sold for £40 said to be in good condition. Now lost.

E1SA 169R/13 Jul 1951/AUS. Found in 1990 in a very poor state; restored and running again from 1994.

E1SA 170R/28 Jun 1951/DK. Went to the Danish Jowett agent E Sommers who fixed a hard-top to it and sold it to a Swedish customer. No further history is known of this car.

E1SAL 171R/24 Aug 1951/BR. Went to Sao Paolo, logged later for sale in Rio de Janeiro. This is the first LHD production Jupiter. No further history is known of this car.
E1SAL 172R/3 Sep 1951/USA. Shipped to Angell Motors of Pasadena. No further history is known of this car.
E1SAL 173R/29 Sep 1951/USA. Shipped to Angell Motors of Pasadena. No further history is known of this car.
E1SAL 174R/6 Nov 1951/Personal Export car reg'd HAK 731 by Jowett to a Mr G S Wise c/o Wells Motor Sales, Toronto, Canada. Subsequent history of this car is unknown.
E1SAL 175R/27 Aug 1951/BR. Shipped to Sao Paolo. No further history is known of this car.
E1SAL 176R/29 Aug 1951/USA. Shipped to Angell Motors of Pasadena. No further history is known of this car.
E1SAL 177R/27 Aug 1951/NL. Shipped to Amsterdam agent H G L Sieberg. A period photo shows what is likely this Jupiter, with reg'n NG-30-24. No further history known.
E1SAL 178R/29 Aug 1951/USA. Shipped to Angell Motors of Pasadena. Known from 1989 in Ca owned by an ex-NASA engineer. Via eBay Dec 2011 rough but complete to Colorado.
E1SAL 179R/27 Aug 1951/BR. Shipped to Sao Paolo. There is a hint via its engine number that it came to California around 1953, but there is no further history known of this car.
E1SAL 180R/27 Aug 1951/USA. Shipped to Angell Motors of Pasadena. That is all we have this on car.
E1SA 181R/5 Jun 1951/HK. There is evidence that this car migrated to NZ and was most probably scrapped there c.1970
E1SA 182R/20 Jul 1951/NZ. Owner Vic Morrison from 1962. Reg'd AJ 2061 and raced very well by Vic (the 'Jaguar-eater' see Ch 6) to c.1972 when it passed through several owners. Reg'n JJ 182 in the 1990s. Current owner bought it in 2011.
E1SA 183R/24 Jul 1951/Personal Export reg'd HKU 43 by Jowett for a Mr C G Henry for exporting to where?

E1SA 184R/8 Nov 1951/Personal Export for a Mr S Lay to abroad, presumably in November, but to where?
E1SA 185R/19 Jul 1951/AUS. Known from 1974. Reg'n SA 185 in 1984 after restoration. No folding hood, only a detachable hard-top. New owner from 1987. A good runner.
E1SA 186R/12 Jul 1951/AUS. It may be the Des Pinn Jupiter, lightened and highly tuned for events in 1952. See Ch 5. This car (186) currently stored.
E1SA 187R/11 Jul 1951/Personal Export reg'd HKU 90 by Jowett to a Mr B Wananaker. No more known.
E1SA 188R/20 Jul 1951/NZ. First owner claimed he drove 430,000 miles in it to 1980 when restored. Later in a museum near Auckland. From c. 2010 out and about. Reg'n CY 2305.
E1SA 189R/20 Jul 1951/NZ. First registered ER 3985. Known from 1968. Owner from 1995 superbly restored it by c.2000 from a bad state. Now in the late Ray Win's collection of Jowetts: the Ray Win Collection Community Trust.
E1SA 190R/26 Jul 1951/CH. Imported by the Zurich agent Jos Stierli & Co. We have no further history of this car.
E1SA 191R/26 Jul 1951/CH. Imported by the Zurich agent Jos Stierli & Co. We have no further history of this car.
E1SAL 192R/29 Aug 1951/USA. Shipped to Angell Motors of Pasadena. Known from 1958 in Ca. Owner Jim Miller from 1986. He has historic-raced it from 1989 wearing '36'.
E1SA: 193R/3 Sep 1951/USA. Shipped to Angell Motors of Pasadena. We have no further history of this car.
E1SAL 194R/28 Sep 1951/USA. Shipped to Angell Motors of Pasadena. We have no further history of this car.
E1SAL 195R/3 Sep 1951/USA. Shipped to Angell Motors of Pasadena. Worked on by the "King of Kustomizers" George Barris. Various Ford engines fitted over the years. In Arizona from 1964 with the Daugherty family: owned Cash Daugherty from 1990. Some restorative work from 2002.

E1SAL 196R/30 Aug 1951/USA. Shipped to Angell Motors of Pasadena. We have no further history of this car.

E1SAL 197R/28 Aug 1951/USA Ca. Shipped to Angell Motors of Pasadena. In the Johnson family father & son from new. Laid up with broken crank in 1953 with 16,448 miles covered, back on the road in 1990 owner W T Johnson.

E1SAL 198R/28 Aug 1951/USA Ca. Shipped to Angell Motors of Pasadena. We have no further history of this car.

E1SAL 199R/28 Aug 1951/USA Ca. Shipped to Angell Motors of Pasadena. We have no further history of this car.

E1SAL 200R/29 Aug 1951/USA Ca. Shipped to Angell Motors of Pasadena. We have no further history of this car.

E1SAL 201R/29 Aug 1951/USA Ca. Shipped to Angell Motors of Pasadena. Only a 1962 enquiry from Arizona for parts from Jowett Engineering; no further history of this car.

E1SA 202R/7 Aug 1951/AUS. Said to have been raced by the Tasmanian agent Donald Gorringe. Around c.1960 it was customised reg'd WVA 506, undone in 1963 reg'd WTN 539. Once in the 1960s driven across the Nullabor Plain. Car thought to be stored somewhere in Tasmnania.

E1SA 203R/20 Jul 1951/NZ. Original registration BL 7753. For a time, it had the entire front-end of a Standard Vanguard fitted under the Jupiter bonnet. In 1980 new owner located the sawn-off front chassis tubing and restored it to original by 1989 except for a Toyota 5-speed g/b with the car looking very good, runs well, reg'n NF 1663. New owner from c.2005.

E1SA 204R/13 Aug 1951/Reg'd HKU 37 by Jowett for a Mr G A Graham. A photo of it at the front of Jowett's London showroom titled an exhibit for the Oct 1951 London Motor Show. No destination given but a Mr Graham is known to have raced a standard Jupiter in Ceylon, and a B Gordon Graham exported a chassis (46) to Ceylon. That is all we have.

E1SA 205R/7 Sep 1951/AUS. Known from before 1980

when owner sold it to Ed Wolf, both of Sydney. Latest owner bought it in 2000 and completed its restoration in 2005.

E1SA 206R/27 Jul 1951/Reg'd HKU 284 by Jowett for a Mr & Mrs Gene Fowler of Beverley Hills, California. This the first of the four Jupiters bought by the USA film comedian Red Skelton for himself and his immediate entourage (see also 228, 256, 266). Owner 1962–1966 Don Ricardo, once leader of big bands like NBC Orchestra; a collector, restorer and racer of 'antique automobiles'. Known from 1975, restored and to Arizona 1980; from 1996 owned and stored California.

E1SAL 207R/28 Sep 1951/USA. Importer Sanders Motor Sales of Texas. Seemingly found in Ca with chassis cut for a V8. Back to GB in 1999, condition rough. Owner from 2011 began difficult restoration; the car in running order by 2013.

E1SAL 208R/3 Sep 1951/USA Ca. Shipped to Angell Motors of Pasadena. History unknown

E1SAL 209R/28 Sep 1951/USA Tx. Shipped to Sanders Motor Sales of Texas. History unknown.

E1SAL 210R/24 Mar 1952/Shipped to an address in Tripoli after re-work at Jowett, in 1951 having been shipped to the French agent Plisson of Paris as RHD. Definitely an 'E1'.

E1SA 211R/12 Jul 1951/Originally shipped to the French agent Plisson of Paris as RHD. Returned to Jowett in March 1952 and re-sold in GB September 1953 as E3SA 211R with some 1953 updates. Registration KAM 941. Known from 1971. A running car to 1986. New owner 2003 bought it for restoration.

E1SAL 212R/5 Feb 1952/delivered to the Antwerp agent, but believed originally to Plisson for Oct 1951 Paris Salon, then unsold in France. Found 1986 still in Belgium, soon excellently restored reg'n HLY 725. Always in good order in 2011 re-registered 1.OAN.435 in 2011. The car often shown.

E1SAL 213R/1 Sep 1951/USA Tx. Shipped to Sanders Motor Sales of Texas. First buyer in Co. Wichita, Ks. Bob Barnes its third owner from 1953 won an SCCA National Rally in Nebraska in 1953 and then raced it at Aspen

(Colorado) and Okmulgee (Oklahoma) in 1954. By 1962 he in New Jersey. By 1977 it was long-stored. Sold 2008 to an unknown buyer.

E1SAL 214R/28 Sep 1951/USA. Shipped to Sanders Motor Sales of Texas. Very likely the car in the 1990 Pan Americano Race across Mexico. In 2002 for sale on eBay; unsold 2009 in Mexico City: vendor Leonardo Huerto of Ducky Imports.

E1SAL 215R/11 Oct 1951/USA Tx. Shipped to Sanders Motor Sales of Texas. History unknown.

Chassis 216 not built according to Jowett records.

E1SA 217R/20 Jul 1951/NZ. Owners known from 1984 when registered CF 5320. Owned in the same family from 2000.

E1SAL 218R/18 Jul 1951/YV. It was shipped to Commercial di Auto-Movitas, Venezuela. Nothing more known.

E1SA 219R/20 Jul 1951/NZ. Registrations BG 6217 (1951) then BB 6217 (1997) then NB 765 (2000). Known from 1967. Restored from 1986: 'a classy runner' 1996. New owner 2012.

E1SA 220R/20 Jul 1951/NZ. Known from 1957 with DA 7058 registration. By 2009 registered JUPATR owner Alan Stanley.

E1SA 221R/20 Jul 1951/NZ. First registered CS 2260. History known from 1966. later registered GF 1834. New owner 2014. Condition rough, to be restored by 2016.

E1SAL 222R/28 Sep 1951/USA Tx. Shipped to Sanders Motor Sales of Texas. No history known of this car.

E1SAL 223R/24 Sep 1951/BR. Shipped to S.E.I.S.A in Rio de Janeiro. No history known of this car.

E1SAL 224R/27 Sep 1951/USA Tx. Shipped to Sanders Motor Sales of Texas. No history known of this car.

E1SAL 225R/27 Sep 1951/D/Shipped to H A Angell of Westphalia, then of West Germany. No more history known.

E1SAL 226R/1 Oct 1951/USA Tx. Shipped to Sanders Motor Sales of Texas. No history known of this car.

E1SA 227R/9 Aug 1951/Personal Export reg'd HKU 93 by Jowett to a Mr T F Kingston for export to we know not where.

E1SA 228R/27 Jul 1951/Reg'd HKU 286 by Jowett for a Mr & Mrs David Rose of Beverley Hills, California. The second of the four Jupiters bought by the USA film comedian Red Skelton for himself and his immediate entourage (see also 206, 256, 266). In 1977 found in a depleted state in a Los Angeles wreckers yard but by 1983 it had vanished.

E1SA 229R/19 Sep 1951/Personal Export car sold to a Mrs D Yull c/o Berlieri Malek of Accra, the capital of the then Gold Coast (Ghana). Returned to the UK (Devon) in 1953. Photographed in the 1953 MCC-Daily Express Rally driven by G Yull, registration WP 8448 its West Africa mark. Then UK reg'd PTT 243. Next owner drove it in the 1958 Exeter Trial. New owner in 2015 has it under restoration.

E1SA 230R/20 Aug 1951/Personal Export reg'd HKU 228 by Jowett for a Mr Chatham. In 1977 owned by M Pittier of Rolle, Lake Léman, Switzerland. Stored there since the 1960s.

E1SA 231R/20 Aug 1951/CH. Shipped to the Geneva agent H Ziegler. The first Jupiter with red upholstery. That's it.

E1SAL 232R/26 Oct 1951/MEX/Shipped to a Mr A W Tucker of Mexico. Found in 1971 in Puebla as a runner. Owner from 2006 the finder's son who will restore it.

E1SAL 233R/12 Oct 1951/USA Tx. Shipped to Sanders

G Yull driving his ex-Gold Coast Jupiter 229 in the November 1953 MCC Rally. (LAT Photographic)

Motor Sales of Texas to Massachusetts. Next owner from 1963. From New Hampshire to Florida, a very nice restored running car.

Chassis 234 to 241 were not constructed according to Jowett.

E1SA 242R+/13 Jul 1951/GB. The first of 12 consecutive rolling chassis shipments. The body looks standard but is not, it built by R Watling Greenwood of Worth, Sussex, reg'd GAP 6. Driven by first owner R Holmes in some Sussex events in 1953 see Ch 6. Found in 1966 and body-off restored by 1970. Sold 1989 reg'n KAS 147. The car looking very good, running well.

E1SA 243R+/5 Jul 1951/GB. Rolling chassis shipped to an East Yorkshire agent, who returned it to Jowett and it was built into the std Jupiter E2 SA 886R and shipped out in Sept 1952.

E1SA 244R+/5 Jul 1951/GB. Rolling chassis shipped to a South Yorkshire agent, who returned it to Jowett, it was built into the std Jupiter E2 SAL 939R, shipped out in Sept 1952.

E1SA 245R+/27 Jul 1951/GB. Shipped to Farr & Son of Blackburn for a FHC body to be fitted, first owner S H Whittaker of Preston, Lancs who did not like it, but 2nd owner did, keeping it 10 years. After nine more owners and decline, owner from 2008 has had some work done on it.

E1SA 246R+/26 Jul 1951/GB. Shipped to the Southampton agent. Found still as chassis in 1958. FHC body fitted by 1964 reg'n 538 KOR. Crashed c.1970, body scrapped. Rebuilt as std with panels from three scrapped Jupiters. Running again c.1972. New owner from 1996 has a nice running car.

E1SA 247R+/10 Jul 1951/GB. Abbotts of Farnham fitted a comely FHC body and registered it KOU 605 in November 1952. A roadside photo was found of it as a day-to-day car taken in 1955. It was a runner to 1966. In 1996 bought by Tom Chapman who had it very well restored and running by 2009. Sold in auction in 2014 to disappear.

E1SA 248R+/18 Jul 1951/GB. Handsome open body fitted by Richard Mead of Kenilworth, Warwicks. Reg'd GTL 279 in May 1953. First owner M Beaumont raced and rallied it. He said *"its road-holding was excellent particularly in snow and the wet when one could outperform MGs, TR2s and their like on local club circuits"*. In 1972 its body scrapped but complete chassis survives for something to be fitted to it.

E1SA 249R+/25 Jul 1951/GB. Handsome open body fitted by Richard Mead of Kenilworth, Warwicks. First owner emigrated to NZ with it, NZ reg'n CY 3377, now IN 1951. After restoration work from 1995 the car now a good runner.

E1SA 250R+/5 Jul 1951/GB. Shipped to the Weymouth, Dorset agent. Presentable open bodywork fitted by G Hartwell of Bournemouth reg'n LRU 888. Last heard from in 1960.

E1SA 251R+/5 Jul 1951/GB. Another delightful DHC by Richard Mead of Kenilworth, Warwicks. Full description in *The Autocar* 20 Jun 1952. Registered MBM 305. In use to 1972 when owned by Dr Hampson. Restored 2009-2012, then sold as a runner in 2012 to Australia to Frank Choate. Further restoration carried out there to a very high standard.

E1SA 252R+/13 Jul 1951/GB. Closed body fitted by J E Farr & Sons Ltd of Blackburn Lancashire for F Hamilton Payne of Stalybridge, Manchester, reg'n 4 Nov 1952 as FRJ 351. Bought Mr A Turner in 1966 when found broken down near his place in Colwyn Bay, N Wales. Sold 1969 for storage. Sold in 2015 for full restoration.

E1SA 253R+/19 Jul 1951/GB. Open body fitted by a Cumberland bodyshop, reg'd LRM 577 Aug 1952. Sold to a starlet apparently, then Peter Ustinov who used it for 2 years. Found 1965 by D. Sparrow, running c.1970 but stored since.

E1SA 254R/9 Aug 1951/AUS. Found and bought in 1976 by Rex Maddock. Stored.

E1SA 255R/26 Jul 1951/Personal Export Originally invoiced to Judge C J Hand reg'd HKU 92 by Jowett. The sale failed as in 1 May 1952 it went to JCLtd Service Dept, who then sold it on, as K Hartridge drove it on 29 May 1954 in an Eight-Clubs 40-min High Speed Trial. Sold for £5 in 1976 running *"on two or three cylinders"*. After some years dismantled, new owner from 1999 began restoration on it.

E1SA 256R/27 Jul 1951/Personal Export reg'd HKU 285 by Jowett for a Mr & Mrs Bo Christian Roos of Beverley Hills, California. This was the third of the four Jupiters bought by the USA film comedian Red Skelton for himself and his immediate entourage (see also 206, 228, 266). Believed to have survived in Arizona and then Colorado into the late 1970s.

Film comedian Red Skelton (with cine camera) taking delivery of his Jupiter in August 1951. (LAT Photographic)

E1SA 257R/27 Jul 1951/Shipped to Auto Corporation SA, Casablanca, western Morocco. Nothing more known

E1SA 258R/27 Aug 1951/D/Shipped to H A Angell "Lurster West" maybe H A Angell of Westphalia, importer of Jupiter (287). But this Jupiter (258) was known in New York USA by 1969, from 1990 in Michigan. On eBay 2002 with 275,000 miles covered; not sold. Since then restoration has begun.

Chassis 259 to 263 were not constructed according to Jowett.

E1SA 264R/28 Aug 1951/Shipped to D Benaim, Gibraltar. Military registration G 8028. Brought back to GB 8 Oct 1951 by Major Milligan, and registered RYR 89. All owners known since. Bought by D Nash in 1998. Believed stored.

E1SA 265R/19 Sep 1951/P. Portuguese registration CL-17-82. Jacques Touzet was its first and only owner, buying it in 1954 and using as daily transport to 1964. Touzet brought it to UK twice for work on it by Jowett. The car was totally destroyed in 1994 by a fire in his motor car store, he had a small collection.

E1SA 266R/27 Jul 1951/Personal Export reg'd HKU 283 by Jowett for Mr & Mrs Skelton of Beverley Hills, California. This was the last of the 4 Jupiters bought by the USA film comedian Red Skelton for himself and his entourage (see also 206, 228, 256). Owned in the 1950s by Southern California racing team "Ecurie Fatique". Believed in Arizona and then Colorado in the late 1970s. Sold by Walker Edmiston in 1980. Owned from 2007 in Ca, restored and running from 2011.

E1SA 267R/18 Sep 1951/AUS. A running car in the 1960s with an MG gearbox fitted. By 1988 it was stripped – body-set going to Jupiter 428. Chassis then cut for the ex-Paul Emery Jowett twin-cam cylinder head engine (Ch 8), not so far fitted.

E1SA 268R/4 Oct 1951/SGP. Shipped to Champion Motors Singapore. We have no more history of this car.

Chassis 269 to 274 were not constructed according to Jowett.

E1SA 275R/24 Oct 1951/HK. Shipped to Aero Technical Corp of Hong Kong. We have no more history of this car.

Chassis 276 to 280 were not constructed according to Jowett.

E1SA 281R/19 Sep 1951/P. Portuguese registration CL-17-83. First owner Hermano Areias used it in a 24-hour competition, the '24 Horas da Bola'. Believed scrapped by 1974.

E1SA 282R/18 Sep 1951/GB. Reg'd PEH 796 to L C Procter. He used it in the 1952 RAC International Rally, not listed amongst the first 30 finishers. Also in the November 1952 MCC-Daily Express Rally. That is all we know of this car.

E1SA 283R/4 Oct 1951/SGP. Shipped to Champion Motors Singapore. We have no more history of this car.

E1SA 284R/4 Oct 1951/SGP. Shipped to Champion Motors Singapore. Believed lightened and raced in Singapore. Imported back to GB in July 1955 reg'd TKC 240. A runner to August 1965. Bought 1972 in scrap condition and next owner restored it 1974 to 1984. Sold 2011 as a smart running car.

E1SA 285R/24 Oct 1951/HK. Shipped to Aerotech the Hong Kong importer. Located in Macau, then a Portuguese island colony, reg'n M-17603. Said to have been raced in the Macau Grand Prix of 1954 or 1955. From 2000 with new owner and it was his wedding car in 2011; the car looks good, runs well.

E1SA 286R/2 Nov 1951/Personal Export shipped to a Mr E A Haig of NZ, reg'd AZ 5670 there. First known in 1968. Later reg'n OE 7760. A runner to 1981. Chassis-up light-weight restoration 1989-1994 to road-racing condition. In 2004 its owner put it into storage possibly taking it to Australia.

E1SA 287R/2 Sep 1951/D/Shipped to the German agent H A Angell of Westphalia. First heard from in the 1970s in Germany. Owner from 1986 Hans Herrneder, reg'd that year as ED-WT-81. Fitted with an Opel engine but it may not have run in this form. Currently stored.

E1SA 288R/26 Sep 1951/Kenya/Shipped to Larstolls Ltd, Nairobi. We have nothing more on the fate of this car.

E1SA 289R/5 Oct 1951/Personal Export reg'd HKU 537 by Jowett for a Mr F J Osmond. Nothing more known.

E1SA 290R/5 Oct 1951/NZ. First owner kept the car from new (registered BZ 4941) until he died in 1983. He willed it to the Southward Car Museum of Paraparaumu, North Island.

E1SA 291R+/11 Sep 1951/CH. Importer Jos Stierli of Zurich. Very attractive open body fitted by Gebrüder Beutler, of Thun near Berne, reg'n SG-6966. Found in 1970s by Ernst Oberholzer of St Gallen and very well restored. He drove it to GB for the 1982-83-84 Jowett rallies. From 2005, stored.

Chassis 292 to 314 were not constructed according to Jowett.

E1SA 315R/23 Nov 1951/GB. Reg'd HKU 607 by Jowett for Sir John Hodge. From c.1953–1960 next owner Jack Bates used it in 5 events 1955 to 1957 (see Ch 6) to 2 class 1st and 2 class 2nd in Sussex rallies. Written off 1961 by 3rd owner.

Chassis 316 to 335 were not constructed according to Jowett.

E2SAL 336R/24 Nov 1952. Shipped to Daniel Fajardar of Buenaventura, Columbia. No more known of this car.

E1SAL 337R/18 Jun 1952/F. Delivered to a Miss Ulla Piper c/o the Paris agent Plisson. No more known of this car.

E1SA 338R/7 Nov 1951/AUS. No recent history known.

E1SA 339R/16 Oct 1951/GB. Demonstrator London Motor Show October 1951, reg'n HKU 639. Sold by Jowett in 1956. Present owner from 1975 stores it, it's in poor condition.

Chassis 340 to 399 were not constructed according to Jowett, and 399 was the last of the 128 unused chassis numbers.

E1SAL 400R/12 Oct 1951/USA. Imported by Sanders Motor Sales, Texas. Current owner from 1977 still in Texas.

E1SAL 401R/12 Oct 1951/USA. Imported by Sanders Motor Sales, Texas. Nothing more known of this car.

E1SAL 402R/11 Oct 1951/USA. Imported by Sanders Motor Sales, Texas. Nothing more known of this car.

E1SAL 403R/8 Oct 1951/B. Imported Nouveaux Ets de Gregoire, Brussels. We have no more history of this car.

E1SAL 404R/11 Oct 1951/USA. Imported by Sanders Motor Sales, Texas. Nothing more known of this car.

E1SAL 405R/12 Oct 1951/USA. Imported by Sanders Motor Sales, Texas. Known from before 1980, car stored in Fort Worth. Bought 1995 by Kip Lankenau who runs Kip Motor Co a classic car restoration workshop in Dallas Texas. Very well restored in all respects by Kip Motor Co Inc. Still there.

E1SAL 406R/11 Oct 1951/USA. Imported by Sanders Motor Sales, Texas. Nothing more known of this car.

E1SA 407R/171 Oct 1951/Personal Export reg'd HKU 756 by Jowett for a Liverpool Export/Import agency. Dr A E Bernstein drove it in the 1953 Alpine Rally (Ch 4). It since disappeared.

E1SAL 408R/9 Nov 1951/USA. Imported by Sanders Motor Sales, Texas. Nothing more known of this car.

E1SAL 409R/20 Nov 1951/USA. Imported by Sanders Motor Sales, Texas. Nothing more known of this car.

E1SAL 409R/20 Nov 1951/USA. Imported by Sanders Motor Sales, Texas. Nothing more known of this car.

E1SAL 410R/20 Mar 1952/USA. Imported by Angell Motors of Pasadena but originally for Sanders. Nothing more known.
E1SAL 411R/8 Nov 1951/USA. Imported by Sanders Motor Sales, Texas. Nothing more known of this car.
E1SAL 412R/8 Nov 1951/USA. Imported by Sanders Motor Sales, Texas. In Michigan 1963; bought 1983 by present owner who got it running by or before 2002. Still in Michigan with restoration under way or completed by 2016.
E1SA 413R/1 Nov 1951/Personal Export reg'd HKU 538 by Jowett for a Mr W M Young. Nothing more known.
E1SA 414R/19 Oct 1951/NZ. Known from 1965 owned by E. Blatchford. In a race in the early 1960s in the Jarama team. Still owned by Mr Blatchford.
E1SA 415R/17 Oct 1951/NZ. Known from 1965 reg'd AM 5161. The 1972 owner exported it to UK in 1976 where reg'd LUG 347; from 1982 in three museums. Restored by 2000 by M Kavanagh; new owner 2001 registered it SSM 3.
E1SA 416R/19 Oct 1951/Bermuda/Known in 1964 in New York. Then 1991 in Massachusetts with Jupiter (827). In 2012 both advertised looking rough, but not sold then.
E1SA 417R/19 Oct 1951/NZ. Owned by Malcolm Bergin from 1966 to his death in 1981; restored in his ownership. Still in NZ some place!
E1SA 418R/24 Oct 1951/AUS. Present owner from 1973. Restored and running from 1992. Still his in 2015.
E1SAL 419R/9 Oct 1951/NL. First Jupiter with ivory body colour plus red interior and black hood. No more known.
E1SAL 420R/19 Sep 1951/P. Given Portuguese registration HH-18-02 April 1953 for Guilherme da Palma. That's all.
E1SA 421R/22 Oct 1951/AUS. Found in 1974 in good order by B Kelsall. Scrapped due to damage by a fire before 2000.
E1SA 422R/18 Oct 1951/NZ. Known 1971 reg'd DE 3644. Fourth NZ owner, with reg'n KS 504, sold it in 1993 to Australia. From at least 2000 in race-tuned state, used in hill-climbs, races and the Targa Tasmania classic rally. With its 95bhp engine it beat a Porsche in a race. Stored since c. 2006.

E1SAL 423R/20 Mar 1952/USA Ca. Shipped to Angell Motors of Pasadena. Known from 1963. Bought 2002 by owner of Minnesota, but tricked out of it in 2009. After two more owners, sold 2014 to Gullwing Motors of Astoria NY. and then sold to a person in Poland for restoration.
E1SAL 424R/12 Nov 1951/P. Given Portuguese registration AE-18-17. First owner Luis Garcia, Benito. No more known.
E1SAL 425R/8 Nov 1951/USA Tx. Imported by Sanders Motor Sales, Texas. To Ca by 1970 then owned by Walker Edmiston. In 1979 to Colorado, sold again 1989. Needs work.
E1SAL 426R/8 Nov 1951/USA. Imported by Sanders Motor Sales, Texas. Known in NY 1959-1988, then restored. In 1994 sold to Ohio. From 1995 owners T. & M. Jowett of Ontario.
E1SA 427R/22 Oct 1951/AUS. Known from 1961 as wreck with a 6-cylinder engine. Bought 1990 for much restoration. Sold 1998 for more restoration, still on-going in 2015.
E1SA 428R/7 Nov 1951/AUS. Known from 1977. Bought in poor state in 1987 and restored with body set from Jupiter (267). Superb award-winning restoration completed 1995 with 5-speed gearbox of unknown parentage.
E1SAL 429R/12 Nov 1951/P. Given Portuguese registration HH-18-01. First owner Antonio de Almeida. No more known.
E1SAL 430R/25 Mar 1952/Portuguese West Africa (now Angola). Importer Monteiro Gomez Ltda. No more known.
E1SA 431R/7 Nov 1951/AUS. Known from 1985, and from 1992 its owner restored it. By 2000 being used for mild competition events and Club rallies.
E1SAL 432R/20 Mar 1952/USA. Shipped to Angell Motors of Pasadena. Known in the LA area in 1977 but now lost.
E1SA 433R/31 Oct 1951/AUS. Known from 1968 when no longer a runner (due to a smash). New owner 1985, thorough restoration in progress from 1999.
E1SAL 434R/20 Mar 1952/USA Ca. Shipped to Angell Motors of Pasadena. Known 1957. Professionally restored

2001-2003.

E1SAL 435R/7 Mar 1952/Chile/Bought 1986 still in Chile. Restored 1998 reg'n BT 3F 16. Known running in 2012.

E1SAL 436R/8 Feb 1952/B. Imported by Ets Brondeel the Antwerp Jowett agent. No subsequent history known.

E1SAL 437R/12 Nov 1951/P. Given Portuguese registration HH-18-00. First owner Alfredo Carcalho. Maybe scrapped.

E1SA 438R/31 Oct 1951/AUS. Known from 1974. By 1985 in poor state. Some restoration from 2009. New owner 2014.

E1SAL 439R/20 Mar 1952/USA. Shipped to Angell Motors of Pasadena. Raced 1953/54 by 2nd owner Bill Rush. A wedding present for 3rd owner, stored when the wedding fell through. Car not heard from since 1963.

E1SA 440R/7 Nov 1951/AUS. First owner crashed it 1961. Bought 1993 running and raced c.1994 reg'd GBD 432. In 2009 Targa Tasmania Tour Class, won best Classic Award. To the Netherlands 2013, to Germany 2014 For sale 2015.

E1SAL 441R/8 Nov 1951/USA. Imported by Sanders Motor Sales, Texas. No subsequent history known.

E1SAL 442R/21 Mar 1952/USA. Shipped to Angell Motors of Pasadena. No subsequent history known.

E1SA 443R/29 Oct 1951/AUS. Known from 1967. Restored and running 1975. More work from 2010, very nice in 2015.

E1SA 444R/30 Oct 1951/AUS. Owner Barry Houston from 1979. Top-class restoration by 1988. In regular use 2015.

E1SA 445R/8 Nov 1951/NZ. Known in 1968. Same owner 1974-2014 then bought by new owner for restoration.

E1SAL 446R/8 Nov 1951/USA. Imported by Sanders Motor Sales, Texas. In 1962 in Kansas City Mo needing $600 parts. Sold 1969 as planter for flowers – now long gone.

E1SA 447R/8 Nov 1951/NZ. Fairly certain raced by first owner Dr Orr, and he rolled it in his 2nd race. Known from 1980.

E1SA 448R/9 Nov 1951/NZ. Registered CN 7925 in 1952. Restored 1990 to 2001 with body parts from another Jupiter (189) and given registration JU 51. New owner from 2012.

E1SA 449R/9 Nov 1951/GB. Shipped to a Bradford agent reg'd HKW 360. Known from 1959. After much decline, bought Geoff McAuley in 1989 and he fitted a Fiorano kit-car body to it, on the road 2008. Sold 2010, a nice running open car.

E1SA 450R/14 Dec 1951/GB. Delivered to Edgar Bros of London; invoice code indicates it went abroad, so lost to us.

E1SA 451R/31 Oct 1951/AUS. First owner John Michell of the wool family business. The car got a very enterprising restoration 1999-2004 from its current owner.

E1SA 452R/28 Dec 1951/GB. Delivered to a Lancashire agent, reg'd HFY 845. Known in 1987, almost scrap. Still known 2008. It must have had a chassis change at Jowett when nearly new as another Jupiter had the same chassis number, on the original chassis ex-the Jowett scrapheap:– this TR2-powered 'Ineson Special' was reg'd NWU 1 in 1954 and it did some races – body like a "rabbit hutch" they said, but this chassis in a scrapyard in 1970s. So 2 Jupiters had same chassis number!

E1SA 453R/8 Nov 1951/NZ. Reg'd BG 502 in 1952. Known from 1971 and in 1985 reg'd WA 7448. Bought 1996 restored, on the road 1998. New owner from 2005, car reg'd JUPITA.

E1SA 454R/9 Nov 1951/NZ. First reg'd AV 7817. Restored in the 1970s. In 1982 reg'd KS 506. Then 1986 reg'n JUPITR. Rebuilt with body-set from (681) to good nick by 1994. Then to GB in 2010 reg'd 605 YUB. Car on the road looking good.

E1SA 455R/9 Nov 1951/NZ. Original registration AR 2096. Known 1964 with the R1 engine ex-Pacific Spot speedboat: top speed 110mph [later this engine in (168)]. From 2006 new owners; they had it restored for them 2012-2014.

E1SA 456R/31 Oct 1951/AUS. Known from 1960. Present owner from 1985. The car stored, dismantled.

E1SA 457R/3 Dec 1951/GB. Delivered to Burton-on-Trent Jowett agent; the name of 1st owner G Hartlans is all we have.

E1SA 458R/16 Nov 1951/Shipped to Gold Coast (Ghana) and bought by GB Army Officer Lt John Doran, reg'd AD 1233. Driven in 1955 from Accra to Dakar in Senegal – see Ch 7. Then to Germany with Lt Doran, and rallied there. To GB in 1956 reg'n SGX 64. From 1967 it the first Jupiter to get a total restoration. New owner 1994, used for some years then stored.

E1SA 459R/23 Nov 1951/GB. Delivered to a Glasgow Jowett agent. We have no more history on this car.

E1SA 460R/19 Nov 1951/CY. Delivered to the Colombo agent, the only standard Jupiter to Ceylon. In 1952 a Mr J A Graham won a sports car event in a Jupiter there, so we can assume it was this one. Nothing more known.

E1SA 461R/22 Nov 1951/GB. Delivered to a Glasgow Jowett agent; its 1st owner J B Lalto of Glasgow is all we have.

E1SA 462R/16 Nov 1951/GB. Delivered to a Yorkshire Jowett agent; the name of 1st owner Dr E B Harrison is all we have.

E1SA 463R/19 Nov 1951/GB. Delivered to Hebden Bros the Lancs Jowett agent. Known from the 1960s, bought for restoration in 1976 finished 2002. Owned Budge Rogers the ex-Bedford & England rugby player 2004-2008. It was then sold to New Zealand where it remains.

E1SA 464R/27 Nov 1951/GB. Delivered to a Lancashire Jowett agent; A H Cooke the name of 1st owner is all we have.

E1SA 465R/11 Dec 1951/GB. Delivered to the Whitstable, Kent, Jowett agent and reg'd GFN 324. Known from 1960. Owner from 1981 with the car on the road in 2000 after 35 years storage. It runs well, looks good. For sale 2015.

E1SA 466R/23 Nov 1951/GB. Delivered to a Yorkshire Jowett agent and reg'd OWB 179. Known from 1970. By 1990 stripped. Sold 2014 for restoration.

E1SA 467R/9 Nov 1951/GB. Delivered to a Yorkshire Jowett agent and reg'd HKU 888. Known from 1965. Restored and running 1993 to 2003 but believed stored since.

E1SA 468R/3 Dec 1951/GB. Delivered to the Edinburgh Jowett agent and reg'd JSF 282. Raced by Frank Collins 1954-58. Sold to the Netherlands in 1964, owner from 1972 restored it reg'd 99-DU-82. It featured in the 1991 film "Oh Boy". Sold 2011 to Germany, with reg'n VER KG 78 H – a good runner.

E1SA 469R/23 Nov 1951/GB. Delivered to a Suffolk Jowett agent. The name of 1st owner G V K Burton is all we have.

E1SA 470R/19 Nov 1951/GB. Delivered to a Scottish Jowett agent; all we have is name of 1st owner J Donochry of Paisley.

E1SA 471R/12 Dec 1951/GB. Delivered to a Leicester Jowett agent and registered KBC 444. In 1968 dismantled for scrap.

E1SA 472R/23 Nov 1951/GB. Delivered to the Yorkshire Jowett agent E Foulds reg'n KWY 821. He drove it in the 1952 Lands End Trial and a night rally in 1955 (Ch 6) before selling it to John Hagar that year. Photo below. We have no more.

E1SA 473R/12 Dec 1951/GB. Delivered to the Lincoln Jowett agent reg'd FFE 513. Last ran in 1965. A stripped bodyless chassis by 1989. Bodywork fitted from scrapped Jupiters, on the road in 1993. New owner from 2008 improved it further.

The Jupiter (472) of Edward Foulds, with TR2 owner John Hagar on the grass. (E Foulds)

E1SA 474R/7 Dec 1951/GB. Delivered to a Birmingham Jowett agent reg'n LOV 450. Last ran 1969. Found in 2004. New owner in 2009, very good restoration completed by 2015.

E1SA 475R/12 Dec 1951/GB. Delivered to the Brighton Jowett agent and reg'd LUF 420. Crashed late 1960s, body removed and lost. Chassis bought 1970. Panel set obtained from the scrapped Jupiter (936); rebuild awaited.

E1SA 476R/4 Dec 1951/GB. Delivered to a Birmingham Jowett agent reg'n LOV 692 for C Ingham, who drove it to Switzerland for a holiday. Nothing more known.

E1SA 477R/29 Nov 1951/GB. Delivered to a Manchester Jowett agent and reg'd MND 444. Scrapped in 1962.

E1SA 478R/26 Nov 1951/GB. Delivered to a Manchester Jowett agent and reg'd FBA 308. Known from 1970, some restoration by 1983. Exported to Norway in 1997 with more restoration and re-registration to W-1555.

E1SA 479R/26 Nov 1951/GB. To the Bournemouth Jowett agent for Wallis & Co of Nottingham. Nothing more known.

E1SA 480R/4 Dec 1951/GB. Delivered to the Birmingham Jowett agent Frank Grounds. No more history known.

E1SA 481R/23 Nov 1951/GB. Delivered to a Sheffield Jowett agent and reg'd OWA 845. Known from new; running to 1969, restored 1982-85, with further work by next owner. New owner from 2011, a very smart running car.

E1SA 482R/12 Dec 1951/Shipped to Southern Rhodesia (now Zimbabwe). Nothing more known.

E1SA 483R/12 Dec 1951/Shipped to Singapore reg'd AH 3850 in Malaya. Found 1981 in Melbourne. In 2000 owner restored it. In 2007 said to be 'nearly ready for the road'.

E1SA 484R/28 Nov 1951/GB. Delivered to a Yorkshire Jowett agent reg'n KBT 702. Stolen in 1996 but some panels survive.

E1SA 485R/31 Dec 1951/GB. Delivered to a Lancashire Jowett agent reg'n HBU 144. First owner Lewis Pellowe in the 1952 Morecambe Rally (Ch 6). He later had a bad accident in it, it went back to Jowett for repair. We have no more history.

E1SA 486R/19 Dec 1951/GB. Delivered to a Lancashire Jowett agent reg'n OTJ 428. Known on and off from 1963. Owner from 1989 we think still stores it.

E1SA 487R/20 Dec 1951/GB. Delivered to a Yorkshire Jowett agent reg'n HPY 696. Known to have won its class at July 1952 Redcar Flying Km trials, driver R V Russell, (Ch 6). Written off in 1959 – but rebuilt maybe: alleged seen in c.1968.

E1SA 488R/23 Jan 1952/PEx/Personal Export car, reg'd HKU 878 to a Capt A S Biggs c/o Fox & Hounds, Tadworth, Surrey. Subsequent history of this car is unknown.

E1SA 489R/31 Dec 1951/GB. Delivered to a Wiltshire Jowett agent for Lionel Stevens. Nothing more known of this car.

E1SA 490R/14 Feb 1952/GB. Delivered to a Gloucestershire agent reg'n LDF 290. Owner 1966 to 1972 did work on it as a runner. In 1979 shipped to the USA. In 1984 in Georgia USA.

E1SA 491R/17 Dec 1951/GB. Delivered to the Southampton agent reg'n JTR 777. Known from 1962, running to 1966. Restoration from a poor state to on-the-road 2014-15.

E1SA 492R/12 Dec 1951/Shipped to a Singapore importer. No further history known.

E1SA 493R/10 Dec 1951/GB. Delivered to a Birmingham agent reg'n AFA 875. Known from new. Owner from 1967 has restored it, the car normally on the road.

E1SA 494R/12 Dec 1951/GB. Delivered to the Doncaster agent reg'n LDT 3. First owner C F Eminson used it in at least five sporting events 1952-53 (Ch 5, Ch 6) He recalled "a nice little car not hotted up in any way". Known scrapped in 1966.

E1SA 495R/11 Dec 1951/GB. Delivered to a Yorkshire agent reg'n KBT 696. Bought 1965 by a Dr Nileshwar. In India 1968 to 1970. Restored for new GB owner from 2003.

E1SA 496R/15 Jan 1952/GB. Delivered to a London agent reg'n XME 740. May have been raced at Goodwood 1953. Owner from 2009 keeps it in very good running order.

E1SA 497R/22 Jan 1952/GB. Delivered to a Belfast agent reg'n NZ 3395. In 1953 Circuit of Ireland Trial driven by a Mrs Mitchell. Seen in Lincolnshire in 1971. Owner from 1979 restored it 1990s. In 2001 owner and car to France, used in local outings. Back in the UK from 2013.

E1SA 498R/29 Feb 1952/GB. Delivered to a Surrey agent reg'n RPF 981. Owner bought it 1972. Dismantled by 1996, being worked on from 2012.

E1SA 499R/19 Feb 1952/GB. Delivered to a Northampton agent, believed reg'n CVV 198. Last heard from c.1960.

E1SAL 500R+/29 Nov 1951/DK. The sole LHD rolling chassis, to Danish agent E Sommers who built a lovely FHC body on it (Ch 9). The car used to 1966 when in very poor state. Some restoration by 1973. Full restoration by new owner 1988-2001. Has its first reg'n B 55 again. Car looks, runs like new.

E1SA 501R/16 Jan 1952/GB. Delivered to a Cardiff agent reg'n GBO 888. Seen, ruinous, in a scrapyard in 1972.

E1SA 502R/26 Feb 1952/GB. Delivered to a Bedfordshire agent reg'n KTM 250. Owner from 1965 stores it needs work.

E1SA 503R/15 Jan 1952/GB. Delivered to a Lincolnshire agent reg'n JBE 4. Second owner KLW Cook used it in competition 1953/54. Work done on the car in the 1970s. Owned Noel Stokoe since 1985. Car looks good and runs well.

E1SAL 504R/20 Dec 1951/USA. Shipped to Angell Motors of Pasadena. No subsequent history known.

E1SA 505R/31 Jan 1952/GB. Delivered to a Cumberland agent reg'n EHH 707. Known from 1967. Restored to a high standard in the 1970s. New owners from 1996.

E1SAL 506R/20 Dec 1951/USA. Shipped to Angell Motors of Pasadena. No subsequent history known.

E1SAL 507R/20 Dec 1951/USA. Shipped to Angell Motors of Pasadena. Owned Fred McWherter, IL, from 1990.

E1SAL 508R/20 Dec 1951/USA. Shipped to Angell Motors of Pasadena. Known in California from 1963. In a poor state, chassis sold c.2007 to Mark Moriaty to restore the ex-Cushenberry Jupiter-chassis Dream Rod custom car, see photo above. Its body-set came to the UK for the restoration of a depleted Jupiter.

Dream Rod (508) originally built on a different Jupiter chassis by Bill Cushenberry for 1963-64 ICAS tour. (Street RODDER)

E1SA 509R/5 Feb 1952/GB. Delivered to the main London agent reg'n MXA 506. Raced, hill-climbed for first 18 months by its owner Neil Freedman; see Ch 4, Ch 5. It was a push-car at the Northants Santa Pod raceway 1971-74. Restored 2001-04. Owner from 2002 had previously owned it 1964 to 1969.

E1SAL 510R/20 Dec 1951/USA. Shipped to Angell Motors of Pasadena. Known from 1960s. Restored 1966-72. To France 2002 reg'n 8081-TZ-97. Sold there 2012 a very good car.

E1SAL 511R/20 Dec 1951/USA. Shipped to Angell Motors of Pasadena. Known from 1960s. Bought 2000, by 2015 stored.

E1SAL 512R/20 Dec 1951/USA. Shipped to Angell Motors. Chassis stripped, body went to UK for a Jupiter restoration.

E1SA 513R/21 Jan 1952/GB. Delivered to a Surrey agent. Taken to NZ by a Dr Forbes who used it for his rounds, then traded for an MG which Forbes said was '*nowhere near as good*'. Bought 1977 restored 1977-83 with reg'n JJ 1951.

E1SAL 514R/21 Dec 1951/USA. Shipped to Angell Motors of Pasadena. In CA it got a Ford V8-60 installed. To TX in 1967 and bought by Texan Fred McWherter in 1991.

E1SAL 515R/21 Dec 1951/USA. Shipped to Angell Motors of Pasadena. In Detroit MI 1970s to 1985 when exported to UK. Owner from 1992 is to restore it.

E1SAL 516R/21 Dec 1951/USA. Shipped to Angell Motors of Pasadena. Known from new. In 1999 exported to UK. Owner from 2005 is restoring it.

E1SAL 517R/21 Dec 1951/USA. Shipped to Angell Motors of Pasadena. Known from 1969. In 1999 in a poor state exported to UK and bought by owner who restored it.

E1SAL 518R/21 Dec 1951/USA. Shipped to Angell Motors of Pasadena. History unknown.

E1SAL 519R/21 Dec 1951/USA. Shipped to Angell Motors of Pasadena. Owned & restored 1990-2013.

E1SA 520R/30 Jan 1952/GB. Delivered to a London agent. Believed to be MXP 417 in various competitive events in 1953 driven by R B Goddard. Class winner Clacton Rally; MXP 417; see Ch 6. It was scrapped in the 1960s.

E2SA 521R/14 Jan 1952/GB. Delivered to a Hertfordshire agent. First owner Freddie Still used it in 9 events 1952-53. Class winner 1952 Margate Rally. See Ch 4, Ch 5, Ch 6. In use to 1966. Some work in 1980s, bought E & G Nankivell in 1992; professionally restored, an excellent running car since.

E2SA 522R/12 Mar 1952/GB. Delivered to a Rugby dealer. Thought be Jupiter reg'n MAC 2 for Mike Sharp who drove it in the RAC Rally and the MCC-Daily Express rallies of 1952; see Ch 4, Ch 5 and Ch 6. Believed scrapped.

E1SAL 523R/7 Jan 1952/USA. Shipped to Angell Motors of Pasadena. In a poor state by 2001 when bought and restored to a very high standard by 2007.

E1SAL 524R/7 Jan 1952/USA. Shipped to Angell Motors of Pasadena. Owned from 1970 by Jim Miller needing restoration.

E1SAL 525R/8 Jan 1952/USA. Shipped to Angell Motors of Pasadena. In same family from 1958. To be restored.

E1SAL 526R/8 Jan 1952/USA Ca. Shipped to Angell Motors of Pasadena. No further history known.

E1SAL 527R/8 Jan 1952/USA. Shipped to Angell Motors of Pasadena. Some restoration from 1985.

E1SA 528R/29 Jan 1951/HK. Shipped to Aerotech the Hong Kong importer. No more known.

E1SAL 529R/7 Jan 1952/USA. Shipped to Angell Motors of Pasadena. Last known in 1966, presumed scrapped.

E1SAL 530R/7 Jan 1952/USA. Shipped to Angell Motors of Pasadena. Car owned by a Mr Jones and driven to Ohio in early 1970s; then a Ford engine and g/b fitted. Car well restored 2010 but retaining the Ford power plant.

E1SAL 531R/8 Jan 1952/USA. Shipped to Angell Motors of Pasadena. No history of this car known to us.

E1SAL 532R/8 Jan 1952/USA. Shipped to Angell Motors of Pasadena. No history of this car known to us.

E1SAL 533R/8 Jan 1952/USA. Shipped to Angell Motors of Pasadena. No history of this car known to us.

E1SAL 534R/8 Jan 1952/USA. Shipped to Angell Motors of Pasadena. Known from 1959 in Kansas. Had Jeep engine. In Ohio from 2010. In 2011 shipped to Italy in poor state.

E1SAL 535R/8 Jan 1952/USA. Shipped to Angell Motors of Pasadena. Sold at auction in 1997 with a Ford Capri engine installed. Last heard from in 2002 in Arizona.

E1SA 536R/4 Feb 1952/GB. Delivered to the Wm Robb agent of Fife, Scotland reg'n KSP 1, then London reg'n 81 HYN in 1964. Dismantled by 1974. Restoration by owner started 2011.

E1SAL 537R/7 Feb 1952/USA. Shipped to Angell Motors of Pasadena. No history of this car known to us.

E2SA 538R/30 Jan 1952/GB. Delivered to a London agent reg'n MUW 599. Known from 1956. Car always in good nick.

E1SA 539R/7 Feb 1952/GB. Delivered to a Surrey agent reg'n RPF 16. First owner F Defty used it in events 1952, 1953, see Ch 4. Next owner badly crashed it c.1970. Sold in bits in 2005.

E1SA 540R/21 Jan 1952/GB. Delivered to the Southampton agent but no further history known.

E1SA 541R/16 Jan 1952/GB. Delivered to a Leicester agent reg'n HJF 602. Full history known from purchase in 1965 by its 2nd owner Allan Wright (first secretary of re-formed JCC). Restored, sold 2011 to its third owner.

E1SA 542R/15 Feb 1952/GB. Delivered to a Lancashire agent. Reg'n OTB 73 and a running car up to 1965.

Restored from 1978. Owner from 2000 has a very good car.

E1SA 543R/20 Feb 1952/GB. Sold by a Scottish dealer reg'n SW 8760. Restoration from 1972. For its new owner in 2010, there was more restoration carried out on this nice runner.

E1SA 544R/31 Jan 1952/GB. Sold by a Sussex dealer but reg'd HKW 429 by Jowett for first owner Robbie MacKenzie-Low who raced and rallied it, sometimes with its pink hard-top fitted, see Ch 5 and Ch 6; then it was his road car for some years. New owner from 1971 used it but it's now stored.

E1SA 545R/15 Jan 1952/GB. Sold by a Northumberland agent reg'n FNL 300. Known from 1967. A wreck bought by H Brierley, well-restored 1990-96. Present owner from 2013.

E1SA 546R/21 Jan 1952/GB. Bought by a Jersey, Channel Island garage reg'n NOJ 14163. Back to mainland 1955 a crashed wreck, on the road by 1957 reg'd 992 LMD. Owner from 1987 carefully restored it; ready and on the road 2015 looking good.

E1SA 547R/22 Feb 1952/GB. Sold by a Kent dealer to J. Langley of Oxfordshire. Nothing more known of this car.

E1SA 548R/29 Jan 1952/HK. Shipped in primer to Aerotech the Hong Kong importer. First owner was of the Fleet Air Arm in Hong Kong. He had it painted 2-tone grey using Battleship and Aircraft Greys. To GB in 1959 reg'd XXT 59. All owners known, current owner from 1999. Car looks good, runs well.

E1SA 549R/29 Jan 1952/HK. Shipped in primer to Aerotech the Hong Kong importer. Nothing more known of this car.

E1SAL 550R/6 Feb 1952/USA. Shipped to Angell Motors of Pasadena. Known from 1959. Bought by Jim Miller in 1991 as a running car, restored by previous owner.

E1SAL 551R/6 Feb 1952/USA. Shipped to Angell Motors of Pasadena. No further history known of this car.

E1SAL 552R/7 Feb 1952/USA. Shipped to Angell Motors of Pasadena. No further history known of this car.

E1SA 553R/23 Feb 1952/GB. Sold to a Kent agent. That's all.

E1SA 554R/17 Mar 1952/GB. Sold to an Essex agent reg'n UEV 555. Fully restored 1988-2000, then Australia and owner from 2004 had more good work done to it. Reg'n NXA 78E.

E1SA 555R/23 Jan 1952/GB. Sold to a London dealer reg'n XME 608. Seen in scrap condition by the author in 1972.

E1SA 556R/22 Feb 1952/GB. To Aberdeen dealer reg'n ERS 565. Photo (1) at their showroom, (2) in 1952 lapping the Crimond circuit, and (3) on a postcard taken in front of an Odeon Cinema in London. Nothing more known.

E2SA 557R/13 Feb 1952/GB. Sold to a Yorkshire agent reg'n JKY 832. In 1953 Cats Eyes Rally N Roarke (Ch 6). Known from 1962. Owner from 1975 now stores it.

E2SA 558R/11 Feb 1952/GB. Sold to a Kent agent reg'n OKP 822. Known from 1969. Rough stored from 1974. In 1977 to the Netherlands. Well restored 1983 reg'n DE-19-43 in 1989. To Hungary in 1999. Owner from 2011 of Budapest.

E1SA 559R/1 Feb 1952/GB. Sold to a Nottinghamshire agent reg'n OAV 861. Known from 1963, daily use to c.1974. Bought in 1976 as a running car, now stored needing work.

E1SB 560R/11 Feb 1952/GB. The only 'SB' Jupiter, the Mk1a prototype. Registered by Jowett HKW 197. Uniquely just the bonnet had strakes. Road tested by several magazines. In the 1953 London-Languedoc-Sète Rally, appearing in *Milestones for the Motorist* published by D Noble. Just its bonnet survives. See photo overleaf.

E2SA 561R/15 Feb 1952/GB. Shipped to the Exeter, Devon agent. We have no further history of this car.

E2SA 562R/24 Jan 1952/GB. Shipped to the Renfrewshire agent reg'n JYS 603. Known from 1967. Restored 1985-87. Bought in 2002 to Sweden. Swedish, reg'n TAX 049.

E2SA 563R/23 Jan 1952/GB. Shipped to a Lancashire agent reg'n KYG 606. Last a daily runner in 1968. By 1985 in depleted state. Restoration currently (2015) under way.

E2SA 564R/23 Jan 1952/GB. Shipped to a Bradford agent

On its return from Sête, the staff of the restaurant Les Lavandières near Bourges in central France admire the Jupiter (560). Marianne Noble at the wheel. (Dudley Noble)

reg'n HKW 386. Used by Ken Brierley in competition 1954 to 1958 see Ch 6. Scrapped in 1968.

E2SA 565R/23 Jan 1952/GB. Shipped to a Lancashire agent reg'n OMB 522. Used in Wirral MC Sprint by E P Scragg in 1952, see Ch 5. Owned 1955-1961 by Peter Craven, twice World Speedway Champion. At some point dismantled, new owner from 1984 has had quite some restoration done.

E2SA 566R/23 Jan 1952/GB. Shipped to a Lancashire agent reg'n MLV 797. Dismantled and scrapped by 1990.

E2SA 567R/23 Jan 1952/GB. Shipped to a London agent. Long lost so almost certainly scrapped.

E2SA 568R/22 Feb 1952/GB. Shipped to the Bristol agent reg'n OHY 423. First owner a Dr Oliff who used it for his rounds. Sold 1967 as a runner, but it has since disappeared.

E2SAL 569R/11 Jan 1952/B. Shipped to the Antwerp, Belgium agent. Nothing more known of this car.

E2SA 570R/14 Feb 1952/GB. Shipped to a London agent. Bought new by Lord Nunburnholm for his daughter.

Original registration unknown. Bought c.1972 in Scotland and restored from a low state by 1990, registered JSF 281 (ex 468).

E2SA 571R/29 Jan 1952/GB. Shipped to a Devon agent and registered NOD 759. Crashed in 1958 and left in the open. Owner from 1989 carrying out a slow restoration.

E2SA 572R/22 Jan 1952/Nigeria/Reg'n G9075 WAN. In 1954 to Gold Coast (Ghana) reg'n AD5863, then for new owner PH2925. To UK in 1955 reg'n QE 612 used to 1963. After storage, bought in 1977 and rebuilt, back on the road 1987 reg'n FSV 612. A very good running car with fixed hard-top.

E2SA 573R/4 Feb 1952/GB. Shipped to a London agent yet reg'd ORL 812 a Cornish mark. Known from 1971. Owner from 1998 had it professionally restored by 2015.

E2SA 574R/1 Feb 1952/GB. Shipped to a London agent but no further history known.

E2SA 575R/4 Feb 1952/GB. Shipped to a London agent reg'n XME 857. Known from 1962. Badly stored from 1977. Bought 2008 for restoration which by 2015 continues.

E2SA 576R/14 Feb 1952/GB. Shipped to a Hampshire agent and sold to a Londoner. No more history known.

E2SA 577R/7 Feb 1952/GB. Shipped to a Yorkshire agent, but believed scrapped in 1967 or thereabouts.

E2SAL 578R/6 Feb 1952/USA. Shipped to Angell Motors of Pasadena. Known only in 1972/73 still in California.

E2SA 579R/1 Feb 1952/GB. Shipped to a Glasgow agent reg'n KGA 548. Known from 1961. Body-off restoration from 1977 completed 2001 by next owner, with separate seats, roll-over bar and clip-on hood, painted bright yellow, a good runner. sold 2013 to Chemnitz, Germany. Again for sale 2015.

E2SAL 580R/6 Feb 1952/USA. Shipped to Angell Motors of Pasadena. Possibly Hunter Hackney's rally winner see Ch 4. Owners known from 1960s. Private restoration completed by Kip Motor of Dallas Tx. Sold at auction 2014.

E2SAL 581R/7 Feb 1952/USA. Shipped to Angell Motors of Pasadena. Only one California owner before being exported to England in 1989. The car very well restored reg'n HSL 610.

E2SA 582R/8 Feb 1952/GB. To the Reading, Berkshire agent reg'n HBL 11. Known from 1954. From 2002-2007 reg'n RFG 510, then AUM 92 then AOR 366. After more work, sold via eBay 2012 to person or persons unknown.

E2SA 583R+/4 Feb 1952/GB. Shipped to Lancs agent R F Ellison for the coachbuilder Farr to build a FHC for the son Selwyn Farr; reg'n EBV 429. Owned from mid-1960s by J Evans who crashed it prior to 1970 when it was stripped and scrapped.

E2SA 584R/7 Feb 1952/GB. Shipped to a Dorset agent reg'n FPR 474. Known from 1981. Bought 1986 and restored by 1993. A reliable running car.

E2SA 585R/12 Feb 1952/GB. Shipped to the Roxburghshire agent reg'n CKS 334. Full history known. Bought 1987 in a poor state so given full restoration, running by 1990 looking good.

E2SA 586R/8 Feb 1952/GB. Shipped to a Derbyshire agent reg'n MVO 704. In the 1952 and 1953 Circuit of Ireland Trial, driver B Hibbert (Ch 6). Owner from 1991 has it still a running car.

E2SAL 587R/7 Feb 1952/USA. Shipped to Angell Motors of Pasadena. No history known.

E2SA 588R/15 Feb 1952/GB. Shipped to the Edinburgh agent for a Mrs H C Murphy. Nothing more known.

E2SA 589R/6 Feb 1952/GB. Shipped to a Bradford agent reg'n HKW 480. Dismantled, bought 1979. Now under restoration.

E2SAL 590R/11 Feb 1952/USA. Shipped to Angell Motors of Pasadena. No history known.

E2SAL 591R/6 Feb 1952/USA. Shipped to Angell Motors of Pasadena. No history known.

E2SAL 592R/6 Feb 1952/USA. Shipped to Angell Motors of Pasadena. No history known.

E2SAL 593R/6 Feb 1952/USA. Shipped to Angell Motors of Pasadena. Only known 1975-1989 in Colorado.

E2SAL 594R/7 Feb 1952/USA. Shipped to Angell Motors of Pasadena. Known from 1971. Owner from 1975 still in Ca.

E2SAL 595R/6 Feb 1952/USA. Shipped to Angell Motors of Pasadena. Known 1970 to 1988 in Ca in poor condition.

E2SAL 596R/11 Feb 1952/USA Ca. Shipped to Angell Motors of Pasadena. No history known.

E2SA 597R/15 Feb 1952/GB. Shipped to a Somerset agent reg'n MCD 28. In events 1952, 1953 F Masefield-Baker then H Appleby in 1955 and A Dowsett in 1956, see Ch 6. Known from 1961; refurbished and run from about 1971.

E2SA 598R/13 Feb 1952/GB. Shipped to the Falmouth agent believed reg'n ORL 123 and last known 1955-58.

E2SA 599R/15 Feb 1952/GB. Shipped to a Kent agent for J T Johnson of Folkestone. We have nothing further on this car.

E2SA 600R/7 Mar 1952/Bermuda. Moved to Virginia USA in late 1950s; known there from 1970. Owner from 2005 in Georgia had some restoration done by 2015.

E2SA 601R/11 Mar 1952/GB. Shipped to a Surrey agent for Lt Col Morgan. We have nothing further on this car.

E2SA 602R/10 Mar 1952/GB. Shipped to the Bedfordshire agent Alf Thomas, reg'd KTM 555 for Ken Crutch who used it in competition in 1953 (Ch 5, Ch 6). The car now lost.

E2SA 603R/11 Mar 1952/GB. Shipped to a Bradford agent for Kenneth Ashworth. We have nothing further on this car.

E2SA 604R/18 Feb 1952/GB. Shipped to a Lancashire agent. We have nothing definite further on this car.

E2SA 605R/15 Feb 1952/GB. Shipped to the Inverness agent reg'n FST 777 in 1953 then SK 4432 in 1954. Owners known right through. Owner from 1966 restored it in the late 1960s. New owner in 1999. A good running car after more work.

E2SA 606R/19 Feb 1952/GB. Shipped to a Yorkshire agent for F S R Smith. We have nothing more on this car.

E2SAL 607R/11 Feb 1952/USA. Shipped to Angell Motors of Pasadena. Nothing more known of this car

E2SAL 608R/11 Feb 1952/USA. Shipped to Angell Motors of Pasadena. Nothing more known of this car

E2SAL 609R/11 Feb 1952/USA. Shipped to Angell Motors of Pasadena. Nothing more known of this car.

E2SAL 610R/11 Feb 1952/USA. Shipped to Angell Motors of Pasadena. Known from 1959. To Canada in

1990 where owner superbly restored it from a poor state by 1996. A show winner.

E2SAL 611R/13 Feb 1952/USA. Shipped to Angell Motors of Pasadena. Known in 1996 in a field. Since gone.

E2SAL 612R/12 Feb 1952/USA. Shipped to Angell Motors of Pasadena. Nothing more known of this car.

E2SAL 613R/12 Feb 1952/USA. Shipped to Angell Motors of Pasadena. Nothing more known of this car.

E2SAL 614R/11 Feb 1952/USA. Shipped to Angell Motors of Pasadena. Nothing more known of this car.

E2SAL 615R/12 Feb 1952/USA. Shipped to Angell Motors of Pasadena. Known in Virginia from 1968. In Ma 1994-98. In 1999 to Scotland in poor nick. Owner from 2006 had done much restoration on it by 2013. Registration 971 YUE.

E2SA 616R/2 Feb 1952/GB. Shipped to a Lancashire agent, registered NTJ 998. Burnt remains seen 1977; now all gone.

E2SA 617R/4 Mar 1952/S. Shipped to Stockholm agent. Known from new, on the road to 1963. In 1981 dismantled and restoration started. Present owner from 1992.

E2SA 618R/25 Feb 1952/GB. Shipped to an Edinburgh agent reg'n DS 3131. Rallied by first owner R Goodburn (Ch 6). To Cornwall late 1960s then to Devon. Bought 2015 in good nick.

E2SA 619R/27 Feb 1952/GB. Shipped to a Sussex agent reg'n NPO 5. Second owner drove it for 4 years including to Switzerland to ski. Scrapped 1966 after a crash.

E2SA 620R/26 Feb 1952/GB. Shipped to the Oxford agent reg'n FUD 194. Maurice Tew used it in rallies in 1953 e.g. the Lisbon International, the last international event for a Jupiter see Ch 4, Ch 6. A runner bought 1965, well restored by owner.

E2SA 621R/26 Feb 1952/GB. Shipped to the Oxford agent for Harold Cox of Lincoln College Oxford. We have no more.

E2SA 622R/7 Mar 1952/GB. Shipped to the Epsom agent and registered RPF 978. Known from 1965. Bought in 1993 and by 1997 in nice running condition.

E2SA 623R/24 Apr 1952/GB. Shipped to a Yorkshire agent and registered PUM 356. Last road licence expired 1966.

E2SA 624R/6 Mar 1952/GB. Shipped to the Cumberland agent for Anthony Capstick. Nothing further known of this car.

E2SA 625R/1 Apr 1952/GB. Shipped to a Staffordshire agent. reg'n KDA 111. Known from 1957, some restoration 1983. Stripped for restoration 1998. Bought March 2013 for lightweight restoration for racing; in work 2015.

E2SA 626R/11 Feb 1952/GB. Shipped to a Gloucestershire agent reg'n RAE 850. Known from 1970. Some restoration work in the 1970s. Owner from 2008 restored it by 2014.

E2SA 627R/28 Feb 1952/GB. Shipped to a Staffordshire agent for Thomas Harrison. Nothing further known of this car.

E2SA 628R/25 Feb 1952/GB. Shipped to a Bradford agent reg'n HKW 610. Owned 1955 by a Cambridge undergraduate. In Craigantlet Northern Ireland hill-climb in 1955. He said "It had roadholding second to none". Last licence expired 1962.

E2SA 629R/29 Feb 1952/GB. Shipped to a Buckinghamshire agent reg'n PBH 583. Known from 1971. Restored by 1985. In 2015 its condition very good.

E2SA 630R/11 Mar 1952/GB. Shipped to a Surrey agent for F E Lynch. No further history known of this car.

E2SA 631R/26 Feb 1952/GB. Shipped to a Manchester agent for Mrs P Lytham. Nothing more known of this car.

E2SA 632R/12 Mar 1952/GB. Shipped to a Staffordshire agent for K J Wilkinson. Nothing more known of this car.

E2SA 633R/13 Mar 1952/GB. Shipped to a Gloucestershire agent reg'n MDG 475. Known from 1964. Rebuilt from 1970 to mid-1990s. New owner 2015; car restored and running well.

E2SAL 634R/13 Feb 1952/USA Ca. Shipped to Angell Motors of Pasadena. Nothing more known of this car.

E2SAL 635R/13 Feb 1952/USA Ca. Shipped to Angell Motors of Pasadena. Nothing more known of this car.

E2SA 636R/29 Feb 1952/GB. Shipped to the Bristol agent reg'n CGL 837. Present owner bought it in 1981.

E2SAL 637R/19 Feb 1952/NL. sold via H G L Sieberg the Amsterdam agent reg'n 15-98-GH. Known from 1970. Restored 1992. Sold 1994 to the Danish Sommers museum.

E2SA 638R/11 Mar 1952/GB. Shipped to a Lancashire agent reg'n BCW 337. Known from 1955. Owner in 1999 took it to Tenerife. New Tenerife owner in 2010. A nice running car.

E2SA 639R/24 Mar 1952/GB. Shipped to a Surrey agent reg'n RPG 231. Owner from 1971 has a very nice running car.

E2SA 640R/4 Apr 1952/GB. Shipped to an Edinburgh agent believed reg'd JWS 187. Used by Fl Lt G F Norris in 1954 competitions. Nothing more known.

E2SAL 641R/22 Feb 1952/B. Shipped to the Antwerp, Belgium agent. Nothing more known of this car.

E2SA 642R/4 Apr 1952/GB. Shipped to the Carlisle agent reg'n LAO 786. Last known owners in the 1960s.

E2SA 643R/7 Mar/GB. Shipped to a Lancashire agent. It could be reg'n BDJ 905 owned F Lennon 1953-54. No more known.

E2SA 644R/17 Mar/GB. Shipped to a Manchester agent. Nothing more known of this car.

E2SA 645R/17Mar/GB. Shipped to a Kent agent reg'n OKP 7. A runner up to 1967. Owner from 2005 restored it by 2010.

E2SA 646R/12 Mar/GB. Shipped to a Kent agent reg'n MOE 87. Known from 1966 in poor nick, almost derelict by 1980 when restored by its owner. In excellent order by 1983.

E2SA 647R/14 Mar/GB. Shipped to a Surrey agent reg'n RPG 776. Known from 1959, running to 1977. Restored, sold to Italy 1992. New owner 2013 - a good running car.

E2SA 648R/18 Mar/GB. Shipped to a Hertfordshire agent reg'n NRO 964. Known from 1965. Restored from 1989. New owner from 2005 has the car in very good order.

E2SAL 649R/20 Mar 1952/USA Ca. Shipped to Angell Motors of Pasadena. Known from 1960s to at least1991.

E2SA 650R/19 Jun 1952/GB. Shipped to a London agent reg'n NXN 499. Known from the late 1960s. Owner Mike Smailes competed in it with many successes from 1971. Bought by Ib Rasmussen of Denmark in 2005 where it competed with more successes. Registered in Denmark B 499.

Ib Rasmussen (650) in a Danish event. (Rasmussen)

E2SA 651R/17 Mar 1952/GB. Shipped to a Sussex agent reg'n NPO 133. Used in competition by first owner G A Dudley (Ch 6). Known from 1967. Owner from 2000 has restored it.

E2SA 652R/12 Mar 1952/GB. Shipped to an Essex agent reg'n KER 437. Owner from 1969 well-restored it for hill-climbs. To France with him in 2004, reg'd 4707-TQ-87. A tidy runner.

E2SA 653R/27 Jun 1952/GB. Shipped to a Somerset agent reg'd NLX 901 in London. Known from 1967. Owners from 1999 have a very nice running car.

E2SA 654R/23 Jun 1952/GB. Shipped to a Scottish agent reg'd KGE 445. To USA in 1965. In Florida from 1991 and restored there, reg'n 093 452. From 1999 a very nice running car.

E2SAL 655R/7 Mar 1952/B. Shipped to Ets Brondeel the Antwerp agent. No further history known.

E3SA 656R/14 May 1953/GB. Shipped to a Kent agent reg'n RKJ 836. The first of several Jupiters built a year earlier but finished later. Fully dismantled by 2007, restored 2011 when sold. More work on it by 2013 to a high running standard.

E2SA 657R/4 Apr 1952/GB. Shipped to a Bradford agent reg'n HKW 918. Last used mid-1966. Now lost to us.

E2SA 658R/20 Mar 1952/GB. Shipped to a Birmingham agent reg'n MOC 898. Bought by Graham Berry in 2009 in very original condition, back on the road November 2010.

E2SA 659R/7 Apr 1952/GB. Shipped to the Lincoln

agent and registered FFE 648. Running up to mid-1969. Restored in the 1990s. More restoration by present owner from 2010.

E2SA 660R/23 Jun 1952/GB. Shipped to a Cheshire agent reg'n PFM 606. Present owner bought it in 1982.

E2SA 661R/12 Mar 1952/GB. Shipped to a Manchester agent reg'n JDK 381. Cowap timed at Prescott hill-climb in Sept 1952 at 57.64s and 58.0s (Ch 6). This car now lost to us.

E2SA 662R/5 Sep 1952/GB. Shipped to a Northants agent reg'n KRY 170. Known from 1969. In same family since 1982 when some restoration began.

E2SA 663R/9 Apr 1952/GB. Shipped to an Essex agent. No further history known.

E2SA 664R/25 Apr 1952/GB. Shipped to an Edinburgh agent reg'n JS 9669. Known from 1981. On the road 1988. By 1996 had body-set fitted from (693) and re-registered MXP 272. By 2000 fully restored. Sold to France 2003 then in 2006 to Belgium where made a very good car. In 2009 reg'n XPQ 908.

E2SA 665R/10 Apr 1952/GB. Shipped to a Bradford agent reg'n HKY 133. First owner John Sykes used it in motor sport *"with much fun"*. In 1960 its new owner bought and used it. Rebuilt in the 1980s, and by 2001 his son owned it, with restorative work done by 2010 to a high standard.

E2SA 666R/7 Apr 1952/GB. Shipped to a Manchester agent. No further history known.

E2SA 667R/3 Apr 1952/GB. Shipped to a Durham agent reg'n CBR 99. Known from 1957. Current owner from 1999. Excellent restoration 2003-09 by Mike Koch-Osborne. A very very good running car.

E2SA 668R/9 Apr 1952/GB. Shipped to an Essex agent reg'n VEV 21. Known from 1956, a runner to 1970. New owner from 2010 began restoration from 2011.

E2SA 669R/1 Apr 1952/GB. Shipped to a Birmingham agent and it is thought registered MOC 883. Lost from 1959.

E2SA 670R/27 May 1952/GB. Shipped to a Scottish agent reg'n SW 8769. In Ireland 1970-1989. Back to GB in 1990 and well restored. New owner from 2006.

E2SA 671R/27 May 1952/GB. Shipped to a Durham agent reg'n NPT 795. Not heard from since 1967.

E2SA 672R/17 Mar 1952/GB. Shipped to a London agent reg'n MXP 610. Known from 1975. Well restored from poor state 1987-1991. New owner from 2015.

E2SA 673R/2 Apr 1952/GB. Shipped to a Scottish agent reg'n FHS 338. Known from 1966 when a good running car. Meticulous rebuild 1981-89. New owner from 2014.

E2SA 674R/18 Jun 1952/GB. Shipped to a London agent reg'n NLT 331. Known 1993, fully restored by 2000. Bought 2002.

E2SA 675R/2 Apr 1952/GB. Shipped to a Surrey agent. We have no further history on this car.

E2SA 676R/28 Apr 1952/GB. Shipped to an Essex agent. We have no further history on this car.

E2SA 677R/4 Jul 1952/GB. Shipped to a Hertfordshire agent reg'n OJH 161. Was JOAC founder Stan Blyther's car 1957 to 1965. Dismantled before 2003. Bought for restoration 2006.

E2SA 678R/29 Jun 1953/GB. Shipped to a Hertfordshire agent reg'n GBA 743. New owner in 2000, car awaits restoration.

E2SA 679R/22 May 1953/GB. Shipped to the Northampton agent reg'n LMJ 517. Owner Eddie Shrive drove in trials 1954-55. Known from 1960. To Eire in 1969, crashed in 1970. In 2000 new owner, with the car under slow restoration.

E2SA 680R/22 May 1953/GB. Shipped to the Ipswich agent reg'n ECF 494. Owner Bill Smith used it in rallies and trials 1952-54, see Ch 6. It was professionally restored 2010-2015.

E2SA 681R/23 May 1952/GB. Shipped to a Scottish agent. It was in NZ by 1982 but it is now dismantled and lost to us.

E2SA 682R/23 Apr 1952/GB. Shipped to a Welsh agent reg'n HDM 949. Known from new to now: a smart running car.

E2SA 683R/8 Apr 1952/GB. Shipped to the Kings Lynn, Norfolk, agent. First reg'd OPW 456 in May 1953. Full history known, restored by 1983. New owner from 2014.

E2SA 684R/23 Apr 1952/GB. Shipped to the Norwich,

Norfolk, agent, reg'n EVG 853. Known from the mid-1950s. Sold 1974 in a depleted state. Restored 1982-88 to a high standard in the 1990s. New owner from 2010.
E2SA 685R/3 Apr 1952/GB. Shipped to a Lancashire agent, reg'n FBA 737. Reported scrapped 1970 or before.
E2SAL 686R/19 Mar 1952/Finland/believed in use to 1977. New owner from 2004.
E2SA 687R/20 Jun 1952/GB. Shipped to a Welsh agent, Flintshire reg'n JDM 184. Known 1969 as a runner. Rebuilt c.2010. A new owner from 2015: the car a good runner.
E2SA 688R/1 Apr 1952/GB. Shipped to a Northants agent, reg'n BEG 570. Bought in stripped state 1994.
E2SA 689R+/25 Mar 1952/GB. Rolling chassis to a London agent, and lost to us. Could have been the 'Primrose Saloon'?
E2SA 690R/3 Jul 1952/GB. Shipped to an Essex agent, reg'n VNO 118. Known from 1972. Believed scrapped.
E2SA 691R/3 Apr 1952/GB. Shipped to a Lancashire agent, reg'n ERN 383. Restored 2000 to 2008. New owner 2015.
E2SA 692R/4 Apr 1952/GB. Shipped to a Sussex agent reg'n GNJ 756. Likely the first owner was champion boxer Don Cockell. Known from 1962. To Northern Ireland 1993. Slow restoration nearly done 2015.
E2SA 693R/9 Apr 1952/GB. Shipped to a London agent reg'n MXP 272. Known from 1960s. In 1990s, body and registration of this car put on (664). Chassis bought Mike Smailes 2000 and a Nickri glass fibre body fitted. Car roadable 2012 with registration (from 664) now JS 9669.
E2SA 694R/1 Apr 1952/GB. Shipped to the Hull, Yorkshire agent reg'n NAT 146. Known from 1965, professionally restored c.2000. Bought ex-Jowett man Phill Green as a very smart runner in 2008. For sale in 2015.
E2SA 695R/16 Apr 1952/GB. Shipped to an Essex agent reg'n FJN 326. Known from 1974. Fully restored by 1984. A very good car with present owner from 2011.
E2SAL 696R/19 Mar 1952/BR. Shipped to the Bahia, Brazil, Jowett agent. Nothing more known of this car.
E2SA 697R/10 Apr 1952/GB. Shipped to the Chester, Cheshire agent reg'n BHF 308. Known from 1953. Fully restored by 1989. A good runner, new owner from 2000.

E2SA 698R/21 Apr 1952/GB. Shipped to a Glasgow agent, but we have no further history of this car.
E2SA 699R/4 Apr 1952/JAP. Shipped to the Tokyo agent, but its engine in Ca so the car may have gone to USA. That's all.
E2SA 700R/2 Apr 1952/GB. Shipped to a Kent agent reg'n KOY 350. Owned since 1974 by George Mitchell almost fully dismantled. Likely this Jupiter John Surtees's first road car.
E2SAL 701R/9 Mar 1952/BR. Shipped to Vianna Braga and known from 1960, registered CIO 5492. Owner Jean Carlos from 1960s. Has VW 1600cc engine, runs well looks good.
E2SAL 702R/20 Mar 1952/USA. Shipped to Angell Motors of Pasadena. History unknown.
E2SAL 703R/21 Mar 1952/USA. Shipped to Angell Motors of Pasadena. Known from 1965. In scrapyard 1989. To GB 1999. Restored by 2008 reg'd 316 XUD but had bad smash. Body and more onto another Jupiter. Chassis repaired and bought 2010 and it is being rebuilt with body from a scrapped Jupiter.
E2SA 704R/4 Apr 1952/GB. Shipped to a North Wales agent, reg'd HUN 482. Full history known. Restored from dismantled state 1975. Owned from 2010 a very sound running car.
E3SA 705R/1 Oct 1953/GB. Sold by a London agent with reg'n 143 AMM. Restored by 1994. On the road 1995.
E2SAL 706R/21 Mar 1952/USA. Shipped to Angell Motors of Pasadena. History unknown.
E2SA 707R/9 Apr 1952/GB. Shipped to a Hampshire agent, reg'n MEL 96. Runner to 1970. By 1978 had an MGA engine. From 1986 much depleted some panels going to Jupiter (563).
E2SA 708R/16 Jul 1953/GB. Shipped to a Lancashire agent, reg'n BHG 703. Known from 1965. Totally stripped 1968/69. Chassis to Bill Ray in 1989, he built his own design open body, finished by Mike Koch-Osborne and running by 2001.
E2SAL 709R/21 Mar 1952/USA. Shipped to Angell Motors of Pasadena. Known from 1960s. Dismantled in 1978 and its badly damaged body tub and broken chassis

left to rot behind abandoned filling station in San Jose, California.

E2SAL 710R/14 Aug 1952/USA. Ordered via Angell Motors of Pasadena. First owner a USA army man based in Germany who got it from Jowett so it was registered HKW 407. That's all.

E2SA 711R/14 Aug 1953/GB. Shipped to a Staffordshire agent, reg'n KDA 943. Scrapped in 1968, engine survives.

E3SA 712R/14 Aug 1953/GB. Shipped to a Manchester agent, but only its engine survives.

E2SA 713R/24 Apr 1952/GB. Shipped to a Manchester agent, reg'n MVM 488. Known from 1971. Restored in 1980s. New owner from 2000, the car excellent condition.

E3SA 714R/14 Aug 1953/GB. Shipped to a Lancashire agent. We have no later history on this car.

E2SAL 715R/21 Mar 1952/USA. Shipped to Angell Motors of Pasadena. Known from 1962. From 2014 under restoration in Ca by the expert Scott Renner for owner living in Australia.

E2SAL 716R/25 Mar 1952/USA. Shipped to Angell Motors of Pasadena. No further history known.

E2SA 717R/24 Apr 1952/GB. Shipped to an Edinburgh agent, reg'n JWS 95. Known from 1955. Owner from 1963 restored it 2011-2013. On the road runs and looks good.

E2SA 718R/20 Jun 1952/GB. Shipped to a Sussex agent, with Bradford reg'n HKY 344. Raced to 4th place at Goodwood 26Jul52 by John Lewis (Ch 6) who also raced it at Castle Coombe Oct52. Crashed at Goodwood Mar53, repaired as he raced at Goodwood 12Sep53. Lost to us from 1955/56.

E2SAL 719R/26 Mar 1952/USA. Shipped to Angell Motors of Pasadena. No further history known.

E3SA 720R/28 May 1953/GB. Shipped to a Lancashire agent, reg'n BHG 501. Known from 1958. Looking good, it was bought 1981 by the Bradford Industrial Museum, on show.

E2SAL 721R/26 Mar 1952/USA. Shipped to Angell Motors of Pasadena. No further history known.

E2SA 722R/29 May 1952/GB. Shipped to a Scottish agent, reg'n HS 1 for Sir W J Lithgow of the then big shipbuilding concern. Re-reg'd JHS 365 for 1955 sale.

Professionally restored by 1990. New owners from 2003, a fine running car.

E2SA 723R/29 May 1952/GB. Shipped to a Staffordshire agent reg'n KDA 678. Known from 1970. Restored and used in Historic competition 1985 to 1989.

E2SA 724R+/late March1952/GB. Initially a rolling chassis, then built into **E2SAL** 938R q.v.

E2SA 725R+/31 Mar 1952/GB. Shipped as rolling chassis to a Kent agent. Closed body built by Adams & Robinson for P Fotheringham-Parker for the 1953 Monte Carlo Rally but not ready in time. Reg'd 32 MMY for next owner Willment Bros, racing car people. Bought 1969 by Edmund Nankivell. Restored 1971-73, a smart runner.

E2SA 726R+/31 Mar 1952/GB. Shipped as rolling chassis to a London agent. Possibly was the Gilliver Saloon, see Ch 9.

E2SA 727R/23 Jun 1952/GB. Shipped to the Croydon agent reg'n KRK 203. Known from 1974. In 1980 said to be dismantled, under restoration. New owner from 2013.

E2SAL 728R/27 Mar 1952/USA. Shipped to Angell Motors of Pasadena. Known from 1984 when bought by Mike Rogers.

E2SA 729R/16 May 1952/GB. Shipped to Hereford reg'n JVJ 148. The 'Green Goddess' known from 1957-58 when owned by explorer/author Blashford-Snell. New owner 2014 is restoring the car.

E2SAL 730R/28 Mar 1952/USA. Shipped to Angell Motors of Pasadena. No further history known of this car.

E2SAL 731R/26 Mar 1952/USA. Shipped to Angell Motors of Pasadena. Known from 1983 in NY state. Bought 2007.

E2SAL 732R/25 Mar 1952/USA. Shipped to Angell Motors of Pasadena. Known from 1954. Bought 2008 by Ken Nelson.

E3SA 733R/23 Jul 1953/GB. Shipped to the Burnley, Lancs agent reg'n BHG 914. Full history known. By 1975 just a stripped chassis. New owner from 1992 fitted a Romahome camper body to it with Javelin front-end and other parts. Running in 2007 registered KMW 988 from the Javelin.

E2SA 734R/8 Apr 1952/GB. Shipped to a London agent

reg'n MYM 925. Bought Dennis Sparrow in 1973 as original unrestored car but stored since then.

E2SA 735R/1 Sep 1952/GB. Shipped to a Berkshire agent reg'n JBL 419. Known from 1974, a runner to 1978. Restored 1999-2004. To France in 2008 reg'd 735-ANY-29 in very good condition, regularly used in classic car rallies in Brittany.

E2SA 736R/17 Jul 1952/GB. Shipped to the Oldham, Lancs agent reg'n HBU 900. Found in 1972 in poor state. Bought 2011 and restored for the road by 2015.

E2SA 737R/10 Apr 1952/GB. Shipped to a Lancashire agent reg'n BEN 197. Last heard from in 1966.

E2SA 738R/20 Aug 1952/GB. Shipped to a Hertfordshire agent reg'd OJH 778 then RSV 846. Known from 1974, in need of total restoration. New owner in 2003. Restoration nearly done by 2006 with reg'n OJH 778 again.

E2SA 739R/11 Jun 1952/GB. Shipped to a Surrey agent reg'n RPL 519. A runner to 1963. By 1974 reduced to a bare stripped frame. During 2009-2010 built up to complete running car and sold 2011 as a smart runner.

E2SAL 740R/24 Mar 1952/USA. Shipped to Angell Motors of Pasadena. Known from 1969. In 1992 'complete and goes'. In c.2000 to Sweden, bought and very well restored 2004-06. In 2013 to Denmark and registered C499.

E2SAL 741R/27 Mar 1952/USA. Shipped to Angell Motors of Pasadena. Early owners Pacific Auto Rentals, a Los Angeles firm who rented cars to movie studios. Known 1977-84 in Minnesota. From 1990 owner in USA state of Georgia.

E2SAL 742R/27 Mar 1952/USA. Shipped to Angell Motors of Pasadena. No further history known.

E2SAL 743R/26 Mar 1952/USA. Shipped to Angell Motors of Pasadena. In 1976 dismantled, stored. New owner 2002.

E2SAL 744R/26 Mar 1952/USA. Shipped to Angell Motors of Pasadena. No further history known.

E2SAL 745R/27 Mar 1952/USA. Shipped to Angell Motors of Pasadena. Known from 1976. To GB 1990. It 95% restored 1990-99 via Graham Berry. Bought 2006 by owner who completed its restoration, reg'd 153 XUB.

E2SAL 746R+/9 Apr 1952/D/Shipped to Danish agent as LHD rolling chassis. Returned to Jowett, built into RHD car (937).

E3SA 747R/30 Sep 1953/GB. Shipped to a London agent reg'n 977 AMC. History known from 1957. New owner from 1980.

E2SA 748R/11 Jun 1952/GB. Shipped to a Staffordshire agent reg'n KDA 937. In rallies and hill-climbs 1952/53 driver Ian Sievwright see Ch 5, Ch 6. Known from 1959 and restored 1994. New owner from 2012.

E2SA 749R/25 Apr 1952/GB. Shipped to a Birmingham agent reg'n YRE 161. Running to 1965 or later. History known from 1975. Bought 1982 by owner believed to be storing it.

E2SA 750R/26 Jun 1952/GB. Shipped to a Yorkshire agent. Warranty to a Mr Piston. Nothing more known.

E2SA 751R/1 Jul 1952/GB. Shipped to a Scottish agent but reg'd in London April 1953 as NXH 439. Owner from 1987 stores it needing restoration.

E2SA 752R/23 Jun 1952/GB. Shipped to a Glasgow agent reg'n KGD 967. Known from 1972. By 1990 chassis stripped, incomplete. New owner bought it 2005.

E2SA 753R/23 Jun 1952/GB. Shipped to a Derbyshire agent possibly the Jupiter reg'd RRB 844. Known only in 1963.

E2SAL 754R/11 Apr 1952/USA. Shipped to Angell Motors of Pasadena. No further history known of this car.

E3SA 755R/11 Aug 1953/GB. Shipped to a Bradford agent reg'n DJX 141. Known from 1967. Shipped to NZ in 1971. Under restoration from 2012.

E2SAL 756R/10 Apr 1952/USA. Shipped to Angell Motors of Pasadena. Known from 1973. To GB in 1999 then to France in 2008. Restored by 2015.

E2SA 757R/13 Jun 1952/GB. Shipped to a London agent reg'n YMC 900. In the 1953 RAC Rally crewed by Ross & Phillips. Not heard from since 1961.

E2SAL 758R/10 Apr 1952/USA. Shipped to Angell Motors of Pasadena. Known from 1980. Owned and restored to racing spec. by Scott Renner 1990-1991 and regularly Historic raced.

E2SAL 759R/11 Apr 1952/USA. Shipped to Angell Motors of Pasadena. No further history known of this car.

E2SAL 760R/10 Apr 1952/USA. Shipped to Angell Motors of Pasadena. No further history known of this car.

E2SA 761R/29 May 1952/GB. Shipped to a Glasgow agent with London reg'n NLX 909 of March 1953. Driven by Alec Gordon in five rallies in 1953 (Chs 4, 5) Nothing known since.

E2SAL 762R/11 Apr 1952/USA. Shipped to Angell Motors of Pasadena. Known from first owner W Horton. Exported to GB in 1988. A running car by 1990 reg'd CSK 274.

E2SAL 763R/11 Apr 1952/USA. Shipped to Angell Motors of Pasadena. Bought in poor state in 1980.

E2SAL 764R/11 Apr 1952/USA. Shipped to Angell Motors of Pasadena. No further history known of this car.

E2SAL 765R/11 Apr 1952/USA. Shipped to Angell Motors of Pasadena. Known from 1977. New owner 2002.

E2SAL 766R/11 Apr 1952/USA. Shipped to Angell Motors of Pasadena. Known from 1962. Last seen 1978 in poor state.

E2SAL 767R to 772R/all Apr 1952/USA. All shipped to Angell Motors of Pasadena, with no further history known.

E2SAL 773R/25 Apr 1952/USA. Shipped to Angell Motors of Pasadena. Known from 1965. To GB in 2005 and restoration in progress from 2009.

E2SAL 774R/24 Apr 1952/USA. Shipped to Angell Motors of Pasadena. Owner from 1993: body-off restoration from 2001.

E2SAL 775R/24 Apr 1952/USA. Shipped to Angell Motors of Pasadena. No further history known of this car.

E2SAL 776R/25 Apr 1952/USA. Shipped to Angell Motors of Pasadena. Known from 1977 a 'stripped-out wreck'. To GB in 1999. Bought 2001 for restoration.

E2SAL 777R/24 Apr 1952/USA. Shipped to Angell Motors of Pasadena. No further history known of this car.

E2SAL 778R/25 Apr 1952/USA. Shipped to Angell Motors of Pasadena. Known from 1975. To Arizona in 1977. Sold 2014.

E2SAL 779R/25 Apr 1952/USA. Shipped to Angell Motors of Pasadena. No further history known of this car.

E2SA 780R/16 Jun 1952/GB. Shipped to a Lincolnshire agent with reg'n KBE 595 in 1953. Crashed/scrapped in 1967.

E2SAL 781R/24 Apr 1952/USA. Shipped to Angell Motors of Pasadena. No further history known of this car.

E2SAL 782R/24 Apr 1952/USA. Shipped to Angell Motors of Pasadena. Known from 1971. Owner known from 1975.

E2SA 783R/27 Jun 1952/GB. Shipped to a Staffordshire agent reg'n XRE 953. Known from 1968. Scrapped 1972.

E2SAL 784R/25 Apr 1952/USA. Shipped to Angell Motors of Pasadena. No further history known of this car.

E2SAL 785R/25 Apr 1952/USA. Shipped to Angell Motors of Pasadena. Known from 1990. New owner from 2002.

E2SAL 786R/25 Apr 1952/USA. Shipped to Angell Motors of Pasadena. No further history known of this car.

E2SAL 787R/30 Apr 1952/USA. Shipped to Angell Motors of Pasadena. Known from 1957. To Arizona 1980 and well restored. To Australia 1993. Owner 2000 with reg'n BPW 253. It is a very nice running car.

E2SA 788R/15 May 1952/GB. Shipped to a Birmingham agent reg'n MOF 554. Known from 1961. Restored 1978-1980. New owner from 1988. A nice runner.

E2SAL 789R/29 Apr 1952/USA. Shipped to Angell Motors of Pasadena. Known from 1970. With Volvo engine not a runner.

E2SA 790R/18 Jun 1952/GB. Shipped to a Yorkshire agent but nothing further known of this car.

E2SAL 791R/29 Apr 1952/USA. Shipped to Angell Motors of Pasadena. Known from 1977. Bought B. Jowett in 1991, the car under slow restoration.

E2SAL 792R/30 Apr 1952/USA. Shipped to Angell Motors of Pasadena. No further history known of this car.

E2SAL 793R/2 May 1952/USA. Shipped to Angell Motors of Pasadena. Known since 1960s. To GB in 1978 reg'd FSV 108 after restoration. New owner from 2008.

E2SAL 794R/29 Apr 1952/USA. Shipped to Angell Motors of Pasadena. Known from 1958. By 1980 in Minnesota; the car a runner but to be restored.

E2SAL 795R/30 Apr 1952/USA. Shipped to Angell Motors of Pasadena. Known from 1978. Owner from 1986 of Washington State then Idaho. By 2015 restored and looking good.

E2SAL 796R/2 May 1952/USA. Shipped to Angell Motors of Pasadena. No further history known of this car.

E2SAL 797R/1 May 1952/USA. Shipped to Angell Motors of Pasadena. No further history known of this car.

E2SAL 798R/2 May 1952/USA. Shipped to Angell Motors of Pasadena. Not heard from since 1968.

E2SAL 799R/30 Apr 1952/USA. Shipped to Angell Motors of Pasadena. Known from 1969. In scrapyard 1989 for sale.

E2SAL 800R/2 May 1952/USA. Shipped to Angell Motors of Pasadena. In Oklahoma 1957 to 1993 when exported to GB and after restoration reg'd NFF 445.

E2SAL 801R, 802R, 803R/all 2 May 1952/USA. All shipped to Angell Motors of Pasadena. No more known of these cars.

E2SAL 804R/3 May 1952/USA. Shipped to Angell Motors of Pasadena. Known since 2002. Bought Ken Nelson in 2009 with restoration well under way as of 2015.

E2SAL 805R to 812R/all in May 1952/USA. All shipped to Angell Motors of Pasadena. No more known of these cars.

E2SAL 813R/8 May 1952/USA. Shipped to Angell Motors of Pasadena. Known since 1967 when in concours-winning state. Owned still in good nick from 1997 by Rick Jowett of Texas.

E2SAL 814R/9 May 1952/D/New to agent W Gloeckler of Frankfurt. Nothing further known of this car.

E2SAL 815R/7 May 1952/USA. Shipped to Angell Motors of Pasadena. Known from 1975. Just chassis exported to GB in 1990. Bought Graham Berry, it was restored using imported body-set released from the original Dream Rod custom car. Reg'n XSK 478. Exported to Canada in 2000, auctioned 2015.

E2SAL 816R/7 May 1952/USA. Shipped to Angell Motors of Pasadena. Known from 1962. Bought 1992 by Jim Miller, it was restored by 2000 with 'Stars & Stripes' paint job. Came to France for the 2000 Le Mans 50th. Always a good running car.

E2SAL 817R/8 May 1952/USA. Shipped to Angell Motors of Pasadena. Known in 1970s but believed long gone.

E2SAL 818R/4 Jun 1952/D/New to agent W Gloeckler of Frankfurt. In Sweden by 2010 in good condition.

E2SAL 819R/18 Jun 1952/S. Imported by the Gothenburg agent Alpen & Gundersen. Stored by owner from 1960.

E2SAL 820R/22 Aug 1952/USA. Shipped to Angell Motors of Pasadena. Known from 1963. To Germany in 2008. In 2011 to Poland. In 2012 sold to another Polish owner.

E2SAL 821R/14 Aug 1952/USA. Shipped to Angell Motors of Pasadena. No further history known of this car.

E2SAL 822R/22 Aug 1952/USA. Shipped to Angell Motors of Pasadena. Known from before 1961. In use to 1973. Owner from 1984 getting it restored 2014.

E2SAL 823R/22 Jul 1952/Personal Export car reg'd by Jowett HKY 232 for Capt R H Jones. Nothing more known.

E2SAL 824R/22 Aug 1952/USA. Shipped to Angell Motors of Pasadena. No further history known of this car.

E2SAL 825R/22 Aug 1952/USA. Shipped to Angell Motors of Pasadena. Reported in 1978 to exist.

E2SAL 826R/14 Aug 1952/USA. Shipped to Angell Motors of Pasadena. No further history known of this car.

E2SAL 827R/27 Jun 1952/USA. Importer Hoffman Motor Car Co of New York. Known from 1964. For sale 2012.

E2SAL 828R/27 Jun 1952/USA. Importer Hoffman Motor Car Co of New York. Nothing more known of this car.

E2SAL 829R/20 Aug 1952/USA. Shipped to Angell Motors of Pasadena. Known 1962-1978 as a running car.

E2SAL 830R/19 Aug 1952/USA. Shipped to Angell Motors of Pasadena. Known from 1978. To Canada 1966 and well-restored by its owner. New owner in 2000 still in Canada.

E2SAL 831R/19 Jun 1952/Personal Export car reg'd by Jowett HKY 225 for Mr L H Sugg. By 1968 in Connecticut USA. In 2015 still in same family from nearly new.

E2SAL 832R/22 Aug 1952/USA. Shipped to Angell Motors of Pasadena. Destroyed in 2002.

E2SAL 833R/13 Jun 1952/F. Sold to a Mr A Gomez via Plisson the Paris agent. Nothing further known of this car.

E2SAL 834R/11 Aug 1952/USA. Shipped to Angell Motors of Pasadena. No further history known of this car.

E2SAL 835R/19 Aug 1952/USA. Shipped to Angell Motors of Pasadena. No further history known of this car.

E2SAL 836R/22 Aug 1952/USA. Shipped to Angell Motors of Pasadena. No further history known of this car.

E2SAL 837R/19 Aug 1952/USA. Shipped to Angell Motors of Pasadena. No further history known of this car.

E2SA 838R/19 Jul 1952/GB. Shipped the Brighton Sussex agent reg'n MCD 545. First owner A R Sandibanks of Edinburgh. In 1953 RSAC Rally entrant C G Marshall but the car did not finish. Known from 1970. Restored in the 1990s. Bought 2014 by Dr L. Jowett & G. Walker.

E2SA 839R/2 Jul 1952/GB. Shipped to a Yorkshire agent but registration not known. Dismantled 1966 and scrapped.

E2SA 840R/2 Jul 1952/GB. Shipped to the Belfast agent reg'n PZ 1007. To GB, restored in 1970s for Mrs Elizabeth Davis's use, which she drove for many years. New owner 2014.

E2SA 841R/7 Jul 1952/GB. Shipped to the Liverpool agent and registered NKD 258. Known from 1967 and bought 1969 by Keith Clements who used it, improved it, travelled a lot in it, see Ch 7. Never needed rebuild, never off the road.

E2SA 842R/7 Jul 1952/GB. Shipped to a Middlesex dealer. We have no further history of this car.

E2SA 843R/27 Jun 1952/GB. Shipped to a Yorkshire agent reg'n WRF 444. Known from its very early days. Bought 2005 in very original condition by S. Wood.

E2SA 844R/21 Aug 1952/GB. Shipped to a Buckinghamshire agent reg'n HJB 326. Known from 1975. E Tonner drove it from Bristol to Rome & back no problems c.1971. Superbly rebuilt 1982-1992. New owner 1997.

E2SA 845R/4 Jul 1952/Personal Export car reg'd by Jowett HKY 226 for Mr R J Leaman. Nothing more known.

E3SA 846R/20 May 1953/GB. Shipped to a Buckinghamshire agent reg'n BHG 427. First owner Tom Blackburn raced and rallied it in 1953 & 1954 see Ch 5, Ch 6. Now gone.

E2SAL 847R/13 Jun 1952/F. Shipped to Plisson the Paris agent. Nothing further known of this car.

E3SA 848R/20 Aug 1953/GB. Shipped to a London agent

reg'n 966 AMC. Known from 1966. Under full restoration from 1983. Body back on chassis 2005.

E2SA 849R/2 Sep 1953/GB. Shipped to a London agent reg'n XVW 179 c. Dec 1953. Seen in scrap form in 1960s.

E3SA 850R/14 Aug 1953/GB. Shipped to a London agent. It was 2nd in SJCC Driving Test 29 Aug 1954. No more known.

E2SA 851R/1 Jan 1953/Personal Export car reg'd by Jowett JAK 824 for a Miss Granville. Nothing more known.

E3SA 852R/10 Jan 1953/Personal Export car to Gordon Hale. and car shipped to Lagos Nigeria. Nothing more known.

E3SA 853R/26 Aug 1953/GB. Shipped to a London agent. Nothing more known.

E3SA 854R/10 Jul 1953/GB. Shipped to the Burnley, Lancashire agent. No more known.

E3SA 855R/29 May 1953/GB. Shipped to a Scottish agent reg'n KSG 532. Body burnt out 1953, rebuilt with non-standard glass-fibre and aluminium body. First logged owner L Paladini from the early 1960s. He hill-climbed it to 1967. Present owner bought it in 1978, car currently stored.

E3SA 856R/23 Aug 1953/GB. First to an Edinburgh agent then a London agent. First owner in Newcastle, No more known.

E3SA 857R/23 Aug 1953/GB. Shipped to a London agent reg'd OLK 685. Known since 1960. Owner from 1968

The Nankivell's Jupiter (560) on tour in France in 2003. (CJ)

daily use to 1976, he restored it 2003-2009 into good condition.

E2SA 858R/20 Mar 1953/GB. Shipped to a London agent reg'd YMP 935. Known from 1965. Laid up in 1990, still stored in 2015.

E2SA 859R/10 Mar 1953/GB. Shipped to a London agent reg'n LBY 254. Owner from 1972 restored it lightweight for HSCC racing 1975-2001. In 2008 to Richard Gane for more HSCC events. New owner from 2015.

E2SA 860R/9 Jul 1953/GB. Shipped to a Glamorgan dealer reg'n HKG 669 late 1953. Known from 1969. Restored 1980s. To Switzerland 1983, a very good car. Swiss reg'n SG-32287.

E2SA 861R/18 Aug 1953/GB. Shipped to a Surrey agent reg'n RKO 10. Known from 1960. Professionally restored 1975-78. Present owner from 2007. A nice running car.

E2SAL 862R/30 Jun 1952/USA. Importer Hoffman Motor Car Co of New York. Known from before 1978 in Pennsylvania. By 1990 in Kentucky in poor condition.

E3SA 863R/23 Jul 1953/GB. Shipped to a Lancashire agent reg'n RTD 111. Known from 1968. Owner from 1997 restored it by 1999. A very good car.

E2SA 864R/24 Jun 1952/Personal Export car reg'd by Jowett HKY 227 for a Mr Birmingham. Nothing more known.

E3SA 865R/29 Aug 1953/GB. Shipped to a Manchester agent reg'n GBA 131. Known scrapped before 1990.

E3SA 866R/22 May 1953/GB. Shipped to a Manchester agent reg'n NXN 494. Owner from 1960 to 1970s was Jowett spares man Charlie Dodd who restored it. Present owner from 1982.

E2SA 867R/3 Jul 1952/GB. Shipped to a Bedfordshire agent reg'n LTM 445. Last used 1965, believed scrapped.

E2SA 868R/3 Jul 1952/GB. Shipped to a Yorkshire agent reg'd GVY 555 as their demonstrator. No more history known.

E2SA 869R/7 Jul 1952/GB. Shipped to a Yorkshire agent reg'n PWB 208. Last heard from in 1961.

E2SA 870R/25 Jun 1953/GB. Shipped to a Manchester agent. Nothing more known of this car.

E3SA 871R/13 Aug 1953/GB. Shipped to a London

agent reg'n 7881 H. Known from 1961. Restored from dismantled state 2009-11. Re-registered 705 YUE in April 2011. New owner by 2013: the car a very good runner.

E3SA 872R/7 Aug 1953/GB. Shipped to a Lancashire agent reg'n GBA 895. In N. Ireland 1970-72. Bought 1973 Jack Gipe of California visiting GB but it's stored in London since then.

E2SA 873R/10 Sep 1952/GB. Shipped to a Surrey agent reg'n SPB 725. Known from 1968. Rebuilt in 1980s by then owner David Taylor. New owner 2003, the car a very good runner.

E3SA 874R/24 Aug 1953/GB. Shipped to a London agent but no further history known.

E2SA 875R/8 Sep 1952/GB. Shipped to an Essex agent reg'n UVW 849. No more known about this car.

E3SA 876R/8 Jun 1953/GB. Shipped to the Norwich agent reg'n FVG 332. Known from 1956. Bought 1967 by P. Dixon to race in HSCC events to 1983. Sold and restored by 2010. To France 2011. Now in Brittany, a very good car.

E3SA 877R/22 Jul 1953/GB. Shipped to a London agent reg'd NYM 671. Known from 1959. Owner from 1971 took it with him to the USA in 1975.

E3SA 878R/19 Sep 1953/GB. Shipped to a London agent reg'n 956 AMC. Owner from 1976 keeps it always a running car.

E3SA 879R/18 Aug 1953/GB. Shipped to a London agent but no further history known.

E3SA 880R/19 Aug 1953/GB. Shipped to a Birmingham agent reg'n OGX 224. Owner from 1971 rebuilt it before 1972 when sold as a road car. Sold again 2011 a nice runner.

E3SA 881R/10 Aug 1953/GB. Shipped to a Surrey agent reg'n TPF 601. Known from 1954. In good order sold 1989 to Mauritius to the BWW/Daihatsu agency there. In 2003 registered D 588. New owner from 2009. A drivable car for sale 2015.

E2SA 882R/3 Sep 1952/Personal Export car reg'd by Jowett HKY 762 for a Dr Maurice Livera. Confirmed in Sri Lanka in 1987 reg'n EL 4103. Owner in 1970 restored it. In 2000 transferred to his son. A runner still in Sri Lanka.

E2SA 883R/4 Jul 1953/GB. Shipped to a Gloucestershire

agent reg'n LDG 988. Known from 1972. Owner from 1991 had the car restored and running again from 2011.

E2SA 884R/13 Mar 1953/GB. Shipped to a Gloucestershire agent reg'n BFL 578. Known from 1965. Owner from 2013 repaired its fire damage.

E3SA 885R/4 Jul 1953/GB. Shipped to a Lancashire agent but with Bradford reg'n JKU 945 for a USA army man. Found in 1978 in Tucson Arizona but believed scrapped after that date.

E3SA 886R/4 Jul 1953/Algeria/First shipped as rolling chassis (243) in July 1951 but returned unbuilt to Jowett who built it into this complete car, exported to Algiers. No more known

E3SA 887R/12 May 1953/GB. Shipped to a Birmingham agent reg'n JUN 68. Known from mid-1950, last used 1961. Very incomplete by 1969. Owner from 1989 has gathered missing parts for restoration quite well advanced by 2015.

E2SA 888R/16 May 1952/GB. Shipped to a Lancashire agent and registered FRJ 132. Known from 1971. Restored 1989 to 1995 by owner K Foulds. In 2006 sold to someone in Macau.

E3SA 889R/21 Jul 1953/GB. Shipped to the Nottingham agent and reg'd RAU 436. Known from 1963. Owner from 1988 keeps it in good original running condition

E3SA 890R/28 Apr 1953/GB. Shipped to the Sheffield agent reg'n PWE 755. Known from 1969. Bought in 1983 and restored by 2012.

E2SA 891R/26 Nov 1952/BR. Shipped to the Recife, Brazil agent but nothing more known.

E2SA 892R/28 Nov 1952/Personal Export car reg'd by Jowett JAK 557 for a Mr Kendall. Found in 1984 in Canada but its remains believed scrapped by 2001.

E2SA 893R/1 Apr 1953/GB. Shipped to a Leeds agent reg'n RUA 449. Known from 1967. Had bad accident in 1972, only a few parts remain in 2015.

E3SA 894R/24 Jul 1953/GB. Shipped to a London agent reg'n NYM 449. Last on the road 1967. Stored since 1975.

E2SA 895R/3 Sep 1952/Algiers/Shipped to the Anglo-American Garage but nothing more known of this car.

E3SA 896R/20 May 1953/GB. Shipped to the Oxford agent reg'n TJO 887. Known from 1969. New owner from 2004, the car in need of restoration.

E3SA 897R/20 Apr 1953/GB. Shipped to a Staffordshire agent. Warranty to Shelley Potteries Ltd. Nothing more known.

E3SA 898R/30 Jun 1953/GB. Shipped to a Birmingham agent reg'n JUN 592. In 1954 owner Max Trimble raced and rallied it, saying "*it was a superb car especially in its day*". See Ch 6. Owner from 1982 restored it in 1990s to very good order.

E3SA 899R/3 Jun 1953/GB. Shipped to a Surrey agent reg'n TPD 543. Known from 1975. Owner from 2002 restored it by 2008 from poor state to excellent nick.

E3SA 900R/3 Jun 1953/GB. Shipped to a Lancashire agent reg'n GFR 766. Known from 1977. Restored by 2006 when sold in good order to Eire, with Irish reg'n ZV 65749.

E3SA 901R/14 May 1953/GB. Shipped to the Chester agent reg'd RMA 500. Full history known. A runner in 1969 for new owner, then stored. Now his son has begun its restoration.

E3SA 902R/14 Jul 1953/GB. Shipped to an Oxford agent then 7 Oct 1953 to the Renfrew agent and bought by a Loch Lomond hotelier. We have no more history of this car.

E3SA 903R/27 Apr 1953/GB. Shipped to a Norwich agent reg'n FVG 87. Known from 1954. Restored in the 1980s. New owner from 2004; a good-looking running car.

E3SA 904R/20 May 1953/GB. Shipped to the Peterborough Northants agent. Nothing more known of this car.

E2SA 905R/10 Oct 1952/GB. Shipped to a London agent reg'n NLA 45. Known from 1968. Professionally rebuilt 1975. To Australia in 1981. New owner there from 2003.

E2SA 906R/3 Sep 1952/Algiers/Shipped to the Anglo-American Garage but nothing more known of this car.

E2SA 907R/26 Nov 1952/BR. Shipped to the Recife, Brazil agent but nothing more known.

E3SA 908R/3 Jul 1953/GB. Shipped to the Burnley Lancashire agent. Original owner L S Cordingley in the 1954

Driving Tests at Blackpool see Ch 6. Nothing more known.

E2SA 909R/20 Mar 1953/GB. First to a Northants agent, then 1 May 1953 to a Manchester agent reg'd OKC 687. Known from 1960, a runner in 1967. From 2000 in a small collection.

E2SA 910R/5 Mar 1953/GB. Shipped to the Burnley Lancashire agent reg'n BHG 181. First owner J Waddington used it in local rallies. From 1971 dismantled. In 2013 chassis to an owner who as of 2015 gets bodywork to re-assemble it.

E2SA 911R/20 Mar 1953/GB. Shipped to the Lincoln agent and must have gone to South Africa as its engine found there.

E3SA 912R/16 Apr 1953/GB. Shipped to a Norwich agent but we have nothing more on this car.

E3SA 913R/18 Jun 1953/GB. First to the Torquay agent then Jan 1954 to a London agent reg'd OLO 429. Stored from 1964. Owner from 1972 did some racing; stored from 1978.

E2SA 914R/19 Mar 1953/Personal Export car reg'd by Jowett JKU 729. In South Africa 1970 registered TJ 95780.

E3SA 915R/31 Mar 1953/GB. First to a Norwich agent then Apr 1953 to a Manchester agent reg'd OKC 491. Owner from 1969 restored it 2002-11 to very good order.

E2SA 916R/9 Jun 1953/GB. Shipped to a Manchester agent reg'n GBA 438. Owner from 1977 restored it by 2012.

E2SA 917R/22 Jun 1953/GB. Shipped to a Manchester agent reg'n OKD 725. Known from 1955. Bought 2009 by R. Gane and restored by him to light-weight Le Mans specification with 100+ bhp engine. Raced with successes from June 2013.

E3SA 918R/23 Jun 1953/GB. Shipped to a London agent reg'n PNK 627. A Company Car to 1957. Sold 1972 to a USA airline pilot. In USA from 1992. To Poland 2015 to be restored.

E3SA 919R/14 Aug 1953/GB. Shipped to a London agent, then 8 Sep 1953 Personal Export for Mr E T Hodgson. That's it.

E3SA 920R/30 Jun 1953/GB. Shipped to a Birmingham agent then it went to a London agent. Reported scrapped.

E3SA 921R/29 Jun 1953/GB. Shipped to a London agent reg'n NYM 283. Known from 1968. Running again 2008, sold 2009 to Morgan dealer/racer Richard Thorne who prepared it for lightweight racing by 2010 in French events.

E2SA 922R/17 Nov 1952/GB. Shipped to a Berkshire agent but reg'd HKY 770 July 1952. Owned 1955-59 by Ken Taylor for rallies (Ch 6). From 1961-64 owner England Rugby player Budge Rogers. In 2006 new owner. A very nice running car.

E3SA 923R/29 Jul 1953/GB. Shipped to a Northumberland agent reg'n FJR 759. Known from September 1955. Owned 1965-75 as a runner by Jimmy Shand, world famous accordionist. Bought 2013, car under restoration.

E3SA 924R/23 Jun 1953/GB. Shipped to a Manchester agent reg'n OKC 950. During 1963-69 owned by Aubrey Forshaw, chairman of Pan Books, who advised Ian Fleming about all things "motor car" when he was writing his James Bond books. This Jupiter is known to have been scrapped.

E3SA 925R/23 Jun 1953/GB. Shipped to a London agent reg'n NXX 416. To Australia in 1971. Owner from 1979 has the car in usable state but it could do with some work.

E2SA 926R/16 Mar 1953/GB. Shipped to a Scottish agent but we have no later information on this car.

E2SA 927R/19 Sep 1953/Shipped to Bermuda, returned 1957 to GB on the 'Queen Mary' reg'd TOW 997. Restored at leisurely pace 1993-2013. New owner from 2014.

E3SA 928R/16 Mar 1953/GB. Shipped to a Scottish agent reg'n JSR 964. New owners from 2012.

E3SA 929R/20 Jun 1953/GB. Shipped to a Birmingham agent reg'n LJW 979. In the MCC Rally of November 1953 crewed by Harrison & Guest. See Ch 4. No more known.

E3SA 930R/25 Jun 1953/GB. Shipped to a Yorkshire agent reg'n MWU 540. Present owner bought it 1971.

E3SA 931R/14 Apr 1953/ZA. Shipped to the Capetown agent. Known from 1970. Owner from 1978. Fully restored 2015.

E3SA 932R/5 Jun 1953/GB. Shipped to a Lancashire agent reg'n BHG 633. Known from 1957. Last driven in 1999. Bought 2014 for full restoration.

E3SA 933R/26 Jun 1953/GB. Shipped to a Norwich agent reg'n FVG 634. Known 1962. Bought 2006 for full restoration.

E3SA 934R/3 Jul 1953/GB. Shipped to an Edinburgh agent reg'n KWS 137. Known from first owner. Restored 2009-2011. Present owner bought it 2013.

E3SA 935R/23 Oct 1953/GB. Shipped to a London agent reg'n 189 AME. Known from 1960s. In c.1980 it housed poultry. Bought 1982 and fully restored by 1996 and looking good.

E3SA 936R/30 Oct 1953/GB. Shipped to a London agent reg'n 980 AMC. Known from 1962. Destroyed 1972.

E3SA 937R/27 Jun 1953/GB. Shipped to a London agent reg'n NXY 763 originally to the Danish agent as rolling chassis (746) but returned to Jowett for full build to standard bodywork. Restored 1970. In Lord Cranworth collection 1971-1982, then sold. Running again by 2015.

E2SAL 938R/22 Aug 1952/USA. Shipped to Angell Motors. First a rolling chassis (724) then built up. No more known.

E2SAL 939R/10 Sep 1952/JAP. Shipped to a Tokyo agent. Initially was a rolling chassis (244) but returned to Jowett for completion to standard bodywork. No more history known.

E2SC 940R/17 Nov 1952/GB. Shipped to K Brauer of Liverpool reg'd by Jowett JAK 76. It's the first production Mk1a and on the Jowett stand at the Oct 1952 London Motor Show. Bought 1970 in poor condition by Harry Brierley and restored by him. With present owner from 2003.

E3SC 941R/22 Jun 1953/GB. Sold to Major John Gibson of Eire after a spell in the Jowett London showroom, reg'd by Jowett JKW 400. Irish registration ZU 120. Under restoration: owned from 1982 still in Eire.

E2SC 942R/21 Oct 1952/GB. Registered to Jowett Cars Ltd JAK 74. This was the demonstrator for the 1952 London show. A very good running car; with current owner from 1998.

E2SC 943R/9 Dec 1952/GB. Shipped to a Northumberland agent reg'n RVK 105. Known from 1967. Said to have an R1-spec. engine. Bought by current owner in 2001.

E3SC 944R/16 Jul 1953/GB. Shipped to a Staffordshire agent as 'E2' reg'n 2258 E. From 1973 reduced to a bare frame after a crash. Frame bought by the very talented Allan Fishburn in 2008, to accurately build into the 'Jupiter Mk2' which at Jowett was intensively drawn up, detailed, with plasticine model made; it would have been based on the Eberhorst frame. Allan accurately built the car that the Jupiter R4 might have been; on the road 2012. For more see Ch 8. Sold 2015.

E3SC 945R/23 Jul 1953/GB. Shipped to a Surrey agent but via a Manchester agent. Agent, date, colour a good match for the Mk1a Jupiter reg'd TPJ 100 last heard from in the late 1950s.

E3SC 946R/19 May 1953/GB. Shipped to a London agent reg'd JUN 70. Known from 1957. In 2001 needed a new bonnet, fitted from an ex-Works Monte Carlo Rally car. Bought 2009, the car restored and running well.

E3SC 947R/20 May 1953/GB. Shipped to a London agent reg'd NXH 709. David Dixon drove it in events 1954-55, see Ch 6. Bought Geoff McAuley in 1969 and used by him for HSCC competition, with considerable success, see Ch 7.

E3SCL 948R/13 Jan 1953/USA. Importer Hoffman Motor Car Co of New York. From 1962, owner in NY State keeps it in good condition.

E3SC 949R/4 May 1953/GB. Shipped to a Manchester agent although it had been for the Geneva agent. No more known.

E3SC 950R/6 Feb 1953/GB. Shipped to the Brussels agent. RHD as it says, but nothing more known of this car.

E3SCL 951R/3 Jun 1953/USA. Shipped to the New York agent Major R D Seddon. First owner Larry Fox of Illinois, who placed 28th from 29 in an Indiana Hillclimb in Nov 1953. Still in Illinois, bought 2000, with the car in pieces.

E3SCL 952R/3 Jun 1953/USA. Shipped to the New York agent Major R D Seddon. Known from 1956 in Massachusetts. Rebuilt and re-trimmed by its 1967 sale.

Owner from 1998 in New Jersey, with the car further refurbished.

E3SC 953R/20 Aug 1953/Personal Export reg'd JKW 72 by Jowett for a Mr W R Constable of the Netherlands Antilles.

E3SCL 954R/2 Feb 1953/Colombia/Shipped to someone in Bogota. In 1999 Julio Tellez of Bogota enquired for parts.

E3SCL 955R/11 Jan 1954/to Broadway Motors Southern Rhodesia. Definitely LHD. Probably the car there in the late 1970s registered S 37766/SRH as a runner. No more known.

E4SCL 956R/15 Feb 1954/P. Shipped to the Lisbon agent, but not sold til 1956 to H Sordeiro registered IA-19-71. That's it.

E3SC 957R/8 May 1953/Personal Export registered by Jowett JKU 925 for a Mr R Metcalf of Sierra Leone. Back to GB by 1957, used to 1964. Some restoration by 1998. In 2014 bought and more work done. With new owner in 2015.

E4SCL 958R/5 Mar 1954/A. Shipped to the Vienna agent, but nothing more known.

E3SCL 959R/2 Feb 1953/Colombia. Shipped to the Bogota agent but nothing more known.

E3SCL 960R/13 Jan 1953/USA. Importer Hoffman Motor Car Co of New York but nothing more known.

E3SCL 961R/6 May 1953/B. Shipped to the Antwerp agent but nothing more known.

E3SCL 962R/7 Jul 1953/Cuba. Shipped to Eduardo Gutierrez of Falla, Cuba, but nothing more known.

E3SCL 963R/3 Jun 1953/USA. Shipped to the New York agent Major R D Seddon. Good guess this is the car Bill Lloyd raced on 29 Aug 1953 at Floyd Bennett Field, Brooklyn, to a good win over 15 MG-TDs and a Singer (Ch 5). No more known.

E2SC 964R/3 Dec 1952/GB. Shipped to a Surrey agent yet Bradford-registered JAK 592. Known from 1962 when sold to Pierre Strinati of Cologny near Geneva registered GE 30268 as his road car. He sold it c.1968 then bought it back in 1991 and had it well restored for his collection.

E3SCL 965R/3 Jun 1953/USA. Shipped to the New York

agent Major R D Seddon. No more history known.

E3SC 966R/3 Dec 1952/GB. Shipped to a London agent to an owner in Reigate. No more history known.

E3SCL 967R/3 Jun 1953/USA. Shipped to the New York agent Major R D Seddon. In Connecticut from 1972. To Michigan in 1976, then bought Ken Nelson in 2010 for restoration.

E4SC 968R/26 Feb 1954/Personal Export registered by Jowett KAK 775 for USAAF 2nd Lt R E Alterman, who owned it to 1965 in Monterey Park Ca. He rallied it in England and used it to tour Europe before export to the USA in the mid 1950s. Owned from 1983 by Californian owner and very well restored by him; from 1995 he and car moved to Canada.

E3SCL 969R/25 Nov 1953/F. Shipped to Plissons the Paris agent, but no further history known.

E4SCL 970R/15 Feb 1954/P. Shipped to the Lisbon agent and registered FE-19-71. Raced by first owner José Batista, timed at 94.6mph in speed trial on 25 Jul 1954. Next known owner A S Aitken of Maryland USA had bought it in Portugal in 1961. Owner-restorer from 1992 living in Texas.

E4SCL 971R/28 Nov 1953/USA. Shipped to the new CA agent World Wide Imports Inc. Seen by EN in an LA

Werner Bald and Jupiter (971) 'Storm and Urge' in the 2000 Rally around Hamburg. (Bald)

car showroom in 1970. Exported to Germany late 1980s, bought 1990 by Werner Bald of Hamburg with restorative work done there. Hamburg registration HH-0750 and very nice running car. See photo on previous page.

E3SC 972R/16 Jan 1953/GB. Registered by Jowett as JAK 998. Direct sale to Mr W J Tee, proprietor *Motor Sport* magazine. Its owner from 1970 has done some restoration 1990-1995.

E3SC 973R/13 Mar 1953/Cyprus/Sold by the Famagusta agent to a customer in the Cyprus Turkish sector. No more known.

E3SC 974R/8 May 1953/GB. to a Manchester agent but much reduced from 1972 and considered scrapped.

E4SCL 975R/2 Mar 1954/Direct Export to a certain Mr Ian McDiarmid. Nothing more known.

E3SC 976R/20 Apr 1953/GB. to a Glasgow agent and the warranty was to W J Skelly, the man who raced JGA 123 (41).

E2SC 977R/29 Dec 1952/HK. Shipped to the Hong Kong agent and registered XX 447. To GB in 1959 reg'd XUU 804. This car always in the JOAC. Owner from 1970 keeps it always looking good and running well with its overdrive etc.

E4SCL 978R/5 Feb 1954/GB. Direct sale to Mr Myles John Cooke; it has an export invoice code in the Factory records.

E3SCL 979R/24 Jul 1953/Personal Export reg'd JKW 741 by Jowett to USAAF/RAF Bentwater. This RAF base was used by the USAAF 81st Fighter Wing 1951 to 1993. That's it!

E3SC 980R/6 Jul 1953/GB. to an Essex agent reg'd GJN 466. Known from 1972. Restored to good running nick 1983 to 1995 then sold to present owner in 2004.

E3SC 981R/22 Jul 1953/Personal Export reg'd JKW 679 by Jowett to a Dr Goodall. Found in S Rhodesia in 1970 reg'n RSD 7501. By 1986 it was in Bloemfontein, South Africa. Car being restored from 2012.

E2SC 982R/24 Dec 1952/GB. to the Leicester agent reg'n JAY 420. Known from 1962. Again a runner by 1972, well restored 1996. New owner from 2009, car a very nice example.

E3SC 983R/9 Apr 1953/S. Imported by the Swedish

agent and in records as RHD but nothing more known.

E3SC 984R/30 Apr 1953/GB. Shipped to the Leicester agent reg'n JJU 655. First owner T A G Wright won a Novice Award in a national rally Nov 1953 (Ch 6). Owner from 1972 well-restored it fitting an overdrive. Owner from 2011 R. Jowett.

E3SC 985R/2 Jan 1953/GB. Shipped to a Birmingham agent reg'n JNT 230. This car is believed to be no more.

E3SC 986R+/2 Mar 1953/Lebanon/The last rolling

At the 1987 Pirelli Classic Car Run to Le Mans (984) became the first Jupiter to drive around the Le Mans circuit since 1952, this time with Dennis Sparrow at the wheel. (CJ)

chassis to leave Jowett, to a Beirut importer for a Mr Farlane. That's all.

E3SCL 987R/24 Apr 1953/Hawaii/Imported by R Bacon & Co. First known in 1968 owned by H Train, Washington DC. Last owner 1966-77 in Maryland. Car destroyed in a fire.

E4SCL 988R/17 Mar 1954/Personal Export. Found in New Jersey in 1971. Sold 1999 by M Reinwald of NJ back to GB. Well-restored by 2000, reg'd NSL 471.

E3SCL 989R/14 Aug 1953/Personal Export to a D G Corbett of the Brazilian Consulate in Boston Massachusetts. That's all.

E3SCL 990R/13 Nov 1953/F. Shipped to Plissons

the Paris agent. To Virginia USA from France in 1964. Rescued from abandonment in a parking lot in 1984. Sold 2007 to owner in France. This car now well-restored and running.

E3SCL 991R/3 Jun 1953/USA. Shipped to the New York agent Major R D Seddon. Owner of NY known only in 1985.

E3SC 992R/19 Jun 1953/GB. Shipped to a Northumberland agent reg'n STN 474. Owner from 1972 spent good money on it. In Majorca 1978-82 and to France in 1985 for the Angoulême classic car event. Bought 1997 by a collector and it went to Greece. A good running car.

E3SC 993R/1 Jul 1953/GB. Shipped to a Manchester agent but no further history known.

E3SC 994R/3 Jul 1953/GB. Shipped to a Sussex agent reg'n OPX 495. First owner Edward Pitt drove it in the London-Languedoc-Sête Rally of August 1953. Next owner Eric Jenner loaned it to Mr & Mrs Moore for the TEAC Cat's Eyes Rally February 1955. Owner in 1971 Capt. Mike Jackson of a parachute Regiment based in Northern Ireland. He crashed it in 1973. Restored by next three owners. Owner from 1985 has it as a running car with a little work still being done.

E3SC 995R/8 Jul 1953/Personal Export reg'd JKW 560 by Jowett to a Major H D Holsworthy. The car to GB from Sierra Leone in 1956; all owners known. Present owner from 2003 has completed its restorative work.

E3SC 996R/3 Nov 1953/GB. Shipped to a Lancashire agent reg'n CEN 154. Known from 1966 a largely stripped rolling chassis. By 2001 all missing parts collected and the car well-restored by Mike Kavanagh, sold 2014 a very nice running car.

E3SC 997R/19 Oct 1953/GB. Shipped to a Surrey agent but no further history known.

E3SC 998R/3 Nov 1953/Nigeria/Shipped to the Lagos agent but no further history known.

E3SC 999R/5 Nov 1953/GB. Shipped to a Manchester agent reg'n PKB 17. Known from 1969 when a JCC Concourse-winner. Auctioned in 1990 and bought by a Danish car museum who sold it in 2006. Sold from

Denmark back to GB in 2014 now reg'd PKB 17 again. A very nice car.

E3SC 1000R/12 Nov 1953/GB. Shipped to a Manchester agent for a Mrs Marjorie Walkden. No further history known.

E3SC 1001R/21 Jan 1954/ZA. Shipped to the Cape Town agent and first heard from in Pretoria in 1977. Owner from 2010 has the car at least partially restored.

E3SC 1002R/21 Jan 1954/ZA. Shipped to the Cape Town agent but no further history known.

E3SC 1003R/21 Jan 1954/Shipped to Portuguese East Africa but no further history known.

E3SC 1004R/4 Dec 1953/GB. Shipped to a Suffolk agent reg'n FVG 888. Known from 1966. By 1983 long stored in the open. Owner from 1990 carefully restoring it from 2010.

E3SC 1005R/21 Jan 1954/GB. Shipped to a London agent but no further history known.

E4SC 1006R/13 Mar 1954/GB. Shipped to a London agent but logged as scrapped by 2004.

E4SC 1007R/11 Feb 1954/GB. Shipped to the Southampton agent reg'n GJT 620. Known from 1977. New owner from 1990 and the car well-restored by him by 2000.

E4SC 1008R/3 Feb 1954/Jamaica. Shipped with radio fitted to the Xaymaca Agencies, but no further history known.

E4SC 1009R/3 Feb 1954/ZA. Shipped to the Cape Town agent but no further history known.

E4SC 1010R/19 Aug 1954/GB. Shipped to a Lancashire agent but first owner lived in Cheshire. By 1964 it was domiciled in Huntingdon, Cambridgeshire. No more known.

E4SC 1011R/13 May 1954/ZA. Shipped to the Cape Town agent. Owner 1979 Bill Mutschmann in Salisbury Rhodesia, a reporter with CBS News. From 1999 new owner in Muldersdrift, part of Mogale City, West Rand, South Africa.

E4SC 1012R/13 May 1954/ZA. Shipped to the Cape Town agent. No more history known.

E4SC 1013R/14 May 1954/GB. Shipped to the Bristol agent but it first lived in Sussex with London reg'n

PLB 310. Known from 1964. In Yorkshire events 1973 to 1976 (Ken Lees) but not in good nick. New owner from 2012 to fully restore.

E4SCL 1014R/6 Apr 1954/USA. Shipped to the New York agent Major R D Seddon. No more history known.

E4SCL 1015R/1 Apr 1954/Finland/Reg'd there UD-119 and known from 1972. The car a good runner.

E4SCL 1016R/15 Apr 1954/F. Shipped to the new Paris agent operated by ex-rally driver Jacques Savoye. Known from 1980. Bought 2011 by Jean-Marc Fourcaud of the Cahors Auto Retro Club with restorative work under way.

E4SCL 1017R/15 Apr 1954/F. Shipped to the Paris agent Jacques Savoye. Moved to NY USA in 1963. Owner from 1990 Jim Miller of Ca, car on the road and running well.

E4SCL 1018R/2 Jun 1954/F. Shipped to the Paris agent Jacques Savoye. Known from 1980. In 1991 bought as a runner and developed for competition with 1½-litre Alfa Romeo engine, with a 5-speed gearbox and reg'd 68000-SF-74.Was once timed at 200km/hr (125mph).

E4SCL 1019R/16 Jul 1954/USA. Shipped to the New York agent Major R D Seddon. Known in Missouri from 1967. It then moved to the Carolinas, and was bought 1980 by a dealer in New Jersey. Later history unknown.

E4SC 1020R/18 Aug 1954/GB. Shipped to a Lancashire agent but it first lived in North Yorkshire with York reg'n KDN 799. Known from 1958. Owner from 1963 ran it to 1965 then dry stored it.

Jupiters visit a classic car event in northern France in 2012. David Kennedy in his white SC Jupiter (1021). (CJ)

E4SC 1021R/6 Jul 1954/ZA. Shipped to the Cape Town agent. Bought as a wreck in 1972 by owner then of Johannesburg who superbly restored it by 1986 for the Fiva Total 1750-mile 2-week Classic Car Regularity Run to finish 57th from 150 entrants. Came back with the owner to GB in 1992 reg'd PSK 469 always a very smart well-running car.

E4SCL 1022R/26 May 1954/F. Shipped to the Paris agent, Jacques Savoye. Known from 1970. New owner from 1981. The car is complete but needs restoration.

E4SCL 1023R 14 Jun 1954/F. Shipped to the Paris agent Jacques Savoye. Not seen since 1981.

E4SCL 1024R/30 Jun 1954/F. Shipped to the Paris agent, Jacques Savoye. Known from 1981. Bought 1985 and given a superb restoration by classic car specialist Maurice Merlin. On the road 1994. New owner in 2003 reg'd it in Biarritz as 7015-XT-64, a very good running car.

E4SCL 1025R/12 Jul 1954/F. Shipped to the Paris agent, Jacques Savoye. Dismantled, parts sold, chassis gone by 2006.

E4SC 1026R/9 Jun 1954/GB. Shipped to the York agent but went via a Lancashire agent reg'd TTD 88 to first owner in Dundee. Known from 1971. Present owners bought it 2005, it was restored by 2010. A very good car.

E4SC 1027R/9 Jun 1954/GB. Shipped to the York agent reg'd OYE 244. Known from 1971. Owner from 1986 restored it and it always looks good and runs well.

E4SC 1028R/25 Jun 1954/GB. Shipped to a Staffordshire agent reg'n 826 DRE. In use to 1966 but in 1967 abandoned in London so we assume it has gone.

E4SC 1029R/August 1954/Turkey/Shipped for the Izmir Fair. It surfaced in 1998 still in Izmir. Owner from c.2000 of Bursa, Turkey. The car stored, in need of some restoration.

E4SC 1030R/27 Aug 1954/GB. To a London agent reg'n PGP 10. Owned from 1970, it awaits restoration.

E4SCL 1031R/23 Jul 1954/F. Shipped to the Paris agent, Jacques Savoye. In 1970 a runner in Paris. In a collection from 1974. To GB in 1988, owner from 2002 restoring it.

E4SC 1032R/22 Sep 1954/GB. Built in the Jowett Service dept and considered the last all-new Jowett-built Jupiter.

Shipped to a London agent reg'd PLB 552. Known from 1962 when in immaculate condition. New owners from 2003, an excellent running car looking good.

E4SC 1033R/4 Nov 1954/GB. Built in the Jowett Service dept, the last car built by Jowett, its chassis frame being the Exhibition Chassis (2). Shipped to a Bradford agent reg'n KKY 155. Known from 1966. Restored 1990-96. sold 2015.

In the mid-1950s a Mk1a Jupiter was built by Robert Townend of Cottingham, Yorkshire from all-new components obtained from Jowett Engineering. Reg'd VWF 99 on 10th July 1958. Owner from 1990 gave it a body-off restoration by 2002.

The three R1 Jupiters are in the Factory Records. They were constructed on slightly narrower versions of the Eberhorst Jupiter frame:–

E1R1 1/6 Jun 1951/GB. Registered HAK 364, see Ch 3: (1) entrant 1951 Le Mans crewed by Wisdom & Wise. (2) Winner of the 1951 Queen Catharine Monteur Cup at Watkins Glen USA driver George Weaver. (3) Class 4th 1952 Prix de Monte Carlo, driver Marcel Becquart. (4) Le Mans 1952 crewed by Gatsonides/Nijevelt – retired. This R1 was scrapped by Jowett.

E2R1 56/20 May 1952/GB. Registered HKY 48 for the 1952 Le Mans see Ch 3. This R1 was also scrapped by Jowett.

E2R1 62/20 May 1952/GB. Registered HKY 49 for the 1952 Le Mans. Crewed by Marcel Becquart and Gordon Wilkins, it was the class winner see Ch 3. Although scrapped by Jowett, it was rescued from the Jowett scrap heap by a Jowett employee, it is believed, and somewhat crudely rebuilt by 1962 reg'd YKU 761. Bought 1978 by Dennis Sparrow and Peter Dixon. It was then carefully and accurately professionally restored and running by 2000

with its original registration HKY 49 returned to it, taking part in HSCC events and the Le Mans retros of 2001 and 2005 as just some examples. For sale 2016.

The three R4 Jupiters do not have factory records entries and they were not constructed on the Eberhorst Jupiter frame. All the R4s are covered in Ch 8.

Lastly, an open Jupiter on a spare Eberhorst Jupiter frame fitted with a Mk6 Rochdale body was constructed 1954-55 by George Colin Ross, and registered JST 53. He drove it in some local competitive events. Restored for Wally Dale to enter it in the 1989 Pirelli Classic Marathon. The car had a new owner from 2015, a good running car with FIA papers. See Ch 9.

Pirelli Marathon 1989: hard cornering in the Ramsgate test. Robin Barry did the driving with Wally Dale navigating – see Chapter 7. This Rochdale-bodied Jupiter is the last 'in era' all-new Jupiter to have been constructed. (Mary Harvey)

Epilogue:
Sir Hugh Bell remembers his Jupiter GPY 859 (25)

The car was the quickest and best-mannered car I had ever had.

I did Tees, Darlington, to the Thames, Chelsea, door to door in 4 hours 20 minutes [*approximately 245 miles at 55mph average*] on Pool petrol diluted with 50% methanol, comfortably.

There was no dual carriageway north of Hatfield!

Until the Mercedes 300SLR, I thought the Jupiter the best-mannered car in the wet.

It seemed a lucky car and is the only car I never spun!

I was only stopped once by the police – for doing 80mph down the Seven Sisters Road [*in London*], and they let me off! It was about 2 o'clock in the morning.

I remember the Jupiter with the great affection one has for intelligent but difficult children on whom much thought is lavished and who make up for it by intermittent brilliance.*

I recommend the empty narrow twisting hilly roads of Scotland to know it at its best.

---

* Sir Hugh did quite some development work on his very early hard-driven Jupiter including lowering the chassis by 1½ inches, having pistons specially made, fitting a magneto to replace its coil ignition, fitting a special oil cooler, raising the compression ration by shaving a 1mm off the heads and liner tops, adding methanol to the only-available 80-octane Pool petrol, and making a special twin exhaust system that he said made the car "sound like a motor boat". See photo on Page 12.

Appendix:
A Jupiter Chronology

1947: Lazard Bros replaced Charles Clore as majority shareholder of Jowett Cars Ltd. George Wansborough became chairman of Jowett Cars Ltd.

1948 January: ERA Ltd bought by Leslie Johnson from Humphrey Cook who had been, with Raymond Mays, one of ERA's founders in 1933.

1949. Leslie Johnson persuaded Jowetts to enter a Javelin in the Spa 24-hour race in August, saying he ran his Javelin everywhere at 70mph so the car ought to win. Jowetts agreed if ERA paid the entry; the Javelin, with lightened body, was driven to the race in Belgium pulling Horace Grimley's holiday trailer with a spare engine aboard. With Tom Wisdom and Anthony Hume sharing the driving, it won the 2-litre Touring Car class at 65.5mph.

1949 January: Britain's steel shortage hit Jowetts and some workers were laid off – steel allocation depended upon exports. Hume, Leslie Johnson and Laurence Pomeroy (*Motor* Technical Editor) hatched the plan for ERA to design a sports car around the Javelin's mechanicals. Wansborough, on the lookout for a new exportable product, agreed. Pomeroy and Hume drove to Italy in a Javelin to contact Pomeroy's friend, the Austrian-born Professor Dipl Ing Robert Eberan von Eberhorst, at that time working for Cisitalia in Turin.**

May: Eberhorst came to England to work at ERA on the contract from Jowett for five chassis powered by the Javelin engine with output raised to 60bhp. David Hodkin assisted. The Jupiter's chrome molybdenum big-bore chassis was developed.

September: One more chassis given a closed body by Seary & McReady for Harold Radford but under the direction of Leslie Johnson, and a photo of it appeared in the *Daily Graphic* of the 28th. Jowett, thinking of an open car, were not enamoured.

October: London Motor Show at Earls Court. An ERA chassis was on the Jowett stand – chassis terminated at the rear axle support structure, 60bhp achieved by an improved camshaft – and was hailed as a piece of advanced engineering by the British motoring press. Harold Radford's ERA-Javelin coupé was in the London showroom of Jowett Cars Ltd in its basement. It was described as 'captivating' by the motoring journalists.

** Eberhorst had worked for Auto Union and developed in 1938 a car with torsion rod springing at both ends (like the Javelin) and a chrome molybdenum steel big-bore tubular chassis.

November: Wilfred Sainsbury (a Lazards man with much power at Jowett) met Leslie Johnson and told him there would be no further contract as Jowett intended to build the chassis themselves and design their own bodywork for it. Eberhorst was subsequently seen at the Jowett factory about twice but he was shown and photographed with Jupiter No 1 when it was finished.

Early December 1949: Reg Korner, Jowetts Chief Bodywork Designer, was given just four months to design a prototype Jupiter, to be in the USA's British Automobile and Motorcycle Show the following April at Grand Central Palace, New York (John Cobb's 1938 record-breaking Railton was there also). This was the programme for Jowett's five ERA-Jupiter chassis:–
(1) First prototype car, for New York.
(2) First exhibition chassis for Brussels Geneva, Amsterdam, Paris, London.
(3) Second exhibition chassis for the New York show. It then went to Angell Motors of Pasadena.
(4) Lightweight car for Le Mans June 1950.
(5) Second prototype car for road testing then shipment to Canada.
The Hoffman Motor Car Co Inc of New York was to buy (1) and (3) but then declined (3) only keeping the car; (5) went to Wells Motor Sales of Toronto.

1950 Mid-January: Brussels Motor Show had Exhibition Chassis (2) now with tail extension structure but otherwise as ERA made it.

March 8th: *The Autocar* and *Motor* carried articles on the 'Jowett Javelin Jupiter' as it was initially christened, with photos of the chassis but an artist's impression of the car. 60bhp with modified camshaft was claimed and the price for the chassis was given as £495 before tax. The Exhibition Chassis (2) then went to the Geneva Motor Show.

March 27th: First complete car (1) finished on the Saturday after 14 weeks of strenuous effort. It was tested over 22 miles on the Sunday, a somewhat foggy day in Bradford, then photographed and shown to the local press on Monday the 29th. It was then delivered to the Liverpool docks on the Tuesday for shipment to the USA with the second Exhibition Chassis (3). The brochure for the Jupiter had colour drawings by the artist Roy Nockolds. The second

complete car (5) went on 3000-mile proving run in France driven by Charles Grandfield and Horace Grimley, where it averaged 46mph at 31mpg; whatever else it was, a Jowett had to be economical! Many lessons were learned and fed into production when manufacture got going.

April: The lightweight Le Mans car GKW 111 (4), the responsibility of Charles Grandfield, Roy Lunn, Reg Korner and Horace Grimley, ready for testing.

April 18-25: the New York show a success for the Jupiter in its colour – metallic copper with fawn hood – new for the show. Cameron Peck, president of the Sports Car Club of America, out of more than 100 exhibits ordered a Jupiter at £910 and an Aston Martin DB2 at £1,963. There was heady talk of more than a thousand Jupiters going to the USA in reports of "90mph car sold out a year ahead and not even in production". UK prices pre-tax were given as £795 for the car and £495 for the rolling chassis.

1950 May or early June: The second prototype car (5) appeared at the Silverstone paddock for the benefit of the press, before being shipped to Canada in July. It has since returned to the UK.

June 24-25th: The 1950 Le Mans 24-hour race. The Jupiter (4) won its class ahead of an MG (Ch 3).

August 11th: First production chassis (6) shipped to Sweden, and three days later the second (7) went to Stabilimenti Farina of Turin to fit a closed body.

October 6th: Paris Motor Show. The surprise last-minute entry on the Jowett stand was the elegant Stabilimenti Farina FHC Jupiter. Two weeks later this car appeared at the London Motor Show where it was a considerable centre of attraction.

November: first production batch of 5 complete cars were built (chassis 17 to 21) with strakes and no bonnet louvres. (17) was delivered to a M Thévenin, the owner of a motor business in Bordeaux, and went on to take part in the 1951 Monte Carlo Rally. It survives to this day in good order in France. The other four are now lost to us: however they had notable careers with (19) and (21) road test demonstrators, (20) the showroom and exhibition car, and (18) class-winning the 1951 Monte Carlo Rally in which (19) and (21) also took part (Ch 4). A further batch of 5 cars (chassis 41 to 45) were delivered, just, before the end of 1950 with one

(41) being promised for private competition use in GB and the other four going abroad.

1951 January: standard-bodied Jupiters now being assembled, mainly for export but with four exceptions – Bill Skelly, L J Roy Taylor, Godfrey (Goff) Imhoff and W J Tee of *Motor Sport*. Out of the first 60 Jupiters shipped (by 24th January), 39 were rolling chassis. Braking now full hydraulic, no bonnet louvres yet.

February: the LHD prototype Jupiter delivered to Angell Motors of Pasadena. Jupiter pre-tax prices in Britain now stated as £540 for the chassis and £875 for the car. Reports of steel allocation cuts affecting Javelin and Jupiter production. It was announced that 'Javelin' was being dropped from the Jupiter's full name, after comments in the press that "Jowett Javelin Jupiter sounded like a sobriety test"!

March 19th: the 100th Jupiter was shipped – out of this first 100 there were 50 as rolling chassis.

April 1951: production LHD Jupiters available, price $2,850 f.o.b New York, $700 more than the Morgan Pus 4 and the MG TD but a similar price as the Simca 8 and Porsche 356.

June 23-24: a lightweight 'standard' Jupiter won its class at the 1951 Le Mans 24-hour race (Ch 3).

June/July 1951: the last batch of rolling chassis delivered, about 22. The standard Jupiter now has a pair of 4-louvre panels let into the bonnet, while rear lamps are cast-aluminium-housed rather than formed into the rear wings.

August: Film comedian Red Skelton came to England and bought four Jupiters for himself and his immediate entourage, and returned with them to California where two are known to remain to this day, with Skelton's actual car well-restored.

September 15th: Jupiters first and second in class at the RAC TT, Dundrod, Northern Ireland – a tough 4-hour race against strong competition (Ch 5). Very auspicious in view of the Jupiter's UK launch in a month's time.

September 28th: A Jupiter R1 won the Watkins Glen race for 1½-litre sports cars (Ch 3).

October: Paris Salon has the fourth Stabilimenti Farina Jupiter (109). Then at the London Motor Show Jupiters are released to the home market but with a long wait. Price £895 + £498 14s 5d tax. The exhibition chassis now has the rubber-bushed front suspension, a feature not on production Jupiters for another 12 months. Bonnet louvres still let-in panels but in groups of 7 instead of 4, although the Show Car still had the earlier arrangement. Sales now said to be in the upper 30s per month.

1952 January: Jupiter engine power now 62.5bhp at 4500 rpm with 8:1 compression ratio. Jupiter price with tax now £1,518 3s 4d. Javelin deliveries slip from 110 per week over the previous three years to around 75 per week.

January 29th: Marcel Becquart in his Farina Jupiter finished a difficult Monte Carlo Rally in fifth place overall (Jowetts highest in the general category) but second in class (Ch 4).

February 11th: The Mk1a Jupiter prototype (560) delivered to the Experimental Dept for assessment. Symmetrical metal-faced dash (for ease of RHD/LHD build) rather than the walnut-faced dash with the instruments straight ahead. To address certain criticisms, the new model has an externally accessible boot of slightly greater capacity, and a more raked hood line. Rubber bushed front suspension standardised. Ford began takeover negotiations with Briggs Bodies, the firm that supplied Javelin and Bradford bodies.

February to April: Jupiter production hits a peak of 208 over these three months.

April: Design study for the 'Jupiter Mk2' carried out by Phil Stephenson incorporating the 'attenuated Eberhorst frame' with R1-type scuttle but coachwork close to that of the R4 design of 1953. Jowett's designers were looking at the amazing output from the Italian design houses. Jowett never built one, but the talented panel-man Allan Fishburn did just that, completing the car in 2011 (Page 135).

1952 April 5th: Marcel Becquart in the RAC Rally switched to Javelin to beat all other closed cars.

April 7th: Jowett Cars Ltd AGM statement recorded '1951 a very good trading year for Jowetts, but exports fell away badly at the end of 1951 with the closure of export markets like Australia. Javelin production at Idle cut to 50 per week.

June 14-15th: An R1 Jupiter at Le Mans recorded Jowett's third consecutive class win but the other two R1s both broke their crankshafts. After the race, Arthur Jopling, Jowett's Managing Director, told the drivers the Works was pulling out of racing.

August 15th 1952: Jupiter price cut to £1,284 16s 9d after tax. Delivery 'months rather than years'.

September: The eminent engineer Donald Bastow MIMechE, BSc(Eng), MSAE, MSIA, former assistant to W O Bentley (1947 to 1950) joined Jowett from the BSA Engines & Mechanisms Laboratory in the newly-created post of Chief Engineer.

October: London Motor Show, the Mk1a Jupiter announced. It won a silver medal for coachwork design. Most export cars (except Personal Export) and all LHD cars were now Mk1a. The rival Healey 100 now launched at the pre-tax price of £850.

November 1952: Three Javelins and a Jupiter (76) circulated the MIRA test track at constant speed for three weeks to demonstrate the reliability of the Series III engine. Javelin sales fell to 22 per week.

December 1st: Arthur Jopling suspended his order, placed on Briggs in May, for 5000 CD vehicles now fully tooled up and due for imminent production. He requested that Javelin production should cease and that CC Bradford body assembly should continue but at half the 1952 rate: this last request was refused thus sealing Jowett's fate. Jupiter deliveries hit a low of 12 in the last quarter of 1952.

1953 January: Briggs ceased delivery of Bradford and Javelin bodies.

February: Ford takeover of Briggs effected. Crash programme to design and build a new Jupiter sports car began – Experimental Dept told that, if in London's October Motor Show it might save Jowett.

March 5th: Phil Stephenson completed the colour sketch of the 'Jupiter 100' later renamed the 'Jupiter R4'. Stephenson left Jowett three months later.

April: Charles Grandfield, moving spirit behind the Works competition effort, left Jowett in a huff after the appointment of Bastow. Jupiter selling price was lowered to £795 + £332 10s tax. Jupiter sales rose from 11 in April to 15 in May.

May 1953: The continuing assembly and sale of stored Javelin bodies enabled the debt to Briggs to be paid off in full, permitting Jopling to reopen negotiations with Briggs – now under new management – regarding Javelins at 40 per week and the CD range of cars.

June: Briggs refused to resume Javelin production; CD production considered but a hard line taken and no agreement reached. The Jupiter enjoyed a mini-boom with 28 cars sold. The first R4 Jupiter, registered JKW 537, with all-steel body, ready.

July: Jopling reported 'a heavy overall loss for 1952 leaving an adverse balance since liquidated of £286,353. Exports had dropped 75% in 1952 and sales fell at home'.

July 10th: The first R4, JKW 537 with aeroscreens as the only weather protection, photographed with 148 miles on its odometer. No overdrive fitted yet.

August 22nd: The R4, JKW 537, after its continental proving run, with 4766 miles on its odometer had overdrive fitted and a hardtop made.

September 16th: At a press conference Jopling announced the cessation of Javelin production.

October: London Motor Show. A LHD Mk1a Jupiter (now listed at £725 + £303 4s 2d tax) plus a Javelin and a new fibre- and resin-bodied R4 on the Jowett stand. JKW 537 gave demonstration drives through London streets "Thousands could be sold...". Roy Lunn approached by Ford who made him an offer he could not refuse so he left Jowett.

November 4th: The last Jowett-built car, the Jupiter (1033) driven out of the Jowett Factory.

December 1953: International Harvester who had bought Jowett's factory in October (at a good price) for the assembly of their light tractor, began to move their production planning department into the Experimental Department buildings. There would be no redundancies at Jowett.

December 24th 1953: The Motor Show R4 had its last photographic session.

1955: Jowett Cars Ltd bought by Blackburn and General Aircraft Co Ltd and all Jowett shareholders paid off in full: Jowett Cars Ltd had not gone bust.

1957 The Jowett Car Club of Australia Inc. was formed in Melbourne.

1962. The Jupiter Owner's Auto Club was formed. Also the Jowett Club of New Zealand was founded.

1964: The Southern Jowett Car Club, which dates back to 1923, morphed into the international Jowett Car Club, later the Jowett Car Club Ltd.

1976: The North American Jowett Register was founded.

BUGATTI
Type 57 Grand Prix
– A Celebration

Neil Max Tomlinson

A comprehensive, radical look at the history and development of the Type 57 Grand Prix Bugattis. New material challenges traditional beliefs about these historic cars, and rejects some long-standing conventions. Myths are explored and truths are revealed in this book celebrating all aspects of these remarkable cars and their creators.

ISBN: 978-1-845847-89-0
Hardback • 24.8x24.8cm • £50* UK/$85* USA • 176 pages • 158 colour and b&w pictures

For more info on Veloce titles, visit our website at www.veloce.co.uk
• email: info@veloce.co.uk • Tel: +44(0)1305 260068
* prices subject to change, p&p extra

The
Argentine Temporada Motor Races
1950 to 1960

– in 220 contemporary photos

Hernan Lopez Laiseca

This beautifully illustrated book captures the entire history of the Argentine Grand Prix and the Argentina International Temporada Series, covering all the great races of the golden age of motor sport – when danger and passion defined racing.

ISBN: 978-1-845848-28-6

Hardback • 24.8x24.8cm • £35* UK/$60* USA • 144 pages • 223 b&w pictures

For more info on Veloce titles, visit our website at www.veloce.co.uk • email: info@veloce.co.uk • Tel: +44(0)1305 260068

* prices subject to change, p&p extra

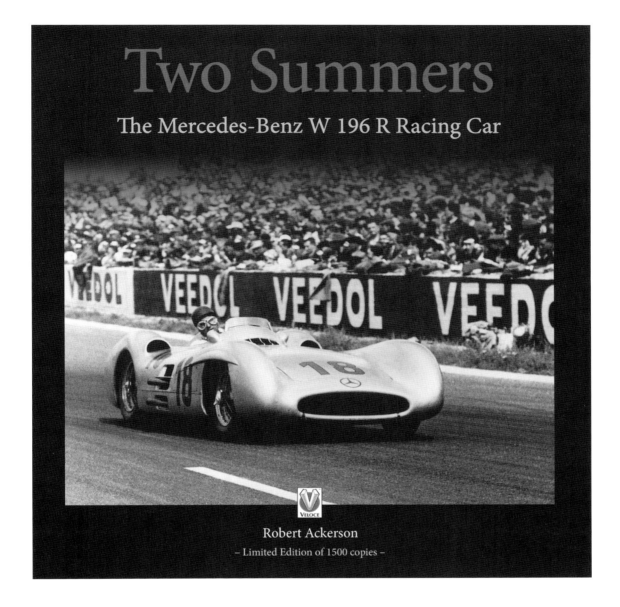

Two Summers

The Mercedes-Benz W 196 R Racing Car

Robert Ackerson

– Limited Edition of 1500 copies –

The story of the Mercedes-Benz W 196 R Grand Prix racing car – its development, roots, and magnificent two-year racing career – has enough drama, emotion and excitement to fill a dozen books, but only this volume captures the car's enduring greatness. Hundreds of photos from the Daimler archives, stunning original artwork, and written with authority, reflection and admiration for the W 196 R.

ISBN: 978-1-845847-51-7

Hardback • 25x25cm • £75* UK/$125* USA • 192 pages • 171 colour and b&w pictures

For more info on Veloce titles, visit our website at www.veloce.co.uk • email: info@veloce.co.uk • Tel: +44(0)1305 260068

* prices subject to change, p&p extra

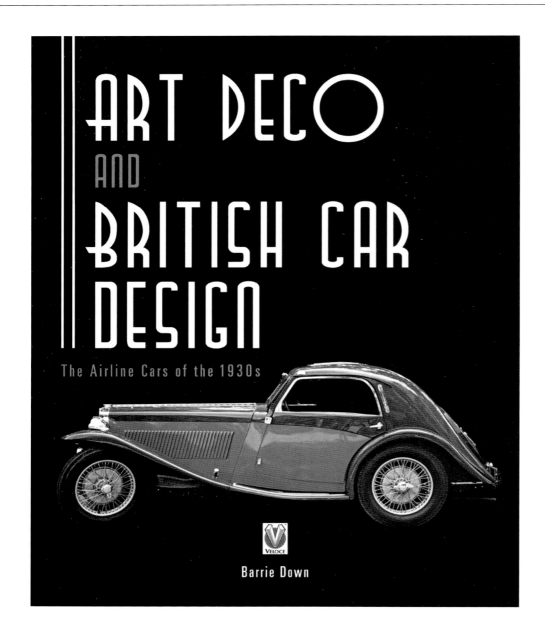

Index